BINOCULAR ASTRONOMY

BINOCULAR ASTRONOMY

CRAIG CROSSEN & WIL TIRION

Published by:
Willmann–Bell, Inc.
P.O. Box 35025
Richmond, Virginia 23235

Published by Willmann-Bell, Inc.
P.O. Box 35025, Richmond, Virginia 23235

Copyright ©1992 by Willmann-Bell, Inc.
First English Edition

Printed in the United States of America

Library of Congress Cataloging-in-Publication Data.

Crossen, Craig.
        Binocular astronomy / Craig Crossen, Wil Tirion. – 1st English
    ed.
            p.   cm.
        Includes bibliographical references and index.
        ISBN 0-943396-36-0
            1. Constellations – Observers' manuals.   2. Constellations-
    -Amateurs' manuals. 3. Astronomy – Observer manuals.
        4. Astronomy – Amateurs' manuals. 5. Binoculars.   I. Tirion, Wil.
        II. Title.
        QB63.C76   1991   91-23506
        523'.8'022'2–dc20   CIP

        92 93 94 95 96 97 98 9 8 7 6 5 4 3 2

Photographs attributed to Barnard are from *Atlas of Selected Regions of the Milky Way*, by E.E. Barnard, Carnegie Institution of Washington, Washington, D.C., 1927.

Photographs attributed to Ross are from *Atlas of the Northern Milky Way* by F.E. Ross and M.R. Calvert, The University of Chicago Press, Chicago, 1936.

Photographs attributed to Georgetown Observatory are from *Photographic Atlas of the Southern Milky Way*, F.J. Heyden and L.C. McHugh, Georgetown College Observatory, Washington, D.C., 1952.

Table of Contents

Preface

This book is a constellation-by-constellation guide to the visually attractive or astronomically interesting celestial objects that can be seen with normal binoculars (instruments of the 7x35, 7x50, and 10x50 type). It has been written for both the individual who has just become interested in astronomy and for the experienced amateur astronomer. If you are in the first group, chances are that you already own a pair of binoculars, or can borrow one from a friend or relative: this book will help you locate the surprisingly large number of double and variable stars, open and globular clusters, planetary and diffuse nebulae, and even galaxies that can be seen in binoculars. If you are an experienced amateur with a telescope as well as binoculars, this book will be a useful guide to the objects and star fields that are better observed in binoculars than in telescopes, and it will help you make the most of trips on which you can bring only your binoculars.

Because the most pleasurable way of observing celestial objects is with the mind as well as with the eye, I have discussed virtually all of the stars, clusters, nebulae, galaxies, and Milky Way fields mentioned in this book at some length. And for most of these objects I have not only tabulated the raw data of their distances, sizes, and brightness, I have also explained their astrophysical interest and how they fit into the scheme of things in our Galaxy. Indeed, Chapters 6 and 7 are in a sense the climax of this book, for Chapter 6 puts the clusters, nebulae, and Milky Way fields mentioned in Chapters 2 through 5 in Galactic perspective, and Chapter 7 explains how the galaxies visible in binoculars are distributed in intergalactic space.

Because 10x50's are perhaps the "ideal" astronomical binoculars (they are reasonably inexpensive and light-weight, but have good magnification and light-gathering power), this book is slanted toward use with that size instrument. If you have 7x50's, 7x35's, or 35 or 40mm zooms, you will not be able to see everything mentioned in this book. On the other hand, if you have "giant" binoculars of the 11x80 or 20x70 class you will be able to see more. However, I have made such a large selection of objects visible in 10x50's, that this book will be useful to owners of giant binoculars and even of small telescopes (especially of small richest-field telescopes).

The photographs in this book have been chosen not merely to illustrate it, but principally to help the observer locate objects discussed in the text. Several of these photographs were taken by amateur astrophotographers, but their quality is professional in the best sense of the word: astrophotography is a difficult, time-consuming, and expensive art, and the skill and patience of the amateurs whose work appears in this book cannot be overpraised. We have also used prints of the historic Milky Way photographs by E.E. Barnard and Frank E. Ross taken during the early decades of the 20th century. These photographs (particularly the Barnard series) are so beautiful that they are as much works of art as they are works of science. However, we have included them principally for their usefulness to the binocular observer: their field sizes are comparable to those of binoculars, and they will give the observer a very good idea of the shapes and relative dimensions of the bright star clouds and the obscuring dust masses that are visible in the Milky Way in binoculars and richest-field telescopes. Keep in mind that many details on these

viii

photographs, some of which have hours-long exposure times, are invisible to the eye not only in binoculars but even in large telescopes. Nevertheless you will discover that these Milky Way fields will look every bit as beautiful in binoculars as they do on photographs.

Princeton, Minnesota
January 16, 1991

A Note on the Astronomical Data

The data in this book for stars brighter than magnitude 3.50 are from "The Brightest Stars" list in the Royal Astronomical Society of Canada's annual *Observer's Handbook*. (During my final proof-read of the text before publication I updated some of the star data—most notably that of Orion Association and Scorpio-Centarus Association members—from the 1991 edition of the *Handbook*.) Data on O, early B, and supergiant stars (other than Orion and Sco-Cen members) are from a catalogue published in 1978 by Roberta M. Humphreys (*Astrophysical Journal Supplement Series* Volume 38, pp. 309–350). Other star data are from a variety of sources, most important of which is *Burnham's Celestial Handbook*. (See the Bibliography, Appendix C.)

The data on clusters, nebulae, and galaxies are likewise from a variety of sources. The information in Chapter 7 ("Galaxies and Galaxy Groups for Binoculars") is drawn almost entirely from the work of Prof. G. De Vaucouleurs (published in a number of places)—except for the apparent magnitudes and sizes of the galaxies, which are my own best judgement from the appearance of each galaxy in 7x50 and 10x50 binoculars. I have updated many galaxy distances with R. Brent Tully's *Nearby Galaxies Catalogue* (Cambridge, 1988). My own astrophysical study has centered on galactic structure, and of the technical books in that area the most useful for the present book has been *Galactic Astronomy: Structure and Kinematics* by Dimitri Mihalas and James Binney (2nd edition, W.H. Freeman and Co., San Francisco, 1981).

The stars and galaxies may well be practically eternal, but astronomical data are not, and the reader must not take the numbers cited in this book to be graven in stone. Distances particularly are subject to continual revision; and star cluster ages are little more than crude estimates. Even stellar spectral types and luminosity classes are subject to differing interpretations (though usually by only a tenth of a spectral type or between two similar luminosity classes). Moreover, the apparent magnitudes and apparent sizes of clusters, nebulae, and galaxies depend on the type of instrument used to look at them and the quality of the observing night. (For clusters, nebulae, and galaxies, I have used values for apparent size and apparent magnitude that reflect what one actually sees in binoculars: the data in standard catalogues are from photographic or photoelectric observations, which seldom correspond with what is visible in binoculars or telescopes.) The reader, therefore, should not be surprised to find slightly (sometimes significantly) different values for the same object's size, brightness, and distance in different books.

Acknowledgements

I would like to express my thanks to the following people for their kind assistance during my work on this book:

To Professor Roberta M. Humphreys of the University of Minnesota's Department of Astronomy and Astrophysics, who graciously answered my questions about stellar associations, supergiant stars, and the southern heavens, and who gave me copies of several of her published papers for my research.

To Professor Lawrence Rudnick, also of the University of Minnesota's Department of Astronomy and Astrophysics, who encouraged my first efforts to write about astronomy.

To Mr. William J. Larson, who generously gave me a sizeable part of his astronomy library when he moved from Minnesota to California. Without such ready access to sources, the research for this book would have been a good deal more time-consuming.

To Mr. Robert Burnham, editor of *Astronomy* magazine and the first editor of this book while it was still in manuscript: in my subsequent rewrite I kept almost all of his editorial changes.

I must also thank Mr. Burnham and Mr. Brian Skiff for reading and commenting on the almost-completed version of this book. I have not accepted all of their suggestions, so any errors in content or inadequacies of style that remain are my responsibility alone.

Willmann-Bell, Inc. and I would like to thank Tom Eby, David Healy, Dr. Jack Marling, Robert Reeves, and Brian Skiff for permission to use the various astrophotos credited to them in this book, Dr. Helga Hühnel and the Kartensammlung und Globenmuseum of the Österreichische Nationalbibliothek in Vienna for permission to reprint the Liechtenstern planisphere, the American Oriental Society of the University of Michigan for permission to use the drawing of Leo and Hydra from a Mesopotamian tablet reprinted in Figure 4–1 of this book, and the Oriental Institute of the University of Chicago for permission to reproduce the drawing of the cylinder seal impression of the Kneeler and the Hydra, Figure 5–1.

Finally, though I have never had the privilege of meeting him, I would like to express my gratitude to the author of *Burnham's Celestial Handbook*, Robert Burnham, Jr., formerly of Lowell Observatory. The present book simply could never have been researched or written without the previous existence of the *Celestial Handbook*. Indeed, my own interest in astronomy might never have been reborn but for the evening of December 26, 1978, when I opened Volume I of *Burnham's Celestial Handbook* and began reading the section on Canis Major.

For Lonnie Durham

Chapter 1

Constellations and Binoculars

This first chapter is intended primarily for the individual who has just gotten interested in astronomy and wants to learn the constellations and how to observe with binoculars. In the first part of this chapter I will explain the concept of the celestial sphere, the important circles on the celestial sphere, the celestial coordinate system, and directions on the celestial sphere. In the second part, after briefly discussing the various ways in which individual stars are designated, I will describe the constellations and explain how to identify them. Finally, in the third part I will discuss the practicalities of observing—not only how specifically to use binoculars to see the various types of celestial objects, but also what you need to know to make any type of observing a pleasant and successful experience. Indeed, even if you are going out simply to learn the constellations, there is a great deal in the third part that you should know about the night.

1.1 The Celestial Sphere

The first step in learning the constellations is to know something about the celestial sphere upon which the stars appear to be fixed. The celestial sphere, its important circles, and the motions of the stars, the Sun, the Moon, and the planets on it, are very abstract topics. However, all courses and textbooks on astronomy begin with a discussion of the celestial sphere and the celestial coordinate system, and they do so for a good reason: it is very difficult to find your way around the heavens, and even to identify the most conspicuous constellations, without some working knowledge about the celestial sphere and the celestial coordinate system. There simply is no way of getting around it. However, there is no need to feel that you must *master* these subjects before you can learn the constellations. Indeed, the best way to understand the concept of the celestial sphere and the daily, monthly, and annual motions of the celestial bodies upon it is from actual observation under the night sky itself.

The Celestial Sphere. The night sky can be thought of as a huge hemispherical dome. Indeed, many ancient

cultures literally believed it to be such, supported at its corners by pillars or mountains resting on the edges of the flat Earth. If you include the part of the heavens beneath the horizon, the sky forms a sphere upon which the more-or-less infinitely distant stars, planets, Sun, and Moon are seen to move in various ways. Of course, not even the stars are truly infinitely distant from us: in fact, astronomers can measure the slight shift of nearer stars with respect to farther stars as the Earth moves in its orbit around the Sun. However, it is useful to think of the celestial sphere's radius as infinite.

The notion of the Heavens as a great sphere is not as natural and obvious as it might seem to us today. There is absolutely no evidence that the ancient Babylonians, who developed some rather sophisticated numerical techniques for computing the motions of the Sun and of the Moon, ever thought of the sky as a sphere. The idea seems to have been introduced by the Greek astronomer Eudoxos of Cnidus early in the 4th century B.C. It created a revolution in ancient astronomy, and the marriage of Babylonian mathematical with Greek spherical astronomy culminated in the mid-2nd century A.D. in the monumental *Syntaxis* (later named the *Almagest*) by the Greek-Alexandrian astronomer Ptolemy. The *Syntaxis* took ancient astronomy as far as it could go; no further significant development in the field was possible until the inventions of the telescope and of calculus.

During the course of a day or of a night, all the heavenly objects appear to move from east to west across the sky. It is, of course, *not* that the celestial sphere itself is rotating from east to west, but that the Earth is rotating on its axis in the opposite sense, that is, from west to east. The stars are for our purposes here considered to be fixed relative to each other on the celestial sphere. (In reality they are moving at velocities of many miles per second through space, but they are so distant that even over thousands of years virtually all of them seem to remain stationary.) However, the Sun, the Moon, and the planets can be seen to move among the fixed stars.

Motion of the Sun on the Celestial Sphere. The Sun moves from west to east among the fixed stars of the constellations of the zodiac, completing one circuit around the sky in a period of 365 1/4 days, the *sidereal year* ("sidereal" means "relative to the stars"). The motion of the Sun among the stars is the result of the Earth's revolution around the Sun: as we orbit the Sun, the background of distant stars behind it changes.

If the Sun's path among the stars, the *ecliptic*, is thought of as a great circle, then, because there are 360° in a circle, the Sun moves approximately 1° a day east among the stars—a distance of about twice its apparent diameter. (The ancient Greeks chose 360 as the number of degrees swept by a radius of a circle as it rotates once around the circle's center because they estimated 360 to be that number of days in a year.) The effect of this 1° per day solar motion is that stars just visible setting in the west at the end of twilight one evening will be invisible the next evening, stars that could not be seen rising in the morning twilight one morning will be just glimpsed before the onset of daylight on the next, and stars that were culminating (that is, reaching the line that passes overhead and connects the north and south points of the horizon, the *meridian*) at sunset or sunrise will be just past (just west of) culmination the next sunrise or sunset.

The period between successive culminations of the Sun (the culmination of the Sun is *astronomical noon*) is exactly 24 hours. But because of the Sun's eastward motion among the stars, the period between successive culminations of any star is only 23 hours and 56 minutes. To better understand this, imagine that the Sun is culminating at the same moment as a star located due north of it (the star, of course, lost in the Sun's glare). Because of the Sun's slow motion eastward among the stars, 23 hours and 56 minutes later the star will culminate but the Sun will still be 1° east of the meridian. Four minutes later the Sun itself will culminate. 24 hours is called the *solar day*, 23 hours and 56 minutes the *sidereal day*. (If the sidereal day was taken as the standard and divided into 24 hours, those hours would be slightly shorter than the 24 hours of our solar day. We use solar rather than sidereal time to keep our clocks in synchronization with the rising and setting of the Sun.)

Motion of the Moon on the Celestial Sphere. The Sun's glare makes it impossible to directly observe its yearly motion through the stars. (The Sun's location among the stars can be inferred from the stars that rise just before sunrise or set just after sunset.) However, it is easy to watch the Moon's west-to-east motion through the zodiac over the course of a month. In fact, during a single night the Moon's location with respect to the bright stars near it will perceptibly change. And

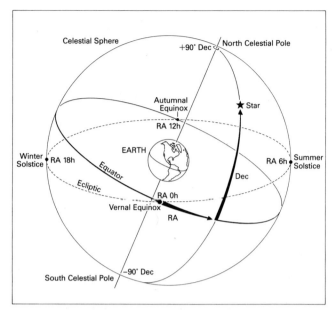

Figure 1–1. *The celestial sphere, with its important circles and reference points.*

if you are a careful observer, you might even notice that the time it takes the Moon to return to one of its phases (first quarter, full moon, last quarter) is *longer* than the time it takes the Moon to return to a specific location among the fixed stars. For example, if one month the Moon is at first quarter near the 1st-magnitude star Regulus in the constellation of Leo the Lion, it will still be only a crescent when it reaches that spot the next month: another couple of nights will have to pass before the Moon once again reaches first quarter, by which time it will be among the stars well east of Regulus. The period necessary for the Moon to return to the same location among the stars is the *sidereal month*, the period for it to return to the same phase is the *synodic month*. The sidereal month is 27 1/3 days long, the synodic month 29 1/2 days. The reason for the discrepancy is that while the Moon is moving west-to-east among the stars, the Sun is moving west-to-east also (though much more slowly); consequently, by the time the Moon has done a full circuit of the zodiac, the Sun has done nearly a twelfth circuit. So, for the same amount of Sun-illuminated Moon to be seen by us, the Moon must be farther east in the zodiac.

The Celestial Poles and the Celestial Equator. Because it is the Earth's daily rotation on its axis that makes the celestial sphere seem to rotate, the axis of rotation of the celestial sphere is simply the projection of the Earth's axis. And just as at the ends of the Earth's axis of rotation are the North and South Poles, so at the ends of the celestial sphere's axis of rotation are the north and south *celestial* poles. The north celestial pole is near the famous North Star, Polaris. If you watch Polaris during the course of a night, you will see that it

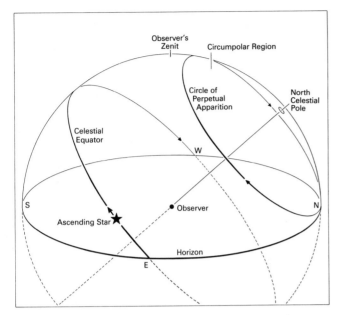

Figure 1–2. *The dome of the sky with its important circles and reference points as they appear from latitude 40° north. The north circumpolar stars and constellations lie between the circle of perpetual apparition and the north celestial pole. As one goes farther north in latitude, the north celestial pole gets nearer the zenith and the celestial equator nearer the southern horizon.*

does not move but that stars near it trace arcs centered upon it. If you could watch these stars right through the next day, you would see that they appear to revolve in circles of various diameters around Polaris (the size of the circle depending upon the star's distance from Polaris). If you stood at the Earth's North Pole (and if it were the 6-months-long polar night), Polaris and the north celestial pole would be directly overhead; and during a 24-hour period the other stars would move in circular paths centered on Polaris and parallel to the horizon. A similar phenomenon could be observed at the South Pole, though there are no bright stars near the south celestial pole and, consequently, no real "South Star."

Halfway between the north and south celestial poles is the celestial equator, which is the projection on the celestial sphere of the Earth's equator. If you stood on the Earth's equator, the north celestial pole would be exactly at the north point of the horizon, the south celestial pole would be at the south point of the horizon, and the celestial equator would arc from the east point of the horizon directly overhead to the west point of the horizon. (The line connecting the east and west points of the horizon and passing overhead is called the *prime vertical,* but only at the Earth's equator does the prime vertical correspond to the celestial equator.) During the course of a night (which will be exactly 12 hours long at the equator, no matter what the astronomical season of the year) the stars will be seen to follow paths

on great semicircular arcs, the arcs of stars near the celestial poles being smaller than the arcs of stars that pass overhead or nearly overhead. Because the celestial poles are halfway around the celestial sphere from each other, they are 180° apart; the celestial equator is 90° from the celestial poles.

For observers midway between the Earth's equator and North Pole (that is, on north latitude 45°), Polaris and the north celestial pole are located halfway up from the north point of the horizon toward the zenith. In general, the height in degrees of the north celestial pole above the north point of an observer's horizon is the same as the observer's latitude. And for mid-northern observers the stars (and Sun and Moon) rise and set on trajectories that make slanting angles with the horizon; the nearer the observer to the Earth's equator, the steeper the angle. At the Earth's equator all celestial objects rise and set perpendicularly to the horizon.

The Circumpolar Stars. The stars that swing down between the north celestial pole and the north point of an observer's horizon, and that therefore never rise or set for the observer, are called the *north circumpolar stars.* Exactly how many stars are circumpolar for an observer depends on the observer's latitude: the farther north you are, the higher the north celestial pole is above your horizon and therefore the larger the part of the celestial sphere that never rises or sets for you. At the Earth's North Pole (and South Pole) *all* visible stars are circumpolar; at the Earth's equator no stars are circumpolar.

Because the south celestial pole is beneath the south point of a northern hemisphere observer's horizon by the same amount that the north celestial pole is *above* the north point of that observer's horizon, there are southern stars that trace circular paths around the south celestial pole and can never be seen at the observer's latitude. The *circle of perpetual occulation* bounds the region on the celestial sphere that is never visible at a given latitude on the Earth's surface. Conversely, the *circle of perpetual apparition* outlines the region on the celestial sphere that never sets at a given latitude. The size of these circles on the celestial sphere depends only on latitude: the higher the latitude, the larger both circles—indeed, the radii of both circles are the same as the observer's latitude.

The Celestial Coordinate System. Just as latitude and longitude specify a place's location on the sphere of the Earth, so *declination* and *right ascension* give a object's location on the sphere of the sky. Like terrestrial latitude, declination (dec) is measured in degrees and goes from 0° at the celestial equator to +90° at the north celestial pole and −90° at the south celestial pole. However, right ascension (RA), though analogous to terrestrial longitude, is measured in hours, minutes,

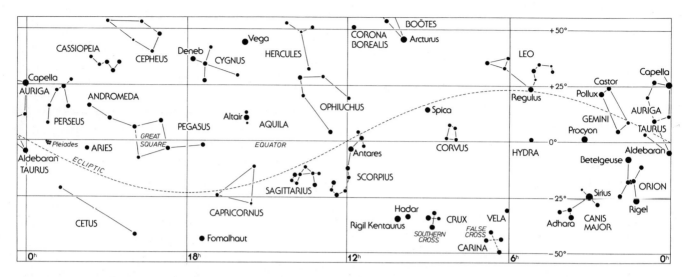

Figure 1–3. *A chart of the heavens between declinations +50° and −50° for 2832 B.C. illustrating the effect of precession. Notice that the Pleiades and the Great Square of Pegasus, presently in the northern heavens, were right on the celestial equator. The Head of Scorpius, today in the southern half of the celestial sphere, was on the celestial equator, and the Belt of Orion, which now is on the celestial equator, was in the southern sky. Adapted from a chart by George Lovi which appeared in the April, 1983* Sky & Telescope *magazine.*

and seconds, each of the 24 hours of right ascension occupying a space on the celestial sphere that resembles a narrow slice cut from an apple. If one star is located sufficiently east of the celestial sphere from another star that it culminates one hour later, then the first star is one hour east in right ascension from the second star. Thus, right ascension is a time derived system, and around the celestial equator (or any other circle of declination) there are $24 \times 60 \times 60 = 86,400$ seconds in right ascension. Declination, on the other hand, though its degrees are also divided into minutes and seconds, is based upon geometric measure: so, around the great circles joining the north and south celestial poles, along which declination is measured, there are $90 \times 60 \times 60 = 324,000$ seconds. Notice that the apparent width of each degree, minute, and second of declination is the same everywhere on the celestial sphere: that is simply because declination is measured around circles of the same size (great circles joining the celestial poles, as was just said). However, the farther north or south on the celestial sphere you go, the *narrower* are the hours, minutes, and seconds of right ascension: they still represent the same amount of *time* elapsed between culminations, but their actual angles are smaller. Think of the apple-slice analogy again: each of the 24 slices is narrower at the top and bottom than in the middle.

The Equinoxes and Solstices. The zero point (0 hours) of right ascension is the *vernal equinox*, the point where the ecliptic—the Sun's path through the stars—crosses the celestial equator in the spring. The point where the Sun crosses the celestial equator on its way

from the northern down to the southern celestial hemisphere in the fall is called the *autumnal equinox*. The most northerly point on the ecliptic is the *summer solstice*, the most southerly the *winter solstice*. For observers in the Earth's northern hemisphere, the day is longest at summer solstice, shortest at winter solstice, and the day and night are both 12 hours long at the equinoxes (as indeed they are everywhere on the Earth at the equinoxes). Despite the glare of the Sun, the locations among the stars of the points of the equinoxes and solstices have been determined precisely: the vernal equinox is in the constellation of Pisces southeast of the asterism called the "Circlet" of Pisces; the summer solstice is just within Taurus about 1° due west of the 4th-magnitude star 1 Geminorum; the autumnal equinox is in western Virgo about 3½° southeast of Beta (β) Virginis; and the winter solstice is in Sagittarius only about 1° northeast of the naked-eye nebula M8.

Precession of the Equinoxes. Unfortunately, the points of the equinoxes and solstices among the stars do not remain the same but slide slowly westward. This phenomenon, called the *precession of the equinoxes*, is the result of the gravitational pull of the Sun and the Moon upon the Earth's equatorial bulge (the Earth's equatorial diameter is some 27 miles greater than its polar diameter), which causes the direction in which the Earth's axis of rotation points to slowly change. Thus, the locations of the north and south celestial poles on the celestial sphere change with time, tracing circles about 27° in diameter in a period just under

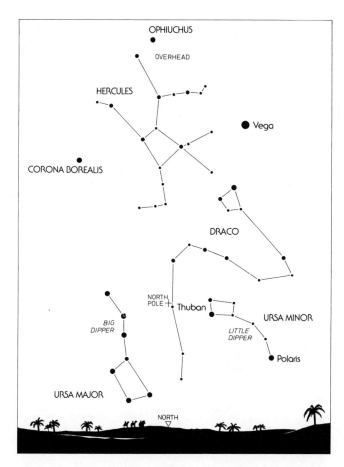

Figure 1–4. *A chart of the north circumpolar stars and the region of Hercules as they would have appeared from the latitudes of Sumeria and Egypt around 3000 B.C. Due to the precession the Pole Star at that time was Thuban, Alpha Draconis. Adapted from a chart by George Lovi which appeared in the April, 1983* Sky & Telescope *magazine.*

26,000 years long. And the places where the celestial equator intersects the ecliptic (the vernal and autumnal equinoxes) slowly shift westward among the stars. 2000 years ago the vernal equinox was in the constellation Aries the Ram, which is why the vernal equinox is sometimes still called the "First Point of Aries."

Precession of the equinoxes is unquestionably the most difficult aspect of the celestial coordinate system to visualize. But is it not as important to understand *why* it occurs as to know *what* it causes—namely, the shift in position over a long period of time of the celestial poles and of the solstices and equinoxes. Because the celestial poles are the ultimate reference point for the celestial coordinate system (the celestial equator, for example, is defined with respect to the celestial poles), over time the circles of right ascension and parallels of declination gradually also shift *their* position with respect to the fixed stars. Thus, all star charts eventually become obsolete. Presently, star charts (including all the charts by Wil Tirion that appear in this book)

are drawn for "equinox 2000.0"—i.e., with the positions that the circles of right ascension and parallels of declination will have among the stars on January 1, 2000. However, many star charts are still in use that were designed for equinox 1950.0. Fortunately, the shifting of the celestial coordinate system is so gradual that it would take a good deal more than 50 years for a star chart to become useless for the unaided-eye or binocular observer.

Directions on the Celestial Sphere. Even experienced observers occasionally lose track of directions in the sky. In telescopes the direction problem is compounded because the field of view is inverted and sometimes reversed. Binoculars fortunately are designed to magnify a field without changing its orientation. To find your way around the celestial sphere, you need to keep only two basic rules in mind. First, because Polaris is almost exactly at the north celestial pole, the direction toward Polaris from anywhere on the celestial sphere is north. Second, the direction of a celestial object's daily motion across the sky is west.

If you are in the middle northern latitudes facing south, the directions on the celestial sphere are easy to determine: north is up toward Polaris behind you and west is the direction in which the stars appear to move, from left to right. But the situation when you look toward the north celestial pole can be more confusing. The north circumpolar stars appear to move counterclockwise around the north celestial pole during the course of a night. Consequently, the stars between your zenith and the north celestial pole are slowly moving from right to left, and the stars between the pole and the northern horizon are moving from left to right. Nevertheless, in terms of the celestial sphere they are all moving west.

Distances on the celestial sphere are measured in degrees, minutes, and seconds along great circles. These degrees, minutes, and seconds are of the same widths as those of declination, but they are measured in any direction across the celestial sphere, whereas declination is measured only along north-south great circles (i.e., great circles that pass through the celestial poles).

1.2 The Constellations

Star Designations. Most of the brightest stars have proper names. The origins of these names are briefly discussed in Appendix A of this book. However, there does not seem to have been any attempt to scientifically label the stars before the 16th century of our era. The earliest star-designation system to stick was introduced by German astronomer Johannes Bayer in his *Uranometria*, which was published in 1603. Bayer labelled the brightest stars in each constellation by the letters of the

| Table 1–1 |
| The Greek Alphabet |

Alpha	α	Iota	ι	Rho	ϱ
Beta	β	Kappa	κ	Sigma	σ
Gamma	γ	Lambda	λ	Tau	τ
Delta	δ	Mu	μ	Upsilon	υ
Epsilon	ε	Nu	ν	Phi	φ
Zeta	ζ	Xi	ξ	Chi	χ
Eta	η	Omicron	o	Psi	ψ
Theta	ϑ	Pi	π	Omega	ω

ancient Greek alphabet (listed in Table 1 1).

In general, Bayer applied these designations in approximate order of brightness. However, there are numerous exceptions to this rule. Indeed, often he applied the Greek letters in simple west-to-east order—as in the Big Dipper, where Alpha (α) marks the star at the front top of the Dipper's bowl, (β) the star at the front bottom of the Dipper's bowl, and so on, to Eta (η) at the end of the Dipper's handle.

The next important system of star labelling was that of the English astronomer John Flamsteed, on whose posthumously-published *Atlas* (1753) the naked-eye stars in each constellation are numbered in west-to-east order. Other more-or-less contemporaneous designation systems used capital or lowercase Roman letters. The Flamsteed numbers are still used today; but the sole significant residual of the Roman letter systems is in variable star designations, for the brightest variables in each constellation are still labelled with either one or two Roman capital letters.

In all these designation systems the letter or number of the star is followed by the possessive form of the constellation's Latin name—as Beta (β) Orionis, 1 Geminorum, VV Cephei, etc. Stars identified by their numbers in the modern standard star catalogues used by professional astronomers are not followed by the constellation name. These catalogues are usually indicated only by their abbreviations, so the stars tabulated in them are referred to in such forms as "GC 31978" and "HD 151804."

The major open clusters, globular clusters, planetary and diffuse nebulae, and galaxies are designated either by an "M" or "NGC" number. The first is from a catalogue of such objects (made, in fact, before their true nature was known) by the late 18th-century French comet-hunter Charles Messier, who got tired of "discovering" comets that turned out to be merely the faint fuzzy objects that he had seen at the same locations before. He therefore made a list of such objects for his own future reference. His catalogue originally had 103 pseudo-comets, but so many clusters and nebulae continued to be found during the 19th century that in 1888

John Dreyer published a *New General Catalogue* (NGC) tabulating thousands of them. And so many more continued to be discovered as larger telescopes came into use that in a few years two *Index Catalogues* (IC) were published as a supplement to the NGC. There are, of course, more recent catalogues of very faint galaxies, clusters, and nebulae that have been compiled, but the M, NGC, and IC lists contain almost all that can be seen in amateur telescopes.

Star Brightness. For readers unfamiliar with it, the magnitude system used to specify star brightness is briefly explained in Appendix B at the end of this book.

The Northern Circumpolar Constellations
[Chart I, page 7. Bright Star Atlas, Maps 1 & 2.]

The place to begin constellation identification is with the Big Dipper, a conspicuous far-northern asterism of 2nd- and 3rd-magnitude stars that seems to be known to practically everyone. For observers north of about latitude +40° the entire Dipper can be seen all night every clear night of the year, its stars slowly tracing arcs centered on the north celestial pole as the hours pass. The Big Dipper's exact location in the northern sky during the early evening depends upon the time of the year: in the Autumn it sits on the northern horizon; in the Winter it seems to balance on the tip of its handle over the NE horizon; in the Spring it is almost straight overhead (and upside down, if you stand facing the north looking up at it); and in the Summer it is high in the NW. Because its stars are so bright, it can be easily spotted even during nights of the full Moon.

The Big Dipper is actually only the hindquarters and surrealistically long tail of the huge constellation **Ursa Major,** the Great Bear. The nose of the Bear is marked by the 3rd-magnitude star Omicron (o) Ursae Majoris, which lies about 15° due west of Alpha (α) Ursae, the top front star of the Dipper's bowl. About 15° to 20° SW and south of the Dipper bowl are three pairs of 3rd- and 4th-magnitude stars that mark three of the Great Bear's feet: Iota (ι) + Kappa (κ), Lambda (λ) + Mu (μ), and Nu (ν) + Xi (ξ). Several individual 3rd- and 4th-mag stars between these three pairs and the Dipper bowl trace the legs of the Bear. (The Bear's fourth foot originally was the Alpha + 38 Lyncis pair, which forms an equilateral triangle with sides 15° long with Iota + Kappa and Lambda + Mu Ursae. However, these two stars were stolen from the Great Bear by Hevelius in the late 17th century for use in his new constellation of the Lynx.)

Ursa Major is rich in interesting objects for binoculars, as will be shown in the section on the constellation later in this book. It even has an unaided-eye object, the Mizar-Alcor double star in the middle of the Dip-

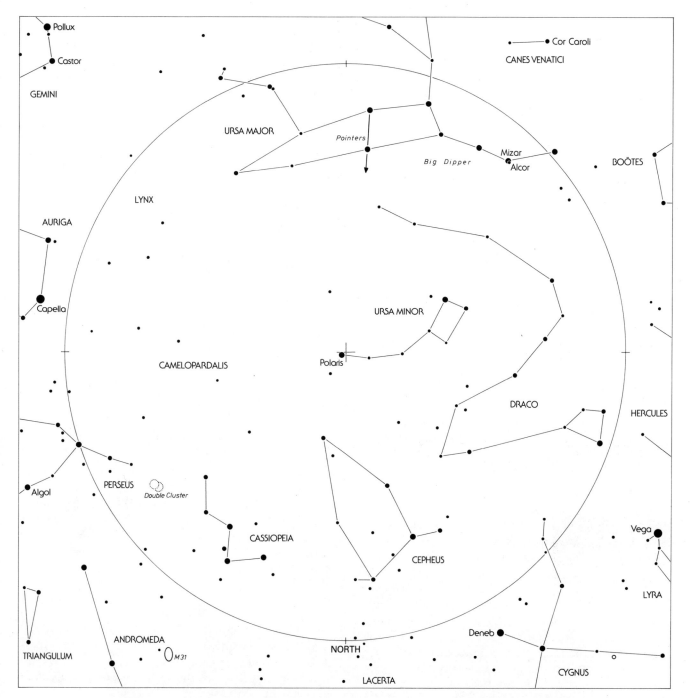

Chart I: The North Circumpolar Constellations for latitudes around 40°N. *The chart is oriented to show the northern sky as it appears for an observer looking North at about 9 p.m. standard time on April 15. To see the position of these constellations 3 months later at 9 p.m. standard time (or 6 hours later the night of April 15–16), rotate the page one-quarter turn counterclockwise. To see them 3 months earlier at 9 p.m., rotate the page one-quarter turn clockwise.*

per's handle. The 4th-magnitude Alcor is nearly 12′ (40% of the Moon's apparent diameter) away from the mag 2 1/2 Mizar and can be resolved by anyone with reasonably good eyesight observing at a location well away from artificial outdoor lights. These two stars are a true gravitationally-connected binary system, but the orbital period of the 4th-magnitude secondary around the brighter star must be thousands of years long.

The Big Dipper is the key to constellation-identification for northern hemisphere observers because its stars point toward other important stars and star groups in the northern sky. Several times during this tour of the heavens we shall return to the Big Dipper to gather ourselves for assaults into the different regions of the sky, but for now we shall follow the line between the two front stars in the Dipper's bowl north to the North Star, Polaris, which lies less than 1° from the true north celestial pole. The distance between the "Pointers," as they are appropriately called, is almost exactly 5°, and the distance from the northern Pointer (Alpha Ursae Majoris) to Polaris is nearly 20°. These two measures provide a rough-and-ready yardstick for estimating distances elsewhere on the celestial sphere, and are always available, because at mid-northern latitudes the Dipper and Polaris are visible the whole night through. Polaris is near enough to the north celestial pole that it appears to remain stationary upon it. However, long-exposure photographs reveal that Polaris, too, traces a tiny arc, the result of its 1° distance from the pole's true location on the celestial sphere.

Polaris marks the end of the handle of the Little Dipper, a much smaller star group than the Big Dipper. Because its handle curves up rather than down (in the manner of the Big Dipper's handle), the little Dipper perhaps resembles a ladle more than it does a dipper. Its stars are generally fainter than those of the Big Dipper, though it includes two of the 2nd magnitude (Polaris and Beta [β] Ursae Minoris) and one of the 3rd (Gamma [γ] UMi). The Little Dipper is actually the constellation **Ursa Minor,** the Little Bear, a group invented by the Greeks sometime around the 6th century B.C. to join the much more ancient Great Bear, which had been mentioned by the two earliest Greek poets, Homer and Hesiod, in the 8th century.

On the opposite side of the north celestial pole from the Big Dipper, and about the same distance from Polaris, is a somewhat misshapen 15° long "W" (or "M"— it depends upon what side of the pole it happens to be on) of 2nd- and 3rd-magnitude stars. These are the brightest members of the constellation **Cassiopeia** the Queen. If you attach the 4th-magnitude Kappa (κ) to the "W", the star pattern resembles another celestial dipper or ladle. Here is one of the many examples of

a group of stars that does not look anything like what the ancient Greeks named it. Presumably, they simply wanted to get Cassiopeia into the heavens.

In Greek mythology Cassiopeia was the wife of Cepheus, King of Ethiopia, and mother of Andromeda, both of whom have also been honored with a place among the stars. According to the story, Cassiopeia offended the sea nymphs by boasting that she was more beautiful than they, so they sent a Sea-monster, Cetus, to ravage the coast of Ethiopia. Neptune, the god of the Sea, proclaimed that he and the sea-nymphs would be appeased only if Andromeda was chained to a sea-cliff and offered as a sacrifice to Cetus. Cepheus and Cassiopeia, with broken hearts, did as the god demanded. However, just as Cetus was about to devour the helpless Andromeda, the hero Perseus chanced along, flying through the sky with the assistance of his winged sandals and carrying in a sack the newly-severed head of the Medusa, a monster-woman with snakes for hair and such hideous features that all who gazed upon her were turned to stone. (Perseus had succeeded in decapitating the Medusa by looking not directly at her but only at her reflection in his highly-polished bronze shield.) Perseus used his baggage to good advantage by showing the Medusa's head to Cetus. Perseus holding the Medusa-head and Cetus are two of the Autumn constellations.

The one celestial sphere that has survived to us from antiquity, the so-called Farnese Globe (thought to have been carved during the 1st century B.C.: it surmounts a marble statue of Atlas found in the ruins of the palaces of the Roman emperors in Rome in A.D. 1575), shows Cassiopeia seated on a simple stool. Her head is oriented toward the south (apparently considered to be at the 4th- and 5th-magnitude stars Nu [ν], Xi [ξ], Omicron [o], and Pi [π] Cassiopeiae) and her arms are outstretched. The Milky Way runs behind the "W"-figure, and therefore Cassiopeia is a constellation rich in objects for binoculars and telescopes. In particular, there is an abundance of open clusters, some of the best of which are described in the section on Cassiopeia later in this book.

WNW of Cassiopeia is **Cepheus** the King. The brightest stars of this constellation are arranged in a crude house-shaped pattern about 30° high. The 3rd-magnitude star at the "gable" of the house, Gamma (γ) Cephei, can be found by extending the line from the Pointers in the Big Dipper to Polaris another 12° beyond Polaris. The house-figure is symmetrical around the NE-SW line from Gamma, its four stars Alpha (α), Beta (β), Iota (ι), and Zeta (ζ) arranged in a square with sides about 8° to 9° long.

Forming a narrow isosceles triangle with Zeta at the south corner of the square of Cepheus are Delta (δ) and Epsilon (ϵ) Cephei. Delta Cephei is the prototype of the cepheid variable stars, pulsating supergiants that change in brightness with clockwork regularity (usually). Delta Ceph itself varies between magnitudes 3.6 and 4.3 every 5 days and 9 hours, and its variations can be followed with the unaided eye by comparing its brightness with that of the mag 3.4 Zeta and mag 4.2 Epsilon.

The last major north circumpolar constellation is **Draco** the Dragon. Despite consisting almost entirely of 3rd- and 4th-magnitude stars, the pattern of Draco does indeed have a remarkably serpentine form. To trace it, begin at the star at Draco's tail-tip, the 4th-magnitude Lambda (λ) Draconis, which lies about one-fourth the distance from the Pointers in the Big Dipper to Polaris. The body of the Dragon curves in a wide arc around the bowl of the Little Dipper and then, at its northernmost point (where its coils are midway between the bowl of the Little Dipper and the magnitude $2\frac{1}{2}$ Alpha [α] Cephei), makes a sharp turn back SW, ending in the fairly conspicuous 8° long asterism of Beta (β)-Gamma (γ)-Mu (μ)-Nu (ν)-Xi (ξ) Dra, the Head of Draco. The ancient Greek astronomical poet Aratos speaks of Draco's head as "nodding" toward the tail of Ursa Major, and the monster is indeed facing in that direction.

There are two large star-poor constellations in the north circumpolar region, **Lynx** and **Camelopardalis** the Giraffe. These are both 17th-century additions to the sky, mere names given to fill in an area whose faint stars were unorganized by the ancient Greeks. Lynx occupies the star-dim space SW of Ursa Major (it is between the Great Bear and the Winter constellations Auriga and Gemini), and Camelopardalis is in the even vaster and blanker area between the head of the Great Bear, Polaris, and Cassiopeia. In both constellations together, which cover an area larger than the whole of Ursa Major, there is only one star as bright as the 3rd magnitude, Alpha (α) Lyncis in the extreme SE corner of Lynx. Insofar as Lynx has a star pattern, it is the 40° long SE-NW line that begins at the Alpha+38 Lyncis pair (which, as already has been mentioned, forms an equilateral triangle with the Iota-Kappa and Lambda-Mu Ursae Majoris pairs) and includes 31, 26, 22, 15, and 2 Lyn, all 4th- or 5th-magnitude stars. Camelopardalis offers even less: look for the bent line of Beta (β), Alpha (α), and Gamma (γ) Camelopardali in the western part of the constellation: Alpha and Beta point toward the bright star Capella in Auriga (see the Winter constellations), and Beta is about one-third the distance from Capella to Polaris.

The Spring Constellations
[Chart II, page 11. Bright Star Atlas, Maps 5 & 6.]

In the main part of this book I will begin with the Autumn constellations. The reason is that the Autumn sky has three distinct regions, each characterized by certain types of objects for the binocular or telescope observer. Here, however, I shall begin with the Spring, because at that time of the year the Big Dipper is high overhead for mid-northern observers and its stars are splendid guides to the Spring heavens.

We start with the two back stars of the Dipper's bowl, which point SW toward the 1st-magnitude star Regulus, some 50° distant. Regulus is the brightest star in the zodiacal constellation of **Leo** the Lion, and is at the base of a 15° tall asterism called "The Sickle," which is formed, in addition to Regulus itself, by Eta (η), Gamma (γ), Zeta (ζ), Mu (μ), and Epsilon (ϵ) Leonis. (As we shall see, there are several other conspicuous asterisms in the Spring sky.) The Sickle marks the shoulder and the head of the Lion; the beast's hindquarters is the right triangle 15° due east of the Sickle consisting of 3rd-magnitude Delta (δ) and Theta (θ) Leo and 2nd-magnitude Beta (β).

Beta Leonis is named Denebola, from the Arabic for "Tail of the Lion," a title given to the star by medieval Arabian astronomers. The name Regulus, however, has even more ancient antecedents. It is Latin for "Little King," but the association of the star with kingship goes all the way back to Mesopotamia, where Assyrian astronomical texts from around 1000 B.C. call the star *Mul Lugal*, "Star of the King." This is one of the many Graeco-Roman star and constellation names that originated in Mesopotamia.

On a clear, moonless night you can see, about 20° due west of Gamma Leonis (the 2nd-magnitude star in the middle of the Sickle), a patch of dim haze comparable in size to the full Moon. This is M44, the Praesepe ("Manger") or Beehive Star Cluster, one of the best objects in the sky for binoculars. To the unaided eye it appears merely like a little shred of faint cloud, but even in 7x35 binoculars it resolves into a couple dozen 6th-, 7th-, and 8th-magnitude stars. M44 is at the center of the constellation of **Cancer** the Crab, another of the 12 zodiacal groups. The cluster is enclosed within a quadrilateral of 4th- and 5th-magnitude stars, Gamma (γ), Delta (δ), Eta (η), and Theta (θ) Cancri. This quadrilateral marks the body of the Crab, its legs extending about 12° SSW to Beta (β), 9° SSE to Alpha (α), and 9° north to Iota (ι). All these are only 4th-magnitude stars. Indeed, Cancer is one of the two faintest of the zodiacal groups (the other being Pisces the Fishes in the Autumn sky). The faintness of Cancer's stars make its star pattern difficult to trace if the sky is brightened by moonlight or city-light.

About 15° due south of M44 (and 20° WSW of Regulus) is a compact (5° in diameter) asterism of a half dozen 3rd- and 4th-magnitude stars. This is the Head of **Hydra** the Sea-serpent, the largest constellation in the sky. Hydra extends for a full 100°, 7 hours of right ascension, from the Winter constellations of Canis Minor and Monoceros on the west almost to the Summer constellation of Scorpius on the east. Its meandering star pattern can be tricky to trace because many of its stars are only of the 4th magnitude, and much of the constellation does not rise very far above the southern horizon-haze for mid-northern observers, but once identified the constellation does indeed appear serpentine.

We start our odyssey down the length of Hydra at the Serpent's head. First, go about 7° SW to the 4th-magnitude star Theta (θ) Hydrae, and another 7° on the same line to Iota (ι). From Iota go 8° SSW to the 2nd-magnitude Alpha (α), called Alphard, "The Solitary One," by the Arabs because no other bright stars are in this area. A line ESE from Alphard takes you first to the 4th-magnitude Lambda (λ) and then, 20° from Alphard, to the 3rd-magnitude Nu (ν) Hya.

Nu Hydrae is a convenient guide to the faint but beautiful star pattern of **Crater** the Cup. SE of Nu, about 5° apart, are the two 4th-magnitude stars, Alpha (α) and Beta (β) Crateris, forming the base of the Cup's foot. To their NE is the semi-circle of 4th- and 5th-mag stars, about 8° in diameter and open to the NE, which forms the bowl of the Cup. The whole star pattern is remarkably similar to the footed wine-goblets that were actually used by the ancient Greeks.

Alpha and Beta Crateris can be thought of as part of the constellation-figure of Hydra as well, because the Greek astronomical texts describe the Cup as sitting on the coils of Hydra and it is shown thus on the Farnese Globe. Beyond these two stars the course of Hydra becomes more ambiguous. Go 5° south from Beta Cra to the 5th-magnitude Chi (χ)-1 Hydrae, and from there SE some 10° to the faint triangle of Xi (ξ), Omicron (o), and Beta Hya. This triangle can be very difficult to spot if the night is hazy: look for it about 15° due south of the bowl of Crater. Some 20° ENE of Beta Hydra is the 3rd-magnitude Gamma (γ) (best found with the assistance of Corvus, as mentioned below). Finally, the tail of the Sea-serpent is at Pi (π) and 58 Hya SW of the late Spring zodiacal constellation Libra the Scales.

There are four minor constellations of the Spring sky that are best found by starting at Leo. South of Regulus is the faint group **Sextans** the Sextant, formed in the late 17th century by Hevelius. The least inconspicuous star pattern in this constellation is the Alpha (α) - Beta (β) - Delta (δ) Sextantis triangle, Alpha located about 12° due south of Regulus and the other two stars 6° east

of Alpha. In the region between the blade of the Sickle and the two back feet of Ursa Major (the Lambda-Mu and Nu-Xi UMa pairs) is **Leo Minor** the Little Lion, another Hevelius innovation. Its main star pattern is the 10° long lozenge formed by Beta-21-28 plus 30-46 Leonis Minoris. Leo Minor occupies one of the least interesting areas of the sky: even for telescopes it offers only a few faint galaxies.

About 15° NE of Denebola on a line toward the end of the handle of the Big Dipper is a roughly triangular concentration of 5th- and 6th-magnitude stars. This is the **Coma Berenices** Star Cluster, a fine object in low power binoculars. It is one of the very few ancient Greek constellations the creation of which can be attributed to a specific century and inventor. (See the section on Coma later in this book for the story.) The area of the sky now considered to be included in the constellation is much larger than the cluster itself. The main star pattern outside of the cluster is the simple right angle formed by Alpha (α), Beta (β), and Gamma (γ) Comae, all 4th-magnitude stars: Gamma is on the north edge of the Coma Star Cluster (though not a true cluster member), Beta 10° due east of Gamma, and Alpha 10° due south of Beta and just over halfway from Denebola ENE to Arcturus in Boötes.

Midway between the Coma Star Cluster and the handle of the Big Dipper is a SE-NW pair of stars about 6° apart. These are the brightest members of **Canes Venatici** the Hunting Dogs, a group invented in the early 16th century to assist Boötes in his nightly driving of the Great Bear across the sky. The SE star of the pair, the 3rd-magnitude Alpha (α), was named Cor Caroli, "Heart of Charles," in honor of Charles I after Charles II restored the English Monarchy in 1660 subsequent to the collapse of the Cromwellian interregnum. This pair of stars is very easy to identify, for the region south of the handle of the Big Dipper is quite star-poor.

From the minor constellations around Leo we go to the constellations of late Spring. The path to these constellations is along the curve of the handle of the Big Dipper. Extend the curve of the handle 30° south to the very bright golden-colored star Arcturus. Another 30° south and slightly east will bring you to another bright star, Spica. As some guidebooks aptly put it, "Follow the *arc* to Arcturus; then make a *spike* to Spica."

Arcturus is the brightest star in the constellation of **Boötes** the Herdsman. Indeed, Arcturus at magnitude -0.04 is the brightest star north of the celestial equator. It is at the base of a very distinctive 25° tall kite-shaped figure, one of the easiest asterisms in the heavens to identify. This kite-shape represents the body of Herdsman, his head at Beta (β), his shoulders at Gamma (γ) and Delta (δ), and his waist the Epsilon (ϵ) - Sigma+Rho ($\sigma + \rho$) line. His knees are marked by

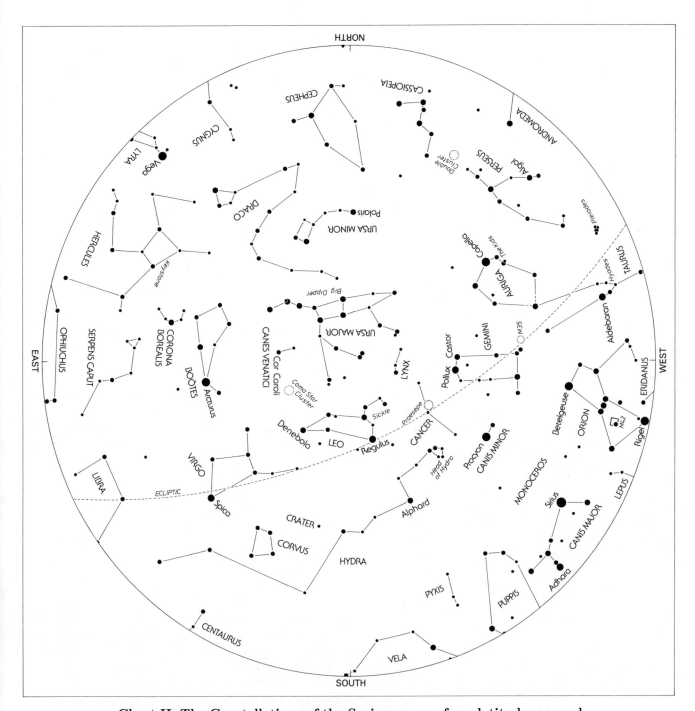

Chart II: The Constellations of the Spring as seen from latitudes around 40°N at about 9 p.m. standard time on April 15, 11 p.m. standard time on March 15, and 7 p.m. standard time on May 15. *The key to the identification of the Spring Constellations is the Big Dipper, which is nearly straight overhead at 40°N latitude during the early evenings of the Spring. Follow the line of the two stars at the back of the Dipper-bowl SW to Regulus, at the base of the Sickle in Leo the Lion. The "arc" of the handle of the Dipper will take you to Arcturus; then make a "spike" from Arcturus straight south to Spica.*

the two little trios of dim stars a few degrees WSW and SE of Arcturus. According to the ancient Greek astronomical texts, Arcturus itself merely marks the hem of the Herdsman's tunic—a rather trivial function for the chief luminary of the northern heavens!

East of the waist and immediately SE of the right shoulder of Boötes is the half circle of 2nd-, 3rd-, and 4th-magnitude stars that forms **Corona Borealis** the Northern Crown. This is one of the few star patterns that reasonably resembles what it was named for, which is not a gold crown but the laurel wreath worn by victors at the Greek athletic and poetry-reading contests and later by Roman generals and emperors. Like the laurel crown itself, the circlet of stars of Corona Borealis is open at one end. (In the main part of this book I include Corona Borealis among the Summer Constellations, but it is best found with the assistance of Boötes.)

Spica is the brightest star in the zodiacal constellation of **Virgo** the Maiden. This constellation covers a very large area in the Spring sky, but other than Spica its awkward and sprawling star pattern is composed only of 3rd- and 4th-magnitude stars. Extending NW from Spica toward Leo is a large leaning "Y" shape consisting of Theta (θ), Gamma (γ), Eta (η), Beta (β), Nu (ν), Delta (δ), and Epsilon (ϵ) Virginis. The region enclosed by Beta, Gamma, and Epsilon Virginis and Denebola in Leo is called "The Realm of the Galaxies" because within it is the richest concentration of galaxies in the sky. NE of Spica is a bent-rectangle pattern of stars formed by Spica itself with Zeta (ζ), Tau (τ), 109, Mu (μ) and Iota (ι) Virginis.

About 15° SW of Spica is the conspicuous quadrilateral of 3rd-magnitude stars that forms **Corvus** the Crow. In Greek astronomical literature Corvus is described as pecking at the tail of Hydra; and thus it is illustrated not only on the 1st century B.C. Farnese Globe, but even on a Mesopotamian astronomical tablet of the 3rd century B.C. The 3rd-magnitude star Gamma (γ) Hydrae is 10° due east of Beta (β) Corvi and 12° south of Spica.

Gamma and, another 10° to the WSW, Pi (π) Hydrae are helpful in finding your way into **Centaurus,** for the two northernmost bright stars of the Centaur are directly south: the 3rd-magnitude Iota (ι) Centauri is 14° due south of Gamma Hydrae, and the 2nd-magnitude Theta (θ) Cen is 10° south of Pi Hya. Centaurus and **Lupus** the Wolf directly to its east are rich in bright stars but are so far south on the celestial sphere that only from the extreme southern continental United States can they be easily observed—and even there binoculars are necessary to pick their very southernmost stars out of the horizon haze.

Some 25° east of Spica is a SW-NE pair of 4th-magnitude stars about 9° apart. These stars mark the balance-beam of the zodiacal constellation **Libra** the Scales. They are easy to find because they are the only reasonably bright stars between Spica and the arc of stars marking the head of Scorpius. Several degrees to the SE of each is a faint star that represents one of the two scale trays. About 12° due south of the midpoint of the balance-beam is the solitary 3rd-magnitude star now labelled Sigma (σ) Librae, but during the 17th and 18th centuries it was included among the stars of Scorpius and designated Gamma (γ) Scorpii.

The Summer Constellations
[Chart III, page 15. Bright Star Atlas, Map 7.]

The best way to find your way around the Summer skies is by first identifying the "Summer Triangle" of 1st-magnitude stars formed by Vega in Lyra, Altair in Aquila, and Deneb in Cygnus. The magnitude 0.0 Vega, the brightest of the three, is about 15° SE of the Head of Draco and on the western edge of the Summer Milky Way. Deneb, at magnitude 1.3 the faintest of the Summer Triangle trio, is some 30° ENE of Vega in the middle of the Milky Way; and the magnitude 0.8 Altair is about 40° SE of Vega on the eastern edge of the Milky Way. Look for the Summer Triangle in the region just east of your zenith during the early evenings of June, and just west of the zenith during the early evenings of August and September. There will be no mistaking it, for these three are the only 1st-magnitude stars in the northern two-thirds of the Summer skies.

Vega's brilliant blue-white luster almost completely overpowers the other stars of its constellation, **Lyra** the Lyre. Nevertheless, Lyra has one of the most attractive star patterns in the sky. Vega makes a little equilateral triangle, about $1\frac{1}{2}$° on a side, with two 4th-magnitude stars, Epsilon (ϵ) and Zeta (ζ) Lyrae, respectively NE and SE of the bright star. Zeta in turn is also at the NW corner of an almost perfect parallelogram, $4\frac{1}{2}$° long and 2° wide, with two 3rd-magnitude stars at its south end, Beta (β) and Gamma (γ), and two 4th-magnitude stars at its north end, Zeta and Delta (δ). Beta Lyrae is the prototype of a special class of variable star characterized by short periods and continuously changing light curves: Beta Lyrae variables are eclipsing binary systems in which two young blue stars are so close together that their mutual gravitational attraction has distorted them into ellipsoids, hence a continuously changing amount of light surface is presented to us as the stars revolve around each other. Beta Lyrae itself varies between magnitudes 3.4 and 4.3 in a period just under 13 days, and its minima can be noticed by comparing its brightness to the mag 3.3 Gamma just to its ENE.

Between Lyra and Corona Borealis spreads the figure of **Hercules,** whose star pattern was known to the ancient Greeks merely as "The Kneeler." At the center of the figure, just over half the distance from Vega to the brightest star in the Crown, is the asterism known as the "Keystone," formed by the 3rd-magnitude Zeta (ζ), Eta (η), and Pi (π) Herculis and the 4th-magnitude Epsilon (ϵ). The shoulders of Hercules are at Beta (β) and Delta (δ), one arm stretching from Delta NE toward Lyra, and the head is at Alpha (α), whose name Ras Algethi is from the Arabic for "Head of the Kneeler." The kneeling leg is defined by the angle made by the 4th-mag stars Sigma (σ), Tau (τ), Phi (ϕ), and Chi (χ) Her, and the other leg by Theta (θ), which lies only a few degrees WSW of Vega, and Iota (ι), the Kneeler's foot at Iota always being represented as planted victoriously on the head of Draco.

Hercules seems to be oriented in the sky head-down. South of him is another giant figure, but oriented head-up. This is **Ophiuchus** the Serpent-bearer. The star marking the head of Ophiuchus, Alpha (α) Ophiuchi (named Ras Alhague, "Head of the Serpent-bearer"), is only about 5° ESE of the star marking the head of Hercules, and on old charts the two heros are sometimes drawn nose-to-nose. Two pairs of stars about 9° WSW and SSE of Alpha are at the shoulders of Ophiuchus, and nearly 20° farther to the SE is a line of four 2nd- and 3rd-magnitude stars, almost 20° long and oriented NW-SE, which designates the waist and (at the NW end) the serpent-grasping left hand (marked by the Delta [δ]- Epsilon [ϵ] pair) of the hero. The ancient Greek texts state that Ophiuchus tramples on Scorpius the Scorpion, which is immediately to the south; but the legs of the Serpent-bearer are represented only by two short straggling groups of faint stars due north of the Heart and the Tail of the Scorpion.

Serpens, the Serpent grasped by the Serpent-bearer, is the only constellation divided into two parts. Serpens Caput, the Head of the Serpent, is west of Ophiuchus, the head itself a triangle of 4th-magnitude stars about 12° due south of Corona Borealis, and the creature's neck extending south in an uneven 20° long line of one 3rd- and four 4th-magnitude stars. (The 3rd-magnitude star, Alpha [α] Serpentis, is sometimes called Cor Serpentis, "Heart of the Serpent.") Serpens Cauda, the Tail of the Serpent, is east of Ophiuchus and stretches up the Great Rift in the Summer Milky Way. It is not particularly easy to trace. Start at Eta (η), Ophiuchi, the magnitude 2$\frac{1}{2}$ star at the SE end of the line that marks Ophiuchus' waist. Just NE of Eta Oph is the triangle of Nu (ν), Xi (ξ), and Omicron (o) Serpentis. NE of this triangle is the 3rd-magnitude Nu Ophiuchi at the right hand of the Serpent-bearer. (The distance from Eta to Nu Oph is around 10°.) Further NE are the 3rd-magnitude Eta Serpentis and, at the tip

of the Serpent's tail, Theta (θ) Ser. Theta and Eta Ser with Nu and Eta Oph form a long NE-SW line at right angles to the Eta-Zeta-Epsilon-Delta Oph line.

Due south of Ophiuchus is **Scorpius** the Scorpion, one of the few constellations that looks exactly like what it is named for. In fact, the resemblance is uncanny. The head and shoulders of the Scorpion are marked by a north-south arc of one 2nd- and two 3rd-magnitude stars, Beta (β), Delta (δ), and Pi (π) Scorpii, a conspicuous group as it rises in the SE during April evenings. Following this is another arc of three stars, the 1st-magnitude Antares flanked on its NW and SE by two 3rd-magnitude guardians. The name Antares means "Rival of Mars" and was given to this star by ancient Greek astronomers because its distinctive ruddy color does indeed resemble the hue of the Red Planet.

SE of Antares and its guardians is the fishhook-shaped Tail of Scorpius, about 15° across its longer dimension. The western side of the fishhook consists of a 9° long north-south line of evenly-spaced stars. The most northerly star is the 2nd-magnitude Epsilon (ϵ) Scorpii. About 4° south of it is the unaided-eye double star Mu (μ) Sco, an east-west pair separated by nearly 6' and of magnitudes 3.1 and 3.6. Nearly 5° south of the Mu pair is another wide unaided-eye double, Zeta (ζ) Sco, the components of which are nearly 7' apart in an east-west line and of mags 3.6 and 4.8. The Mu pair must be physically associated because the two stars are moving through space together with the same direction and speed; but the Zeta stars are a mere chance alignment of a nearer (Zeta-1 is 160 light-years away) with a much further star (Zeta-2 is around 6200 l-y distant). From dark-sky sites in the extreme southern United States a little patch of haze can be seen about $\frac{1}{2}$° due north of the Zeta pair, the rich but remote open cluster NGC 6231.

Just north of the "Sting" in the Tail of Scorpius (represented by Lambda [λ], Upsilon [υ], and G Scorpii) are two more hazy patches, noticeably brighter than the Milky Way glow in this region. These are the two open clusters M6 (the NW patch) and M7. The Bedouin of the Arabian Desert called these two hazy patches *Al Humah,* "The Venom."

Now we return to the northern part of the Summer sky, where we shall start with Cygnus and work our way SW down the Milky Way to Sagittarius.

Deneb, the northeastern star of the Summer Triangle, is the brightest member of the constellation **Cygnus** the Swan, which lies east of Lyra right in the midst of the broad stream of the Summer Milky Way. Because of its shape Cygnus is also known as the Northern Cross, and by a happy coincidence about 8 o'clock in the evening during the Christmas holidays the Northern Cross can be seen (from mid-northern latitudes) standing upright just over the NW horizon.

The Greeks envisioned the Swan as flying SW down the Milky Way, its tail at Deneb (the Arabic word for "tail") and its head marked by the justifiably famous telescopic double Albireo (Beta [β] Cygni), a 3rd-magnitude star SW of Lyra. Notice that the Great Rift in the Milky Way begins at Deneb, from where it extends all the way SW into the far southern Milky Way. The Great Rift consists of relatively nearby (nearby, that is, in Galactic terms) clouds of interstellar dust particles that obscure the light of the stars beyond. These dust particles are extremely small and the density of the interstellar medium is even less than that of the best laboratory vacuum, but the dust clouds are so large, scores of light-years across, that they are essentially opaque.

The brightest stretch of the Milky Way anywhere in the northern celestial hemisphere is the Cygnus Star Cloud, a 15° long oval between Albireo on the SW and the star at the intersection of the arms of the Cross, Gamma (γ) Cygni, on the NE. 3° due east of Deneb is a little patch of glow, the famous North America Nebula, one of the few diffuse nebulae that can be seen with the unaided eye. The "North America" outline of this nebula is quite easy to see in 10x50 binoculars. The North America Nebula's full apparent diameter is about three times the apparent diameter of the Moon!

The next major constellation SW along the Milky Way from Cygnus is **Aquila** the Eagle. Modern drawings of the constellation usually show the Eagle flying NE up the Milky Way, its heart at the 1st-magnitude star Altair (which, like Antares in the Heart of the Scorpion, is flanked by two guardian stars), its wings to the NW (Zeta [ζ] + Epsilon [ϵ] Aquilae) and SE (Theta [θ] Aql) and its tail to the SW (at Lambda [λ]). I have always found this a logical and aesthetically pleasing conception of these stars. However, for once their good taste abandoned them and the ancient Greeks (as we know from the Farnese Globe) envisioned Aquila as flying SE *out* of the Milky Way, Altair and its two companions incongruously assigned to the minor task of marking the Eagle's right wing, with Theta as the Eagle's head, Delta (δ) at its left wing, and Zeta + Epsilon at its tail.

There are several minor constellations in the region between Cygnus and Aquila. About 10° due north of Altair is the small (5° long) group of four 4th-magnitude stars that forms **Sagitta** the Arrow. Despite its size and the modest brilliance of its components, this is a very distinct little constellation that actually resembles an Arrow and is one of the 49 groups we have inherited from the ancient Greeks. The area between Sagitta and Cygnus, though in the Milky Way, is scattered with faint stars and was not organized into a constellation

until the 17th century, when the astronomer Hevelius named it **Vulpecula** the Little Fox. Like many of the other Hevelius constellations, Vulpecula is merely an area on the celestial sphere and has no true star pattern—and certainly no star pattern that could justify Hevelius' fanciful name!

About 10° NE of Altair and some 30° due south of Deneb is a very distinctive little group of five 4th-magnitude stars that the ancient Greeks very appropriately and very poetically named **Delphinus** the Dolphin. Its curved form, set on the edge of the stream of the Milky Way, truly does call to mind the image of a Dolphin leaping out of the waves of the Mediterranean Sea. SE of Delphinus is a small group of 4th- and 5th-magnitude stars called **Equuleus** the Foal, first organized as an independent constellation by the 2nd century B.C. Greek astronomer Hipparchus (better known for his discovery of the precession of the equinoxes than for his invention of Equuleus!). This little star pattern is probably most easily found from the Autumn constellation Pegasus, for it lies just west of the 2nd-magnitude star Epsilon (ϵ) Pegasi.

A minor constellation also lies just SW of the modern tail of Aquila: **Scutum** the Shield, like Vulpecula a creation of the imaginative Hevelius. Scutum is chiefly notable for the brilliant Scutum Star Cloud, which occupies most of the NE quadrant of the small area modern astronomers have assigned to the constellation. As a guide to some of the other interesting objects in this area of the Milky Way, it is helpful to identify the slightly bent line of the 4th-magnitude stars Beta (β), Alpha (α), and Gamma (γ) Scuti (to list them in their north-to-south order), which lies almost exactly along the central line of the Milky Way, the galactic equator.

Finally, SW down the Milky Way from Aquila, and due east of the Scorpion, is the zodiacal constellation **Sagittarius** the Archer. Though this group includes two 2nd-magnitude and eight 3rd-magnitude stars, they are not distributed in a very distinctive pattern, and their arrangement most assuredly does *not* resemble the archer-centaur shown for Sagittarius on virtually all the ancient Graeco-Roman zodiacs that have survived. The 10° long arc of Lambda (λ), Delta (δ), and Epsilon (ϵ) Sagittarii has a superficial resemblance to a bow, and therefore these stars during the Renaissance were named Kaus Borealis, Kaus Meridionalis, and Kaus Australis, the Northern, Middle and Southern Bow, respectively. (These are hybrid names: *kaus* is Arabic for "bow" and the other terms are Latin.) Gamma (γ) is *Al Nasl*, "The Arrow Tip." A more realistic shape is made by the asterism of Lambda, Mu (μ), Phi (ϕ), Sigma (σ), Tau (τ), and Zeta (ζ) Sagittarii, popularly known as "The Milk Dipper" but a title that goes back only to the 19th century.

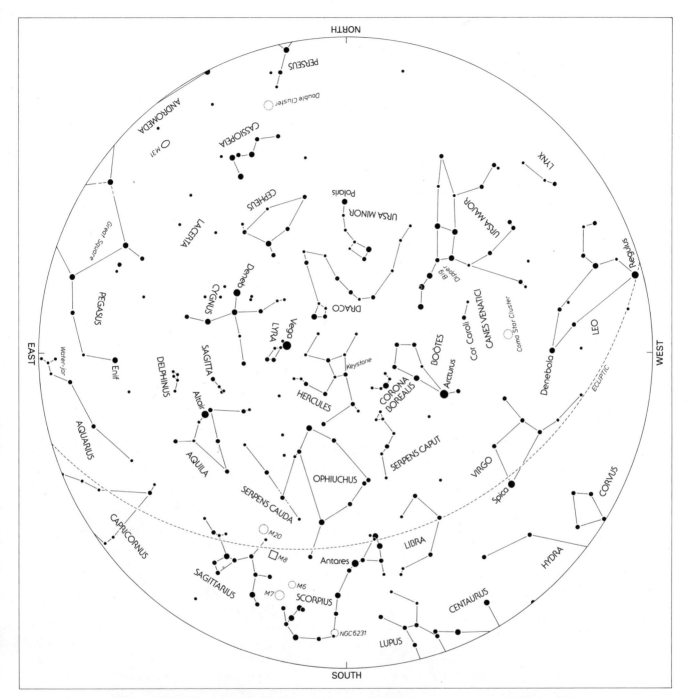

Chart III: The Constellations of the Summer as seen from latitudes around 40°N at about 9 p.m. standard time on July 15, 11 p.m. standard time on June 15, and 7 p.m. standard time on August 15. *The "Summer Triangle" of 1st-magnitude Deneb, Vega, and Altair is a good place to start in identifying the Summer Constellations. You could also start at the conspicuous hook-shape of Scorpius, the tail of which sits just above the southern horizon during the early evenings of mid-summer for mid-northern observers. The Summer Milky Way is the brightest stretch of the Milky Way visible to mid-northern hemisphere observers.*

The brightest star cloud in the entire Milky Way lies north of Gamma and Delta Sagittarii. The "Great Sagittarius Star Cloud" is part of the central hub of our Milky Way Galaxy and therefore lies some 30,000 light-years distant. A couple degrees north of Mu Sgr is the 2° long SW-NE glow of the Small Sagittarius Star Cloud, M24, a better object in binoculars than even the bright but distant Great Sagittarius Star Cloud. Finally, about 4° west and slightly north of Lambda Sgr, just outside the NW edge of the Great Star Cloud, is a hazy 4th-magnitude "star," the Lagoon Nebula, M8, one of the handful of diffuse nebulae that are visible to the unaided eye. It has always seemed particularly appropriate to me that during the warm and humid nights of mid-summer, when the moist southern winds carry the fragrances of growing things and the sounds of frogs in the marshes, that something with the name "The Lagoon" should slowly drift over the southern horizon like a beacon of the equatorial jungles and the South Sea islands.

About 10° due south of the bowl of the Milk Dipper, and about 20° east of the Sting of Scorpius, is an arc of 4th- and 5th-magnitude stars named **Corona Australis,** the Southern Crown. This constellation was canonized by the ancient Greeks later than Corona Borealis, but like its northern namesake it was envisioned as a laurel wreath. Because of its southerly declination, observers in the northern half of the United States must use binoculars to pick Corona Australis out of the horizon haze as it culminates in the early evenings of August and September.

The Autumn Constellations
[Chart IV, page 19. Bright Star Atlas, Maps 3 & 8.]

A line drawn from Polaris through the westernmost star of the "W" of Cassiopeia, and extended south about the same distance (30°), will bring you to the Great Square of Pegasus, the most distinctive asterism of the Autumn Skies. The Great Square is in fact a bit wider than it is high, measuring about $18° \times 14°$. Its NE and SW stars are magnitude 2, and its NW and SE stars mag $2^{1}/_2$ (though the NW star varies irregularly between mags 2.1 and 3.0). The Great Square is conspicuous in part because the stars forming it lack competition in brilliance in this region of the heavens. Nevertheless, a reasonably keen-eyed observer on a transparent night at a dark-sky site will probably be able to count at least two dozen 4th-, 5th-, and 6th-magnitude stars within the Square itself!

The Great Square marks the body of the Winged Horse, **Pegasus,** only the forepart of which has been given a place in the sky. Pegasus is upside-down, its neck and head extending SW from Alpha (α) Pegasi, the

star at the SW corner of the Great Square: from Alpha Peg go 15° SW through Xi (ξ) and Zeta (ζ) to Theta (θ), and from Theta go 7° NW to the 2nd-magnitude star Epsilon (ϵ) Pegasi, named Enif (from the Arabic for "Nose"). Enif is 30° due east of Altair in Aquila. The forelegs of Pegasus are indicated by two ESE-WNW lines of 3rd- and 4th-magnitude stars that begin in the vicinity of Beta (β) Pegasi, the NW star in the Great Square. These lines consist of Eta (η) and Pi (π)-2, and Mu (μ) + Lambda (λ), Iota (ι), and Kappa (κ).

Pegasus is the place to start in exploring the Autumn constellations. First, between the two stars marking the upper foreleg of the Horse, Eta and Pi-2 Pegasi, on the south, and the small triangle of Delta (δ), Epsilon (ϵ), and Zeta (ζ) Cephei on the north, there stretches a scattering of 4th- and 5th-magnitude stars named **Lacerta** the Lizard by the often-mentioned Hevelius. (He acknowledged that he placed a Lizard here simply because that was what would fit!) Lacerta's claim to fame is the fine Milky Way background glow in its northern half.

Next, we go to the star at the NE corner of the Great Square. Despite its name, Alpheratz, which is from the Arabic *Al Faras,* "The Horse," this star has always been shared by Pegasus and the constellation on Pegasus' NE, **Andromeda** the Chained Lady. Modern astronomers have simply conceded the star to Andromeda, designating it as Alpha (α) Andromedae. (As a star in Pegasus it formerly also had the designation Delta [δ] Pegasi.) The main star pattern of Andromeda consists of two diverging lines extending NE from Alpha And. The southern line of the pair, through Delta (δ), Beta (β), and Gamma (γ), contains brighter stars and is therefore more conspicuous than the northern line, which includes Pi (π), Mu (μ), and Phi (ϕ). The chained arms reach SE to Zeta (ζ) and Eta (η), which are about 8° from Delta, and NW through the little triangle of 5th-magnitude Theta (θ), Rho (ρ), and Sigma (σ), 6° from Pi, on another 10° to the group Iota (ι), Kappa (κ), Lambda (λ), and Psi (ψ).

If the line from Beta to Mu Andromedae is extended NW an amount equal to the distance between these two stars, it will end at M31, the Andromeda Galaxy, which appears to the unaided eye as a 5th-magnitude sliver of haze. M31 is the only external galaxy (other than the two Magellanic Clouds in the southern celestial hemisphere, which are merely satellites of our own Galaxy) that is readily visible to the unaided eye (though the night must be dark and moonless, Andromeda must be well above the horizon haze, and the observer must be at a site away from city light). To see M31 best, look just to its side: "averted vision" makes use of the fact that the retina of the human eye is most sensitive just to the side of the center of focus.

A line from Mu through Beta Andromedae extended SE about twice the distance between them will end very near M33, the Pinwheel Galaxy in Triangulum. M33 can be seen as a small amorphous patch of haze, barely brighter than the night sky around it, by exceptionally keen-eyed observers under exceptionally transparent skies at exceptionally dark observing sites. (Unfortunately, one of those keen-eyed observers is not the present writer.) M33 in apparent size is larger than the full Moon, but its surface brightness is only one forty-millionth as great! It is 14° from M31 and seems to be a true gravitationally-bound satellite of the larger galaxy.

Centered about 10° due south of the Great Square is a 5° ellipse of 4th- and 5th-magnitude stars. This asterism is called the "Circlet of Pisces" and represents the western Fish of the zodiacal constellation **Pisces** the Fishes. Despite the faintness of its constituent stars, you will not find the Circlet difficult to spot. The rest of Pisces, however, is not so easy. Beginning just a few degrees NE of the Circlet is a 30° long shallow curve of 4th- and 5th-magnitude stars that represents the Cord from the tail of the western Fish to the Knot, at Alpha (α) Piscium, that binds this Cord to the one from the tail of the northern Fish. The northern Cord, curving NNW away from Alpha Psc, is 15° long and consists of only three stars. The two Cords curve in opposite senses (the southern Cord open to the south and the northern Cord open to the NE) so that they meet tangentially at Alpha. The northern Fish is a crude oval, about 10° long in a north-south direction, of faint 5th-magnitude stars due south of Beta (β) Andromedae. Identifying the two Cords and the northern Fish requires a very clear and moonless night at an observing site well away from city or town lights.

Less than 10° WSW of the Circlet of Pisces, and about the same distance SSE of the 4th-magnitude star in the head of Pegasus, Theta (θ) Pegasi, is a crude leaning "Y" of three stars of the 4th magnitude and one of the 5th. This is the Water-jar held by **Aquarius** the Water-pourer and, like the Circlet of Pisces, is a fairly conspicuous asterism despite its faint components. Beginning about 10° SE of the Water-jar is a 15° long NW-SE oval of mostly 4th- and 5th-magnitude stars arranged in groups of twos and threes. This is the Stream from Aquarius' Water-jar and was catalogued as a separate constellation by the very earliest Greek astronomers. It probably got its name because the doublets and triplets of stars in it resemble the splashing of water. All Renaissance and Enlightenment star charts and globes that I have seen show the Water-pourer himself standing just west of the Water-jar and the Stream (almost always holding a colorful banner out over the back of Capricornus); but in the last 150 years or so he is often drawn on the 20° long line of 3rd-magnitude Al-

pha (α) and Beta (β) Aquarii and 4th-mag Epsilon (ϵ) that extends SW from the Water-jar toward the head of Capricornus.

South of the just-mentioned Alpha-Beta Epsilon Aquarii line is the conspicuous boat-shape of the zodiacal constellation **Capricornus** the Goat-fish, the Alpha-Beta-Epsilon Aqr line pointing directly at the naked-eye double star in the head of the Goat-fish, Alpha Capricorni. The shape of Capricornus did in fact suggest a boat to the ancient Mesopotamians, who during the 3rd millennium B.C. envisioned it as a Ship with a Goat-head prow. Apparently, this star pattern became a composite monster with the head and fore-body of a goat and the tail of a fish only around 2100 B.C.: before that date there are no known examples of goat-fish in Mesopotamian art, but after 2000 B.C. the motif becomes very common.

Most of the ancient southern constellations are "watery" in character. In addition to the already-discussed Pisces the Fishes, Aquarius the Water-pourer, and Capricornus the Goat-fish, there are in the southern autumn heavens Piscis Austrinus the Southern Fish, Cetus the Sea-monster, and Eridanus the River. Farther east, in the southern sky of Winter, is Argo the Ship (now divided into three smaller constellations for convenience), and, stretching across the southern sky of Spring, Hydra the Water-serpent. The idea of the southern heavens as a sort of celestial Sea came to the Greeks from the Babylonians and the Sumerians, for virtually all the above-mentioned watery constellations were adopted by Greece from Mesopotamia. And the Mesopotamians themselves probably got the idea from the simple fact that south of their land (which corresponds to modern Iraq) are the broad waters of the Persian Gulf.

At the NW prow of the boat-shape of Capricornus is the naked-eye double star Alpha Capricorni, its components 6′ apart in an east-west direction and of magnitudes 3.6 and 4.2. This is, however, not a true gravitationally-bound double but just a chance alignment of a nearer with a farther star. The binocular double Beta (β) Capricorni 3° to the south is, however, a true binary system.

Some 20° SE of Capricornus and due south of the Stream of Aquarius is the lonely 1st-magnitude star Fomalhaut, which marks the mouth of **Piscis Austrinus,** the Southern Fish. It is possible to imagine a fish-shape in the crude 20° flattened oval of 4th- and 5th-magnitude stars that extends west from Fomalhaut. The most obvious part of the star pattern is the east-west line of five 4th-magnitude stars that begins with the Delta (δ) + Gamma (γ) Piscis Austrini pair just 3° south of Fomalhaut and extends west through Beta (β), Mu (μ) and Iota (ι) PsA.

Due south of Piscis Austrinus is a 15° long NW-SE

line of stars marking the neck of **Grus** the Crane. A
3rd-magnitude star, Gamma (γ) Gruis, is at the NW
end of this line, a 2nd-mag star, Beta (β) Gru, at its
SE end, and 10° due west of Beta, another and even
brighter 2nd-magnitude star, Alpha (α). This is a fairly
conspicuous constellation, but it is so far south that for
observers in the continental United States binoculars
are necessary to pick these stars out of the horizon haze
as they culminate low in the south during the early
evenings of October. Grus and neighboring **Phoenix**
to its east are the farthest north of the constellations
introduced by the German astronomer Johannes Bayer
to fill the south circumpolar heavens, the area of the
celestial sphere invisible to the ancient Mesopotamian
and Greek constellation-formers.

To explore the constellations of the eastern Autumn
sky we will begin once more at the "W" of Cassiopeia.
SE of Cassiopeia is **Perseus,** its main feature a 15° long
NW-SE "hook" formed by Eta (η), Gamma (γ), Alpha
(α), Delta (δ), Mu (μ), and Lambda (λ) Persei. The rest
of the constellation-pattern consists of two lines of stars,
one going south of Alpha through Kappa (κ), Beta (β),
and Rho (ρ), and the other south of Delta through Epsilon (ϵ), Xi (ξ), and Zeta (ζ). In the conception of
the ancient Greeks as pictured on the Farnese Globe,
one of the hero's legs is along the Epsilon-Xi-Zeta line,
the other bends up to Mu and Lambda (which gives him
the appearance of stepping up), the Medusa's head (the
Beta-Rho-Pi [π]-Omega [ω] asterism) is suspended behind his back by a sack, his right arm is upraised toward
Cassiopeia, and in his right hand he grasps his Scimitar.
In Greek astronomical texts the Scimitar was stated to
be represented merely by the hazy patch of the Perseus
Double Cluster (NGC's 869 + 884), which can be found
halfway between Gamma Persei and Delta Cassiopeia.
The Double Cluster resolves well in binoculars, and is
one of the showpiece objects in the northern heavens for
telescopes.

In addition to the Double Cluster, Perseus has two
other interesting objects for unaided eye observing.
First is the group of 4th-, 5th-, and 6th-magnitude stars
between and around Alpha and Delta Persei: this is a
true gravitationally-bound open cluster called the Alpha Persei Moving Group and includes the bright Alpha (as the name implies) as well as Delta and possibly
Epsilon. The second additional unaided eye objective
in Perseus is Beta Persei, named Algol (from the Arabic
for "The Demon"), an eclipsing binary star marking the
right eye of the Medusa's Head. Algol varies between
magnitudes 2.1 and 3.4 in a period just under three
days, and its light changes can be observed with the assistance of nearby mag 2.9 Epsilon Persei and mag 2.1
Gamma Andromedae. Despite its location in one of the
most sinister asterisms in the sky, there is absolutely

no evidence that the ancient Greeks were aware of the
star's variability.

SW of the Medusa's Head, and due south of Gamma
Andromedae, is **Triangulum** the Triangle. Presently
this is conceived of as the thin right-angled figure
formed by Alpha (α), Beta (β), and Gamma (γ) Trianguli; but the ancient Greeks thought of it as equilateral (their name for it, *Deltoton,* is from the Greek
letter *delta,* the capital form of which is written as an
equilateral triangle), its east vertex at the inconspicuous
5th-magnitude star now designated 12 Trianguli.

About 10° due south of Triangulum is the Head of
the zodiacal constellation of **Aries** the Ram, consisting
of the 2nd-magnitude Alpha (α) Arietis, the 3rd-mag
Beta (β), and the 4th-magnitude Gamma (γ). The rest
of the constellation extends over the area NE, east, and
SE of this asterism, but this area's thin scattering of
faint stars bears absolutely no resemblance to a Ram—
or to anything else, to tell the truth. Aries is a constellation that was invented by the ancient Greeks themselves
(one of the few: most of the star groups we have inherited from them were originated by the Mesopotamians),
and apparently it got its name from the fact that the
vernal equinox was in this region of the zodiac at that
time, which made the pastoral Greeks think of these
stars as the leader of the zodiacal constellations in the
same way that a ram is the leader of a flock of sheep.

15° SE of the Head of Aries is the Head of **Cetus** the
Sea-monster, an uneven pentagon of 3rd-, 4th-, and 5th-
magnitude stars including Alpha (α), Gamma (γ), Xi
(ξ)-2, Mu (μ), and Lambda (λ) Ceti, with Xi-1 marking
a horn and Kappa (κ) the outstretched tongue. (The
horn and the outstretched tongue of the Sea-monster
are shown on the Farnese Globe and therefore were a
part of the original Greek conception of the constellation's image.) About 8° SW of the Head of Cetus is the
location of the red giant pulsating variable star Mira,
"The Wonderful," which sometimes reaches 3rd magnitude but for long stretches of time remains quite invisible to the unaided eye. The curve of both Cords from
the tails of the Fishes of Pisces, which intersect at Alpha
Piscium, points directly toward Mira, and there is reason to suspect that the original Greek Knot-star was not
the inconspicuous 4th-magnitude Alpha Psc but indeed
Mira at maximum light (though there is no evidence
that the Greeks were aware of Mira's variability).

The main body of Cetus is centered about 20° SW
of the Sea-monster's Head, and is outlined by Beta (β),
Eta (η), Theta (θ), Zeta (ζ), and Tau (τ) Ceti. This
is a very conspicuous star pattern in the southern skies
of late Autumn, for there are no other bright stars near
it—and even precious few faint stars in it. Indeed, the
large area SW, south, and SE of the body of Cetus
is one of the most star-poor in the entire sky. The

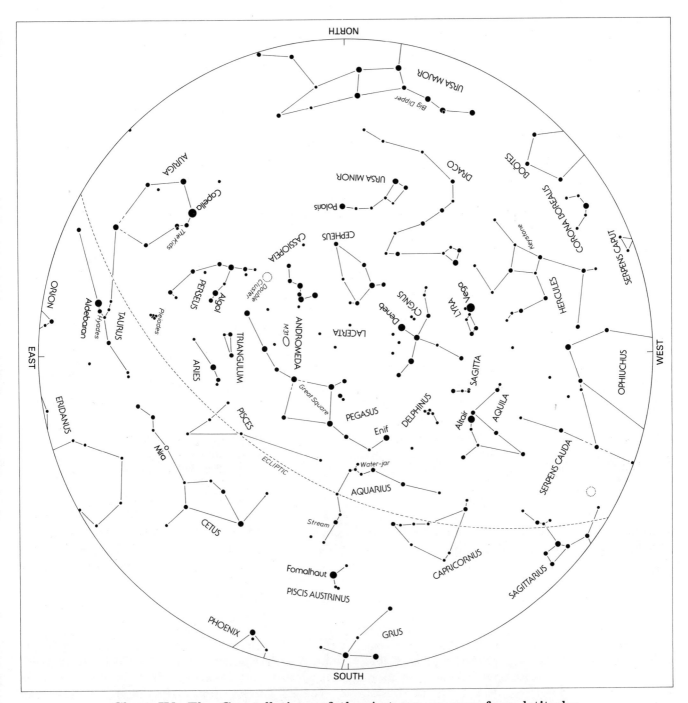

Chart IV: The Constellations of the Autumn as seen from latitudes around 40°N at about 9 p.m. standard time on October 15, 11 p.m. standard time on September 15, and 7 p.m. standard time on November 15. *The Great Square of Pegasus dominates the Autumn sky, and is a good starting point for identifying the autumn constellations. The lone 1st-magnitude star of Autumn, Fomalhaut, rides low in the south; however, during the evenings of September the "Summer Triangle" of 1st-magnitude Deneb, Vega, and Altair are still high in the west, and the bright Milky Way star clouds in Cygnus are still favorably positioned for binocular observing.*

astronomers of ancient Greece ignored this area, and it was not until the mid-18th century of our era that the French astronomer Lacaille divided it into **Sculptor** the Sculptor's Workshop on the west and **Fornax** the Chemist's Furnace on the east—not that its poor scattering of faint stars has the least resemblance to any artistic or scientific apparatus: in fact, the brightest star in the large region covered by both constellations, 4½ hours of right ascension long and 15° high, is the mag 4.0 Alpha Fornacis.

Though in the main body of this book I include **Eridanus** the River among the constellations of Winter, I will describe it here because it is, like the southern constellations of Autumn (excluding Bayer's and Lacaille's innovations), a "watery" group and has the same appearance as they: a star pattern constructed mostly of faint 3rd-, 4th-, and 5th-magnitude stars but fairly conspicuous and logical in design. Eridanus is one of the constellations that actually resembles what it has been named for. The River's "headwater" is the 3rd-magnitude star Beta (β) Eridani, located just 4° NNW of the 1st-magnitude Rigel in Orion. First Eridanus flows about 20° west and then SW to another 3rd-magnitude star, Gamma (γ) Eri, named Zaurak, Arabic for "Boat." Then it curves in a mighty bend 15° across first NW, then south, and finally through the nine stars labelled Tau (τ) back east to a point 10° due south of Zaurak. 10° farther SE are the four Upsilon's (v), from where the River flows back SW, then west through Theta (θ) and Iota (ι), and finally another 20° SW to the 1st-magnitude star Alpha (α), whose name Achernar is from the Arabic for "End of the River." You will need binoculars to pick out from the horizon haze the constellation's more southerly stars.

The Winter Constellations
[Chart V, page 23. Bright Star Atlas, Map 4.]

Orion the Hunter is probably the best-known of the 88 constellations. (Remember, the Big Dipper is merely an asterism, *not* a full-scale constellation.) The 3° long NW-SE line of three 2nd-magnitude stars that forms the Belt of Orion lies almost exactly on the celestial equator and is a conspicuous landmark in the Winter heavens. It points SE toward the brightest star in the sky, Sirius the "Dog Star," and NW toward Aldebaran and the Hyades Star Cluster, the "V"-shape of which marks the face of Taurus the Bull.

Just south of the Belt of Orion hangs the Sword of Orion, also about 3° long but oriented north-south. Its stars are fainter than those in the Belt, but the middle one, the binocular double Theta (θ) Orionis, is surrounded by a faint glow of M42, the Orion Nebula, one of the few diffuse nebulae visible to the unaided eye.

The Belt and the Sword of Orion are enclosed within a rectangle, some 18° tall and 8° wide, formed by the bright stars that mark the shoulders and knees of the Hunter. The stars at the NW and SE corners of the rectangle are of the 2nd magnitude, but those at the NE and SW corners are both 1st-magnitude stars and a color contrast pair: Alpha (α), Betelgeuse, in the right shoulder of Orion, is a red supergiant irregular variable with an average magnitude of around 0.7; and Beta (β), Rigel, at the Hunger's left knee, is a blue supergiant with an apparent magnitude of 0.1, the seventh brightest star in the sky.

The star pattern of Orion is remarkably true-to-life. In addition to the features just described, there are stars marking the Hunter's head, club, and shield. The head is indicated by a little triangle of 3rd-magnitude Lambda (λ) and 4th-mag Phi (ϕ)-1 and Phi-2, a tight group located just over the midpoint of the line joining the Giant's shoulders. His right arm and club are the stars NNE and north of Betelgeuse, Mu (μ), Nu (ν), Xi (ξ), and the two Chi's (χ). And the shield (or lion's skin, according to some old representations) that he holds before himself to take the impact of the charging Taurus is formed by the 15° long, gently curved north-south line of the two Omicrons (o) and six Pi's (π).

If you are unfamiliar with Orion, look for it high in the SE during the early evenings of January, or on the meridian just after twilight during February. In the early evenings of March it will still be conspicuous high in the SW. It truly is a beautiful sight as it glitters astride the meridian on frigid January nights: in the arctic air its brilliant stars sparkle with a crystalline, hard-edged sharpness. To Orion's NW is the ferocious figure of the Bull, which the hero seems to drive across the heavens during the course of the night; and to his SE follows his faithful Dog, Canis Major, itself rich with bright blue stars.

Due south of Orion are two small winter constellations. The Hunter seems to stand directly upon **Lepus** the Hare, which consists of a quadrilateral of 3rd-magnitude stars (Alpha [α], Beta [β], Mu [μ], and Epsilon [ϵ]) with a pair of 4th-magnitude stars just to its ESE (Gamma [γ] and Delta [δ]) and a gentle arc of three faint stars to its NE (Zeta [ζ], Eta [η], and Theta [θ]). This star pattern could be likened to any number of things, but the little arc of faint stars does indeed resemble the curve of a Hare's back.

15° south of Lepus is a NW-SE pair of 3rd-magnitude stars, about 4° apart, that marks the body of **Columba** the Dove. A scattering of 4th-magnitude stars east and west of this main pair completes the Dove's figure. Lepus dates from ancient Greek times; but Columba is no older than the late 16th century of our era.

NW of Orion is the zodiacal constellation of **Taurus** the Bull. Basically, only the Bull's Head is figured in the stars; however, the Head is oriented in a manner that suggests the Bull is charging Orion. (This is something of a contradiction to how the east-to-west motion of the celestial sphere makes it appear as if Orion is driving the Bull before himself.) As has already been mentioned, the Belt of Orion points NW toward the "V" of the Hyades Star Cluster, which marks the face of the Bull. The Bull's horn-tips are at Beta (β) and Zeta (ζ) Tauri, 15° NE of the ends of the "V" of the Hyades and 8° from each other in a SSE-NNW direction. At the end of one arm of the Hyades "V" is the 1st-magnitude star Aldebaran, marking an eye of the Bull, its noticeably ruddy color suggesting the beast's rage. Aldebaran, however, is not a true member of the Hyades: the cluster proper is centered about 150 light-years away from us, whereas Aldebaran lies at less than half that distance, 68 light-years.

12° NW of the Hyades is another unaided-eye star cluster, the Pleiades. This group is one of the half-dozen best objects in the entire sky, the blue-white luster of its brightest members filling the field with silvery brilliance. In binoculars dozens of faint Pleiades stars can be counted, but the number visible to the unaided eye depends upon the observing conditions of the night and the acuity of the observer's vision. You should see at least six, arranged in a pattern suggesting a dipper with its handle to the east. (Since there were *seven* Pleiades in the Greek myths, daughters of Atlas and Pleione, the fact that usually only six are visible gave rise to various Greek legends about the "Lost Pleiad.") On dark nights I have identified nine stars in the cluster. However, experienced observers with excellent eyesight have reported seeing 15. The Pleiades cluster is larger than it appears at first glance, for the Moon could fit into its "dipper-bowl." The cluster is about 410 light-years away, almost three times the distance of the Hyades.

Taurus shares the star at the tip of its northern horn, Beta Tauri, with the constellation immediately to the north of the Bull, **Auriga** the Charioteer. Auriga is a nearly perfect pentagon of one 1st-magnitude, two 2nd-magnitude, and two 3rd-magnitude stars. Capella is a circumpolar star for the northern United States, virtually all of Canada, and most of Europe. From these latitudes Capella can be observed twinkling low in the lingering golden midsummer twilights over the far northern horizon, while the stars of Scorpius and Sagittarius glitter in the dark south.

Capella is found by following the line joining the top stars in the Big Dipper's bowl about 70° to the west. Just SW of Capella is a thin little triangle formed by 3rd-magnitude Epsilon (ϵ) and Eta (η) Aurigae with 4th-mag Zeta (ζ). This group is called "The Kids" because the bright star's name, *Capella*, is Latin for "Little She-goat." In the area east of Beta Aurigae are scattered nine faint stars labelled Psi (ψ) Aurigae and considered to represent the multi-strapped flail held by the Charioteer.

The Winter Milky Way cuts through the pentagon of Auriga and passes SE behind the feet of **Gemini** the Twins, the next zodiacal group east from Taurus. The persons of the Twins are represented by two roughly parallel NE-SW lines of stars, each line crowned on its NE by a bright star. These bright stars are each named after one of the Twins, the northern star being Castor (magnitude 1.6 Alpha [α] Geminorum) and the southern Pollux (mag 1.2 Beta [β] Gem). The line of stars that traces the figure of Castor are Alpha, Tau (τ), Epsilon (ϵ), Mu (μ), and Eta (η) Gem. Pollux is Beta, Delta (δ), Zeta (ζ), and Gamma (γ), a line that points SW toward Betelgeuse in Orion. A couple degrees NW of the stars marking the feet of Castor, Mu and Eta Gem, can be seen (on dark, clear nights) the small hazy patch of the open cluster M35, a fine binocular object. You can confirm your identification of the stars Castor and Pollux by drawing a line from the NE and SW corner stars in the Big Dipper's bowl.

About 22° due south of Pollux and 26° due east of Betelgeuse is the magnitude 0.4 star Procyon, the brightest star in the constellation **Canis Minor** the Little Dog. The only other bright star in this unpretentious little group is Beta (β) Canis Minoris, about $4\,1/2$° NW of Procyon. This constellation seems to have been invented during the 1st century B.C., for there is no reference to a celestial "Little Dog" in early Greek astronomical literature. The name Procyon *does* go back to the earliest surviving Greek astronomical texts, but it means simply "Before the Dog" and derives from the fact that Alpha Canis Minoris rises just before the true Dog Star, Sirius. Despite its location on the eastern edge of the Winter Milky Way, Canis Minor offers almost nothing even to the telescope observer.

The Winter Milky Way cuts in a broad NW-SE band between Canis Minor and Orion. Despite the presence of the stream of the Milky Way through it, this large area, bounded by Orion on the west, the feet of Gemini on the north, Canis Minor on the NE, and Canis Major to the south, has no stars as bright as the 3rd magnitude and therefore was ignored by the ancient constellation-formers. It was not until the late 16th century that the scattering of 4th- and 5th-magnitude stars here was consolidated as **Monoceros** the Unicorn. Monoceros, though poor in bright stars, is rich in open clusters, of which several of the best are discussed in the section on the constellation later in this book. As a preliminary survey of this large region and as preparation for finding the clusters, identify the 4th-magnitude star 13 Monocerotis, located 9° due east of Betelgeuse, the 13° long line of 4th-mag Delta (δ), 18, and Epsilon (ϵ) Mon, which points NW directly toward Betelgeuse, and the Beta (β) + Gamma (γ) Mon pair 12° due east of the Sword of Orion.

The Belt of Orion points 20° SE at the brightest star in the heavens, the magnitude −1.4 Sirius. This ancient Greek name means "Scorching One" and refers to the fact that during Graeco-Roman times the star rose and set simultaneously with the Sun during July and August, the hottest time of the northern hemisphere Summer. It was a more auspicious star in the eyes of the ancient Egyptians, for in the 4th and 3rd millennia B.C. it rose just before the Sun during June, the time of year when the Nile River commenced its annual life-giving flood. (Ancient Egyptian civilization had become so ossified by the 2nd millennium B.C. that Sirius kept its good reputation with the Egyptians long after it ceased to rise just before the Sun during June.) The star's bluish-white color is easy to see with the unaided eye, though as it rises or sets, refraction through the dense layers of atmosphere near the horizon acts as a prism and makes the star twinkle with all the hues of the rainbow—which is why the Sumerians of Mesopotamia called it *Mul Tiranna*, the "Rainbow Star."

Originally the name "Orion's Dog," which appears even in Homer, probably applied to the star Alpha Canis Majoris alone. But sometime previous to the 4th century B.C., the constellation of **Canis Major** as we know it had been invented. One of the Dog's forelegs is marked by the 2nd-magnitude star Beta (β) Canis, several degrees west and slightly south of Sirius and known to the Arabs as *Murzim*, the "Announcer," because it precedes the bright Sirius through the sky. The head of the Dog is the triangle of 4th-magnitude Theta (θ), Iota (ι), and Gamma (γ), just east and NE of Sirius. The body of the Dog goes SE through Pi (π) and the two Omicrons (o), ending about 10° SE of Sirius in a striking triangle of bright stars, mag 1.5 Epsilon (ϵ), mag 1.8 Delta (δ), and mag 2.4 Eta (η). This is a fine star-rich region and is especially beautiful in binoculars, which bring out the pale yellow color of Delta, the ruddy orange of Sigma (σ), and the crystalline silver-blues of Epsilon and Eta.

10° due east of the Epsilon-Delta-Eta CMa triangle is a pair of 3rd-magnitude stars about 4° apart on a nearly east-west line. These stars, Rho (ρ) and Xi (ξ) Puppis, mark the stern of the celestial representation of the Argo, the Ship on which Jason and the Argonauts sailed in the Quest for the Golden Fleece. A large number of the Greek constellations have Argonautic connections. Hercules and Castor and Pollux were on the Quest. So was Orpheus, whose Lyre has been immor-

talized in the constellation Lyra. The Centaur represented by the constellation Centaurus, Chiron, was the young Jason's mentor. The ship's surgeon, Aesculapius, was later honored with a place among the stars as the constellation of the Serpent-bearer, Ophiuchus. And of course, the zodiacal Aries was thought of as the Ram that had grown the Golden Fleece.

The large number of Argonautic constellations, as well as the group of constellations in the Autumn skies associated with the Perseus-Andromeda myth, leave no doubt that the ancient Greeks tried to coordinate their myths and their constellations. For the most part they adapted their myths to the star groups they had received from the Mesopotamians. But they also substituted, inventing new constellations to fit in with their indigenous legends. The whole Perseus-Andromeda family of constellations replaced the older Mesopotamian constellations in that region of the sky— with the exception of the Scimitar of Perseus, which indeed had been a Mesopotamian constellation occupying at least some of the stars of the later Greek star group Perseus.

Despite the fact that the Greeks envisioned only the back half of the Argo in the sky, it was such a huge constellation that astronomers last century divided it into three manageable pieces, **Puppis** the Stern, **Vela** the Sails, and **Carina** the Keel. Unfortunately, Argo is so far south on the celestial sphere that for most of the continental United States much of the Ship does not rise above the southern horizon at all, and the part that does never ascends very high and therefore is dimmed by horizon haze.

However, begin your exploration of the celestial Ship at Rho Puppis, the more easterly of the two 3rd-magnitude stars east of the Delta-Epsilon-Eta Canis triangle. From Rho Puppis go 16° due south to the mag 2.2 Zeta (ζ) Puppis. Another 7$\frac{1}{2}$° south of Zeta Puppis is the mag 1.8 Gamma (γ) Velorum, the brightest star in Vela the Sails. Vela is outlined by a long oval of 2nd-, 3rd-, and 4th-magnitude stars stretching about 2$\frac{1}{2}$ hours in right ascension east from Gamma Vel. Zeta Puppis and Gamma Velorum are two of the most interesting stars visible to the unaided eye anywhere in the heavens. Zeta Puppis is an extremely hot and extremely luminous star: its surface temperature is 50,000° K, and its true brightness is 60,000 times that of the Sun. Gamma Velorum A (telescopes reveal that Gamma Vel is a fine double) is the brightest and nearest of the "Wolf-Rayet" stars, which are young and highly luminous supergiant stars that are experiencing ongoing mass loss by a process that seems to be something like a continuous explosion of material from the star's upper layers.

To complete your survey of Puppis, return to the

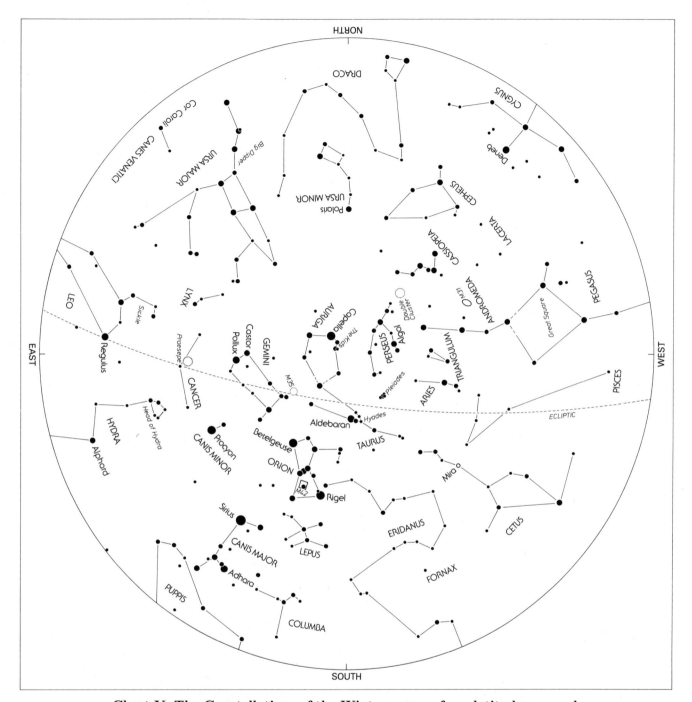

Chart V: The Constellations of the Winter as seen from latitudes around 40°N at about 9 p.m. standard time on January 15, 11 p.m. standard time on December 15, and 7 p.m. on February 15. *The Belt of Orion, a 3° long line of 2nd-magnitude stars, is about halfway up from the southern horizon to the observer's zenith and provides a good guide to the other Winter star groups because it points NW toward the "V" of the Hyades Star Cluster in the face of Taurus the Bull and SE toward the brightest star in the Sky, Sirius the Dog Star in Canis Major. The Winter Milky Way is rather faint and narrow in Perseus, but widens and brightens toward the SE in Monoceros and Puppis.*

AUTUMN				
Object(s)	Type	Constellation	Chart(s)	Text page(s)
NGC 7000, the North America Nebula	Diffuse nebula	Cygnus	2, 8	140
Milky Way from Deneb NW to Lac & Cep	Rich Milky Way field	Cyg-Cep-Lac	2	36, 41, 140, 143
μ Cephei, the Garnet Star	Red star (& variable)	Cepheus	2	40–1
Delta (δ) Cephei	Double star (& variable)	Cepheus	2	40
NGC 7789	Rich open cluster	Cassiopeia	1, 2	45–6
NGC's 869 and 884, the Perseus Double Cluster	Open cluster pair	Perseus	1	48
α Persei Group	Large open cluster	Perseus	1	49
M31, the Andromeda Galaxy, M32 and NGC 205	Galaxy group	Andromeda	3	154–55
NGC 752	Large open cluster	Andromeda	3	50
M33, the Pinwheel Galaxy	Galaxy	Triangulum	3	154–55
NGC 7293, the Helical Nebula	Planetary nebula	Aquarius	8	34–5
NGC 253	Galaxy	Sculptor	3	156

WINTER				
Object(s)	Type	Constellation	Chart(s)	Text page(s)
M45, the Pleiades	Large open cluster	Taurus	3	59–61
The Hyades and α Tau	Large open cluster	Taurus	4	58, 60
M36, M38	Open clusters in rich Milky Way field	Auriga	4	70
M35	Open cluster	Gemini	4	71
NGC 2174	Diffuse nebula	Orion	4	65
Orion's Belt (δ-ϵ-ζ Ori)	Rich star field	Orion	4	65
M78	Reflection nebula	Orion	4	65
M42, the Orion Nebula,+ θ Orionis	Diffuse nebula with double star	Orion	4	63–65
Σ752	Double star	Orion	4	65
NGC 2237 and NGC 2246, the Rosette	Diffuse nebula with open cluster	Monoceros	4	73–4
Milky Way from central Mon to the SE	Rich Milky Way field	Mon-Puppis	4	73, 76
M41	Open cluster	Canis Major	4	69
δ, ϵ, η, o^1, o^2, σ CMa	Color contrast group	Canis Major	4	67
M46, M47	Open cluster pair	Puppis	4, 5	76

SPRING				
Object(s)	Type	Constellation	Chart(s)	Text page(s)
M44, Praesepe	Open cluster	Cancer	5	84
U Hydrae	Red carbon star	Hydra	5	86–7
M81 and M82	Galaxy pair	Ursa Major	1, 2	158
M101	Galaxy	Ursa Major	1, 2	156–57
M51, the Whirlpool Galaxy	Galaxy pair	Canes Venatici	2, 6	157
M65, M66 and NGC 3628	Galaxy group	Leo	5	158–59
Coma Star Cluster	Large open cluster	Coma Berenices	6	94
γ, ϵ, β Corvi	Color contrast group	Corvus	6	88
M83	Galaxy	Hydra	6	157-58
NGC 5128	Galaxy	Centaurus	6, 10	157-58
Omega (ω) Centauri, NGC 5139	Globular cluster	Centaurus	6, 10	100
Alpha (α) Librae	Double star	Libra	6	98–9

SUMMER				
Object(s)	Type	Constellation	Chart(s)	Text page(s)
Head of Scorpius (β-δ-π Sco)	Rich star field; star colors	Scorpius	7	114–15
Heart of Scorpius (α-σ-τ Sco)+M4	Color contrast stars; Globular cluster	Scorpius	7	114–16
NGC 6231	Open cluster of supergiant stars	Scorpius	7	116, 119
M7	Large open cluster	Scorpius	7	119–20
The Great Sgr Star Cloud	Part of Galactic Hub	Sagittarius	7	122, 125
M8, Lagoon Nebula, and M20 Trifid Nebula	Diffuse nebulae	Sagittarius	7	125–26
M24, Small Sgr Star Cloud	Star cloud	Sagittarius	7	126–28
M17, the Swan Nebula	Diffuse nebula	Sagittarius	7	128–29
M22	Globular cluster	Sagittarius	7	122
Scutum Star Cloud	Star cloud	Scutum	7	130–32
Scan from γ to ζ Aql: B142-3 and the Great Rift	Dark nebulae in the Milky Way	Aquila	7	132–34
Dumb-bell Nebula	Planetary Nebulae	Vulpecula	7,8	135
ϵ, ζ, δ Lyrae	Field of double stars	Lyra	7	136–37
Cygnus Star Cloud	Star cloud	Cygnus	7, 8	138–40

Table 1–2. *The above table is a seasonal list of some of the best objects for an unexpected hour of observing under dark skies. The objects mentioned are favorably located for observing during 10–11 p.m. local standard time from around 40° N lat. during the middle of their respective seasons. They are given in the most convenient order for getting from one object to the next.*

Rho-Xi Puppis pair and go SW through Pi (π) Puppis (which is about 8° south of Eta Canis) and on to Nu (ν) Puppis. Pi and Nu Puppis are not difficult to identify because they are 3rd-magnitude stars in a region of the sky where there are few stars even of the 5th magnitude.

However, 10° SSW of Nu Puppis is the northwest-ernmost star in Carina the Keel, the brilliant mag -0.7 Alpha Carinae, named Canopus, the second brightest star in the sky. Canopus marks one of the two rudder-oars of Argo, and there is good, though indirect, evidence that it was the original end of Eridanus. Most of Carina is to the SE of Canopus, and south of Vela, and therefore is very poorly situated for observers even in the far southern continental United States.

1.3 Observing With Binoculars

Probably most households are not without binoculars. If you are new to astronomy and already own a pair of binoculars of the 7x35 or 7x50 type, or can borrow one from a friend, there is no reason why you should bother to buy a telescope—at least right away. Binoculars are much more portable, require no set-up time to use, and, because they have wide fields of view oriented right side up, they are much easier to find celestial objects with.

The disadvantages of binoculars are their low magnifications and modest apertures. They are, however, more powerful than one might suppose. 50mm glasses gather about 50 times as much light as the dark-adapted human eye; but to gather 50 times as much light as 50mm binoculars you'd need a 14-inch telescope!

No observing guide that I have read does justice to the capabilities of a good pair of binoculars used at a dark-sky site. With my 10x50s I have identified a half dozen planetary nebulae, over twenty diffuse nebulae (including two supernova remnants), six dozen galaxies, and scores of open clusters, most of which my glasses could at least partially resolve. Naturally, the nebulae and galaxies, and many of the open clusters, appeared merely as small disks or patches of haze. There are, however, a surprising number of objects and fields for which binoculars actually provide *better* views than such popular telescopes as 6-inch Newtonian reflectors and 8-inch Schmidt-Cassegrains. These include large open clusters like the Hyades and Pleiades (which simply do not fit in the small fields of view of telescopes), Milky Way star clouds, and extended low surface brightness nebulae and galaxies like the Rosette and North America nebulae, the face-on spirals M33 in Triangulum and M101 in Ursa Major, and the huge emission complexes IC 1396 in Cepheus and IC 1848 in Cassiopeia. All of these, which are in fact difficult, even impossible, for 6- or 8-inch telescopes, are actually rather easy to see in binoculars.

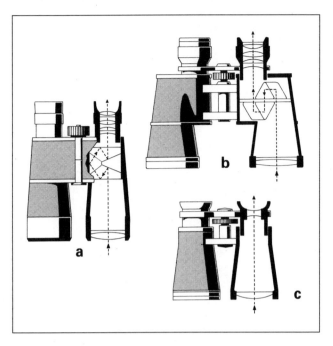

Figure 1–5. *The three principle types of binoculars:* **a** *Roof Prism;* **b** *Porro Prism; and* **c** *Field or Opera Glasses. Field or opera glasses are unsuitable for astronomical use. While the very best (and very expensive) binoculars have desirable features the author used binoculars that he purchased from Sears & Roebuck in 1978 for $40.00 to prepare this book.*

The reason binoculars are so good for Milky Way fields and extended low surface brightness nebulae and galaxies is that they yield much greater "image brightness" than telescopes. The high magnifications of telescopes spread an extended object's light out, but binoculars magnify it only enough to maximize its contrast with the sky background.

Binocular Designs (Fig. 1–5)

Binoculars are essentially just two refractor telescopes mounted in parallel. They differ from conventional refractor telescopes in having prisms in the optical path between the light-gathering objective lens and the image-magnifying ocular. The prisms fold the light path, thus decreasing the tube length and preventing the image seen in the ocular from being inverted, as it always is in the conventional refractor telescope. Because most binoculars have porro prisms, which cause a "jog" in the light path through the instrument, they are built with the axes of the oculars off-set from the axes of the objectives.

Some models, however, use roof prisms, which have a straight-through light path and allow the glasses to be constructed in a simple H-shape—a lighter and more compact design. Roof-prism binoculars are, however, more expensive than the porro-prism type. Do not confuse roof-prism binoculars with field glasses or opera glasses, which also have an H-shape but use a mere erecting lens in front of the eyepiece to deliver an upright image. Field and opera glasses have magnifications of only 2x or 3x and are much inferior to prism binoculars for astronomy.

Binoculars are classified by a two-number system that gives their magnification and the diameter (in millimeters) of their objectives. Thus, 7x50 binoculars magnify seven times and have objective lenses 50 millimeters in diameter. (There are 25.4 millimeters per inch, so 50 millimeters is almost two inches.) Zoom binoculars are labelled with their power range: 7–21x40 zoom instruments, for example, have 40mm objectives and magnify from 7 to 21 power. For astronomy, the size of a binocular's objective lens is more important than the instrument's magnification because you want as much light-gathering power as possible. To compute the relative light-gathering power of two different size binoculars, simply square their objective diameters and divide the larger figure by the smaller. Thus you'll find that 50mm binoculars gather about 1.6 times as much light as 40mm glasses and twice as much as 35mm instruments.

Binoculars also have different fields of view—even glasses with the same magnifications and objective diameters can have different field widths. Usually the field of view is specified on the instrument and expressed either in degrees or in feet at 1000 yards' distance from the observer. Because distances on the celestial sphere are measured in degrees, you should know your binocular's field in degrees. If it's not given on the instrument or in the user's manual, you can estimate it by looking at the Pointer Stars of the Big Dipper, which are about 5° apart.

Choosing Binoculars

If you already have good quality binoculars of at least 35mm aperture, don't bother getting a larger instrument, at least not right away. 7x35s are sufficient to see over half the objects discussed in this book. Glasses with 20mm or 30mm objectives are somewhat small for astronomical observing, but even 20mm lenses gather about nine times as much light as the dark-adapted human eye and are therefore an appreciable step up from naked-eye observing.

For astronomy the best binoculars are 10x50 extra wide angle instruments. Giant binoculars (11x80s, 20x70s, 20x60s) offer superior magnification and light-gathering power to 10x50s but are so heavy that you will need a tripod to observe with them for any length of time. Also they are expensive, running $250 and

more, not including the tripod. You might as well put that kind of money into a telescope.

In many books and articles you will see 7x50s recommended over 10x50s for astronomy, usually on the grounds that it is easier to hold 7x glasses steady. That might be true, but there are a lot of galaxies and nebulae visible in 10x50s which cannot be seen in 7x50s. (The extra magnification not only increases the size of the galaxies and nebulae, it also enhances their apparent contrast with the sky background.) Furthermore, 10x is necessary to resolve small open clusters and tight double stars. Therefore, I recommend that unless you already have 7x50s, get 10x50s. If you indeed do find 10x glasses difficult to hold steady, you can always find something to brace yourself against—a fence post, a picnic table, your car, etc.

Zoom binoculars offer the observer flexibility—low powers for Milky Way fields and large galaxies and nebulae, and high powers for resolving open clusters and double stars. However, zoom binoculars are notorious for their poor image quality. The 7–21x40 instrument I used in some of my observing for this book cost well over $100 and was made by a reputable optical firm. But it gave sharp images only at the center of the field and did not focus at all at the extremes of its power range. Moreover, it was so poorly color-corrected that Sirius, for example, appeared as a white spot inside a dark blue disk! Now, if you already have a zoom binocular, don't junk it, even if it is as poor as the one I used. Enjoy the advantage its higher powers will give you on open clusters and double stars. But if you are in the market for your first pair of binoculars, I advise getting single-power glasses.

There are several things to keep in mind when shopping for binoculars. To begin with, do not buy a pair that lack fully-coated optics ("fully-coated" means that both the lenses and the prisms are coated). The coating decreases the reflectivity of the glass surfaces, maximizing the amount of light that makes its way through the optical system to your eye. Next, when you are looking at binoculars in a store, check to be sure that there are no scratches on the lenses, that the focus operates smoothly, and that it is well-constructed. If, for example, the ocular barrels can be wobbled (as with one pair I inspected), then it's a lemon.

Whether buying from a store or through the mail, be sure that you can field-test the binocular and return it if it proves optically unsatisfactory. Most retailers, department stores, and mail order companies are willing to refund a customer's money on merchandize returned in resalable condition, but if in doubt get the promise in writing before you buy. When field-testing the glass, first see how sharp the focus is. The stars should appear as pinprick points without color fringes (assuming your eyes do not suffer from astigmatism). Then check that the stars are in focus out to the edge of the field—it's no use buying "extra wide angle" binocs if the outer parts of the fields are blurry. Finally, handle the binoculars long enough to find out if weight will be a problem.

Observing Equipment

Besides binoculars, and this book, all you need for observing is a flashlight. Use a regular flashlight for finding your way out to your observing site and a penlight for consulting the star charts in this book. The penlight's lens should be covered with red cellophane because red light impairs night vision less than white or yellow light. (You can probably get red cellophane from most dime and drug stores. Even if they don't carry it as retail item, they will almost certainly stock it for display wrapping.) In a real pinch, a layer or two of grocery bag paper taped in place will suffice. No doubt you'll also find it convenient to have a folding table or some other portable flat surface for this book. If there is a wind, anchor it by clamping it down with those spring-steel clips sold for holding tablecloths to picnic tables.

Choosing an Observing Site

The most important factor to consider in selecting a place from which to observe is convenience—if it takes you an hour to get there, you simply will not be able to observe all that often. Unfortunately, if you live right in a large metropolitan area, you probably *are* an hour from a decently dark sky. If you live in the outer suburbs, however, light pollution will still be a bit of problem, but your own backyard is an adequate potential observing location.

Basically what you need for observing is a place out from under the worst of the light pollution of cities and towns and where most of the sky is unobstructed by trees or buildings. (On occasion, though, trees and buildings can block yard lights, street lights, and vehicle headlights. The glare of a farmyard light even a quarter mile distant will prevent your eyes from fully dark-adapting.) Try to find a location where you can see almost down to the southern horizon and therefore as much of the southern constellations as possible. To minimize the annoyance from mosquitoes, select a spot away from swamps or ponds and near the crest of a hill.

If the observing site you choose is on private property, be sure to ask the owner's permission to use it. If it is municipal or public property, keep in mind that some parks and recreational areas officially close at 10 or 11 in the evening. The police have broad discretion in such matters, and if they happen by they will probably ignore you or merely ask what you are doing. However, if they have received a call from some excitable person about "muggers lurking in the park," you may have some explaining to do.

Selecting an Observing Night

The best nights for observing are those without haze, humidity, or moonlight. A crescent Moon is never bright enough to interfere (and is interesting to look at in binoculars, particularly as it sets or rises), but from first to last quarter, you will have to observe after moonset or before moonrise. (Moonrise and moonset times for each day are given in most almanacs and in the annual *Observer's Handbook* of the Royal Astronomical Society of Canada.)

The Moon is predictable, but in most parts of the country weather isn't—at least not with the accuracy an observer would want. Sometimes the meteorologists will promise a clear night, but an hour later—just as you get to your observing site—the clouds roll in anyway. If you have just driven 40 miles, you'll be irritated. Unfortunately, such aggravations come with the territory. The American Southwest has weather that is generally good for observing most nights year-round. The rest of us must keep an eye on the sky (particularly to the west) during the late afternoon and learn how to spot the approaching line of thunderstorms (in summer) or the cloud shield of developing low pressure system (in autumn, winter, and spring). Humid, hazy afternoons almost invariably mean a poor night for observing. Before you go out to observe, watch the television weather reports and pay particular attention to the time-lapse radar and satellite shots. They will show if precipitation or clouds are headed your way.

Keeping Warm

Even a summer night can be cool, but usually denim jeans and medium-weight jacket or hooded sweatshirt will be enough. For spring and autumn, however, you need a good deal more to stay comfortable. (The southeastern U.S. is an exception because the high humidity keeps nighttime temperatures from falling too far below the daytime ones.) Start with your feet, which will be the first to get cold. Wear boots and two layers of socks, the inner layer cotton (to wick moisture away from your foot) and the outer layer wool (which provides the insulation). Long underwear and denim jeans should keep your legs warm down to 20°F unless there is a strong wind. The best type of long underwear I know is the double-layered variety, which pairs a cotton inner layer to a wool outer layer.

There are two approaches for keeping the upper half of your body warm: (1) a single heavy goose-down or synthetically insulated arctic coat, or (2) several layers of wool garments beneath an outer nylon or cotton poplin "shell" jacket (to stop the wind). I live in Minnesota. I also snowshoe and winter camp, so I'm set up for layered dressing. (Layering is best for heavy cold weather activities because you can take off or put on layers to adjust to variable weather conditions and to the amount you exert yourself.) For observing in cool weather in a wind, I wear a long-sleeve double-layer undershirt, a turtleneck, a denim shirt, a wool sweater-vest, a hooded sweatshirt, a medium-weight wool jacket, and an army field jacket. The wide, deep pockets of army field jackets are excellent for carrying flashlights, notebooks, candy bars, portable radios and cassette players, or almost anything else you might need or want for an observing session. In fact, army field jackets are perhaps the ideal garment for all outdoor activities.

The head and hands are particularly exposed to the cold and, like your feet, require special attention. Unlined gloves are adequate down to about 40°F but below that you need to wear lined gloves (those with removable wool liners are especially good) or mittens. Because one-fourth of the heat generated by your body can be lost through your head, you must keep it covered. (Lumberjacks used to say, "When you feet get cold, put your hat on.") In the absence of wind, a wool stocking cap should be enough. However, if there is a wind and unless your coat has a lined hood, you will need something more—such as one of those troopers' hats worn by many law enforcement officers in winter.

Winter Observing

Winter observing (December, January, and February) from Canada and the northern United States rates a special section. In order to enjoy it you must not only want to observe, you must also enjoy the challenge of defying bitter cold. It is not an activity for the sedentary or the ill-prepared. When temperatures drop below zero you are risking frostbite, particularly to the face. Bare flesh exposed to −10°F air pushed by a 20 mile per hour wind will freeze within minutes.

Even with above-zero temperatures and no wind, it's not easy to stay warm during a winter observing session. Your feet and hands take a beating from the cold—the feet because they have nothing to do (which slows circulation) and the hands because of the cold of the binoculars and because you will find it necessary to take them out of your mittens to write notes or to turn the pages of this book. For the hands I recommend ski mittens or wool-lined "wood choppers." For the feet, use arctic pac boots. Buy them a half-size larger than your normal shoe size so you can put a felt innersole in the bottom—the more between your foot and the cold

ground the better—and can wear a couple pairs of socks (cotton inside wool, as before). To the clothes I wear during autumn and spring observing I add alpaca-lined flight-pants, a second wool jacket, and (in place of the field jacket) a paratrooper parka with a fur-trimmed hood (the fur keeps face-heat from being lost so fast). This combination has kept me warm down to −25°F. Most of you will not—thank goodness—have to observe at such extreme temperatures.

The cold causes a number of annoying equipment difficulties: ink in pens flows poorly, flashlight batteries lose power, and the focusing mechanism of the binoculars becomes stiff. When the binoculars have cooled down to air temperature (which takes a little over half an hour), their oculars will tend to frost over. And you don't even need to breathe on the lenses to make frost, since the moisture and heat of your eyes themselves are enough. When you notice that star images in the oculars are beginning to haze, fold back the rubber protective caps. The binoculars will be a little more difficult to hold steady, but the free flow of air between the eyepieces and your eyes will carry most of the moisture away. When you take the cooled binoculars back inside, water will condense on the lenses: *do not* wipe the water off. Let it evaporate naturally.

Observing is supposed to be enjoyable, so if the rigors and aggravations of winter star gazing aren't to your taste, don't push yourself—stay inside, stay comfortable, and read a good book. You can always catch Orion in March or after midnight next November. Besides, the clarity of the winter sky is overrated. The arctic air masses that plunge south from Canada into the central and eastern United States during winter are in fact usually thick or even hazy.

Hazards of The Night

Even if you don't plan to observe any nearer the wilderness than your own suburban back yard, you might encounter some fellow creatures that make life interesting. In the southern parts of the United States scorpions and/or poisonous snakes sometimes can be found even in the suburbs, particularly where there is swamp or brushland nearby. If you live in such an area, never go outside at night without a flashlight. Never reach blindly into a bush, under a rock, into piles of debris, or onto ledges. And never lie on the ground to observe—use a picnic table, a reclining lawn chair, your car hood, or some other elevated surface.

About the only nasty creature suburban observers in Canada and the northern United States need to consider are skunks. Don't laugh—skunks aren't just a smelly joke. They sometimes carry rabies. Moreover, receiving full blast of skunk secretion directly in the face can induce convulsions. Skunks, unfortunately, are not as afraid of humans as most other wild animals, so you can't assume they will stay out of your way. But if you watch where you are going at night with a flashlight and occasionally sweep your vicinity with its beam while you observe, you should avoid any problems with them.

At rural sites your chances of seeing a skunk or some other animal are enhanced, though still actually rather small. If you have lived in cities or suburbs all your life and are therefore unaccustomed to the various sounds of country night, you probably will feel more secure having a baseball bat within reach. But don't expect to have occasion to use it. Animals, wild or domestic (except for snakes), no more like things lurking in the night than you do, and they will generally give you a wide berth.

The national parks of the United States and the provincial parks of Canada are excellent places for vacation observing. However, you ought to give a thought to bears. As a rule, the black bears of the eastern U.S. and Canada are more mild-mannered than the aggressive grizzlies of the western mountains. Most bears will find you quite uninteresting if you are not carrying food, except in the unlikely event that they are starving. But any bear accompanied by its young should be considered extremely dangerous.

Observing Techniques

Night Vision. It takes several minutes for the human eye to adapt to low-light conditions. In fact, after the rapid initial adjustment your eyes will continue to dark-adapt slowly for another hour. Avoid all bright lights while observing and consult charts and books only with a flashlight or penlight shielded with red cellophane. Your night vision will generally improve as you observe. Beginners don't see well at night and therefore will not be able to see as faint objects in binoculars or telescopes as the seasoned observer. Nicotine, among its many other undesirable effects, inhibits the dilation of the eye's iris and consequently impairs dark adaption. If you can't stop smoking altogether, at least refrain from it before and during your observing.

Averted Vision. The retina of the eye is most sensitive just outside the center of vision. Therefore, when you are viewing a low surface brightness galaxy or nebula, or trying to resolve the faint stars of a cluster or star cloud, do not look directly at the object, but just to its side. At first you will find the acrobatics of looking at one spot while concentrating on another difficult, but it soon becomes second nature.

Steadying the Binoculars. Though individuals vary, 7x glasses are about the highest power instrument that you can use free-standing. While observing with 10x or zoom binoculars, steady yourself by leaning against a fence post, the side of a building, your car, or any other firm object. To observe in the region of the zenith you will have to lie on something (a reclining lawn chair, your car hood, a picnic table, a flat-bed wagon, etc.), and your head will need support. The binocular case works well and you can set it on edge to give your head more elevation when you want to observe lower in the sky. How long you can hold your binoculars steady will of course depend on your arm's strength. To reduce arm fatigue, try to prop at least one elbow against something while you observe.

Learning to Look. Even if you know better than to expect the splashy full-color photographs you've seen in astronomy books and magazines, your first glance at most celestial objects through binoculars or even a telescope will disappoint you. In fact, most beginning observers will not be able to see many of the subtler objects and details mentioned in this book. However, seeing is an acquired ability, perfected through practice, and the more eyepiece time you accumulate, the more acute your eyes will become to faint objects and subtle details. When I first began observing with binoculars I could not see the Rosette Nebula at all, but now it is not difficult for me even under poor sky conditions.

The most important thing in observing is to really *look*—a mere glance at an object or a field is simply not enough. You must keep your eyes at the oculars for at least a full minute at a time. This gives your eyes the chance to adjust to the light conditions in the field of view, making them more sensitive to the faint star-specks at the limit of resolution. It also reveals the subtle difference between the hazy patch of a galaxy or nebula and the sky background. To avoid eye fatigue, blink as you feel the need. Another technique to improve acuity is to jiggle the binoculars a bit while looking at faint object: your brain is good at spotting motion, even with dim objects, and this can help. It also reduces eye fatigue.

Star Colors

Star colors appear more striking in binoculars than in telescopes—probably because with binoculars both eyes are involved in the seeing and therefore color fatigue, to which the human eye is particularly susceptible, occurs less rapidly. For good star-color observing, it is of course necessary that your binoculars be well color-corrected. If they are not, you will see color fringes on each side of the star images (blue on one side, red on the other), or the star image will be embedded in a blue disk (the unfocused blue light of the star).

Stars have a variety of colors, but the exact color you see for any given star depends on two factors (besides the optical quality of your binoculars)—the atmosphere and your eyes. The effect of the atmosphere on star colors is predictable. It virtually always reddens stars, so the more humid or smoggy a night is, the worse the blue tones of blue stars will be washed out and the more the tints of yellow, orange, and red stars will be deepened. And because near the horizon we look through the most atmosphere, rising or setting stars are always reddened, even on transparent nights.

The human eye, however, is not so predictable. Color sensitivity not only differs from person to person, it can even vary in the same person from one night—or one eye—to the next. In general, the color sensitivity of the human eye is greater to red than to blue, so in 50mm binoculars you will be able to see red-toned stars down to the 6th magnitude but blue-toned stars down to only about the 4th magnitude.

Astronomers express star color by a quantity called color index, the difference between a star's magnitude as it appears on a blue-sensitive photographic plate and its magnitude as it appears to the typical human eye (or on a photographic plate with the same color sensitivity as the human eye). Appropriately standardized, color index yields an unambiguous number. However, in this book I have chosen to stick with color names because they are more familiar to most people. Though some of the color names might seem over-descriptive, I have picked them carefully. For example, I call Rigel and most other B-type stars "silver blue" because to my eye they have a sharp icy sparkle that the more pedestrian "blue-white" fails to communicate. And since many K-type stars (such as the 61 Cygni pair) seem to have an almost metallic gleam, I call them chrome orange-red. But please remember that the tints you see will depend on your eye's color sensitivity and on the atmospheric conditions under which you observe. You will find, in any case, that star colors are among the most beautiful things to view in your binoculars.

Chapter 2

The Constellations of Autumn

The autumn heavens are dominated by the Milky Way, which for observers in the middle north latitudes passes through the zenith at this time of year, bridging the sky from horizon to horizon. The major Milky Way constellations of autumn are Cepheus, Cassiopeia, and Perseus, but during the early evenings of September Cygnus is still virtually overhead. In fact, though Cygnus is usually classified as a summer constellation (and this book conforms to that custom), the cool transparent nights of early autumn, when the sky is free of summer haze and humidity, is a particularly good time to observe it.

Despite the prominence of the Milky Way, the autumn sky is singularly poor in bright stars. The one 1st-magnitude star of autumn is Fomalhaut, which drifts in mysterious solitude over the southern horizon for a few hours each September and October evening. There are plenty of 2nd- and 3rd-magnitude stars in the constellations of Cassiopeia, Perseus, Andromeda, and Pegasus (all in or near the Milky Way), but only one star in these four constellations is brighter than magnitude 2.0 (Alpha [α] Persei at magnitude 1.8). Farther away from the Milky Way even 3rd-magnitude stars become scarce, and though the star patterns of Capricornus, Piscis Austrinus, Aquarius, Pisces, and Cetus have a subtle logic and delicate beauty, they achieve this mostly with dim 4th- and 5th-magnitude stars.

The southern part of the autumn sky was known to the ancient Greeks, and before them to the cultures of Mesopotamia (from whom the Greeks got most of the constellations they passed on to us), as "the Sea" or "the Water." The aquatic motif in this part of the sky seems virtually as old as western civilization itself. During the 4th and early 3rd millennia B.C., when the Sumerians of southern Mesopotamia first formed many of the ancient constellations, the Sun was in Capricornus, Aquarius, and Pisces during November, December, and January—then as now that region's rainy season. The rains and the spring floods of the Tigris and Euphrates Rivers were particularly important to the farmers because fresh water was needed to wash away the salt deposited in the fields by irrigation during the dry season. Aquarius thus appears in Mesopotamian art as a hero pouring out the fresh waters of life.

For the binocular observer the constellations of the autumn Milky Way are rich in beautiful and interesting objects—open clusters, star fields, and even some emission nebulae. Away from the Milky Way, however, good objects are more scattered. The eastern non-Milky Way constellations of autumn contain several galaxies easily visible in most binoculars, but the western autumn constellations are poor in galaxies even for telescopes and contain only a handful of other types of deep-sky objects to observe.

2.1 The Early Autumn Constellations

Capricornus, the Goat-Fish, Map 8.

Capricornus is a herald of autumn. When Sagittarius reaches the meridian during July midnights, Capricornus is already fully risen in the southeast. Like the other constellations of the celestial "Sea," Capricornus is poor in bright stars. Its only 3rd-magnitude objects are Delta (δ) at magnitude 2.8 and Beta (β) at magnitude 3.1, but its boat-like shape is distinctive. The shape, however, does not resemble a goat, let alone a fish-tailed goat!

The earliest known representation of a goat-fish appears on a Mesopotamian cylinder seal carved around 2100 B.C. The seal design shows the creature as the foot-stool of the enthroned Sumerian water-god Enki, who holds before himself his signifying attribute: a water-jar emitting two streams up which swim fish. The form of the goat-fish on this seal is in all points identical to the form of the goat-fish as it appears on Graeco-Roman period zodiacs—even to the extended foreleg. This is one example of the power Mesopotamian astronomy in all its forms—mathematical as well as mythological and iconographic—exerted over early Greek astronomy. Contrary to the assertions of some well-known writers on popular science, Greek astronomy did *not* begin with the Pre-Socratic Greek philosophers, it evolved from Mesopotamian astronomy.

The goat-fish was a very common fill motif on Old Babylonian cylinder seals of the early 2nd millennium B.C., and it appears on at least one Syro-Cappadocian seal cut during or just after the Old Babylonian period. Almost certainly, therefore, Syria was the route through which the image and the constellation of the goat-fish was transmitted from the old civilizations of the Euphrates to the early Greeks.

Capricornus is not rich in objects for binoculars or telescopes. In fact, *Burnham's Celestial Handbook* catalogues only one galaxy brighter than magnitude 13.0 in Capricornus—astonishing for an area of the sky this large and this far away from the Milky Way's obscuring dust. Readers with Wil Tirion's *Sky Atlas 2000.0* or Bečvář's *Atlas of the Heavens* will notice that Capricornus, Aquarius, Pegasus, western Pisces, Piscis Austrinus, and small Equuleus and Microscopium are all galaxy-poor.

Alpha (α) and Beta (β) Capricorni. Capricornus has two nice double stars for binocular observers, Alpha and Beta Cap, both of which fit in the same binocular field of view. The Alpha pair is a naked-eye double. In binoculars you should see a definite yellow or orange-yellow color to both stars. Unfortunately, the two stars are merely an optical double: chance has aligned a nearer star with one about five times farther away. The Beta pair, however, though also extremely wide and easy to split in even the smallest field-glass, is a true gravitationally-bound system. The 6th-magnitude star orbits its primary in a period that must be thousands of years long. The Alpha pair, the Beta pair, and the 5th-magnitude Nu (ν), less than 1° east-southeast of Alpha, form a nice group in binoculars—surprisingly rich for this otherwise star-poor area.

Table 2–1
$\alpha^1 + \alpha^2$ Cap and $\beta^1 + \beta^2$ Cap

Star	Sep. ($''$)	PA (°)	App Mag	Spectra	Dist (l-y)	Abs Mag
α^1			3.6	G9 III	100	+1.1
α^2	376	291	4.2	G3 Ib	500	−1.7
β^1			3.1	K0 II+A5		−2.2
β^2	205	267	6.2	B9	360	+0.9

Microscopium, the Microscope, Map 8.

Microscopium was created by the 18th-century French astronomer Nicolas Louis de Lacaille to fill the blank region due south of Capricornus. It is one of the most barren constellations in the entire sky. Its brightest star Gamma (γ) is only magnitude 4.7 and even for 8-inch telescopes Microscopium offers nothing more than a handful of unremarkable doubles and a few faint galaxies. Microscopium is so far south (it lies between declinations −28° and −46°) that for most of the United States its few naked-eye stars are lost in the horizon haze.

About all a binocular observer can do with Microscopium is identify the constellation's Greek-lettered stars—at least useful for getting to know where Microscopium is. (This is all the mid-northern observer gets from several other minor southern constellations—Phoenix later in the autumn, Horologium, Caelum, and Pictor in the winter, Pyxis and Crater in the spring, and Norma and Corona Australis in the summer.)

Piscis Austrinus, the Southern Fish, Map 8.

The glory of Piscis Austrinus is Fomalhaut. At magnitude 1.2, this star is only the 18th brightest in the sky, but it lies so far from any comparably bright object that it quite completely dominates the southern skies of autumn. Fred Schaaf in *Astronomy* magazine appropriately described Fomalhaut as "a solitary lighthouse on the southern shore of the Water." There is something mysterious and melancholy about this star as it drifts in solitude low over the southern horizon for a few hours each autumn evening. It seems an appropriate symbol for a season when the trees lose their leaves, the grass withers, and the nights grow long and cold.

Fomalhaut comes from the Arabic *al-Fum al-Hut*, "the Mouth of the Fish," the position it marks in the constellation. This name was given to the star by medieval Arab astronomers when they rediscovered the astronomy of Greece and Rome and adopted the classical constellations. The Bedouin, however, knew Fomalhaut as *al-Difda al-Awwal*, "the First Frog," because it rose just before the Sun near the beginning of spring.

The idea of a fish in this region of the sky originated in Mesopotamia: Assyrian texts of the late 2nd and the early 1st millennia B.C. refer to our Fomalhaut as *Kua*, the "Fish." This is just another example of a constellation we have inherited from ancient Greece that can be traced back to the even more ancient civilizations of the Euphrates.

In binoculars Fomalhaut has a beautiful blue-white color, but it must be viewed on transparent nights while it is near the meridian (at its maximum altitude), otherwise atmospheric haze will wash out the blue tint. Fomalhaut is 23 light-years distant and its absolute magnitude is +2.0, corresponding to true luminosity of 14 Suns. It has an A3 V spectrum.

Approximately 2° south of Fomalhaut, some two-thirds the distance from Fomalhaut to Delta (δ) PsA, is a pair of stars just below naked-eye brightness separated by a few minutes of arc in a southwest to northeast direction. The northeastern star of the pair, catalogued as GC 31978, is of magnitude 6.5 and has the same distance and space velocity as Fomalhaut. This can hardly be coincidence, so there must be some physical connection between it and its bright neighbor. However, at a distance of 23 light-years the 2° apparent separation between the two stars corresponds to a true separation of at least one full light-year—more if GC 31978 is slightly closer or farther than Fomalhaut. In any case, the actual gravitational attraction between the two stars is negligible.

Burnham suggests that Fomalhaut and its faint companion are the survivors of a low-density star cluster—one so scattered and star-poor that the gravitational attraction between the members was insufficient to hold the cluster together. However, in a cluster of this sort the low-luminosity, low-mass members like GC 31978 (which is a K5 dwarf star with only 10% the Sun's luminosity) are the first to disperse, "evaporating" early from the cluster. The Coma Star Cluster, for example, has lost nearly all members fainter than about a third the Sun's luminosity.

Grus, the Crane, Maps 8 and 10.

Grus is the farthest north of the twelve southern constellations published by Johann Bayer of Germany in 1603. These twelve constellations filled in the area of the celestial sphere too far south to be seen by the constellation builders of the ancient Near East. Actually, Bayer did not invent most of the twelve "Bayer constellations"— he merely published what he learned about the southern heavens from mariners who had sailed to the Southern Hemisphere. The area in the southern heavens without ancient constellations provides a reliable and interesting way to estimate the date when at least the most southerly of the ancient constellations were formed.

The part of the southern sky not visible from any northern hemisphere site is a circular region centered upon the south celestial pole. However, if you take Wil Tirion's *Bright Star Atlas* maps 9 and 10 (the southern sky) and trace a circle that encloses the twelve Bayer constellations, you will find that the circle is centered approximately midway between Alpha (α) and Gamma (γ) Hydri—quite far indeed from the present south celestial pole, which is located in Octans.

The reason for this is that precession of the equinoxes has carried the south celestial pole away from the location it had when the most southerly of the ancient constellations were created. The hole that Bayer filled preserves, fossil-like, the region of sky that was invisible when the earliest constellations were created. The south pole back then must have been between Alpha and Gamma Hydri. We can calculate the approximate date when the south pole lay here, and it turns out to be about 2600 B.C.

This is really a terminal date, since no doubt most of the constellations were created well before 2600 B.C. However, the above method shows that even the final stage of the creation of the constellations we inherited from the Greeks cannot have been more recent than the middle of the 3rd millennium B.C.! This is solid evidence for the extreme antiquity of the major constellations.

Back to Grus: Its northernmost bright star is Gamma, a magnitude 3.0 star with a declination of −38°. It can be seen with the assistance of binoculars, assuming you have an unobstructed southern horizon and a good transparent night, from as far north as Quebec City, Winnipeg, and Vancouver. You also have to have a good idea of when the star will be crossing the meridian. Fortunately, this is not difficult to estimate, for Grus lies due south of Piscis Austrinus and therefore culminates with it.

Grus is appropriately named, for the line of Gamma, Lambda (λ), Mu 1 (μ^1) and Mu 2, and Delta 1 (δ^1) and Delta 2 suggest a crane's long neck, but exactly how much of it you can see depends on your latitude. If you are observing from about 40° north you can even glimpse (with binoculars) Alpha and Beta (β) Gruis, two 2nd-magnitude stars in the body of the Crane. However, only from the extreme southern parts of Florida and Texas will Alpha and Beta culminate high enough above the horizon haze for their fine color-contrast to be observed: Alpha is a B7 V star of magnitude 1.7 that should appear blue-white, and Beta is a mag 2.2 M5 III star that will look ruddy-orange. These stars are less than 5° apart and therefore fit easily in the same field of view in most 7x binoculars.

Aquarius, the Water-pourer, Map 8.

Aquarius is a large constellation: in terms of area, it is the ninth largest constellation overall and second largest of the zodiacal twelve. Though containing only three 3rd-magnitude stars, Alpha (α) at 3.0, Beta (β) at 2.9 and Delta (δ) at 3.3, Aquarius has an intriguing and visually attractive constellation-pattern. The Water-jar is the tight little asterism of Gamma (γ), Zeta (ζ), Eta (η), and Pi (π) Aquarii. The Stream of water pouring from the jar is a 17° oval of 4th-, 5th-, and 6th-magnitude stars, including Lambda (λ), Tau (τ) 1 and Tau 2, Delta (δ), the three c's (86, 88, 89), the three b's (98, 99, 101), A 1 and A 2 (103 and 104), the three i's (106–8), Omega 1 (ω^1) and Omega 2, and the three Psi's (ψ). The figure of the Water-pourer is nowadays usually drawn stretched out over the back of Capricornus; but Renaissance celestial globes and star charts always pictured him standing behind Capricornus, his shoulders marked by stars Alpha and Beta and his left hand extending to Epsilon (ϵ).

Figure 2–1. *Drawings of the impressions of two cylinder seals carved in Syria in the early 2nd millenium B.C. (From W.H. Ward's Seal Cylinders of Western Asia.) The Mesopotamian Water-pourer stands holding a (poorly shown) vase at his chest from which issue two streams of water. His head is flanked by star-figures. On each side of the Water-pourer stand, above, two-winged sphinxes and, below, two female worshippers. The sphinxes in the top design, the vultures at the extreme right in the bottom design, and the ankh ("key of life") between the lower Aquarius and the female to his left, are all Egyptian motifs. Syrian seals of the 2nd millenium B.C. frequently show this mixture of Egyptian and Mesopotamian subjects, though the latter always predominate (in part simply because the cylinder seal itself was a Mesopotamian device). Duplicated star images are extremely rare on Mesopotamian or Syrian cylinder seals and virtually prove the astronomical association of the Water-pourer in these two seal designs.*

Cylinder seals were invented in the late 4th millennium B.C. by the Sumerians and used in Mesopotamia for the next 3500 years. They were small carved cylinders of stone (hematite, agate, crystal, lapis lazuli, or limestone) or shell, usually with a hole for a string drilled through the longitudinal axis. The geometrical, mythological, and religious or political designs engraved and/or drilled on their surfaces helps date them (different designs being popular during different periods), and were meant to function as the "signature" of the owner of the seal, who would roll it over the still-wet clay of a tablet, upon which the unique design of the seal would be conspicuously embossed. (Then the tablet would be oven-dried.) Tens of thousands of cylinder seals have been excavated in Mesopotamian and Syrian archaeological sites, as well as innumerable baked-clay tablets (principally legal and economic documents) with ancient cylinder seal impressions on them.

All the doublets and triplets in the Stream suggest bubbling water as it cascades out of the Water-jar—which is no doubt why the ancients thought of it as "the Stream" in the first place. In the *De Astronomia* (III, 40) of Hyginus (early 1st century A.D.), the stream is described as pouring into the mouth of the Southern Fish.

The Water-pourer is another Graeco-Roman constellation that can be traced back to Mesopotamia, where the figure was shown either standing or on one knee but always holding a jar from which issues *two* streams of water—a detail faithful to the actual star patterns of the Water-jar and the streams as they are seen in the heavens. Representations of the Water-pourer appear in Mesopotamian art as early as the Akkadian period (2400–2250 B.C.), but two of the most striking (left) are on a pair of Old Babylonian period (c. 1700 B.C.) cylinder seals. They show a star above each of the Water-pourer shoulders and put the astronomical significance of the figure in Mesopotamian art beyond all doubt. These seals, by the way, were carved in Syria and are further evidence (see the section on Capricornus) that Syria was the intermediary in space and time between the astronomy of the Sumerians and Babylonians and the astronomy of the early Greeks.

Despite Aquarius' large area, it has only three objects of interest for binocular observers. Two of these, however, are planetary nebulae, which as a class are the most difficult type of deep-sky object for binoculars (because most of them are very small)—excluding such exotica as supernova remnants and quasars.

The Helical Nebula, NGC 7293, Map 8. In apparent size the Helical (or Helix) Nebula is by far the largest of the planetary nebulae. It measures about $16' \times 12'$, which means that its apparent diameter is about half the Moon's. However, if all the Helical Nebula's light was concentrated into a single point, the resulting "star" would have an apparent magnitude of only 6.5. The Full Moon's magnitude is about −12, so in an area about one-fourth of the Moon's the Helical Nebula has only one forty-millionth as much light! This is a good example of "low surface brightness." It's amazing that this kind of object can be seen in *anything*, let alone binoculars. However, binoculars, with their wide fields of view and low magnifying power, are the ideal instruments for these tenuous extended objects. The Helical is actually much easier to see in 10x50 binoculars than in, say, a 6-inch f/8 reflector at 45x. The extra magnification of the telescope merely spreads out the nebula's already diffuse glow. If you have never looked for this kind of object, keep in mind that you are searching for something with an exceedingly ghostlike and unstellar character. The nebula will likely turn out to be both larger and fainter than you expected. No detail will be visible in the Helical, not even the large central hole. In binoculars the nebula appears simply as a uniformly glowing disc, slightly elongated in a north-south direction.

Since it lies in a rather star-poor region, the nebula can be difficult to locate. Start at 3rd-magnitude Delta (δ) Aquarii and go 4° southwest to the two 5th-

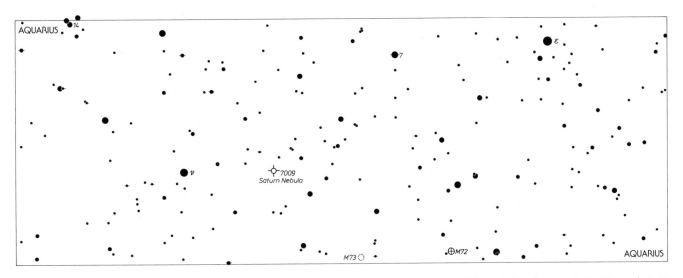

Identification Chart 2–1. NGC 7009 *The faintest stars shown are of magnitude 9.5, and the chart scale is 18mm (=0.71 inch) per degree. North is to the top, east to the left.*

magnitude stars 66 and 68 Aquarii. Another 3° to the southwest is the 5.5-magnitude Upsilon (*υ*) Aqr. The nebula is just over 1° west of Upsilon. The Helical is at the southern vertex of the much-flattened isosceles triangle it forms with Upsilon Aqr and a 7.5-magnitude star 2° west-northwest of Upsilon.

The distances of planetary nebulae are not well-determined. Since it is by far the largest and brightest planetary, the Helical is almost certainly also the nearest, but estimates of its distance range from 90 to 600 light-years.

Planetary nebulae form when very old red giant stars of one or two solar masses become so unstable that they puff off their outer layers one or more times. The stellar core thereby exposed is very hot, but so small that it is not very bright—the star at the center of the Helical Nebula, for example, is only of magnitude 13.3. The ejected outer layers, which expand at the rather modest velocity of 10–20 miles per second, are transient. They shine by fluorescence induced by the ultraviolet radiation from the hot central star, but in only about 40,000 years dissipate into interstellar space. Thus, planetary nebulae are a brief interval in the evolution of an unstable red giant toward a stable, but essentially dead, white dwarf. It is possible that all solar-mass stars form planetary nebulae near the end of their energy-producing lives.

The Saturn Nebula, NGC 7009, Map 8. At apparent magnitude 8.0, the Saturn Nebula is the fourth brightest planetary north of declination −40°. It is, however, only about 30″ in diameter, so in binoculars it appears merely as an 8.0-magnitude "star." Use the accompanying chart to pick it out from the field stars.

The Saturn Nebula is one of the easiest of the planetaries to locate because it is in a fairly star-poor field. (The two faint spikes that project about 15″ from either end of the planetary's oval disc, and from which it is named, require at least an 8-inch telescope to be seen.) The Saturn Nebula's distance, like those of virtually all other planetaries, is uncertain. It may be 3,000 or 4,000 light-years away.

Globular cluster M2, Map 8. In binoculars the globular cluster M2 appears as a bright, compact, fuzzy-edged disc about 10′ in diameter and of magnitude 6.5. Since M2 is approximately 50,000 light-years distant, its true diameter is 150 light-years and its integrated absolute magnitude is about −9.5. This gives it a luminosity of 525,000 Suns. M2 is one of the most luminous of the 200+ globular clusters known to be associated with our Galaxy, but it is only half as bright as the mighty Omega (*ω*) Centauri, the brightest of the lot with an integrated absolute magnitude of −10.2.

M2 is about 5° north of Beta (*β*) Aquarii in a very star-poor region. It is so compact that on a casual sweep of the area you could mistake it for a star, especially in 7x binoculars. However, if you are alert its high surface brightness, fuzzy-edged disc should be easily recognizable.

Globular clusters are not striking objects in binoculars and unfortunately M2 is typical of the best of them. Some hint of resolution of the brightest stars of the nearest globulars is possible in 10x50 glasses, but globular clusters need telescopes of at least 6-inch aperture to begin to look their best. It is, however, one of the pleasures of binocular observing to see anything of such distant and interesting objects.

Pegasus, the Flying Horse, Map 8.

During the early evenings of late October, the Great Square of Pegasus dominates the sky, riding high on the meridian. Pegasus therefore has always seemed the "Halloween constellation" to me. The Great Square is not a true square, but measures about 18° long by 14° high. Its conspicuousness is due in part to the fact that it encloses a very star-poor area, containing no stars brighter than magnitude 4.6 and only three brighter than magnitude 5.0.

The Great Square originally was not part of the winged horse. The Sumerians, who in the 4th millennium B.C. created the first of the great civilizations of Mesopotamia, knew the Great Square as a field of one "iku" area. (One iku was about 0.85 acres.) There is no evidence that the Sumerians or the Babylonians after them ever made the Great Square into a winged horse. In fact, it seems that none of the characters in the Perseus-Andromeda story were in the Mesopotamian heavens. However, the Sumerian conception of the Great Square was adopted in Egypt, for on the planisphere of the Temple of Hathor at Dendera (the only circular representation of the celestial dome that has been found in Egypt) there appears between the two fish of Pisces a square enclosing wavy lines—clearly the celestial field, the wavy lines alluding to irrigation (which was necessary in both Egyptian and Mesopotamian agriculture).

The corner stars of the Great Square are inconveniently distant from each other even in the wide field of 7x glasses, but they are worth the trouble of comparing because they show interesting color-contrasts.

Star	App Mag	Spectrum	Color	Dist (l-y)	Abs Mag
α Peg	2.5	B9.5 III	Blue-white	74	+0.7
β Peg	2.1 to 3.0	M2 II–III	Reddish-orange	210	−1.9 to −1.0
γ Peg	2.8	B2 IV	Flat blue	490	−3.1
α And	2.1	B9 p	Blue-white	90	−0.1

Table 2–2
The Stars of the Great Square of Pegasus

(You can follow the changes in the brightness of Beta Pegasi with the naked eye by comparing it to the other three stars of the Great Square, whose magnitudes conveniently spread throughout Beta's whole range.)

Globular cluster M15, Map 8. Despite being the seventh largest constellation, Pegasus is scant in deep-sky objects. Besides the nice color-contrast of the Great Square's corner stars, Pegasus offers the binocular observer only M15, a globular cluster located about 4° west-northwest of Epsilon (ε) Pegasi. This globular is fairly compact, so even in 10x binoculars its tiny fuzzy-edged disc might not be immediately distinguishable

from its nest of field stars. M15 is about as bright (magnitude 6.5) and large (10′) as M2, but is somewhat closer (34,000 light-years to M2's 50,000); therefore it is intrinsically both smaller and fainter. M15 has a diameter of 100 light-years and an integrated absolute magnitude of −8.6, both fairly average for a globular cluster but considerably less than M2's values.

M15 is notable for being one of the two globulars (the other is M22 in Sagittarius) in our Galaxy's family of more than 100 known to contain a planetary nebula, a telescopic object of magnitude 13.8 and 1″ in diameter on the northeast side of the globular. Because of its association with a globular cluster, the M15 planetary is the only one of the more than 1000 planetaries known in our Galaxy with a well-determined distance and therefore an accurately-known integrated absolute magnitude (−1.3) and true diameter (about one-fifth of a light-year).

2.2   The Milky Way Constellations of Autumn

Cepheus, the King, Maps 1 and 2.

For observers in the middle northern latitudes Cepheus is technically a circumpolar constellation, meaning that it never sets but instead swings down between the pole and the horizon. However, circumpolar constellations are best observed when they lie above the pole, and for Cepheus this occurs during the early evenings of autumn.

Cepheus shares its stretch of the autumn Milky Way with the unassuming little constellation Lacerta, which borders it to the south. Lacerta offers better Milky Way fields for sweeping, but the central line of the Milky Way, the galactic equator, cuts through extreme southeastern Cepheus, passing just southeast of Delta (δ) and Epsilon (ε) Cephei.

Because the Milky Way divides in northern Cygnus, the Cepheus-Lacerta section of the Milky Way has two branches. The main Milky Way stream passes through northern Lacerta and goes into Cassiopeia, but a large tributary branch heads straight north from Cygnus, goes between Alpha (α) Cephei and the triangle made of Delta, Epsilon, and Zeta (ζ) Cep, and comes to a dead-end in the irregular square of Alpha, Beta (β), Iota (ι), and Delta Cep. This tributary branch is the best Milky Way field for binoculars in Cepheus. It is not as bright as the main stream in northern Lacerta, but over its faint background glow is a rich scattering of 4th-, 5th-, 6th-, and 7th-magnitude stars. The gap between this branch and the main Milky Way is caused by a thick cloud of interstellar dust that blocks the light of the stars beyond.

Photograph 2–1. *The IC 1396 complex in southern Cepheus as photographed by E.E. Barnard. The brightest star in the loose cluster in the center of the field is the multiple Σ2816, the O6 component of which provides the ultraviolet radiation that fluoresces the gas in the complex. The dust involved with IC 1396 can be seen to be structured in irregular clouds and patches that unevenly dim the star clouds beyond. The sense of obscuration is particularly strong scanned into IC 1396 from the Milky Way in northern Cygnus. In binoculars and richest-field telescopes the nebulous glow of IC 1396 looks practically circular; however in this photo the dark dust clouds can be seen to be arranged in a noticeably flattened structure the long axis of which is oriented SW-NE (lower right to upper left) paralleling the course of the galactic equator (which lies to the SE outside the field of the photo).*

Identification Chart 2–2. (Overleaf) Milky Way Objects in Northern Cygnus and Southern Cepheus. *The faintest stars shown are of magnitude 7.5, and the chart scale is 9mm (=0.35in) per degree.*

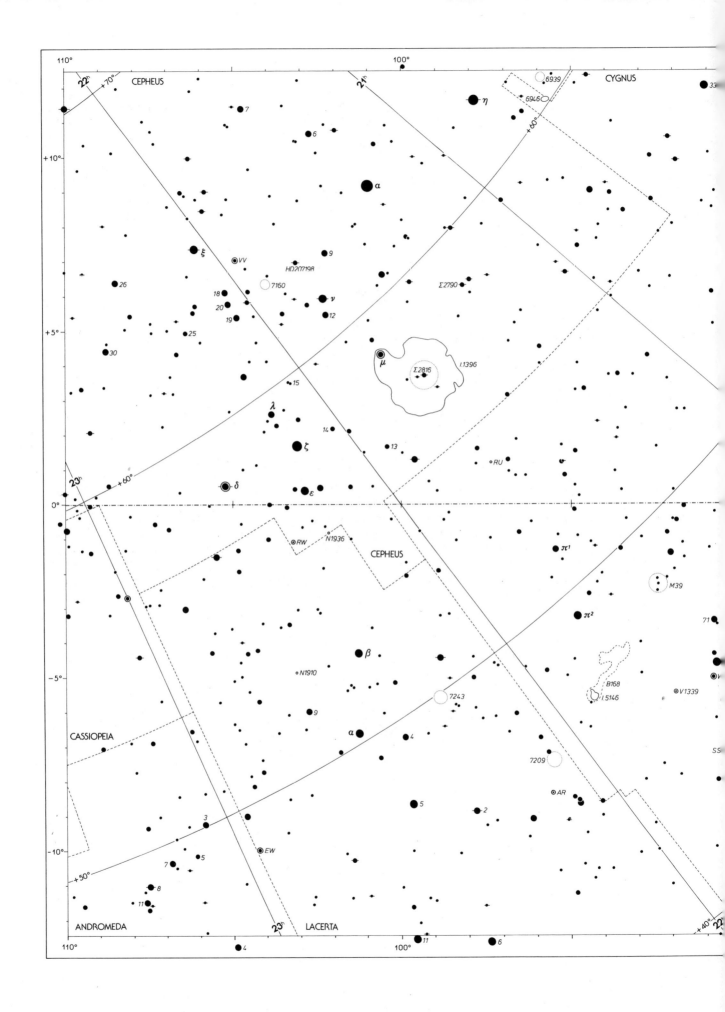

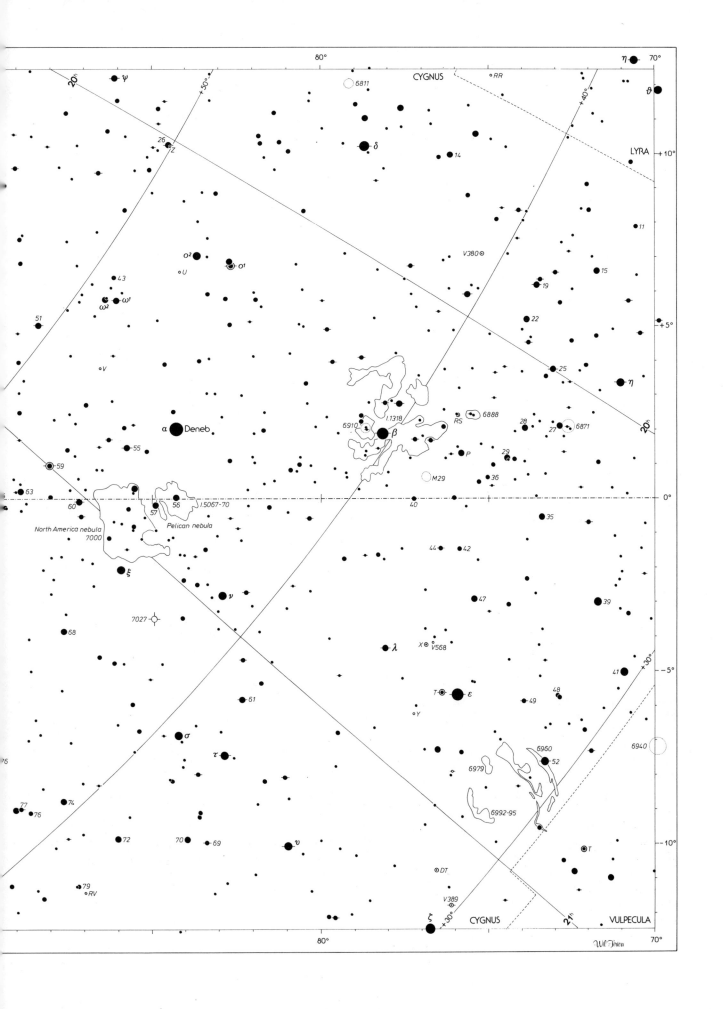

20ʰ

80°

η 70°

ϑ

°RR

6811

ψ

LYRA +10°

26
Z

δ

14

11

V380⊙

15

O²
°U

O¹

43

19

ω² ω¹

22

+5°

51

25

°V

η

α Deneb

I.1318

RS 6888

28

27 6871

55

6910

β

P

29

59

M29

36

63

60

57 56

I.5067-70

40

35

North America nebula
7000

Pelican nebula

44 42

ξ

47

39

ν

7027

λ

X⊙
V568

68

41 -5°

61

T⊙ ε

48

49

σ

°Y

6960

τ

52

6979

6940

76

74

6992-95

77
76

72

70 69

ν

T -10°

79
°RV

DT

V389

ζ

-30°

21ʰ

80°

70°

Wil Tirion

Diffuse nebula IC 1396, Map 2. The *Bright Star Atlas 2000.0* shows that Mu Cephei lies just outside the northern edge of a large diffuse nebulosity, IC 1396, which is about $2\frac{1}{2}°$ in diameter. Though seldom mentioned in observing guides, IC 1396 is not at all difficult in 10x50 binoculars. (It is not so easy for 7x50's, however, since 7x does not darken the sky background as much as 10x and consequently produces less contrast between the sky and the nebula.)

If you have never seen this kind of object in binoculars or a telescope before, it will be difficult for you to imagine what IC 1396 will look like. It is very large, its diameter being equal to half the distance between the Pointers in the Big Dipper, but its light is indescribably tenuous and insubstantial. To get some idea of what to expect, first look at M31, the Andromeda Galaxy. The surface brightness of IC 1396 is comparable to the surface brightness of the outer fringes of M31.

When you have identified IC 1396, gaze at the field for a minute or two, slowly scanning over and around the nebula to allow your eyes to become acclimated to its ethereal light and to the subtle difference between the nebula-glow and the surrounding sky. If the night is transparent and very dark (no moonlight or city-glow), you perhaps will become aware of opaque masses around the fringes of the nebula, making bays and broad channels into it. These are masses of obscuring matter between us and the nebula, for IC 1396 lies deep within great clouds of interstellar gas and dust—in fact, it is merely the illuminated part of these clouds of interstellar matter.

IC 1396 is an emission nebula, glowing by the fluorescence induced in it by the ultraviolet radiation of very hot stars. The chief illuminating star of IC 1396 is Σ 2816, a magnitude 5.6 object a little less than $1\frac{1}{2}°$ south-southwest of Mu (μ) Cephei and right in the center of the nebula. The primary of Σ 2816 (a small telescope at about 50x will show that this star is a beautiful triple) has an O6.5 V spectrum, implying a surface temperature of about 37,000°K. (Our Sun's surface temperature, by contrast, is merely 5800°.) A star like this emits most of its energy at ultraviolet wavelengths.

The distance of Σ 2816 and IC 1396 is around 3,000 light-years, implying that the nebula's true diameter is about 130 light-years. IC 1396 and Mu Cephei are at approximately the same distance and in fact are physically related: they are both members of Cepheus OB2, a complex of young, bright stars and the vast cloud of nebulosity from which these stars have evolved. Indeed, a good many of the 4th-, 5th-, 6th-, and 7th-magnitude stars in this part of Cepheus are members of Cepheus OB2, including Lambda (λ), Nu (ν), 9, 13, 14, 19, and VV Cephei. The stars of Cepheus OB2 have been born only within the past few million years.

Table 2–3 The Brightest Members of Cepheus OB2		
Star	Spectrum	Mag
μ Cephei	M2 Ia	4.07(var)
ν	A2 Ia	4.30
9	B2 Ib	4.74
VV	M2ep Ia+B9	4.90(var)
λ	O6 I	5.05
19	O9.5 Ib	5.11
14	O9 V	5.54
Σ 2816 A+B	O6.5 V	5.62
Σ 2790	M1ep Ib+B	5.66
13	B8 Ib	5.82
HD 207198	O9 Ib/II	5.96

Variable star Delta (δ) Cephei, Maps 1 and 2. This star is the famous prototype of the Cepheid variables, pulsating supergiant stars that change in brightness with clockwork regularity. They also exhibit a relationship between their periods and their luminosities (the longer the period, the greater the intrinsic brightness) that makes them useful as distance indicators, especially for nearby galaxies. Delta Cep varies between magnitudes 3.6 and 4.3 in a period (maximum brightness to minimum and back to maximum) of 5 days, 8 hours, and 48 minutes. The star's light changes can be easily followed with the unaided eye or in binoculars by comparing it to nearby Zeta (ζ) and Epsilon (ϵ) Cep, which are of magnitudes 3.4 and 4.2, respectively. (Zeta, Epsilon, and Delta all fit in the same field of view in most binoculars.)

About 1000 light-years distant, Delta at maximum reaches a very respectable absolute magnitude of -3.9, a luminosity of 3,300 times the Sun's. (It is because of their large luminosities that we can see Cepheid variables in many nearby galaxies.) Delta Cephei's spectrum varies from F5 Ib at maximum light to G3 Ib at minimum; thus, the star is hottest at maximum and coolest at minimum—typical behavior for Cepheids.

Delta Cephei is also a double star, its two components forming a true physical system of mutually orbiting stars. The magnitude 6.3 B7V companion is located $41''$ almost due south of the primary, and can be seen without difficulty in firmly-held 10x binoculars (7x is not quite powerful enough.) It is best to look for the 6.3-magnitude star when the variable primary is near its minimum light, for then there will be less glare and the fainter star will be easier to spot. The true separation of the two stars is at least a fifth of a light-year.

Mu (μ) Cephei, the "Garnet Star," Map 2. Star colors are exceedingly subjective, different observers sometimes reporting wildly dissimilar colors for the same object. But everyone agrees that Mu Cephei is one of the deepest-toned stars in the sky. To me it has never looked the "garnet" or blood-red which some observers report, but simply a chrome orange-red—nevertheless a striking enough color! Even in 35mm glasses the star's hue is immediately evident. It is useful to contrast Mu with nearby silver-white Alpha Cephei, a magnitude 2.5 A2 IV star.

Mu Cephei is an M2 Ia supergiant similar to Betelgeuse in Orion. And like Betelgeuse, Mu Cep is a semi-regular variable, ranging between magnitudes 3.6 and 5.1. Betelgeuse, however, does not have Mu's fine, deep-red color. At least part of the reason for this is that we see Mu Cephei through heavy clouds of interstellar matter which redden its light. These clouds also dim the star by perhaps as much as $2\frac{1}{2}$ magnitudes. Without the dimming, Mu Cep at maximum brilliance would be a 1st-magnitude object. Because the exact amount of obscuration is uncertain, the star's distance and true luminosity are also uncertain. In a 1978 paper, Roberta Humphries of the University of Minnesota estimated Mu to be about 2,700 light-years away and gave its peak absolute magnitude as -8.2—a brilliance of 160,000 Suns. This would make Mu Cephei the most luminous star of its type presently known in our Galaxy.

Open cluster NGC 6939 and Galaxy NGC 6946, Map 2. About 2° southwest of Eta (η) Cephei are two small, circular, very low surface brightness patches of light only about 40′ apart. The northwestern of the two patches is the distant open star cluster NGC 6939. It is about 8′ in diameter, has an integrated apparent magnitude of 10.2, and is not difficult to see even in 35mm or 40mm binoculars—though at 7x it will appear rather small. Southeast of NGC 6939 is NGC 6946, a very, very difficult object in 7x50s and altogether invisible in apertures of less than 50mm. Though it is about the same size as NGC 6939 it is only magnitude 11.1, and therefore its surface brightness is even less. However, 6946 is worth trying for because it is a galaxy, a nearly face-on Sc or SBc spiral estimated to be between 10 and 20 million light-years away. (Its distance is uncertain because we see it through the outer fringes of the Milky Way and it is subject to an unknown amount of dimming by the dust of our own Galaxy.) To assist in finding NGC 6946 are two 6th-magnitude stars located about $1\frac{1}{2}$° south-southwest of Eta Cephei and so oriented that a line through them extended southwest about twice their separation ends at the galaxy.

To see any galaxy with binoculars is a pleasure, but NGC 6946 is not just any galaxy. It is notable because six supernovae have been observed in it during less than 70 years. The first occurred in 1917 and the most recent in 1981. A mere four supernovae have been observed in our own Galaxy in the last thousand years, though others hidden by dust are known to have occurred. Only M83 in Hydra, with five supernovae in 60 years, has nearly equalled the supernova output of NGC 6946. No one knows why these two galaxies should have such an high rate of supernovae, but both have structural peculiarities. M83 has three spiral arms, and NGC 6946 has a tiny, irregular, central hub into which is rooted only one of its two spiral arms. Whatever stresses are distorting these galaxies no doubt are also perturbing the interstellar matter in them, and this might trigger the formation of massive stars that quickly evolve and go supernova.

Lacerta, the Lizard, Maps 2 and 8.

Between Eta (η) Pegasi on the south and Delta (δ) Cephei on the north lies a scattering of 4th-, 5th-, and 6th-magnitude stars that was named Lacerta, the Lizard, by the 17th-century Danzig astronomer Johannes Hevelius. According to R.H. Allen, Hevelius put a lizard into this narrow rectangle of sky unfilled by the ancients simply because that was the only sort of figure that would fit.

Lacerta has two fine Milky Way fields for binoculars. The first is southern Lacerta to the west and southwest of magnitude 3.6 Omicron (o) Andromedae, a region liberally scattered with 5th and 6th-magnitude stars. This field is at its best in 7x binoculars, but is attractive even in 10x glasses. Most of these bright stars, including 8, 10, 12, and 16 Lacertae, are members of the small stellar association Lacerta OB1, centered about 2,000 light-years away.

The Milky Way background behind the Lacerta OB1 stars is faint, but as you sweep north toward Cepheus its glow gets brighter. The brightest Milky Way background in Lacerta is in the region around Alpha (α) and Beta (β) Lacertae. As you gaze at this field you will become aware of scores of momentarily visible star-specks glittering in the Milky Way glow—an effect rather like the sparkling of moonlight on snow. This part of the Milky Way is an extension of the beautiful star clouds in the M39 region of Cygnus.

The glory of the northern Lacerta Milky Way is enhanced by two star clusters, NGC 7209, which is about $2\frac{1}{2}$° due west of 2 Lacertae, and NGC 7243, 2° west of Alpha. Both clusters are about 20′ in diameter. In binoculars 7243 is resolved into a coarse, loose group of 10 or 12 faint stars; 7209, however, appears as a hazy patch with a mottled texture from partial resolution of its clumps of brighter stars.

Cassiopeia, the Queen, Maps 1 and 2.

From northern Lacerta the main stream of the Milky Way runs northeast through western Cassiopeia and into the northern half of the "square" of Cassiopeia (Beta [β], Alpha [α], Gamma [γ], and Iota [ι] Cassiopeiae). Though not as brilliant as the Lacerta

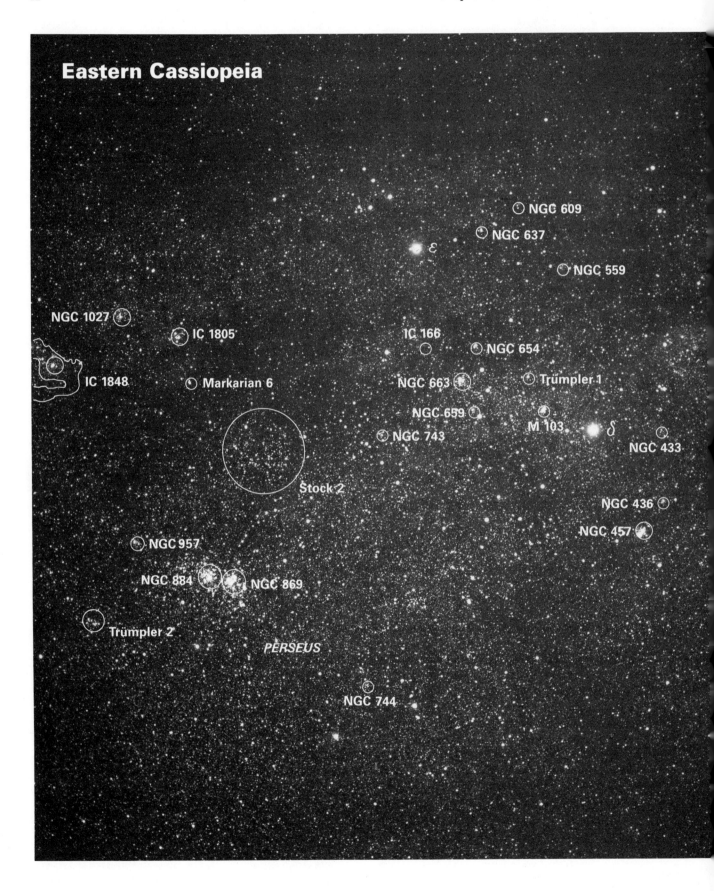

Table 2–4				
Brightest Open Clusters in Cassiopeia				
Open Cluster	Int App Mag	App Diam	Dist (l-y)	Apr Mag of Brightest Star
Stock 2	4.4	45′	1000	8.2
NGC 457	6.4*	20′	8200	8.6*
NGC 129	6.5	12′	5200	8.6
NGC 654	6.5	6′	5200	7.4
IC 1848	6.5	12′	7100	7.1
NGC 7789	6.7	25′	6300	10.7
M52	6.9	16′	4900	8.2
NGC 225	7.0	15′	2000	9.3
NGC 663	7.1	15′	9000	8.4
M103	7.4	6′	8500	10.6
NGC 659	7.9	6′	6800	10.4

*excludes ϕ Cas and HD 7902

Milky Way, the Cassiopeia stream is attractive to scan in binoculars. It even has something of that rich, sparkling half-resolution that makes the northern Lacerta Milky Way so beautiful. While looking at the Milky Way in the square of Cassiopeia, contrast the colors of Alpha and Gamma: Alpha, a K0 II–III star of mag 2.2 is orange-yellow, whereas Gamma, a B0 IV variable presently about magnitude 2.4, is bluish-white. (Gamma has been as bright as magnitude 1.6 and as faint as 3.0.) East of the square of Cassiopeia the Milky Way becomes fairly faint and has no well-defined streams or branches.

Cassiopeia is exceptionally rich in open clusters. Burnham catalogues 25 open clusters in Cassiopeia, a number equalled in his other lists only by Puppis. A good many of these 25 clusters can be detected in binoculars—with my 10x50s I have identified fourteen—but since they are all very distant, most appear either as small patches of indistinct clumpy haze or as tiny knots of three or four faint stars. However, four of Cassiopeia's clusters are good binocular objects:

Open cluster M52, Maps 1 and 2. About halfway between Delta (δ) Cephei and Kappa (κ) Cassiopeiae, on the northern edge of the Milky Way, is a small, fairly bright (magnitude 6.9) patch, M52. This open cluster is so compact that it is not easy to identify in 7x binoculars—look for a "star" with fuzzy edges—but at 10x the hazy disc of the cluster is more obvious. An 8th-magnitude star can be seen just west of the cluster.

M52 is about 4,900 light-years away and therefore has a true diameter of about 20 light-years. It is notable for having the rather high central density of 50 stars per cubic parsec, which is why the cluster is so compact and has such high surface brightness in binoculars. A sphere with the central star density of M52 and a radius of 4.3 light-years (the distance from our Sun to its nearest neighbor, Alpha Centauri) would contain 480 stars!

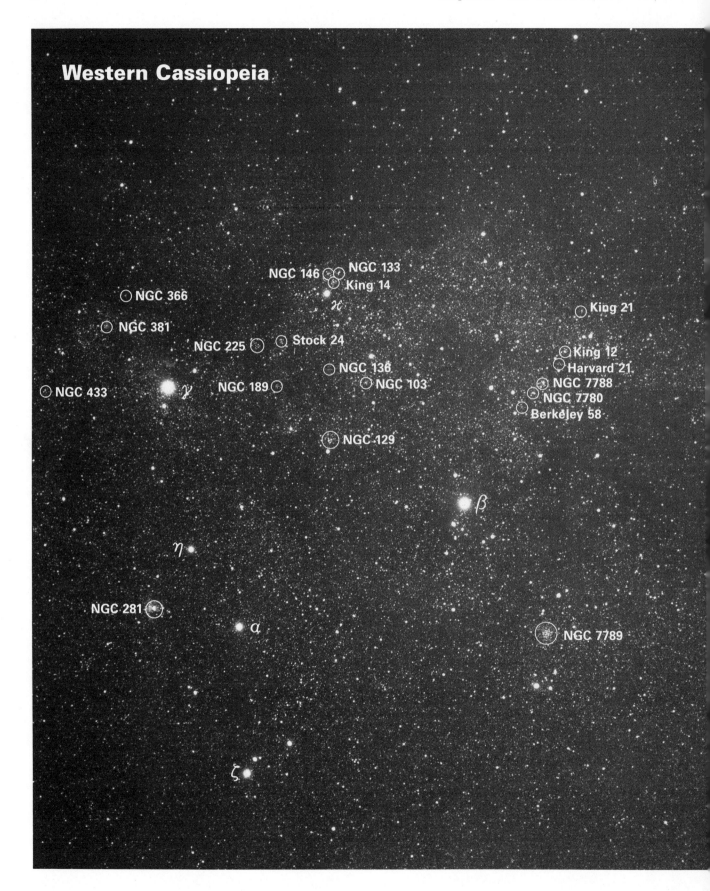

Western Cassiopeia

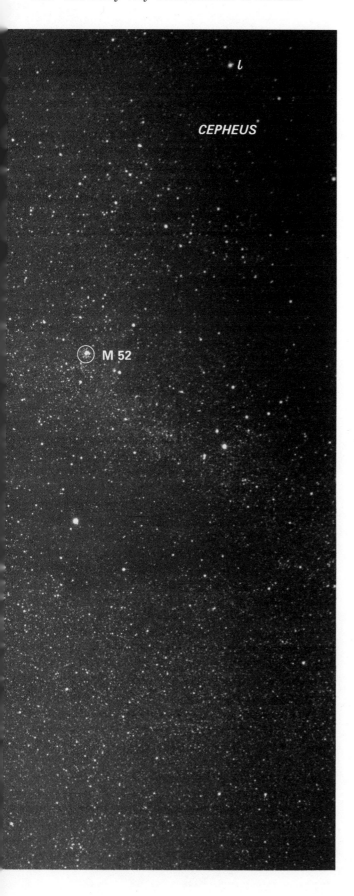

Open cluster NGC 457, Maps 1 and 2. NGC 457 extends northwest from magnitude 5.0 Phi (φ) Cassiopeiae in a roughly rectangular group some 20′ long. Unlike M52 this cluster can be well resolved in binoculars, with perhaps a score of 9th- and 10th-magnitude stars visible in 10x50s. The smaller, light-gathering power of 35mm or 40mm glasses loses some of the fainter cluster members, making NGC 457 appear less rich. This cluster is a delicately beautiful object that looks like a setting of diamond chips with Phi Cas a big multi-carat stone sparkling at one end.

The motion and reddening of Phi are comparable to those of the cluster stars, so it apparently is a true cluster member and not merely a foreground object. Since NGC 457 is about 8,200 light-years distant, Phi has an absolute magnitude of −8.5—a luminosity of 200,000 Suns. Its spectrum is F0 Ia. The magnitude 7.0 star just few minutes southwest of Phi, catalogued as HD 7902, is also a member of NGC 457; it has a B6 Ib spectrum and an absolute magnitude of −6.5. The brightest star in the main body of the cluster is an M2 Ib red supergiant of apparent magnitude 8.6 and absolute magnitude −5.0, almost the twin of Antares in Scorpius.

Open cluster NGC 663, Maps 1 and 2. NGC 663 is a fairly large, 15′ diameter open cluster easily found about $2\,1/2°$ east-northeast of Delta (δ) Cassiopeiae and the same distance southwest of Epsilon (ϵ) Cas. In 50mm binoculars the cluster resolves into at least as many stars as NGC 457, but is not as pleasing to the eye—its stars are scattered about in loose clumps, giving it a ragged, thrown-together look. In 7x35 glasses, NGC 663 is even less impressive: a couple 8th-magnitude stars attended by a scattering of a half dozen fainter cluster members.

However, NGC 663 is about 9000 light-years distant and therefore is intrinsically a very large and bright cluster. Its true diameter is over 30 light-years and its integrated absolute magnitude is about −8.5. NGC 663 is a member of the Cassiopeia OB8 association. This association also includes the open cluster M103, located about $1\,1/2°$ west-southwest of NGC 663 and just 1° northeast of Delta Cas. Even in the higher powers of zoom binoculars, M103 is not an impressive object, appearing merely as a 6′ long line of two or three pairs of stars.

Open cluster NGC 7789, Maps 1 and 2. The best open cluster for binoculars in Cassiopeia is NGC 7789, midway between Rho (ρ) and Sigma (σ) Cas. Since this cluster is 25′ in diameter but has an integrated apparent magnitude of only 6.7, it has fairly low surface brightness. Nevertheless, it is not difficult to see as a hazy patch even in 7x35 binoculars. In 10x50s with averted vision, the cluster's haze has a dim, grainy texture from partial resolution of its brightest stars, which are 11th-magnitude objects. NGC 7789 is perhaps 6,300 light-years away and has a true diameter of over 30 light-years. It is one of the oldest of the open clusters, having formed about 1.6 billion years ago.

Presumably, open clusters have been formed during most of the 10 or 15 billion years our Galaxy has existed, but few of them get even as old as NGC 7789. Indeed, the majority of open clusters are much younger than NGC 7789. For example, the Hyades group is about 700 million years old, the Pleiades around 60 million, and NGC 2244 (in the center of the Rosette Nebula in Monoceros) is only some 500,000 years old. Open clusters are usually not very populous or compact, so the gravitational force holding their stars together is not very strong. By astronomical standards of time, they disintegrate rapidly. The very ancient globular clusters, which seem to have formed at the very beginning of our Galaxy's existence, are extremely populous and concentrated, and are therefore gravitationally stable and resist disruption. The oldest known open cluster is NGC 6791 in Lyra, which is perhaps 9 billion years old and therefore almost as ancient as the youngest globular clusters.

Emission nebula IC 1848, Map 1. The most intriguing, rewarding, and difficult object in Cassiopeia for the binocular observer is the extended emission nebula IC 1848, located in extreme eastern Cassiopeia about 4 1/2° northeast of the Perseus Double Cluster. This is the same type of object as IC 1396 in Cepheus, but with an even lower surface brightness. Nevertheless, under good sky conditions an experienced observer using 8x40 binoculars and averted vision can unambiguously see IC 1848 as a faint amorphous region of haze. 10x50s show the nebulosity's crude rectangular shape—it measures 90′ × 45′, the long axis oriented almost due east-west. This nebula is beautifully star-studded. There is a 6.5 magnitude star towards its west end, a couple of 7th-magnitude stars in its center, and a good many fainter stars scattered randomly over its ghostly glow.

IC 1848 is not especially easy to find, for it lies in an area where even 6th-magnitude stars are scarce. Since it is 4 1/2° due north of Eta (η) Persei and the same distance northeast of the Double Cluster, it forms an isosceles triangle with these two objects. If you know the width of your binocular's field of view, you can find the nebula by placing Eta Per and the Double Cluster near the edge of the field and then estimating the location of a point 4.5° away from both.

IC 1848 is about 7,500 light-years away, roughly the distance of the Double Cluster. The 4.5° apparent separation of the two objects implies a true separation of at least 600 light-years, more if IC 1848 is a bit nearer or a bit farther. IC 1848 is one of the largest emission nebulae known in our Galaxy, measuring about 200 light-

years by 100. It is a region of the Perseus Spiral Arm where star formation is presently occurring.

Perseus, the Rescuer, Maps 1, 3, and 4.

The faintest stretch of Milky Way in either celestial hemisphere runs through Perseus. Toward Perseus and down into northern Taurus lie relatively nearby masses of interstellar gas and dust which obscure the star clouds beyond. Even in binoculars, southern Perseus and northern Taurus look murky and thick. Scan southeast from the star-rich Double Cluster region or sweep due west into Perseus from the bright Milky Way of central Auriga to see what I mean.

Despite the clouds of obscuring matter, Perseus has several good open clusters for binoculars. All but one lie on the periphery of the constellation, where they are outside the obscuring masses. The exception, the Alpha (α) Persei Cluster, lies in *front* of the dust clouds. The most famous object in Perseus, however, is a variable star:

Beta (β) Persei (Algol), Maps 1 and 3. Algol comes from the Arabic *Ras al-Ghul*, "the Demon's Head." The Demon was the name given to the Beta (β)-Pi (π)-Rho (ρ)-and Omega (ω) Persei asterism by Greek astronomers and represents the snake-haired Medusa, whose severed head Perseus was carrying as he came to save Andromeda from Cetus. The association of the Medusa's head with this asterism suggests that the ancient Greeks might have been aware of Beta's variability, but there is no corroborating evidence. As far we know, Algol was first recognized as a variable star about 1667 by the Italian astronomer Geminiano Montanari.

Algol's brightness ranges between magnitudes 2.1 and 3.3 in a period of 2 days, 20 hours, 49 minutes. It is an eclipsing variable, meaning that it consists of two stars in orbit around each other. At intervals, the fainter secondary star covers up about 80% of the bright primary, dimming the total light from the system. Besides the deep primary eclipse, there is a shallower secondary one halfway between the primary eclipses when the secondary star moves behind the primary. The entire primary eclipse lasts only about 10 hours, so in the course of one night it's possible to watch the star fade and then return to its normal 2nd-magnitude brightness. (*Sky & Telescope* magazine publishes the predicted times of Algol's minimum for each month.) Unfortunately there are no good comparison stars near Algol to help you follow its eclipses. For want of anything closer, use Gamma (γ) Andromedae, a magnitude 2.1 star about 10° due west of Algol, and Epsilon (ϵ) Persei, magnitude 2.9 and 8° due east.

Algol lies about 100 light-years away and is actually a triple system. The two stars that eclipse are

Photograph 2–2. *The Perseus Milky Way, from a plate in the Ross-Calvert Atlas of the Northern Milky Way. The Double Cluster is conspicuous in the northwest (upper right) part of the field. The loose scattering of bright stars near the southeast (lower left) corner is the Alpha Persei Moving Cluster. East-northeast of the Double Cluster (and about two-thirds the distance from the center of the photograph to the upper edge) is the east-west rectangle of stars associated with the diffuse nebula IC 1848 in Cassiopeia. (None of the nebula-glow shows up on this print.) Just west-northwest of the IC 1848 cluster, and north-northeast of the Double Cluster, are two tiny knots of stars on an east-west line: these are the open clusters Melotte-15 (right-west) and NGC 1027, neither of which, unfortunately, are good binocular objects. Notice that the left half of the field is much poorer in faint stars than the right half: this is because of relatively nearby clouds of interstellar dust that obscure distant stars in the region of the Milky Way around the Alpha Persei Cluster.*

B8 V and K0 IV objects of absolute magnitudes 0.0 and +3.5, respectively. However, they are orbited by an F2 V star with an absolute magnitude of +3. Algol's primary eclipses occur when the orbit of the K0 star carries it in front of the B8 component. The secondary eclipses, when the B8 star transits the disc of the K0 star, are only a few hundredths of a magnitude deep because the K0 star, though significantly larger than the B8 primary, is much cooler and therefore contributes only a small percent of the total light of the system.

Because of the B8 spectral type of its primary, Algol appears blue-white in color. Rho (ρ) Persei, about 2° south of Algol in the other eye of the Medusa, is an M4 star with a strong red color providing an excellent color-contrast to Algol for the binocular observer. Unfortunately Rho cannot be used as a comparison star for following Algol's eclipses because it, too, is a variable star, a semi-regular red giant with a magnitude range of 3.3 to 4.0.

The Double Cluster, NGC 869 and NGC 884, Map 1. The Double Cluster is visible to the unaided eye as two spots of haze less than 1° apart. In binoculars they resolve into two swarms of stars, both fitting in the same field of view even at high powers. Each cluster is slightly concentrated toward its center (where there is a pale background glow of unresolved stars) but has no clearly defined outer boundaries: they simply merge into the rich star field that surrounds them. The Double Cluster looks good in any binoculars but is so rich in 6th-, 7th-, and 8th-magnitude stars that it appears at its best spread out at 15–20x (if you have zoom binocs). Notice the peculiar chain of ten or twelve stars that extends north of NGC 869, the western cluster, in a $2\frac{1}{2}$° long line that curves slightly west.

In the past there was some question about whether or not the Double Cluster is a true double in the physical sense. For one thing, NGC 884 seems to be younger than NGC 869. For another, some researchers believed that the two clusters are at significantly different distances from us. R.E. Schild in 1966 published distances of 8100 light-years for NGC 884 and 7000 light-years for NGC 869. Now, this difference is hardly more than the error inherent in the methods of distance measurement. However, if it is an accurate difference, it implies the possibility that the Double Cluster is merely a line-of-sight pairing. On the other hand, the two clusters have about the same radial velocity, which does suggest that there is some physical connection. This connection probably is that both clusters formed from the same great cloud of interstellar matter (several million years apart) and share the original space motion of that cloud.

If the two clusters are really as distant from each other as Schild estimated, then each cluster is embedded in its own association, and the rich star field that surrounds the Double Cluster is actually a "composite" of the two associations. On the other hand, if the clusters are at about the same distance, then both are enveloped by the same association.

If we compromise on a distance of 7,500 light-years for the Double Cluster and if the light from the two clusters is slightly dimmed by interstellar matter before it reaches us, then the 35′ apparent diameter of both clusters corresponds to true diameters of 70 light-years. Also, the apparent magnitudes of 4.7 for NGC 884 and 4.1 for NGC 869 imply integrated absolute magnitudes of −8.7 and −9.3—luminosities of 250,000 and 440,000 Suns, respectively. These are two of the largest and most luminous open clusters known in our Galaxy, as large and bright as a typical globular cluster. They are also very massive open clusters: NGC 884 contains about 3300 and NGC 869, perhaps 3900 solar masses. (Globular clusters, however, contain hundreds of thousands of solar masses.)

The Double Cluster and its surrounding association are exceptionally rich in hot, blue supergiant stars like Rigel in Orion, the brightest being the magnitude 5.2 A2 Ia 9 Persei, which has an absolute magnitude of at least $-7\frac{1}{2}$. There are also about 20 red supergiants in the star field surrounding the clusters, many variable and most in the NGC 869 half of the field (one of the hints that the two clusters are of different ages).

Within a few degrees of the Double Cluster lie several other interesting things for binoculars. About $4\frac{1}{2}$° to the northeast in Cassiopeia, is the large emission nebula IC 1848 (discussed under Cassiopeia). About 3° due north of the Double Cluster is a field some 2° in diameter rich in 9th- and 10th-magnitude stars. This is the open cluster Stock 2, only about 1000 light-years away. About 2° west-northwest of Stock 2 is a second star field also approximately 2° in diameter, but less populous and more ragged in appearance. Both star fields fit easily in the same binocular field of view, and their different appearances provide an interesting contrast.

Just 3° east of the Double Cluster is the edge of the dark obscuring matter that covers most of Perseus. This boundary runs for about 4° on a north-northwest to south-southeast line, passing just west of Eta (η) Persei, and is so abrupt that it can be seen with averted vision in 10x50 binoculars. With careful looking on a very dark night you might even be able to see, due west of Eta Persei and just outside the main body of the dark clouds, two long thin streaks of outlying obscuration. They look remarkably like the long thin cirrus outliers that sometimes parallel the cloud shield of an autumn or winter low-pressure system. These outlying streaks of obscuration are very difficult objects to see. To have any chance of spotting them, keep your eyes (which *must* be well dark-adapted) at the binoculars for a minute or two, thus allowing them to adjust to the light conditions in the field and to become sensitive to the subtle difference between the streaks of obscuration and their background.

The Alpha (α) Persei Cluster, Maps 1 and 3. The Alpha Persei Cluster is a coarse, elongated group jeweled at the ends by Alpha (α) and Delta (δ) Persei. It is so large (about 4° long) that it looks much better in the wide fields of binoculars than in the small fields of telescopes—in fact, it is a bit better in 7x than in 10x glasses. This is the eighth nearest open cluster to the solar system, its distance being about 750 light years. In addition to Alpha and Delta, the cluster includes Psi (ψ), 29, 30, 31, and 34 Persei. Epsilon (ε) Persei, though almost 10° from the main body of the cluster and perhaps 100 light-years more distant, shares the cluster's motion through space and therefore is very likely an outlying member. The membership of many of the cluster's over 100 stars has been established by their motion, and consequently this group is sometimes referred to as the Alpha Persei Moving Cluster.

Three stars in the main body of the cluster offer a nice color contrast in binoculars and small telescopes: Alpha, an F5 Ib supergiant of apparent magnitude 1.8, is off-white or cream-white; Delta, a B5 III mag 3.0 star, is silver-blue; and Sigma (σ), though only of magnitude 4.5 (and not a cluster member), is a K0 object that looks distinctly orange. The absolute magnitude of Alpha is about −4.4, corresponding to a luminosity of almost 5000 Suns. The Alpha Persei Cluster is estimated to be only about 14 million years old.

Open cluster M34, Maps 1 and 3. The open cluster M34, located about 5° due east of Gamma (γ) Andromedae and 4° west-northwest of Algol, is a 20′ diameter, magnitude 6.0 object, which under good sky conditions can be seen with the unaided eye as a dim fuzzy spot. In binoculars M34 appears as a knot of seven or eight stars of magnitude 8.5 surrounded by a loose but even distribution of fainter cluster members. Higher powers are useful for spreading out the central core, but the cluster as a whole retains more of a sense of "clusterness" at 8x or 10x. M34 is about 1,500 light-years away, so the 9′ central core has a true size of only four light-years—about the distance between the Sun and Alpha Centauri.

Another Perseus open cluster visible under good sky conditions to the unaided eye is NGC 1528, which is in the northeastern part of the constellation about 1½° northeast of Lambda (λ) Persei. This cluster is as large as M34 and only slightly fainter (magnitude 6.5). In 10x50 binoculars it appears as a fairly thick crowd of star-specks embedded in the faint background haze of unresolved cluster members.

The California Nebula, NGC 1499, Maps 1, 3, and 4. NGC 1499 is an emission nebula shaped as a thick, shallowly curved arc about 2½° long and 1° wide. It is located just northeast of the magnitude 4.0 Xi (ξ) Persei, an extremely hot O7.5 III star that's the source of the ultraviolet radiation which has "turned on" the nebula. The California is not an easy object even for giant binoculars. It is at the limit of visibility in 10x50s, and unless you have just the right sort of viewing conditions you may not see it at all. My experience is that the California and other marginally visible, low surface brightness objects show up best on nights when there is a little atmospheric humidity. This appears to be the result of a heavy atmosphere scattering the light of such objects, smearing some of the brighter sections' light over the fainter sections, thus increasing the contrast of the whole with the night sky. But even on such nights, NGC 1499 is something only for an experienced eye observing from a dark-sky site, and at best it will appear in averted vision as a ghostly glow shaped in a thick, slightly curved, box-like arc. (The "California" shape of the nebula is not obvious in binoculars.)

NGC 1499 and Xi Persei are part of the Perseus OB2 association, which also includes Zeta (ζ), Omicron (o), 40, and 42 Persei. This association is one of the nearest, being about 1,300 light-years away. Its brightest member is Zeta Persei, a B1 Ib supergiant of apparent magnitude 2.9 and absolute magnitude −6. The individual stars of the association are moving outward from the group's center with an average velocity of 12 km/sec, which—given the association's diameter of about 100 light-years—implies that Perseus OB2 must have been formed only about 1.3 million years ago.

2.3 The Late Autumn Constellations

Andromeda, the Chained Princess, Maps 1, 3, and 8.

Andromeda lies just outside the Milky Way. Though this means that there are no star fields, associations, diffuse nebulae, or open clusters here (with the interesting exception of NGC 752, discussed below), it also means that we are away from the obscuring dust of our Galaxy and therefore can see distant galaxies.

The showpiece object in Andromeda is, of course, M31—the Andromeda Galaxy, which is discussed (along with its satellite galaxies, M32 and NGC 205) in Chapter 7 of this book. Andromeda and the other non-Milky Way constellations of late autumn have several excellent binocular galaxies, and this part of the sky is intrinsically richer in galaxies than the early autumn constellations farther west (the reason for which is also discussed in the final chapter of this book).

Andromeda has a couple of things for binoculars besides M31 and its two satellites. One is the open cluster NGC 752, an excellent binocular cluster. Also, the three brightest stars in Andromeda, though they are rather far apart, are an interesting color-contrast set as shown in Table 2–5.

Open cluster NGC 752, Map 3. NGC 752, located about 5° south and just slightly west of Gamma (γ) Andromedae, is a very large (45′) and quite populous open star cluster that under ideal conditions can be seen with the unaided eye as a pale smudge of light. Because of this cluster's large size and the loose distribution of its stars, NGC 752 looks better in the wide fields of binoculars than in most telescopes. In 10x50s at least two dozen cluster members are visible, the impression of richness being enhanced by the fact that the stars are of rather uniform brilliance. Its sixteen brightest stars range only from magnitude 8.9 down to magnitude 10.0. (The 7th-magnitude star on the east edge of the group is not a true cluster member.)

NGC 752 is about 1,300 light-years away and is peculiar on two counts. First, it lies well out of the Milky Way, where most open clusters congregate. Second, its 70 or 80 members all have absolute magnitudes between +1 and +4: it therefore lacks the faint, low-mass dwarf stars that are usually a cluster's most numerous component. Both of these peculiarities result from the fact that NGC 752 is very old for an open cluster. This requires some explanation.

Because open clusters form along the galactic plane (where the gas and dust are), the vast majority of open clusters are found in the Milky Way near the galactic equator. They do not stay there indefinitely, however. As they orbit the Galactic Center, they pass through massive clouds of interstellar matter, or come near other clusters, and are perturbed into orbits that carry them away from the galactic plane. Since the effect of any one encounter is usually not too extreme, it takes a number of such encounters—and therefore a very long time—for a cluster to get into an orbit that takes it as far off the galactic plane as NGC 752 is (600 light-years). Consequently, only very old open clusters are found at any appreciable distance away from the galactic plane. NGC 752, for example, is estimated to be about 1.7 billion years old.

The encounters with other clusters and with interstellar clouds of matter also stir up the stars within a cluster, accelerating some stars to escape velocity. Thus, the red and yellow dwarfs of a cluster generally drift away from it and join the field stars of our Galaxy's disk. In 1.7 billion years NGC 752 has lost all its ordinary stars fainter than absolute magnitude +4. The some-what younger Coma Berenices star cluster (500 million years

Table 2–5 The Brightest Stars in Andromeda					
Star	App Mag	Spectrum	Color	Dist (l-y)	Abs Mag
Alpha (α)	2.1	B9p	Blue-white	100	−0.3
Beta (β)	2.1	M0 III	Ruddy orange	170	−1.6
Gamma (γ)	2.1	K3 II	Pale orange	260	−2.4

old), star-poor from its birth and therefore particularly vulnerable to star-loss, already has no members fainter than absolute magnitude +6. The Coma Cluster will disperse long before it can reach the age of NGC 752.

Just outside the southwest edge of NGC 752 is 56 Andromedae, an easy double star for binoculars since the components are 6th-magnitude and 190″ apart. In 50mm glasses the deep-orange color of both stars is visible. Unfortunately, this is not a true physical double, but merely a line-of-sight pairing of a nearer with a more distant star.

Triangulum, the Triangle, Map 3.

Triangulum is one of the few constellations that originated with the ancient Greeks (who otherwise received their star patterns from the earlier cultures of Mesopotamia). The Greeks' Triangle was the equilateral figure formed by Alpha (α), Beta (β), and 12 Triangulum, which resembles the Greek capital letter delta, Δ. However, in the 17th century astronomer Johannes Hevelius stole 12 Trianguli for his now defunct constellation Triangulum Minor, which he made from 12, 10, and 6 Trianguli. Hevelius' larceny reduced the original Triangle to the scalene figure of Alpha, Beta, and Gamma (γ).

Visually, Triangulum and Triangulum Minor actually do form two discrete compact asterisms rather pleasing to the eye in an area of sky strewn with attractive little asterisms. To the northwest of Triangulum lies the Head of the Medusa, which consists of β, Pi (π), Rho (ρ), and Omega (ω) Persei. Due south of Triangulum the group of Alpha, Beta, and Gamma Arietis form the Head of the Ram. And about 5° east-southeast of Triangulum Minor is another obsolete constellation created during the Renaissance, Musca Borealis, the Northern Fly, marked by 33, 35, 39, and 41 Arietis.

Triangulum has one object for binoculars, the Pinwheel Galaxy, M33. It is discussed in Chapter 7.

Aries, the Ram, Map 3.

Aries is the least interesting of the constellations of the zodiac for binoculars or telescopes. There is, however, a

Figure 2–2. *Drawing (from W.H. Ward's* Seal Cylinders of Western Asia*) of the design on a Neo-Assyrian (c. 800 B.C.) cylinder seal now in the collection of the Pierpont Morgan Library. The celestial Laborer goads the celestial Bull, which pulls the celestial Plow. Above are a crescent, a star, and the 7-dot design that in Assyrian art represented the Pleiades star cluster. Before the Bull is a grain-plant, probably an allusion to the celestial Ear of Grain (the Greek Stachys and Roman Spica: our Alpha Virginis) because Alpha Vir lies very nearly on the ecliptic, which the Mesopotamians thought of as a heavenly Plow-furrow.*

pleasing color contrast between the stars of the Head of the Ram, all of which fit comfortably in the same binocular field: Alpha (α) (Hamal) is a yellow-orange star of magnitude 2.0; Beta (β) is blue-white and magnitude 2.7; and Gamma (γ), a fine double in small telescopes at about 50x, is sky-blue at magnitude 3.9. (Because of the star's faintness, Gamma's color is not easy to see in 35mm binoculars.) Their distances are 75, 52, and 160 light-years, respectively.

Aries is a latecomer to the zodiac, probably being formed in the 2nd millennium B.C. when precession pushed the vernal equinox into this area from Taurus. There is certainly no resemblance in the stars to a ram, but the idea of a Ram as the leader of the constellations of the zodiac would have been natural to the agrarian Greeks who probably named these stars. The Sumerians, more than two thousand years earlier, had called the Alpha, Beta, Gamma Arietis group *Lu Hunga*, "the Hired Laborer." They envisioned him as guiding a celestial Plow (our Triangulum plus Gamma Andromedae) around the sky to form the furrow of the ecliptic. In such a scenario Taurus no doubt was thought of as the Ox pulling the Plow.

Shown above is the impression of a Neo-Assyrian cylinder seal of the 9th century B.C., which almost certainly illustrates the celestial Laborer with his Plow and Ox. The astronomical character of the scene is indicated by the large 8-pointed star and the 7-dot pattern

over the Ox's back. In Assyrian art the latter stood for the Pleiades—which, of course, is in the constellation of the Bull (and located over the Bull's back as well). This type of plowing scene, though usually not in so flagrantly an astronomical context, appears on Mesopotamian cylinder seals back even into the mid-3rd millennium B.C.

Pisces, the Fishes, Maps 3 and 8.

Pisces and Cancer are the only two constellations of the zodiac that do not have a single star of the 3rd magnitude or brighter. Cancer does not even have a very distinct constellation-pattern. Pisces' pattern, on the other hand, though composed of 4th-, 5th-, and even a few 6th-magnitude stars, is logical and pleasing to the eye. The Western Fish is represented by the graceful asterism called the Circlet of Pisces, which lies due south of the Great Square of Pegasus. It consists of Gamma (γ), Theta (ϑ), Iota (ι), Kappa (κ), Lambda (λ), 7, and 19Piscium. The cord that runs from the Western Fish to the knot marked by Alpha (incorrectly named *Alrisha*, "the Cord") gently arcs through two hours of right ascension and includes Omega (ω), 51, Delta (δ), Epsilon (ϵ), Zeta (ζ), Mu (μ), Nu (ν), and Xi (ξ) Psc. The cord from Alrisha to the Northern Fish follows Omicron (o), Eta (η), and Rho (ρ) Psc. The Northern Fish, however, isn't much, being a ragged line made up of the three Psi (ψ) stars, Chi (χ), Phi (φ), Upsilon (v), Tau (τ), 82, and Sigma (σ) Piscium. It is probable that the original Northern Fish, which the Greeks had inherited from the Mesopotamians, included Beta, Mu, Nu, Pi, Delta, Epsilon, Zeta, and Eta Andromedae (Andromeda the constellation being a Greek invention) and therefore was of a more fish-like lozenge shape.

Pisces, like the other major non-Milky Way constellations of autumn, is large in area but sparse in interesting objects for binoculars or telescopes. However, Pisces' four objects for the binocular observer are quite a varied group.

19 (=TX) Piscium, Maps 3 and 8. The easternmost star in the Circlet of Pisces, 19Piscium, could justifiably be called "The Jewel of the Circlet," for it has a remarkable poppy-red color. This star is one of the brightest and nearest of the "carbon stars"—red giant variables whose spectra reveal atmospheres rich in carbon. The deep red color of carbon stars is the result of their extremely low surface temperatures (2600° Kelvin or less), which allow tri-carbon molecules, exceptionally efficient absorbers of blue and violet light, to form in their atmospheres. Carbon stars are thought to be highly evolved objects that have exhausted all the hydrogen in their cores, and which are deriving energy from the nucleosynthesis of helium into carbon. Their atmospheres have become carbon-rich either because they have lost their outer hydrogen envelope, leaving the carbon-rich interior exposed or, more probably, because they have undergone such strong convective mixing that the carbon from deep within has been dredged up to the surface.

Carbon stars usually vary in brightness by about one magnitude in semi-regular periods of a few hundred days, but their behavior can be highly individualistic. For example, 19 Piscium has a very small range (magnitude 5.5 to 6.0) and is completely irregular. Since the absolute magnitude of carbon stars when they are at peak brightness is thought to be near −2.0, 19 Piscium is perhaps around 1,000 light-years away. The only carbon stars that are probably nearer are U Hydrae and Y Canum Venaticorum.

Galaxy M74, Map 3. M74 is a face-on Sc spiral galaxy located about $1\,1/2°$ east-northeast of Eta (η) Piscium. This is a very difficult object to see even in 10x50 binoculars for although its diameter is $9'$, its integrated apparent magnitude is only $9\,1/2$ and its surface brightness is extremely low. However, a trained eye observing with 10x50 binoculars under good sky conditions should be able to see M74 as an amorphous smudge of light. The galaxy is not visible in 7x50s, but it turns out to be slightly easier at the higher powers of 40mm zooms than it is in 10x50s: the higher power darkens the sky background and provides greater contrast for the tenuous glow of the galaxy-light.

The redshift of M74 is 426 miles per second, which implies that it is around 40 million light-years away. If this distance is right, M74 has a true diameter of about 100,000 light-years and an integrated absolute magnitude of −19.4, a luminosity of 4.8 billion Suns. M74, therefore, is about as large as our Milky Way Galaxy but only half as luminous—a consequence of its looser structure.

Zeta and Psi 1 Piscium, Map 1. Two double stars in Pisces split well at 15x and are therefore good objects for zoom binoculars. Zeta (ζ) has components of magnitudes 4.2 and 5.3 separated by $24''$; their position angle is 63°. The other double, Psi 1 (ψ^1), consists of two stars of nearly equal brightness (mags 5.3 and 5.6) separated by $30''$ in P.A. 160°. Psi 1 can be split in tripod-mounted 10x binoculars. It is an exceptionally beautiful double in 6-inch telescopes, for the larger aperture brings out the fine silver-blue color of the two components, both of which have B9 spectra.

Cetus, the Whale, Map 3.

Cetus is a vast constellation. In terms of the area within its boundaries as set by modern astronomers, Cetus is the fourth largest in the sky. Like the other constel-

lations of the celestial Sea, Cetus' pattern is distinct and visually interesting, the head being marked by Alpha (α), Lambda (λ), Mu (μ), Xi 2 (ξ^2), Nu (ν), and Gamma (γ) and the body by Beta (β), Eta (η), Theta (ϑ), Zeta (ζ), and Tau (τ). Cetus' body is quite conspicuous, for all its stars are of magnitude 3.9 or greater and it is set in one of the most star-poor regions of the sky.

Cetus has more bright stars than any of the other constellations of the celestial Sea (except for Eridanus). The best-colored of Cetus' bright stars is Alpha (Menkar), a magnitude 2.5 M2 III object with a fine reddish-orange tone. Contrast it with the nearby bluish Gamma (magnitude 3.6, A2 V) and Delta (magnitude 4.0, B2).

Cetus' brightest star, however, is Beta, a K0 III star of magnitude 2.0 colored a rather nondescript yellow. Beta Ceti has a strange kinship with Fomalhaut. As was mentioned in the section on Piscis Austrinus, because Fomalhaut rose just before the Sun early in the spring, the Bedouin of the Arabian Desert knew it as *Al-Difda al-Awwal*, "the First Frog." Beta Ceti, which rises just after Fomalhaut and therefore can be glimpsed in the morning twilight a few days after it, was called *Al-Difda al-Thani*, "the Second Frog." On some star charts Beta Ceti is still called Diphda or Dipda, though more common is the name given to it by the medieval Arabian astronomers after they adopted the Greek constellations: Deneb Kaitos, "the Tail of Cetus."

If you have the *Sky Atlas 2000.0* or the older *Atlas of the Heavens*, you will notice that Cetus is definitely richer in galaxies than any of the autumn constellations thus far discussed. There is a scattering of galaxies around north-central Cetus from the Zeta-Theta-Eta region up toward Mu and Zeta Piscium. And in eastern Cetus are two compact galaxy groups, one just east of Delta Ceti and the other about 8° due south. The reason for the galaxy-richness of Cetus is explained in the last chapter of this book.

Like Pisces, the few binocular objects Cetus has are a varied and interesting group:

Omicron (*o*) Ceti, or Mira, Map 3. Mira, "the Wonderful," is the most famous and first-discovered (in 1596) of the pulsating red giant long-period variables (called LPVs for short). It can be followed throughout its entire light cycle with only 35mm binoculars. At typical maximum Mira reaches about magnitude 3.5, though some of its maxima have been magnitude 2.5 or even brighter and others only magnitude 4.5. Mira's typical minimum lies between 9 and 9.5. The star's period is about 330 days, with the rise from minimum to maximum taking only a third of the whole cycle.

In terms of its period (300+ days) and range (5 to 6 magnitudes), Mira is a typical LPV. And like other

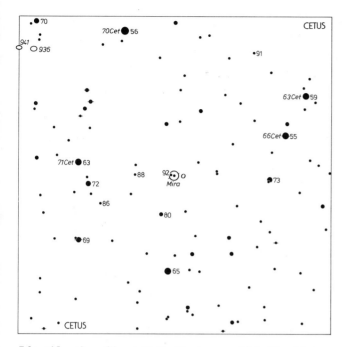

Identification Chart 2–3. Omicron Ceti. *The faintest stars shown are of magnitude 9.5, and the chart scale is 18mm (=0.71 inch) per degree. North is to the top, east to the left. Comparison star brightnesses are to the nearest 10th magnitude, with periods omitted.*

LPVs, its spectrum changes with its brightness. At maximum Mira is an M6 star with a temperature of 2500° Kelvin. But at minimum it cools to 1900°K and reddens to M9. The ruddy color of Mira will help you locate the star when it is not near maximum. For color contrast, compare Mira to the bluish Gamma and Delta Ceti several degrees to the northeast.

Mira is the nearest LPV, being about 220 light-years distant. This means that at maximum its absolute magnitude is about −1 and at minimum, around +5. At minimum, therefore, Mira is intrinsically slightly fainter than the Sun. An interesting fact is that though the visual brightness of a typical LPV decreases by 6 or 7 magnitudes (two or three hundred times) from maximum to minimum, the total energy output of these stars as measured over all wavelengths decreases by only about one magnitude (2.5 times). The reason is in the selective sensitivity of the human eye. We see only a narrow range of the entire electromagnetic spectrum, the range we call visible light. We cannot see gamma-rays, X-rays, ultraviolet or infrared light, microwaves, or radio waves. However, as an LPV cools and fades most of its radiation shifts from visible wavelengths into the invisible infrared. Thus, the large light range of LPVs is mostly an optical illusion, the by-product of our eyes' insensitivity to infrared light.

Planetary nebula NGC 246, Map 3. NGC 246 is one of the three planetary nebulae that show a discernable disc in 10x50 binoculars, the other two being the

Helical Nebula (NGC 7293) in Aquarius and the Dumbbell Nebula (M27) in Vulpecula. Of the three, NGC 246 is the smallest ($4' \times 3.5'$), faintest (magnitude 8.5), and the most difficult to see.

The problem is its size. At 10x, objects of $4'$ diameter are just about the smallest that can be seen as non-stellar objects rather than as star-like. In 10x50s NGC 246 appears as a tiny smudge of faint haze. This is an object where higher powers are very useful and NGC 246 is much easier at 16x in even 40mm glasses than in 10x50s. Fortunately, this planetary is at a well-marked location. It lies at the south vertex of an almost perfect equilateral triangle with Phi 1 (φ^1) and Phi 2 Ceti. Its distance is about 1,200 light-years, and consequently the nebula's true diameter must be around 1.25 light-years.

Galaxy M77, Map 3. The face-on Sb spiral M77 is the brightest galaxy in a galaxy cluster spread over an area 2° in diameter just east of Delta (δ) Ceti. With an apparent magnitude of 10.0, M77 is visible even in 35mm binoculars but is so compact that at the low magnifications of binoculars it merely looks like a star. To pick it out from the foreground stars of our own Galaxy in the field of view, use the accompanying finder chart. M77 is well worth the trouble of locating because it is the prototype of the unusual Seyfert galaxies, named after the American astronomer Carl Seyfert. Seyferts are galaxies with small but extremely bright central hubs, the spectra of which indicate that huge clouds of gas, each containing as much as 10 million solar masses, are blasting out of their nuclei at velocities of several hundred miles per second. The strangest thing, however, is that Seyfert spectra resemble those of quasars. Some astrophysicists therefore suggest that the bright nuclei of Seyferts are simply low-luminosity quasars. M77 is also possibly the most distant object visible in binoculars, for its redshift implies that it is 65 to 70 million light-years away. If this distance is correct, then M77 has an integrated absolute magnitude of −21.5 and is four times as luminous as our Galaxy.

Sculptor, the Sculptor (Maps 3 and 8), and Fornax, the Furnace (Map 3).

South of Cetus is one of the most star-poor regions of the celestial sphere. Here the 18th-century French astronomer Nicholas de Lacaille inserted two of the fourteen southern "filler" constellations he invented and squeezed in between the older Bayer groups. Lacaille did not have much to work with—Sculptor and Fornax together have only two stars brighter than magnitude 4.5—but he had a vivid imagination, as the original names of Sculptor and Fornax show: l'Atelier du Sculptor, "the Sculptor's Workshop," and Fornax Chemica, "the Chemical Furnace."

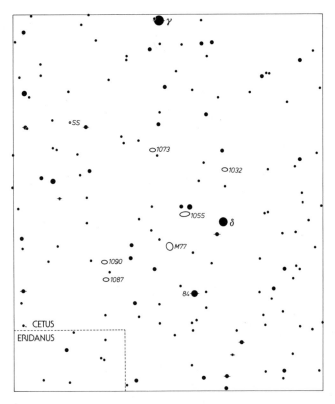

Identification Chart 2–4. M77. *The faintest stars shown are of magnitude 9.5, and the chart scale is 18mm (=0.71 inch) per degree. North is to the top, east to the left.*

Sculptor and Fornax (as they are known today) lie so far south that for most of the United States they are lost in the horizon haze, and you need binoculars merely to identify their Greek-lettered stars. What they lack in stars they make up for in galaxies, however. Each contains a Local Group galaxy and a galaxy cluster. The Sculptor Galaxy Group and the more distant Fornax Cluster are both described in some detail in Chapter 7 of this book. (Two of the Sculptor Group galaxies are among the best galaxies for binoculars.) The Local Group galaxies in the two constellations are called the Sculptor System and the Fornax System. Both are dwarf spheroidal galaxies and lie very near our Milky Way Galaxy. The Fornax system is about 650,000 light-

years away and the Sculptor System is only 270,000 light-years distant.

Dwarf spheroidal galaxies are small, elliptically-shaped, low-star-density objects. Burnham compared the Sculptor System to what you would get if you expanded the great Omega (ω) Centauri globular cluster to fifty times its actual size and then emptied it of 99% of its stars. The difference between dwarf spheroidals and dwarf elliptical galaxies like the M32 and NGC 205 satellites of the Andromeda Galaxy is merely one of degree. Both have decreasing star density outward from the center, but dwarf spheroidals are simply much poorer in stars throughout. Both types also lack gas and dust and contain only ancient, modest-luminosity red and yellow stars.

Because of their scattered character, dwarf spheroidal galaxies of the Sculptor and Fornax type systems have extremely low surface brightness. They are best shown on long-exposure photographs, where their brightest stars show up as a loose collection of pin-points. Dwarf spheroidals are the most numerous type of galaxy in the Local Group and are probably the most numerous type of galaxy throughout the universe.

The Sculptor System has a diameter of 75′ ($2\frac{1}{2}$ times the Moon's apparent diameter) and lies 4° due south of Alpha (α) Sculptoris. The Fornax System, 65′ across, is $2\frac{1}{2}$° southwest of Beta (β) Fornacis, immediately east of Lambda (λ) Fornacis. These galaxies have true diameters of about 6,000 and 12,000 light-years, and integrated absolute magnitudes of −11.7 and −13.6, respectively.

Observers in the southern half of the continental United States and in Hawaii can look for the planetary nebula NGC 1360 in Fornax. NGC 1360 measures about $7\frac{1}{2}$′ × 5′ and has an integrated apparent magnitude of 9.4. In most binoculars it should be seen as a small, moderately bright patch. Because NGC 1360 lies in the star-poor spaces of northeastern Fornax, it is not easy to find. Start at Tau 5 (τ^5) Eridani and go almost 4° due south to a wide, east-west pair of 6.5 magnitude stars. The nebula lies just south of the midpoint of the line between these two stars.

Chapter 3

The Constellations of Winter

Winter is the harshest observing season. Not only is it cold, but skies in many parts of the country tend to be cloudy. The reason is that during the winter the jet-stream winds of the troposphere, pushed far north during summer, swing south over southern Canada and the United States, carrying polar low pressure disturbances which spin out cloud shields that overcast whole states for days at a time. And these winter storm systems frequently come in families of four or five, meaning (for the midwestern and northeastern U.S. and adjoining areas of Canada) that you are fortunate if you get more than two clear nights in a row. Sometimes low pressure areas follow upon each other so closely that you can watch the clouds of one retreat eastward in the morning, only to spot the high-altitude cirrus outliers of the next system appearing in the southwest at sunset the same day! It makes planning a winter observing night—particularly for the city-bound observer who wants to drive out to a dark-sky site—a frustrating proposition.

However, one has to put up with the cold and take one's chances with the clouds, for the winter constellations are the most brilliant of the year. Of the sixteen 1st-magnitude stars visible from mid-northern latitudes, eight are in the winter constellations: Capella in Auriga, Aldebaran in Taurus, Pollux in Gemini, Betelgeuse and Rigel in Orion, Procyon in Canis Minor, and Sirius and Adhara in Canis Major. The winter constellations are also rich in 2nd- and 3rd-magnitude stars, with Orion alone having five 2nd-magnitude stars and Canis Major, another three.

The richness of bright stars in the winter constellations is a result of the Milky Way, because 1st-magnitude stars—like open clusters and diffuse nebulae—concentrate along the Milky Way. The winter Milky Way, which has a brighter glow than most of the autumn's, slashes in a diagonal band from Auriga down between Orion and Gemini, through dim Monoceros, over the back of Canis Major, and finally into Puppis, where (for observers in mid-northern latitudes) it becomes lost in the horizon haze. Wil Tirion's Map 4 shows this quite nicely. On the best nights 10x50 binoculars will enable you to follow the twinkling half-

resolution of faint Milky Way stars to within about 8° of the horizon. (The actual Milky Way glow is not visible so near the horizon, just the glittering of momentarily resolved stars.)

The winter constellations offer some of the most spectacular sights available to binoculars. The Pleiades is the best open cluster for binoculars in the entire sky. The Belt and the Sword of Orion is probably the best star field for binoculars. And the Great Orion Nebula (M42) is the only diffuse nebula visible in middle north latitudes that reveals structural detail in binoculars. In addition, the 1st- and 2nd-magnitude stars of winter have a variety of colors and many lie sufficiently near each other to be conveniently contrasted in binoculars. Since there are so many young, hot stars in the winter sky (particularly in Orion and Canis Major), the theme color of the season is an icy or silver blue—a blue very like that which the snow on east facing slopes reflects at sunset from the blue sky above. Winter is the season for lovers of blue.

3.1 The Off-Milky Way Constellations of Winter

The division of the constellations in this chapter requires a word of explanation. Our solar system's place in the Galaxy lies on the inner edge of a spiral arm, and when we look toward the winter Milky Way we are looking back into that spiral arm. Because of peculiarities in the structure of our spiral arm, open clusters, stellar associations, and bright and dark nebulae which are in our foreground actually lie slightly off the centerline of the Galaxy. This allows us to look over and beyond these objects into the core of our spiral arm. Thus, the sweep of the Milky Way (the spiral arm) is paralleled by a line of nearby clusters, associations, and nebulae that begins in Perseus and extends down through Taurus, Orion, and Canis Major. (You'll find a more detailed explanation in the chapter on galactic structure near the end of the book.)

Eridanus, the River, Maps 3, 4, and 9.

Eridanus, the most easterly of the constellations of the ancient celestial Sea, has the winding form appropriate to a river. Like the aquatic constellations of autumn, however, its pattern is formed mainly by 4th- and 5th-magnitude stars. If Eridanus were straight it would be some 130° long, but in that great length there are only three 3rd-magnitude stars and 1st-magnitude Achernar. Achernar shines at magnitude 0.5, has a B3V spectrum, and lies about 60 light-years away. It is situated at the extreme southern end of the River, and its name is derived—or distorted—from the Arabic phrase meaning "the End of the River." Since it is at declination −57°, Achernar can be glimpsed with the unaided eye only from southern Texas and Florida.

With a clear night and an unobstructed southern horizon, binocular observers from as far north as Jacksonville, Mobile, Baton Rouge, and Austin should be able to steal a look at Achernar as it transits the meridian about $1\frac{1}{2}°$ above the horizon around 8 p.m. local mean time during mid-December. The spectral type of Achernar implies that it has a bluish color, but only in the Florida Keys will the star climb far enough above the horizon to overcome atmospheric reddening and let you see it in its proper color.

Eridanus has the sixth largest area of the 88 constellations; but besides Achernar, the only thing in it for the binocular observer is Gamma (γ) Eridani (Map 3), a magnitude 3.0 star with an M1 III spectrum and a beautiful chrome-orange color. It is also worth using binoculars to trace Eridanus as far down to the southern horizon as you can from your latitude. Detailed star atlases show that the region around the nine Tau (τ) Eridani stars is well populated with faint galaxies. If you have the *Sky Atlas 2000.0* or *Atlas of the Heavens*, you'll see these galaxies form part of a long band that is fairly rich in galaxies. This band begins in eastern Cetus, includes the galaxies around the Tau Eridani stars, extends south down through eastern Fornax (in extreme southeastern Fornax is the rich and compact Fornax Cluster), and continues into the far southern sky, where it includes loose galaxy groups in northeastern Horologium and in Dorado.

Lepus, the Hare, Map 4.

Although Lepus, with its four 3rd-magnitude stars, is not an inconspicuous constellation, it offers the binocular observer only one object, the double star Gamma (γ). This double is an easy split even in 7x glasses, for its components are 95″ apart and the secondary is only 2.6 magnitudes fainter than the primary. This brighter star has an F6 V spectrum and a magnitude of 3.6, and the companion is a dwarf K2 object of magnitude 6.2.

Despite the large separation between its two components, Gamma must be a true physical binary since both stars have the same proper motion and are therefore moving through space together. The system is about 29 light-years away, which means that the primary is three times, and the secondary one-fourth, as luminous as the Sun. The true separation between the two stars is at least 90 billion miles (1000 times the distance between the Earth and the Sun), so the secondary star orbits its primary in a period that must be thousands of years long.

Columba, the Dove, Map 4.

Columba was first created during the Renaissance to accompany the neighboring ancient constellation of Argo, which some Renaissance astronomers identified with Noah's Ark. The ancient Greeks apparently did not have a name for the stars of our Columba. (In Mesopotamia the stars of Columba seem to have been included in the River, then envisioned as flowing southeast toward Canopus rather than toward the southwest.)

Nevertheless, Alpha (α) and Beta (β) Columbae are a fairly conspicuous pair of 3rd-magnitude stars only about $2\frac{1}{2}°$ apart. They show a nice color contrast in binoculars: Alpha, a B7 IV star of magnitude 2.6, is blue-white; and Beta, a K1 III object at magnitude 3.1, is yellow-orange. Alpha is about 180 light-years away and Beta, some 120 l-y distant. Their absolute magnitudes are −1.1 and +0.1, respectively.

Observers in the southern U.S. with 10x50 or zoom binoculars can look for NGC 1851, a globular cluster in the rather star-poor region of southwestern Columba. This globular is quite bright (magnitude 7), but fairly compact (5′ in diameter), so it will appear as a tiny, bright fuzzy-edged disc, easily mistaken for a star. It might not look very impressive in binoculars (few globulars do), but NGC 1851 is one of the handful of globulars known to emit X-rays. That these globulars give off so much high-energy radiation implies that something violent is happening in their centers, but exactly what is a matter for speculation.

Canis Minor, the Lesser Dog, Map 4.

Though Canis Minor lies on the eastern edge of a stretch of the Milky Way rich in open clusters, it is remarkably poor in deep-sky objects. In fact, that comprehensive source, *Burnham's Celestial Handbook*, lists not a single nebula or cluster in Canis Minor. Even little Pyxis,

Kathy located 11-23-98
Quite interesting

which lies on the eastern edge of the Milky Way near Puppis, is credited by Burnham with four open clusters. Without Procyon, Canis Minor would be boring indeed.

Procyon (Greek for "before the Dog," alluding to the fact that it rises just before Sirius) has an apparent magnitude of 0.4, a distance of 11.3 light-years, and an F5 IV–V spectrum. It is the eighth brightest star in the sky and the sixth nearest star visible to the unaided eye. Procyon's absolute magnitude is +2.7, which means that it is seven times as bright as the Sun. By a strange coincidence, Procyon, like Sirius, has a white dwarf companion—a magnitude 10.8 object so close to its bright primary that it is very difficult to see even in large telescopes.

The color of F-type stars like Procyon is rather nondescript. Procyon itself appears cream or off-white. However, Beta (β) Canis Minoris, about $4\frac{1}{2}°$ northwest of Procyon, is a magnitude 2.8 star whose silver-blue color offers a nice contrast to Procyon. And Gamma (γ) Canis Minoris, less than 1° north of Beta, is a 4th-magnitude star with a rich reddish-orange tone that contrasts with the colors of both Alpha and Beta. All three stars fit very well in a 7x field.

Camelopardalis, the Giraffe, Map 1.

The large area north of Perseus and Auriga is very poor in stars and was never organized into constellations by the ancients. In the early 17th century the Dutch astronomer Petrus Kaerius remedied the neglect of the ancients by filling this area with Camelopardalis, the Giraffe. Needless to say, the few 4th- and 5th-magnitude stars scattered through this region hardly suggest the shape of a giraffe, even to the most overheated imagination. Kaerius put a giraffe here mostly because that was what would fit.

Though the galactic equator cuts through its extreme south-western corner, Camelopardalis has no bright stars (Beta [β] at magnitude 4.2 is its brightest) and only a couple small open clusters. For binocular observers the Camelopardalis Milky Way offers just one thing of interest, a strange 3° long star-chain located about 6° west-northwest of Beta Camelopardali. This star-chain runs roughly northwest to southeast and is in two slightly curved segments. The northwest segment contains ten 8th- and 9th-magnitude stars and ends in one of 5th-magnitude, and the southeast segment consists of seven more 8th- and 9th-magnitude stars and ends in a 6th-magnitude object located less than $\frac{1}{2}°$ due south of the very tight open cluster NGC 1502. (With higher magnification, NGC 1502 appears merely as a 6th-magnitude star attended by four or five fainter cluster members.)

This star-chain is peculiar; to my knowledge there is nothing like it anywhere else in the sky. However, it is merely the result of a chance alignment of stars. Since this chain lies in an area without bright stars, it is not easy to find even in wide-field binoculars. Its southeast end (where it terminates near NGC 1502) lies near the west vertex of an equilateral triangle with Alpha (α) and Beta Camelopardali.

Most of Camelopardalis lies well outside the Milky Way, so it is not surprising that there are a number of galaxies scattered around the constellation. Two of them, NGC 2403 and IC 342, are not difficult to see in 10x50 binoculars and are described and discussed in the final chapter of this book.

Lynx, the Lynx, Maps 1 and 5.

Between Ursa Major on the northeast and Cancer, Gemini, and Auriga to the south and southwest is another star-poor region of the northern winter sky ignored by the ancients. It was filled by the 17th-century astronomer Johannes Hoewelke (Hevelius). He chose to insert a Lynx here because, he said, one has to be lynx-eyed to see any of its stars! There is, however, a 3rd-magnitude star in this constellation, Alpha (α) Lyncis, a magnitude 3.2 M0 giant with an attractive reddish-orange color. 38 Lyncis, about 2° almost due north of Alpha, is a magnitude 3.8 A2 star whose bluish-white tone, just visible in 50mm binoculars, provides a color contrast to Alpha.

There is a fairly bright but little-observed galaxy in Lynx suitable for giant binoculars or the higher powers of 50mm zooms. NGC 2683 is of magnitude 9.6, but measures only $8' \times 1'$ and therefore is so needle-thin that in 10x50s it is only intermittently visible even with averted vision. This galaxy lies 5° west and slightly south from Alpha Lyncis in a very star-poor area and is not easy to locate. The best way of getting to it is from Cancer, for it is exactly 1° due north of Sigma 1 (σ^1) Cancri. There is a 6th-magnitude star less than $\frac{1}{4}°$ to the galaxy's southwest. As its needle-thin appearance suggests, NGC 2683 is a spiral galaxy (of type Sb) that we happen to be viewing nearly edge-on. Its distance is estimated to be about 20 million light-years.

3.2 The Foreground of Our Spiral Arm

Taurus, the Bull, Maps 3 and 4.

Taurus is one of the few constellations that actually looks like what it is named for. One can easily visualize a bull's head in the "V" of the Hyades, with Beta (β) and Zeta (ζ) Tauri marking the tips of the horns. Taurus is also one of the most ancient of the constellations.

One of the recurrent motifs of Neolithic art of the ancient Near East is the *bucranium*, or bull's head. This design feature is often accompanied with dots or circles of dots that might be interpreted as star images. A well-preserved vase dating to the first half of the 5th millennium B.C., found at a site in extreme northern Mesopotamia called Tell Arpachiyah, is painted with rows of stylized bucrania among dots and dot-rosettes. A cylinder seal carved some 3500 years later shows a dot-rosette *within* the horns of a realistic bull's head, with an 8-pointed star below the bull's muzzle. The fundamental design similarity between the late 2nd millennium cylinder seal and the early 5th millennium vase attests to the extreme conservatism of ancient Near Eastern art. (A second cylinder seal of the late 2nd millennium shows a group of 7 dots—the Pleiades—within the curved horns of the bull's head.)

Another theory involving Taurus was offered some years ago by the German scholar Willy Hartner.[1] Hartner suggested that the earliest zodiac of Mesopotamia, the forerunner of the Greek 12-constellation zodiac, consisted of just four groups: the Bull, the Lion, the Scorpion, and an Ibex (a type of wild goat formerly common in the Middle East) involving stars of our Aquarius, Capricornus, southwest Pegasus, and Equuleus. Hartner believed that this four-constellation zodiac was organized around 4000 B.C. when these groups could be glimpsed rising in the morning twilight at the times of the equinoxes and solstices. Now, there is no evidence for a celestial Ibex in any of the surviving Mesopotamian constellation lists (the earliest of which dates to about 2000 B.C.), but we can assume that the fourth group should be a Fish (our Piscis Austrinus) which is indeed catalogued in Mesopotamian texts. Otherwise, Hartner's theory is quite plausible. It was customary even in Greek and Roman agricultural handbooks to give dates by the constellations that were rising in the morning twilight (heliacal rising). Moreover, three of the four groups of Hartner's hypothetical early zodiac had symbolic connections with the times of the year which their heliacal rising around 4000 B.C. marked: the Bull as a symbol of fertility was an appropriate constellation to mark the vernal equinox; the Lion rose in the morning twilight just as the summer heat grew fearsome, driving the wild lions down to the cool Tigris and Euphrates river-banks where they were a menace to the villages' herds and flocks; and the Fish heliacally rose during the rainy season of winter.

Despite the fact that only the horn-tips of Taurus lie within the Milky Way, the constellation contains two of the nearest and visually most beautiful of the open clusters, the Hyades and Pleiades.

---

[1] *Journal of Near Eastern Studies* XXIV (1965), pp. 1-16.

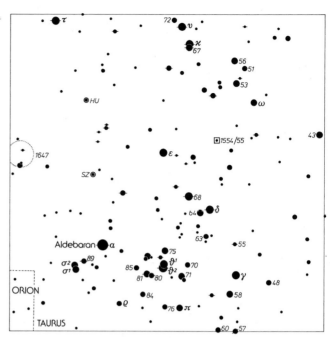

Identification Chart 3–1 for the Hyades Star Cluster. *The faintest stars plotted are of magnitude 8.5, and the chart scale is 9mm (=0.35 inch) per degree. North is to the top, east to the left.*

Table 3–1 The Brighter Stars in the Hyades					
Star	Spectra	Mag	Star	Spectra	Mag
45 Tau	F4 V	5.72	69 $=\nu$	A8 Vn	4.28
48	F5 V	6.32	71	F0 V	4.49
51	F0 V	5.65	74 $=\epsilon$	G9.5 III	3.53
54 $=\gamma$	K0 III	3.65	77 $=\vartheta^1$	K0 III	3.84
55	dF7	6.87	78 $=\vartheta^2$	A7 III	3.40
57	F0 IV	5.59	79	A7 V	5.03
58	F0 V	5.26	80	F0 V	5.58
60	A3m	5.72	81	Am	5.48
61 $=\delta$	K0 III	3.76	85	F4 V	6.02
63	A1m	5.64	86 $=\rho$	A8 V	4.65
64	A7 V	4.80	90	A6 V	4.27
65 $=\kappa$	A7 IV-V	4.22	92 $=\sigma^2$	A5 Vn	4.69
67	A7 V	5.28	101	F5	6.70
68	A2 IV	4.29	102 $=\iota$	A7 V	4.64

The Hyades cluster, Maps 3 and 4. The face of the Bull is formed by the Hyades star cluster, with one of the Bull's eyes marked by flaming Aldebaran (Alpha [α] Tau). Aldebaran is a golden-orange K5 III star that like many other orange and red giants is variable, but its range (magnitudes 0.8 to 0.9) is too small to be observed visually. Aldebaran is only 68 light-years away (less than half the Hyades' distance) and is therefore not a true Hyades member but merely a foreground star. Its absolute magnitude is −0.7, which corresponds to a luminosity of 160 Suns.

The Hyades cluster is centered at a distance of about 150 light-years, making it the second nearest star cluster. (The nearest cluster to us, centered only about

Photograph 3–1. *The Pleiades Star Cluster, as photographed by E.E. Barnard. The exposure of this plate was very long to bring out the details and full extent of the faint reflection nebulae in which most of the brightest stars of the cluster are embedded. The Merope nebula, NGC 1435, around the southernmost of the bright stars of the Pleiades, is the largest and brightest of the reflection nebulae and is just visible in 10 × 50 and giant binoculars.*

78 light-years away, is the Ursa Major Moving Group, which includes the five middle stars of the Big Dipper.) The accompanying chart gives the apparent magnitudes and spectral types of the brightest Hyades.

Actually, the V-pattern is only the core of the cluster, for Hyades members are scattered over an area 24° in diameter and include Kappa (κ) (magnitude 4.1, A7 V), Upsilon (v) (4.2, F0 III), and Iota (ι) (4.5, A7 V). In fact, there are even more remote cluster members—such as Omega (ω) Andromedae, an F4 IV magnitude 4.8 star some 50° from the Hyades proper. The true space diameter of the V-pattern is about 9 light-years; the overall extent of the cluster (excluding the remotest outliers) is around 60 light-years. Several hundred stars have been identified as cluster members, the vast majority being low-mass, low-luminosity yellow and red dwarfs. Over a dozen white dwarfs also have been found in the Hyades.

Because of its large apparent size ($3\frac{1}{2}$° across), the Hyades is much better in binoculars than in telescopes, which "zoom in" too close. In fact, the cluster is better in 7x than in 10x binoculars. The Theta (ϑ) double has a nice color contrast. Theta 1 is orange and Theta 2 is snow-white. (Being 337″ apart, they can be easily split with the unaided eye but the extra light-gathering power of binoculars is necessary to show their attractive colors.) In the same field with the Hyades, only about 4° northeast of Aldebaran, is the large (35′ in diameter) open cluster NGC 1647 which—at a distance of about 1,600 light-years—is over ten times farther than the Hyades. In binoculars NGC 1647 appears as a group of 15 or 20 stars scattered in coarse clumps, behind which is the pale background glow of unresolved cluster members.

The Pleiades cluster, M45, Maps 3 and 4. There are many beautiful objects for binoculars in the heavens, but the most beautiful of all is the Pleiades. This open cluster is stunning in any size binoculars, but perhaps at its best at 15x in 50mm zooms. The thing that makes the Pleiades so glorious is not simply the crowded richness of its 3rd- and 4th-magnitude stars but the silver-blue color of those stars, the glare of which frosts the whole field in ice-blue. This star cluster is only about 60 million years old and its brightest stars are still hot blue giants and subgiants. The apparent magnitudes and identifications of the brightest Pleiades are given in the accompanying chart.

With a distance of 410 light-years, the Pleiades is the fourth nearest open cluster to the solar system. It is about 7 light-years across. However, like the V of the Hyades, our Pleiades is only the core of the star cluster, which in a volume about 30 light-years across has perhaps as many as 500 member stars. Photographs show that the brightest Pleiads are embedded in streaks and

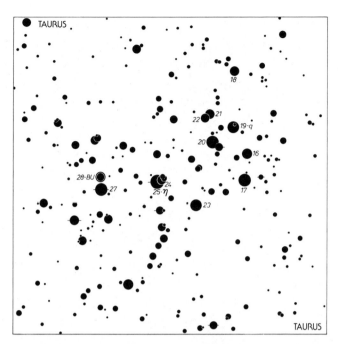

Identification Chart 3–2 for the Pleiades. *The faintest stars plotted are of magnitude 8.5, and the chart scale is 36mm (=1.4 inch) per degree. North is to the top, east to the left.*

Table 3–2 The Brighter Stars in the Pleiades					
Star	Spectra	Mag	Star	Spectra	Mag
16 Tau	B7 IV	5.46	22	A0 Vn	6.43
17	B6 IIIe	3.70	23	B6 IVe	4.18
18	B8 V	5.64	25	B7 IIIe	2.87
19	B6 IV	4.30	27	B8 III	3.63
20	B8 III	3.87	28	B8 Vpe	5.09
21	B8 V	5.76			

Table 3–3 Names of the Pleiades		
16 = Celaeno	20 = Maia	25 = Alcyone
17 = Electra	21+22 = Asterope	27 = Atlas
19 = Taygeta	23 = Merope	28 = Pleione

patches of wispy nebulosity, whose delicacy resembles filamentary cirrus clouds. The nebulosity surrounding and extending south from Merope, catalogued as NGC 1435, can be detected in giant binoculars and small richest-field telescopes.

I once saw the Merope Nebula in 10x50 binoculars. The night did not seem exceptionally transparent, but the nebula was not at all difficult to see with averted vision, appearing as a thick arc of pale light that gently curved from Merope, first south-southeast toward a 10th-magnitude star 11′ distant and then due south. Its total length was about 20′—virtually equal to its photographic length. The nebula was so easy to see that it called attention to itself. I think the reason I had never noticed it previously is that it is not easy to distinguish between the glare of Merope and the subtle glow of the nebula.

The Pleiades nebulosity is composed of fine dust grains that reflect the light of the bright stars near them. It is probably material left over from the original interstellar cloud of gas and dust from which the cluster stars formed—another indication that the Pleiades group is young, for in older clusters (like the 700 million year old Hyades) all residual matter has long since been scattered back into interstellar space. Reflection nebulae are generally of lower surface brightness than emission nebulae like the Orion Nebula, which shine by their own light. The only reflection nebula that is fairly easy to see in normal binoculars is M78 in Orion.

The Pleiades contain some double stars that can be split with binoculars. Alcyone and Maia both have 8th-magnitude companions: Maia's is 3′ southwest and Alcyone's 3′ west-northwest. (Alcyone's companion is actually a triple consisting of three 9th-magnitude stars in an approximately equilateral triangle with sides 1′ long. It can be split into two at 15x, but Alcyone's glare makes it challenging.) Near the middle of the "dipper bowl" formed by Alcyone, Maia, Electra, and Merope is an 8th-magnitude star that in zoom binoculars or tripod-mounted 10x50s can be resolved into two almost equally bright components 39″ apart. Also notice the delicate chain of six stars that begins due south of Alcyone and due east of Merope and extends about 25′, first south and then southeast away from the cluster.

The Crab Nebula, M1, Map 4. M1 is the only supernova remnant you can call relatively "easy" for binoculars. Because it is 9th-magnitude, the Crab is bright enough to be visible in 35mm glasses. But since it measures only 6′ × 4′, even at 10x it appears just as a tiny but fairly bright hazy patch. At magnifications of less than 10x, it looks merely stellar and requires a finder chart to be identified. M1 is located just over 1° northwest of Zeta (ζ) Tauri, a magnitude 3.1 star with a fine blue color. The Crab Nebula is thought to lie about 6,300 light-years away, thus its true diameter is around 6 light-years.

The Crab is the debris of the supernova that old Chinese documents (which called it a "guest star") state first appeared near Zeta Tauri on July 4, 1054 A.D. and remained visible to the unaided eye for almost two years. Comparison of recent with early photographs of the Crab shows that the outer filaments are moving away from the center of the nebula at a rate of 0.2″ per year. This means that to reach its present 6′ × 4′ size, the Crab had to start expanding about 750 years ago. However, astronomers know the expansion rate is accelerating, which means M1 was expanding more slowly

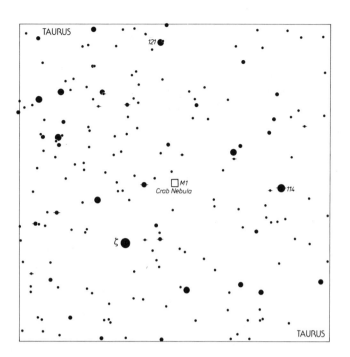

Identification Chart 3–3. M1. *Stars are plotted to magnitude 9.5, and the chart scale is 18mm (=0.71 inch) per degree. North is to the top, east to the left.*

at first and is therefore somewhat older than 750 years. While the changing rate of expansion prevents precise calculation, 900 years is indeed a reasonable estimate of its age.

Because the Chinese records say the guest star was visible in daylight, the Crab supernova must have had an apparent magnitude of at least $-4\frac{1}{2}$ or -5. Given a distance of 6,300 light-years and assuming interstellar absorption dimmed the supernova by one magnitude, its absolute magnitude was probably at least -17 or so, a luminosity of 600 million Suns. Since our Galaxy, a giant spiral, has an integrated absolute magnitude of about -20, it would have taken only 10 or 12 Crab supernovas to have equalled the light output of our entire Galaxy!

The Crab Nebula is one of the most peculiar objects known. (As one astronomer puts it, only slightly facetiously, modern astronomy consists of two parts—studies of the Crab and studies of everything else.) It does not radiate by the same mechanism as other emission nebulae but by the synchrotron process, in which radiation is generated by high-velocity free electrons as they accelerate or decelerate in a strong magnetic field.

Both the high-velocity electrons and the strong magnetic field are supplied by the 16th-magnitude central star of the nebula, the collapsed core of the star that went supernova. This collapsed core is as bizarre an object as the nebula, for it is probably only about 10 miles in diameter but contains twice as much matter as the Sun. At such great density (billions of tons per cubic centimeter) atoms are broken down and their electrons and protons are crushed together into neutrons—hence objects like the Crab Nebula's central star are called neutron stars.

The original star of which the Crab neutron star is the remnant had both a magnetic field and rotated on an axis—as all stars do. When the star went supernova and its core collapsed almost instantaneously, the magnetic field and rotation of the star were carried down into the resulting neutron star. As a consequence, the magnetic field was intensified incredibly (because it now occupied millions of times less volume) and the rotational velocity of the neutron star also increased (in exactly the same way the velocity of a spinning skater increases as the arms are drawn closer to the body).

The magnetic field on the neutron star is so intense (about a trillion times the Sun's) that all the radiation of the star is forced along the lines of magnetic force toward the magnetic poles and only there emitted into space. Since we happen to lie in a direction swept by a magnetic pole as the neutron star rotates, the star behaves like a lighthouse beacon and we see it flash on and off 30 times each second. The pulsed radiation of the Crab neutron star is why it and similar objects are called pulsars.

The pulse rate implies that the surface of the Crab pulsar is spinning at a rate of several hundred miles per second. Any object comparable in size to the Crab pulsar and rotating as fast, but composed of ordinary matter, would simply fly apart. Yet the great density of the pure nuclear matter of a neutron star gives it an incredible surface gravity and the star holds together.

It is the combination of the Crab pulsar's rotational velocity and its strong magnetic field that generates the high-velocity free electrons that shoot out through the Crab Nebula and emit the synchrotron radiation by which the nebula shines. The generation of these electrons is gradually draining the huge kinetic energy of the Crab pulsar's rotation, and the rotational period of the star has slightly but measurably increased since its discovery in 1968. Presumably, all the known pulsars are supernova remnants. However, only three are associated with visible nebulae, and the nebulae of the other two—IC 443 in Gemini and the Gum Nebula in Vela—are not synchrotron-radiating like the Crab but are like much older supernova remnants such as the Veil Nebula in Cygnus. Apparently, the Crab Nebula stage in the life of an expanding supernova cloud is very brief. Furthermore, it seems that not all supernovae result in Crab Nebula type clouds. Neither Tycho's Supernova of 1572 nor Kepler's Supernova of 1604 have left anything more than a few little shreds of faint nebulosity.

Orion, the Hunter, Map 4.

Without doubt, the most striking constellation of all is Orion. In most ancient cultures its star pattern was identified with a warrior, a hunter, or some similar type of national hero. In Egypt it was Osiris, the king and judge of the dead—an appropriate identification in a culture where many of life's rituals concerned the dead. In Sumeria, Orion was called *Sibzianna*, the "True Shepherd of the Sky"—appropriate, again, for a culture immediately descended from neolithic peasants and shepherds. The warlike Greeks knew Orion as "the Warrior," and our word Orion probably derives from the Greek 'ωαριων (in Latin letters *oarion*), or "warrior."

In every detail the star pattern of Orion is remarkably realistic. The shoulders of the Hunter are marked by Betelgeuse (α) and Bellatrix (γ), the knees by Rigel (β) and Saiph (κ), and the head by the small triangle of Lambda (λ) and the two Phi's (φ). The waist is made from Mintaka (δ), Alnilam (ϵ), and Alnitak (ζ); from this starry Belt hangs the Sword, represented by Iota (ι) and the Great Nebula, M42. Upraised in the Hunter's hand is the club Mu (μ), Nu (ν), Xi (ξ), f^1, f^2, Chi 1 (χ^1), and Chi 2. Before him, to take the shock of charging Taurus, he holds a shield or lion-skin, a graceful 15° long arc of stars that begins at 11 and 15 Orionis and sweeps down through the two Omicron's (o), g, and the six Pi's (π). No human artist could have contrived a more beautiful or logical form. Nor could a human artist have executed such a dramatic composition as Orion and Taurus together. Though Taurus rises before Orion does, the Hunter seems to drive the Bull backwards across the sky and eventually forces him below the western horizon.

The Orion Association, Map 4. Orion is not just a fortuitous alignment of stars. The stars of the Belt and Sword, as well as Rigel, Kappa, Sigma, Eta, and Lambda Orionis, are members of the Orion OB 1 association and therefore are physically related. They have all formed from parts of a huge interstellar cloud of gas and dust that still covers most of the constellation. Sections of the Orion Cloud are illuminated by the hot, bright, young stars of the association: very faint nebulous halos surround Epsilon, Iota, and Lambda Orionis. For about 1° south of Zeta (ζ) extends IC 434, a narrow reef of faint light midway upon which is silhouetted the famous Horsehead Nebula. None of these diffuse nebulae are visible in binoculars—their surface brightness are simply too low—but there are a half-dozen other nebulae in Orion that are bright enough to be seen in binoculars.

The Orion complex is over 1,000 light-years deep, for its nearest bright star, Rigel, is about 900 light-years away and its farthest, Kappa, is around 2,100. It

		Table 3–4				
		The Orion Association				
Star	Spectra	App Mag	Dist (l-y)	Abs Mag	Sep ('')	PA (°)
β A B	B8 Ia B5 V	0.08(var) 7.6	900	−7.1 −1.5	9	202
κ	B0 Ia	2.04	2100	−7		
ε	B0 Ia	1.70	1600	−6.8		
ζ A B	O9/B0 Ib B0 V	2.05 4.2	1600	−6.5 −4.3	2.6	164
δ A B	O9 II+O9 II B2 V	2.20(var) 6.87	1500	−6.1 −1.6	53	0
ι A B	O9 III B7 III	2.76 7.3	2000	−6 −1.5	11	141
λ A B	O8 III B0 V	3.56 5.54	1800	−5.2 −3.2	4.4	44
σ A C D E	O9 V+B3 A2 B2 O9f	3.8 10 7.5 6.5	1400	−4.2 +2 −0.5 −1.5	11 13 42	236 84 61
η A B	B1 IV B	3.59 4.98	940	−3.7 −2.3	1.5	77

For ϑ_1 and ϑ_2 see the section on the Sword of Orion, below.

is over 700 light-years wide (the distance from Kappa on the south to Lambda in the north). Betelgeuse and Bellatrix in Orion's shoulders are not members of the association. They are foreground stars which lie about 520 and 470 light-years distant, respectively.

Stellar associations are necessarily very young by astronomical standards. Unlike open clusters they are not gravitationally bound and tend, therefore, to disperse fairly rapidly. This dispersal occurs because first, the individual motions of the stars carry them away from each other soon after they have formed, and second, the stars in remote parts of the association have differing rates of rotation around the galactic center, which tends to shear the whole aggregation apart. As a result, extremely young associations like the Orion and Zeta Persei groups are roughly spherical in form, whereas older associations are elongated. (A fine example of an older association is the Scorpio-Centaurus Group, whose stars are spread out in a long, flat structure from Crux northeast to Scorpius. See the Centaurus-Lupus section in the spring constellations for more about the Scorpio-Centaurus Association.)

The extreme youth of the Orion Association is also indicated by its lack of red supergiant stars. Many associations contain stars already evolved from the blue supergiant to the red supergiant stage. For massive stars this takes only a couple million years. However, the Orion Association's brightest and most massive stars, Rigel, Kappa, and Epsilon, are still blue supergiants.

Because of its youth, Orion is a feast for lovers of blue. In binoculars these stars look not merely blue-white but silver-blue. Rigel is magnificent! So are the three stars of the Belt, which in 50mm glasses fill the field with an icy glare. Binoculars are actually better than telescopes for viewing the colors of 1st-, 2nd-, and 3rd-magnitude stars. In large scopes the images of such stars are so brilliant that they overexpose on the eye's retina and appear predominantly white. In a 6-inch telescope, for instance, Rigel is merely blue-tinged white and Betelgeuse an orange-tinged white.

As can be seen in Table 3–4, the Orion association is rich in double and multiple stars. At about 100x in small telescopes, the Iota, Lambda, and Sigma systems are beautiful. In 10x binoculars you can just glimpse the 6.7-magnitude companion of Delta and the 6.5-magnitude star of the Sigma multiple. (Zoom binoculars are very helpful on both.)

But the best doubles in Orion for binoculars lie in the Sword:

The Sword of Orion, Map 4. The Great Nebula, M42, is so bright it can be seen without optical aid as a hazy halo around 5th-magnitude Theta (ϑ) Orionis, the star in the middle of Orion's Sword. M42 is one of five diffuse nebulae reasonably easy to see with the unaided eye. (The others are the Lagoon Nebula in Sagittarius, the North America Nebula in Cygnus, the Keyhole Nebula in Carina, and the Tarantula Nebula in the Large Magellanic Cloud.)

In 10x50 binoculars you can see virtually the entire photographic extent of M42, except for the great loop that arcs south nearly as far as Iota Orionis. Photos show that the east side of the nebula is dominated by a long, thick filament that extends from the area of Theta south toward Iota. This filament can be easily seen even in 40mm binoculars; and in 10x50s on superb nights it can be traced from Theta (appearing double in binoculars) halfway to Iota. The filament ends at the western star of the 8th-magnitude pair that lie just east of the midpoint of the line joining the Theta with Iota.

This filament makes M42 the one diffuse nebula (except for the Eta Carinae Nebula [NGC 3372 on Map 9], which is in the far southern Milky Way) that reveals in average-size binoculars not merely shape, but internal structure. Another bright part of M42 lies west-southwest from Theta, and on good dark nights the nebula-glow in this direction can be seen for a distance nearly equal to that from Theta to Iota. Since the region between the great filament and this glow is comparatively faint, M42 has something of a "double-wing" appearance in binoculars and telescopes. The photographic diameter of M42 is about 65′, which at the nebula's estimated distance (1,600 light-years) corresponds to a true diameter of about 30 light-years.

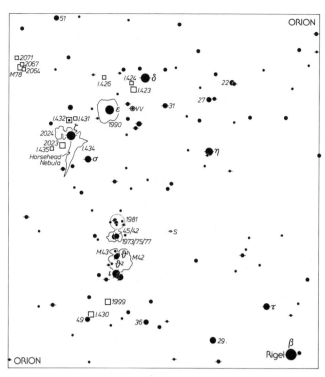

Identification Chart 3–4. Belt and Sword of Orion. *Stars to magnitude 7.5 are plotted, and the chart scale is 9mm (=0.35 inch) per degree. North is to the top, east is to the left.*

Table 3–5			
The Components of Theta Orionis			
Star	Spectra	App Mag	Abs Mag
Theta 1			
C	O7Vp	5.14	−4.5
D	B0	6.3	−3.3
A	A7	6.7–7.7	−2.9
B	O	8.0–8.7	−1.6
Theta 2			
A	O9 V	5.08	−4
B	B1 V	6.5	−2.7
C	B5	8.1–9.8	−1

The brightest part of the Orion Nebula lies in its north central area. Within it we find the wide double Theta Orionis, whose components are 135″ apart and are resolvable even in mere opera glasses. (See Table 3–5.) Both stars of Theta are multiples. Theta 2, the southeastern of the pair, is a triple: due east of its magnitude 5.1 primary are a 6.5-magnitude star 53″ distant and a variable (range 8.1 to 9.8) 129″ away. (The 6.5-magnitude component can be resolved in 7x binoculars, but because of the nebula's background glow the fainter star is difficult to spot even when near maximum brightness.) Theta 1 is the famous Trapezium quadruple star. It is too tight a system to be resolved in binoculars (60x in a telescope is about right), but with a pair of well-focused and firmly-held 10x50's you can see that the image of Theta 1 is not a point, but a tiny disc (compare it to the image of the primary of Theta 2).

The two variable members of Theta 1 are both eclipsing binaries. Theta 2C, however, is an erratic nebular variable, a type of star abundant in regions like the Orion Nebula where star formation is in progress. These nebular variables seem to be newly-formed stars in the last stages of contraction from large, cool globules of dense interstellar matter. The instability that causes their variations is induced by the onset of hydrogen burning (the fusion of four hydrogen nuclei into one helium nucleus) in their core, which conflicts with, and eventually stops, their further contraction.

Theta 2A is of special interest because it is a spectroscopic binary; but its companion, though containing at least several solar masses, emits no radiation at all! The lines in the system's spectrum are all from the O9 primary. This dark secondary is therefore one of the best black hole candidates in the sky.

Emission nebulae like M42 occur when a hot star—one component of Theta 1 Orionis has a surface temperature of about 35,000° Kelvin—lies embedded in a cloud of hydrogen gas. Such extremely hot stars emit a lot of high-energy ultraviolet radiation. This radiation kicks electrons off the atoms of the gas of the nebula. Hydrogen atoms, for example, are split into free protons and free electrons. (The free protons are called H II ions, which is why large emission nebulae are sometimes called H II regions. H I is simply the standard hydrogen atom—neutral hydrogen.) Other atoms in the nebula are also ionized—many of the oxygen atoms, for instance, lose two of their eight electrons, thus becoming O III ions.

When the H II proton recaptures an electron, the electron radiates light as it recombines to form an H I atom. It takes energy to free an electron from an atom, so the electron gives back the energy as it rejoins the nucleus. Specific wavelengths of light are emitted as the electron falls down between given orbital shells in the atom. Some of the emitted radiation is in radio wavelengths, and consequently diffuse nebulae like M42 are strong radio emitters. The visible light of M42 comes principally from wavelengths of 5007 Ångstroms, 4959Å, and 4861Å (1Å = 10^{-8} cm). These three lines all lie in the green range of the spectrum, which is why in moderately large telescopes M42 has a distinctly greenish hue. Photographs also show red and blue tones in the nebula. The red is from the Hα line at 6562Å and the blue is from the Hγ line at 4340Å. No electron in an H II region stays in the hydrogen atom very long. Almost immediately another ultraviolet photon from the hot star knocks it out again, beginning the process anew.

One of my most memorable observing experiences was seeing the spectrum of the Orion Nebula visually.

This didn't happen at the super-sophisticated spectrograph of some observatory telescope, but with a 6-inch reflector and a small spectroscope bought from one of the telescope supply companies. I pointed my telescope at M42 expecting nothing, but when I looked into the spectroscope I was astonished to see three long, thin, glowing lines—the two close oxygen lines at 4959Å and 5007Å and the Hβ line at 4861Å. As the bright region of the nebula (in which the Theta Orionis stars are embedded) drifted across the slit of the spectroscope, the Hγ line at 4340Å was faintly but distinctly visible. Then the spectra of Theta 1 and the three stars of Theta 2 appeared successively. They were thin shafts of light. By positioning the slit just right, I could get three of the needle-like star-spectra superimposed across the tall nebula lines at one time.

The Orion Nebula is only the foremost of several interesting objects for binocular observers in the Sword. Like the other bright Orion association stars, Iota Orionis—the star at the tip of the Sword—has a striking silver-blue color. Just 8′ southwest of Iota is the beautiful double star Σ 747, one of the finest in the sky for binoculars. Though their separation is only 36″, the two stars (which are blue-white B0 and B1 objects) are comparably bright (mags $5\frac{1}{2}$ and $6\frac{1}{2}$) and therefore are an easy split, even at 7x.

At the north end of the Sword is the loose open cluster NGC 1981, a scattered group of about ten stars of magnitudes 8 to 10. (Orion has few open clusters even for telescopes. The huge cloud of gas and dust that covers most of the constellation blocks the light of distant clusters.) About midway between NGC 1981 and M42 is the magnitude 4.7 star 42 Orionis. Surrounding 42 and the slightly fainter 45 Ori several minutes of arc to its east is the reflection nebula NGC 1977, visible in 10x50 binoculars as a very faint and somewhat rectangular area of haze perhaps 30′ long in an east-west direction. This nebula cannot be seen in 7x50s because 7x does not provide enough contrast between the elusive nebular light and the sky background.

Even more difficult, however, is M43, a detached portion of M42 just north of the Theta stars. The neighboring glow of M42 almost drowns it out, but on good nights M43 can be seen in 10x50s as a small northern outcrop of M42. M43 surrounds, and is illuminated by, its own 7th-magnitude B0/1V star.

The Belt of Orion, Map 4. In binoculars the Belt of Orion is hardly inferior in beauty to the Pleiades. The almost perfectly straight line of bright, silver-blue Delta (δ), Epsilon (ε), and Zeta (ζ) (Mintaka, Alnilam, and Alnitak) dominates a field richly strewn with 6th-, 7th-, and 8th-magnitude stars. This is another case where binoculars are superior to large telescopes, for the magnifying power of a telescope simply spreads this field

out and destroys its richness. (The names Mintaka, Alnilam, and Alnitak, by the way, are from the Arabic for the "Girdle," "The String of Pearls," and "The Belt," respectively.)

As I mentioned earlier, firmly-held 10x binoculars can split the companion of Mintaka and the farthest star of the Sigma multiple. Also, 10x50s or 50mm zooms will allow you to glimpse NGC 2024, a large (20′) emission nebula that is centered only about $\frac{1}{4}$° east-northeast of Alnitak. The nebula is almost lost in Alnitak's glare; however, its presence makes the star's glare discernibly asymmetrical, elongated to the east-northeast. NGC 2024 is probably illuminated by the ultraviolet radiation from Alnitak and therefore must be about the same distance from us—1,600 light-years. The nebula's true diameter is around 10 light-years. A 6-inch telescope is necessary to see that NGC 2024 is cut in two by a thick and gently-curving rift of obscuring matter, reminiscent of the one that bisects the Lagoon Nebula in Sagittarius.

About 2.3° northeast of Alnitak, just over half the distance from that star to 56 Orionis, is the compact (6′ × 4′) but fairly bright (magnitude 8) nebula M78. At about 10x or more, M78 appears as a small disc distinctly brighter in its center. Telescopes reveal that there are two close $10\frac{1}{2}$-magnitude stars at the nebula's center. This nebula is bright enough that even 40mm glasses are sufficient to see it, provided the power is 10x or more. (At 7x, M78 appears simply star-like.) M78 is a nebula that shines by reflecting the light of the two $10\frac{1}{2}$-magnitude stars embedded within. It is the only reflection nebula that is relatively easy to see in binoculars because, unlike the vast majority of such nebulae, it has rather high surface brightness. This is the result of the thickness of the dust in this region of the Orion complex. Photographs show that M78 is centered in an area of obscuration about 1° in diameter so thick that few stars shine through it. (Even in binoculars the area around M78 looks oddly star-poor.) Since it is in the Orion Cloud, M78 is probably around 1,500 to 2,000 light-years distant.

Emission nebula NGC 2174, Map 4. In the extreme north of Orion, about $1\frac{1}{2}$° east-northeast of Chi 2 (χ²) Orionis and 2° southwest of Eta (η) Geminorum, lies the emission nebula NGC 2174. This object is seldom discussed in observing guides, but it is large (25′), has moderately high surface brightness, and is visible even in 40mm binoculars with averted vision. NGC 2174 is an interesting object visually, for it is almost perfectly circular. Squarely in its center is a magnitude $7\frac{1}{2}$ star. This star is an extremely hot O6.5 V object (its surface temperature is about 40,000° Kelvin) and it is the source of the ultraviolet radiation which causes the nebula to fluoresce. NGC 2174 and its central star are part of the Gemini OB1 association centered about 5,000 light-years away; the nebula's true diameter is therefore about 36 light-years. The brightest star in the association is Chi 2 Orionis, a B2 Ia supergiant of apparent magnitude 4.6 and absolute magnitude −7.6.

Alpha (α) Orionis, Betelgeuse, Map 4. Though prominent in the constellation, Betelgeuse's membership in the Orion association is doubtful. For one thing, it is only about 520 light-years distant (some sources give 650), and therefore it is considerably nearer than the M42 heart of the association. For another thing, it is a red supergiant (spectrum M2 Iab), and all the other bright stars in Orion are blue giants and supergiants. At the very least this means Betelgeuse is significantly more evolved than the blue stars, which have yet to become red giants and supergiants. However, since star formation is on-going in huge interstellar clouds like Orion, it's possible that Betelgeuse was simply one of the first stars formed here.

In binoculars Betelgeuse has a beautiful orange-red color. Contrast it with Rigel and with Gamma (γ) in Orion's other shoulder. Betelgeuse and Antares are the nearest of red supergiant type stars.

Like most other red giants and supergiants, Betelgeuse is variable, its observed extremes being magnitudes 0.0 and 1.5 and its period irregular (though some astronomers suspect a 6-year cycle lies buried in its random-appearing fluctuations). The star's absolute magnitude therefore ranges between −4.5 and −6, the latter value corresponding to a true luminosity of about 21,000 Suns. To follow Betelgeuse's light changes, compare it to the other 1st-magnitude stars of the northern winter sky: Capella at magnitude 0.1, Procyon at magnitude 0.4, Aldebaran at magnitude 0.9, and Pollux at magnitude 1.2. (The blue tint and the relatively low elevations of Rigel and Adhara make them unsuitable comparison stars for Betelgeuse; Sirius is simply too bright.)

Betelgeuse is perhaps most famous for its great girth. It is so large that even though it lies over 500 light-years away, special techniques allow astronomers to measure the star's diameter directly. The results show that Betelgeuse pulsates like a Mira-type long-period variable, its brightness and size changing together. Because the values are so small, the actual measurements of Betelgeuse's apparent diameter are subject to considerable uncertainty and different authorities cite different numbers. Burnham gives measured extremes of 0.034″ and 0.054″ for the star's apparent diameter, which at 520 light-years corresponds to true diameters of about 450 million and 750 million miles, respectively. If Betelgeuse replaced the Sun, its surface would pulsate between the orbits of Mars and Jupiter.

The apparent diameter of Betelgeuse is about twice the 0.02″ theoretical resolving power of the Hale 200-inch telescope. (In fact, the only star with greater apparent size than Betelgeuse is the Sun.) Astronomers have used computer techniques to remove the effects of atmospheric turbulence on the star's tiny image. The result is a disc mottled with large, relatively brighter patches, implying that certain sections of the star's surface are hotter than others.

Canis Major, the Greater Dog, Map 4.

To the naked eye, Canis Major is almost as striking as Orion. It isn't particularly large, but it contains two 1st-magnitude, three 2nd-magnitude, and three 3rd-magnitude stars arranged in a pattern of delicate beauty. Sirius is at the heart of the Dog, with Gamma (γ), Theta (ϑ), and Iota (ι) marking its head and Beta (β) a foreleg. A straight line south-southeast from Sirius through Pi (π) and Omicron (o) 2 ends in the conspicuous triangle of Delta (δ), Epsilon (ϵ), and Eta (η) at the Dog's hindquarters, with one of the hind legs extending west to Zeta (ζ). Scattered in and around the Delta-Epsilon-Eta triangle are the 3rd- and 4th-magnitude Omicron 1, Omicron 2, Sigma (σ), Tau (τ), and Omega (ω), making southern Canis Major a rich star field for the unaided eye or 7x binoculars.

The stars of Canis Major were associated with very dissimilar myths in various ancient cultures. In Egypt, Sirius was an object of special veneration because it rose just before the Sun at the time of year when the life-giving Nile flood began. The star therefore was associated with the Egyptian symbol of fertility, the cow-goddess Hathor. On tomb walls Hathor is frequently represented with a star between her horns and is shown kneeling upon the raft-like boat, which was imagined to carry her across the heavens.

The Greeks and Romans, however, appreciated Sirius somewhat less. During the 1st millennium B.C., Sirius rose and set with the Sun during summer—a coincidence which led some of the less-perspicacious Greeks and Romans to assume that the heat of summer (which bred malaria and other diseases in the ancient cities of the Mediterranean) was the result of the addition of Sirius' radiation to the Sun's. Our name Sirius comes from the Greek for "the scorching one."

The first civilization of Mesopotamia, the Sumerians, knew Sirius as *Gagsisa*, "the Arrow." Their Bow (*Ban*) was the arced figure formed by Kappa, Epsilon, Sigma, Delta, Tau and Eta Canis Majoris with Kappa and Xi (ξ) Puppis. Apparently, the Egyptians later adopted the Sumerian Bow: the great stone planisphere from the temple at Denderah (now in the Louvre), carved in Egypt during the mid-1st century B.C. but doubtless based upon older models, shows a human figure holding a drawn bow and arrow behind and below the cow-goddess Hathor (our Sirius). Of the dozens of figures on the planisphere only one other holds a bow and arrow, and that is Sagittarius.

In Arabia (before the Arabian astronomers in the 8th and 9th centuries of our era discovered and adopted the Greek constellations), Sirius had the hauntingly beautiful name *Al-Shi'ra al-Abur al-Yamaniyah*, "The Shining One of the Passage to the South." This title referred to a legend of the wedding between the bride Al-Jauzah, represented by our Orion, and the groom Suhail, our star Canopus in Carina. In one version of the story Suhail jilted Al-Jauzah; in another he was forced to leave her. In any case he fled from her to the far southern skies where he is to this day. Abandoned with Al-Jauzah were Suhail's two sisters, Al-Shi'ra (Sirius) and Al-Ghumaisa (Procyon). Al-Ghumaisa means "the Weeping One" and is remembered in our modern name for Beta (β) Canis Minoris, "Gomeisa." Also in the sky are the bridal attendants, represented by Delta, Epsilon, Eta, and Omicron 2 Canis Majoris, collectively called *Al-Adhara*, "the Virgins." Adhara is still the name for Epsilon CMa; and the present name for Eta, Aludra, is a corruption of the Arabic *Al-Udhrat al-Jauzah*, "the Virginity of al-Jauzah."

Alpha (α) Canis Majoris, Sirius, Map 4. Sirius, with an apparent magnitude of -1.42, is the brightest star in the sky. At a distance of 8.7 light-years it is the fifth nearest star to the solar system, the second nearest (after Alpha Centauri) visible to the unaided eye. Sirius has an absolute magnitude of $+1.45$, corresponding to a luminosity of 23 Suns—rather modest for its A1 V spectral type.

Even without binoculars you can see Sirius' fine blue-white color. With binoculars, contrast Sirius with Beta CMa 6° to the west; Beta is a B1 II magnitude 2.0 star with a silver-blue tone. This color difference is the result of a true surface temperature difference: Sirius has temperature of about 9200°K, but Beta's is around 21,000°K.

Sirius is particularly interesting to watch as it rises or sets. Atmospheric turbulence causes the star to twinkle violently and also acts as a prism, making it sometimes appear yellow or even red. These effects also occur with other stars as they rise or set, but are not as noticeable simply because Sirius is so much brighter. The twinkling of Sirius was possibly why the Greek poet Aratos called the star ποικιλος (poikilos), "of varying brightness." The colorful scintillation of Sirius at rising or setting no doubt was the inspiration for the beautiful name the star had in Algeria two centuries ago— Barakish, "of a Thousand Colors."

The famous white dwarf companion of Sirius—a star with 98% the Sun's mass but only 2% its diameter and a density therefore 92,000 times greater—is visible (with difficulty) only in telescopes of several inches aperture. The companion has an apparent magnitude of only 8.7: it is therefore about 10,000 times fainter than the primary and is virtually lost in the bright star's glare. Sirius B is the nearest and, in terms of apparent magnitude, the brightest of the white dwarfs. (A white dwarf visible in 20x giant binoculars is the companion to the magnitude 4.5 Omicron 2 Eridani: Omicron 2B Eri is a magnitude 9.7 star 83″ distant from its primary to the east-southeast.)

The Canis Major Association, Map 4. The star-richness of southern Canis Major is no accident—Delta, Eta, Omicron 1, Omicron 2, and Sigma CMa are all members of an association centered about 2,500 light-years away.

Table 3–6					
The Stars of the Canis Major Association					
Star	App Mag	Dist (l-y)	Color	Spectrum	Abs Mag
Delta	1.8	2,500	yellow	F8 Ia	-7.8
Eta	2.4	2,300	silver-blue	B5 Ia	-7
Omicron 2	3.0	3,100	silver-blue	B3 Ia	-7
Sigma	3.5	2,000	chrome red-orange	M0 Iab	-5.5
Omicron 1	3.8	1,900	chrome orange	K3 Iab	-6

As the list shows, the stars of the Canis Major Association offer beautiful color contrasts for the binocular observer. And they are conveniently close together: the Delta-Epsilon-Eta triangle easily fits in a 7x field. Because this part of the sky never gets very high above the horizon for much of the United States, the Canis Major Association is best observed while it is crossing the meridian. It is also important that the night be transparent and relatively free of haze.

The B2 II star Epsilon Canis Majoris, though only 680 light-years away and therefore actually in front of the Canis Major Association, adds its fine silver-blue to the association's field and provides a convenient color contrast to the reddish-orange Sigma and yellow Delta just to its northeast. Many star charts, following older estimates of Epsilon's brightness which did not sufficiently correct for atmospheric dimming, still show it as 2nd-magnitude. But modern photoelectric measurements made from southern hemisphere observatories give Epsilon's apparent magnitude as 1.49. Thus, Epsilon CMa is technically (by 0.01 magnitude) a 1st-magnitude star and Canis Major joins Orion, Crux, and Centaurus as the only constellations with two 1st-magnitude stars. Most star charts also still show Sigma as a 4th-magnitude object, but modern measurements push it (just barely) into the 3rd-magnitude club.

The fact that it contains red and yellow supergiants indicates that the Canis Major Association is an older, more evolved group than the Orion Association, whose

Photograph 3–2. *Canis Major, from a plate of the Ross-Calvert Milky Way Atlas. The overexposed star image toward the upper right is Sirius. To its right (west) at the edge of the field is Beta Canis Majoris. The Epsilon-Delta-Eta Canis triangle is in the lower center of the field, Epsilon Canis being about midway between the photo's center and its lower edge. (A spurious image occurs just left and slightly above Epsilon.) In the extreme upper left (northeast) corner of the field is the M46 + M47 open cluster pair in Puppis, M46, the eastern cluster, being distinctly larger and richer than M47. The little knot of stars about 60 percent the distance from Sirius to the M46 + M47 pair is the open cluster NGC 2360. Almost straight south of Sirius is the open cluster M41. As this splendid photograph shows, Canis Major lies on the east edge of the Winter Milky Way, the brightest star clouds between Delta and Omicron 2 Canis Majoris. Interstellar dust is rather thin in this direction through the Galaxy, but a few thicker channels of obscuration can be seen in the bright star clouds just east of the Epsilon-Delta-Eta Canis triangle.*

brightest stars are all still blue giants and supergiants. Another evidence that the Canis Major group is relatively old is its lack of nebulosity. The young Orion Association is still rich in gas and dust, but the remnants of the clouds of interstellar matter from which the Canis Major Association stars were formed have all been swept out of it.

Open clusters in Canis Major, Map 4. For telescopes, the finest open cluster in Canis Major is **NGC 2362**, a small (8′) but rich group of about 40 stars of magnitudes 7 to 11 centered on the blue-white Tau CMa. At about 100x in a 6- or 8-inch telescope, this cluster looks like a sapphire with a setting of tiny diamonds. Unfortunately, in binoculars most of NGC 2362 is lost in the glare of Tau—only with the higher powers of zoom instruments can a couple of the fainter cluster stars be glimpsed. However, NGC 2362 is of interest even to the binocular observer because it is one of the youngest star clusters known, perhaps only a couple million years old. It lies about 4,600 light-years away, so Tau, a bluish O9 II star, has an absolute magnitude of around −7, corresponding to a luminosity of over 50,000 Suns.

A better, but still difficult, open cluster for binoculars is **NGC 2354**, midway between Tau and Delta. This cluster has an integrated apparent magnitude of 7, but its individual stars are so faint and scattered (the cluster's diameter is 30′—the apparent size of the Full Moon) that its surface brightness is extremely low. In 10x50 binoculars NGC 2354 appears as a dim, vaguely-mottled patch. Because this cluster's declination is −26°, it never gets very high over the southern horizon for much of the United States and so there is less contrast between the glow of the cluster and the sky background than there would be if you could view it near the zenith. From the northern United States, very careful looking with averted vision is necessary to see NGC 2354 even in 10x50s.

Farther north in the constellation and much easier to see is **NGC 2360**, a cluster located about 3½° due east of Gamma CMa. In binoculars NGC 2360 appears as a 9th-magnitude, 10′ long, oval patch of haze oriented in an east-west direction. It is a much more compact object than NGC 2354, and has much higher surface brightness. With averted vision in 10x binoculars, the cluster's disc will appear faintly mottled from partial resolution of its brightest stars. There is a 6th-magnitude star about ½° west of the cluster. NGC 2360 is much more evolved than NGC 2362 and is estimated to be about 1.3 billion years old. It is set in a fine Milky Way field: the galactic equator cuts through the extreme northeastern corner of Canis Major just ½° northeast of NGC 2360, and since there is relatively little interstellar matter in this direction through the

Galaxy, the Milky Way here is quite bright. In binoculars you can see, embedded in the background glow, myriads of resolved and momentarily resolved stars.

In Canis Major the best open cluster for binoculars, however, is **M41**, located about 4° due south of Sirius. This cluster contains about 50 stars between magnitudes 6.9 and 11 spread over an area some 30′ across. In telescopes M41 should be viewed with the lowest power possible. Because its integrated apparent magnitude is 5.0, M41 can be seen with unaided eye as a small, fuzzy patch. In 10x50 binoculars over a dozen of M41's stars can be seen; and in the higher powers of zooms probably two dozen member stars are visible.

Because M41 lies around 2,400 light-years away, its true diameter is at least 20 light-years and its integrated absolute magnitude is about −4.3, a luminosity of approximately 4000 Suns. The cluster's brightest star, located in its center, is a K3 II object with an apparent magnitude of 6.9 and an absolute magnitude of −2.4. The bright stars of M41 are all either orange giants with spectra around K0 II, or late B main sequence objects, implying the cluster's age is approximately 100 million years.

3.3 The Milky Way Constellations of Winter
Auriga, the Charioteer, Map 4.

In the middle northern latitudes, Auriga's conspicuous pentagon—Alpha (α), Beta (β), Theta (ϑ) and Iota (ι) Aurigae with Beta Tauri—dominates the northeastern sky during the early evenings of autumn and heralds the coming winter. The brightest star of Auriga is Capella, the farthest north of the 1st-magnitude stars. For latitudes north of 44°, Capella is circumpolar. It is beautiful sight as it glitters low in the north during the long twilights of midsummer. At magnitude 0.1 Capella is the sixth brightest star in the sky. It lies about 45 light-years distant and therefore has an absolute magnitude of −0.6, a luminosity of 160 Suns. The star's spectrum shows that it is actually a binary consisting of G giants of absolute magnitudes −0.1 and +0.2 separated by only about 70 million miles. Capella has a fine golden-yellow color best appreciated by contrasting it with the blue-white of Beta Aurigae, a magnitude 1.9 star conveniently located just 6° due east.

Just south-southwest of Capella is the small triangular asterism of "the Kids," made up of Epsilon (ϵ), Zeta (ζ), and Eta (η) Aurigae. (The Greeks and Romans, however, had only two Kids, Zeta and Eta.) The Kids fit perfectly in a 10x field and Zeta and Eta, only ³⁄₄° apart, are a good color contrast pair for 50mm binoculars or a small telescope. Eta is a silver-blue B3 V star of magnitude 3.2, and Zeta is an orange eclipsing binary with a composite K4 II+B7 V spectrum and a range of 3.8 to 3.9—too small to be followed visually.

Another nice color-contrast pair for binoculars is Iota Aurigae and Beta Tauri, which are only about 6° apart. Iota Aur is an orange K3 II star of magnitude 2.7 and Beta Tau has a B7 III spectrum, an apparent magnitude of 1.7, and a silver-blue color. The two stars are 330 and 300 light-years away, respectively, and have absolute magnitudes of −2.4 and −3.2.

The Auriga Milky Way is decidedly brighter than that of Perseus nearby because toward Perseus lie relatively nearby clouds of interstellar gas and dust that obscure the star fields beyond. The best Milky Way fields in Auriga are around the Kids, and from just north of M36 and M38 southeast toward M37. Both fields show a rich half-resolution of multitudes of star-specks buried in the faint Milky Way background glow. To fully appreciate these and similar Milky Way fields, allow your eyes to adjust to the light conditions in the field of view by keeping them at the oculars for at least a full minute at a time but don't stare—blink as you feel the need. This will make the eyes more receptive to the minute sparks of momentarily resolved stars embedded in the Milky Way glow. If the night is particularly good, you might even see that northeast of M38 the star-speckled Milky Way is cut through by thick rifts, channels of obscuring matter in the foreground.

Open clusters M36, M37 and M38, Map 4. The most important objects in Auriga are the three open clusters M36, M37, and M38. These clusters are all about 4,200 light-years away but even in binoculars they have strikingly different appearances. M37 is unresolved (except for a magnitude 9½ star on the cluster's east edge), appearing only as a large (20′) circular patch of haze. M38 is as large as M37, but resolves into perhaps a score of faint stars on a dim, coarsely-textured background glow (the coarse texture is due to partial resolution). M36, though the smallest (12′) of the three, has the brightest stars and is the most completely resolved. At 10x it appears as a tight knot of several 9th-magnitude stars with no background haze.

The different binocular appearances of these three clusters faithfully reflect their different intrinsic characters. M37 is the most populous of the three clusters but is also the oldest (200 or 300 million years) and therefore no longer has any bright blue stars. M38 is not as populous as M37, but is young enough (70 million years) still to have a large number of fairly bright members. And M36, though the least populous of the clusters, is the youngest (20 or 30 million years old) and therefore has the most luminous stars—about a dozen hot bright B2 and B3 main sequence objects.

In 7x binoculars M36, M37, and M38 all fit in the same field of view, though M38 and M37 are crowding the edge. M36 and M38 are only about 2.3° apart and lie in a region of the Auriga Milky Way rich in inter-

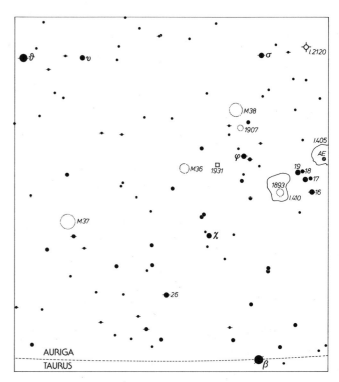

Identification Chart 3–5. Star clusters and nebulae in central Auriga. *Stars to magnitude 7.5 are plotted, and the chart scale is 9mm (=0.35 inch) per degree. North is to the top, east is to the left.*

esting objects. Mention has already been made of the fine Milky Way field north and east of the two clusters. Two other notable things are in the immediate M36 and M38 vicinity. First, about ½° due south of M38 is the 5′ diameter, 10th-magnitude, and very distant open cluster NGC 1907. In 10x binoculars this appears as a tiny patch of haze with a 9th-magnitude star on its southeast edge. Second, about halfway between M36 and Phi (φ) Aurigae is a tiny spot of fuzzy light. It is visible with 10x50s or in the higher powers of 50mm zooms, and it is distinguishable from the field stars chiefly because its image brightness is less. This is the emission nebula NGC 1931, and like NGC 1907, it is very distant.

From M37 and M38 southwest toward Iota Aurigae, the field is rich with 5th-, 6th-, and 7th-magnitude stars, a nice region to sweep in any size binoculars. Notice especially the line of 5th-magnitude stars (including 14, 16, and 19 Aur) midway between M36 and Iota. Each of the northern three stars of this line has a 6th- or 7th-magnitude optical companion several minutes of arc to its west, making a line parallel to the first. To the unaided eye, this double line looks like a large, hazy, partially-resolved star cluster—in 7x binoculars it is a rich and bright star field. About ¾° west-northwest of 19 Aurigae is 6th-magnitude AE Aurigae, a young, hot star moving directly away from the Orion region with the unusually high velocity of 80 miles per second. AE

Aurigae is one of the three "runaway stars" (the other two are Mu [μ] Columbae and 53 Arietis) that seem to have been ejected from the Orion complex by some unknown processes, possibly supernova explosions, at various times in the past.

Centered about 1° southeast of 19 Aur is a 20′ diameter pale glow over which scatter a handful of 9th-magnitude stars. The pale glow is the emission nebula IC 410 and the stars are members of the loose cluster NGC 1893 buried in the nebulosity. The brightest star of the cluster has an O4 V spectrum, implying that its surface temperature is 50,000° Kelvin. The NGC 1893—IC 410 complex is over 10,000 light-years distant and therefore is at least 60 light-years across.

Gemini, the Twins, Map 4.

Because the galactic equator runs between the club of Orion and the feet of the Twins, Orion and Gemini share the same stretch of the winter Milky Way. As a star pattern, Gemini is its most attractive in the early evenings of April when the two lines of stars representing the Twins stand vertically in the northwest.

The heads of the Twins are marked by the bright stars Castor and Pollux, both easily fitting in the same 7x field of view. They are a good color contrast pair. Pollux is an orange-yellow K0 III star, and Castor, a binary whose A1 V and A5 components can be split at 150x in small telescopes, is bluish-white. Though the 17th-century astronomer Johannes Bayer usually assigned Greek letters to the stars of each constellation in order of brightness, Pollux (Beta [β] Geminorum) is distinctly brighter than Castor (Alpha [α] Gem). Their apparent magnitudes are 1.2 and 1.6, respectively. Pollux is 35 light-years away and has an absolute magnitude of +0.9. Castor is 45 light-years distant. Its two components have apparent magnitudes of 2.0 and 2.9 and therefore have absolute magnitudes of +1.3 and +2.2. Both of Castor's stars are spectroscopic binaries. Moreover, Castor has a 9th-magnitude companion 73″ in position angle 164° from the bright pair. Since this star also is a spectroscopic binary, Castor is really a sextuple system.

There is also a good color contrast group in the feet of the Twins. Eta (η) and Mu (μ) are both M3 III stars of a beautiful reddish-orange color and Gamma (γ) is a bluish-white A0 IV object. Gamma lies some 8° southeast of Eta and Mu and therefore is just outside their field of view in most binoculars. Like many red giant stars, Eta and Mu are variable: Mu's range is only from magnitude 2.8 to magnitude 3.0, but Eta varies between 3.1 and 3.9 in a semi-regular period of around 233 days. Its cycle can be followed easily with the unaided eye. For comparison use Mu (its light changes are too slight

to be noticed visually) and Nu (ν), a magnitude 4.1 star about 2 1/2° southeast of Mu. Eta, Mu, and Gamma are 200, 190, and 57 light-years distant, respectively. Their absolute magnitudes are −0.9, −1.1, and +0.7.

Open clusters M35 and NGC 2158, Map 4.

About 2 1/2° northwest of Eta Geminorum is the large and rich open cluster M35, which can easily be seen with the unaided eye on dark, clear nights as a magnitude 5.5 patch of haze. This cluster contains about 120 stars brighter than magnitude 13 spread over an area 30′ across. Since more than twenty of these stars are of the 8th- and 9th-magnitudes, the cluster resolves well in binoculars. M35 is about 2,200 light-years distant, so its integrated absolute magnitude is at least −3.7, a luminosity of around 2500 Suns. The cluster's brightest star is a B3 V object of magnitude 7.5 (absolute magnitude −1.7). It also contains two yellow giants with absolute magnitudes around −0.5. M35 and the Pleiades both seem to be about 60 or 70 million years old.

Only 1/2° southwest of M35 is the extremely distant open cluster NGC 2158. It is very faint (magnitude 11), very small (4′ in diameter), and invisible in 7x35 and 7x50 binoculars. Even in 10x50s NGC 2158 appears only as a tiny, glowing patch behind a couple 9th-magnitude foreground stars. This is, however, a cluster of great interest. For one thing, it is very old. Its brightest members are not the hot bluish stars typical of open clusters, but red giants with absolute magnitudes near −2.5. This is similar to the brightest stars found in the very ancient globular clusters. NGC 2158 is probably over a billion years old.

But the most interesting fact about NGC 2158 is its distance: 16,000 light-years. As we'll see later in the book, this part of the Milky Way lies in the direction opposite the center of the Galaxy—here we are looking directly away from the galactic hub, outward toward the rim of the Galaxy's disc. NGC 2158's great distance in this direction places it very near our Galaxy's outer edge.

Monoceros, the Unicorn, Map 4.

Monoceros, which has only one star brighter than 4th-magnitude (magnitude 3.9 Beta [β]), is the most inconspicuous of the large Milky Way constellations. The ancients left the scattering of 4th- and 5th-magnitude stars in this area of the sky unformed; our Unicorn seems to have been invented during the Renaissance.

However, the brightest part of the winter Milky Way is the stretch through Monoceros and it is a fine scan in binoculars. The whole Monoceros Milky Way is richly strewn with 7th-, 8th-, and 9th-magnitude foreground

Photograph 3–3. *The region of the open cluster M35 in Gemini as photographed by E.E. Barnard for his Atlas of Selected Regions of the Milky Way. North is up and east to the left. M35 is a large, well-resolved group in the upper right of the field. NGC 2158 is the small disk just ½° SW of M35. Due south of M35 in the lower right (SW) quadrant of the field is a knot of stars associated with the diffuse nebula NGC 2174 in Orion. (See pages 65–66.)*

stars. The brightest Milky Way background glow is through the central and south-central parts of the constellation (roughly between 18 and Alpha [α] Monocerotis), where there are multitudes of fine star-specks glittering in the pale Milky Way light. It is a magnificent region in binoculars and richest-field telescopes, but to see it in its full glory you must do more than merely sweep through it. The Milky Way reveals its full splendor only if you allow your eyes to adapt to the light conditions in the field of view by looking through the oculars for a minute or two at a time. It is fatiguing, both to the eyes and to the arms (and even to the mind), but the results will surprise and please you.

Monoceros is rich in open clusters. Most of them are quite distant, for when we look toward Monoceros we are looking over and beyond the Orion complex deep into the core of the spiral arm on the inner edge of which our solar system is located. Despite their remoteness, three of the Monoceros open clusters are easily resolved in binoculars.

Open cluster M50, Map 4. The only Messier object in Monoceros is the open cluster M50, which lies almost exactly midway between Alpha and Beta Monocerotis on the western edge of the best part of the Monoceros Milky Way. This cluster is only moderately large (15′ in diameter), but in 10x50 binoculars six or seven of its brightest stars can be seen on the faint background glow of unresolved cluster members. The cluster's integrated apparent magnitude is 6.3.

M50 is about 2,900 light-years distant. Given the cluster's apparent magnitude, this distance would imply that its absolute magnitude is about −3.6. However, M50 lies in a direction of fairly heavy interstellar dust (the IC 2177 complex is just to the southeast), so its light is dimmed by about one magnitude and its actual absolute magnitude is near −4.5, a luminosity of more than 6000 Suns. The brightest stars of M50 are late B main-sequence objects and yellow giants with absolute magnitudes around −1. This is similar to the bright star populations of M37 in Auriga, M46 in Puppis, and M11 in Scutum, and suggests that M50 has about the same age, 100 to 150 million years.

The Rosette Nebula, NGC 2237 and its cluster, NGC 2244, Map 4. One of the most photogenic astronomical objects is the huge wreath-like Rosette Nebula. Photos of it reveal lots of fine wispy detail, several small blobs and sinuous channels of dark nebulosity, and a large central "hole." In color photos the nebula has a beautiful soft red tone. Nestled in the Rosette's central "hole" lies a sparse cluster of fairly bright stars arranged in a rough rectangle about 20′ long; each corner of the rectangle and the midpoints of both long sides is marked by a star. The cluster is catalogued as NGC 2244, the nebula itself by NGC 2237. Actually each bright section

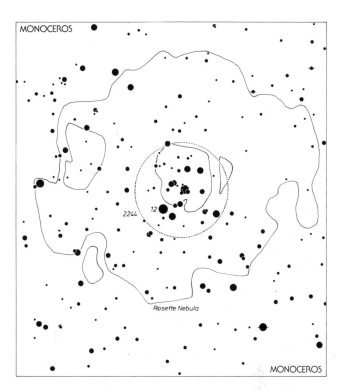

Identification Chart 3–6. Membership for NGC 2244.
Stars are plotted to magnitude 11.0, and the chart scale is 60mm (=2.36 inch) per degree. North is to the top, east to the left.

Table 3–7			
The Brighter Stars in NGC 2244			
Location	Star	Spectra	Mag
Center	HD 46150	O5 V	6.72
SE	HD 46223	O4 V	7.25
NW	HD 46149	O8.5 V	7.61
NW	HD 46106	B0.5 V	7.91
Center	HD 46202	O9 V	8.17
S. Center	HD 46056	O8 Vn	8.19

of the Rosette has its own NGC number, but by custom NGC 2237 usually refers to the nebula as a whole.

The Rosette Nebula's apparent diameter is 80′, about 2½ times that of the Moon. Since it is about 4,900 light-years away, its true diameter is approximately 115 light-years—almost four times the size of the Orion Nebula. The Rosette is one of the larger emission nebulae known in our Galaxy, but much larger ones are seen in other galaxies.

NGC 2244, the open cluster in the center of the Rosette, has an integrated apparent magnitude of 5.3 and on clear, moonless nights can be seen with the unaided eye as a small, fuzzy patch. In binoculars the cluster is easily resolved. In fact, it is so large (20′) and scattered, and the Milky Way background here is so rich in 7th-, 8th-, and 9th-magnitude field stars, that NGC 2244 is almost lost in the clutter. You could scan right over it without recognizing it to be a cluster.

Things aren't helped by the lack of bright stars in the vicinity to assist you in locating the cluster. Probably the best way to find it is to start at Gamma (γ) Geminorum and star-hop. First go 4° south-southeast to magnitude $3\frac{1}{2}$ Xi (ξ) Gem, then 3° south and slightly west to 5th-magnitude S Mon, the brightest star in the cluster NGC 2264 (discussed below). From there go another 3° southwest to 5th-magnitude 13 Mon. The Rosette lies about 2° due south of 13 Monocerotis. The Rosette star cluster's distinguishing feature is its rectangular form, the long axis of which is oriented northwest to southeast.

The brightest star of the Rosette cluster, 5.9-magnitude 12 Monocerotis, is not a true cluster member but merely a yellow K0 III foreground star only a few hundred light-years from us. All the true brightest members are blue stars with surface temperatures around 50,000°K. Such stars are so hot that most of their radiation is emitted in the invisible ultraviolet part of the spectrum.

The intense ultraviolet radiation of the Rosette cluster stars is responsible for the Rosette's nebula glow. It knocks the electrons off the atoms of hydrogen in the nebular gas, and when they are recaptured they emit radiation. Some of this is visible light, some of it is at radio or other wavelengths. The nebula's red color comes from emission at wavelength 6563Å, the so-called Hα emission line, which is radiated by electrons as they fall from the third to the second lowest orbital shells in the hydrogen atom.

The intense brilliance of the NGC 2244 cluster stars is also responsible for the hole in the center of the Rosette. Embedded in the hydrogen gas of the nebula are microscopic grains of silicate and graphite dust. The grains are driven away from the stars by radiation pressure and drag the ionized hydrogen gas along with them. The estimated time to open up a hole free of dust and gas the size of that in the nebula (about 30 light-years across) is around 500,000 years. This, then, is how long it has been since the Rosette cluster stars began radiating. Thus, the Rosette cluster is very young by astronomical standards. In fact, photographs show scattered around the Rosette Nebula many tiny, dark Bok globules, thought to contain contracting proto-stars. The Rosette Nebula therefore is, like the Orion Nebula, a region where star formation is presently occurring.

For the binocular observer, the most astonishing thing about the whole Rosette Complex is that the nebula (except for its central hole) is not all that difficult to see. In 10x50s averted vision is barely necessary and the nebula is even visible in 40mm zooms at about 16x. Probably very nearly the full 80′ photographic diameter of the nebula can be seen in 10x50s, but it will be impossible for the inexperienced observer to anticipate

how ghostly and tenuous the Rosette Nebula actually is. The first time I searched for the Rosette in binoculars (a beautifully transparent, but bitterly cold, January night in Minnesota), I didn't see even a suggestion of it. But when I looked for it again two years later, having learned in the meantime what the phrase "extended, low surface brightness" means by observing M33 in Triangulum, NGC 7293 in Aquarius, and the North America Nebula in Cygnus, I found the Rosette fairly easily.

The Rosette is, however, quite invisible in such standard amateur instruments as the 6-inch f/8 reflector. A moderately long focal length telescope simply magnifies the nebula too much, spreading out its already tenuous light. Binoculars (particularly 10x binoculars) are ideal for the Rosette and other "extended, low surface brightness" objects because they magnify enough to darken the sky background for contrast, but do not significantly reduce image brightness. One of the pleasures of binocular observing is defying the "common wisdom" limitations of aperture!

Open cluster NGC 2264, Map 4. The open cluster NGC 2264 is a 30′ long loose group located about 3° south and slightly west of Xi (ξ) Geminorum. This is sometimes called the Christmas Tree cluster because its stars are arranged in the outline of an arrowhead with the tip pointing south (upwards in the inverted field of telescope). Like the Rosette cluster, NGC 2264 is large and sparse and in such a rich field of 7th-, 8th-, and 9th-magnitude Milky Way stars that it is easy to overlook. But the distinctive arrowhead shape of NGC 2264 will help you identify it. Moreover, its brightest member, the O7 IV–V 15 Monocerotis, is a naked-eye star, an irregular variable with the small range of magnitude 4.5 to magnitude 5.0 (too slight to be obvious visually).

In braced or tripod-mounted 10x50 binoculars, all but two of the twenty brightest cluster members can be seen. The IV–V luminosity class of 15 Monocerotis indicates that it already has begun to evolve away from the main sequence. Because the brightest stars of the Rosette cluster (NGC 2244) are still main sequence objects, NGC 2264 must be a somewhat older cluster than NGC 2244, with an age on the order of several million years.

The distance to NGC 2264 is around 2,300 light-years; the cluster is therefore about 20 light-years long. The distance implies that 15 Monocerotis at maximum has a visual absolute magnitude near −5. However, as with the hot stars in the Rosette cluster, most of 15 Monocerotis' radiation is ultraviolet, and totalled over all wavelengths the star's absolute magnitude is about −8.3. Since this is 13 magnitudes greater than the Sun's bolometric absolute magnitude, 15 Monocerotis radiates as much energy over all wavelengths as 160,000 Suns.

Long-exposure photographs reveal that the stars of NGC 2264 are enmeshed in a large area of faint nebulosity. Silhouetted on the nebulous wisps just south of the 7th-magnitude star at the apex of the Christmas Tree is the remarkable Cone Nebula, a feature that resembles a celestial volcano and which is visible only in very large telescopes. The Cone is an example of a "rim nebula," a dark cloud bordered with bright edges. Rim nebulae form at the turbulent boundary where a hot, ionized gas expands explosively into a cool, dark cloud. Other rim nebulae are associated with M16 (the Eagle Nebula) in Serpens Cauda, M20 (the Trifid Nebula) in Sagittarius, and IC 434, the 1° long reef south of Zeta (ζ) Orionis upon which is silhouetted the Horsehead Nebula.

Minor Open Clusters in Monoceros, Map 4. A number of smaller open clusters are worth noticing as you scan the Monoceros Milky Way. (The following descriptions are based on the clusters' appearances in 10x50 binoculars: if you have 7x50's or 7x35's you will see less, if you are using 50mm zooms or giant binoculars you will see more.) The easiest to locate is **NGC 2232**, which lies just 2° north of Beta (β) Mon and consists of the 5th-magnitude star 10 Monocerotis at the north end of a sparse 30′ long, 10′ wide scattering of 6th to 8th-magnitude objects.

More interesting visually is **NGC 2301**, 2° south-southeast of 18 Mon and 5° west-northwest of Delta (δ) Mon. It forms a fairly conspicuous 15′ north-south line of a half dozen 8th-magnitude stars. (NGC 2301 is the best open cluster in Monoceros for telescopes. It has forty or fifty 9th- to 11th-magnitude members concentrated in two small groups near the northernmost star in the 8th-magnitude line.)

About 3° east-northeast of NGC 2301 and the same distance northwest of Delta (δ) Mon is **NGC 2324**, a compact (9′ in diameter), 9th-magnitude patch of haze. In extreme south central Monoceros, about 3 1/2° southeast of M50, is **NGC 2353**, another of the visually interesting minor Monoceros clusters, consisting of a magnitude 6.0 O9.5 II–III star on the southern edge of a 15′ long spray of much fainter cluster members. Because this is an area with no bright stars, NGC 2353 can be difficult to find. Look for it a little over halfway from Alpha Monocerotis to Theta (ϑ) Canis Majoris.

Finally, in the extreme southeastern corner of Monoceros about 5° east and slightly south of Alpha Monocerotis is **NGC 2506.** An unresolved but fairly large (10′) and bright (mag 8) hazy patch, it is of interest for being about billion years old and therefore one of the most ancient open clusters.

These five minor clusters are all subtle objects, requiring careful looking to appreciate. But each has its own personality and all add to the visual pleasure of scanning the star fields of the Monoceros Milky Way.

Puppis, the Stern, Maps 4 and 9.

Puppis is the Stern of the *Argo*, the ship on which Jason and the Argonauts sailed in their mythological quest for the Golden Fleece. Argo was the largest of the ancient constellations—so large, that for the sake of convenience astronomers last century divided it into Puppis the Stern, Carina the Keel, Vela the Sails, and Pyxis Nautica (now simply Pyxis) the Nautical Box (meaning compass). Except for Pyxis (no ancient Greek ever sailed with a compass!), these divisions follow the lines of Argo as Greek and Roman writers described it. The absence of a Bow goes back to the ancients also, for they thought of Argo as moving through the sky stern-first in the manner of the large vessels of those days, which would back into harbors to ground stern-first on the beach.

Argo is beautiful. The Milky Way runs its entire length, climaxing at extreme northern Carina in the brilliant star clouds around the Eta Carinae Nebula (NGC 3372). There is only one 1st-magnitude star in Argo, but it is Canopus, at magnitude −0.7 the second brightest star in the sky. Argo is, moreover, rich in 2nd- and 3rd-magnitude stars: Puppis contains one 2nd- and six 3rd-magnitude stars, Vela has three each of the 2nd- and 3rd-magnitudes, and in Carina there are three 2nd-magnitude and seven 3rd-magnitude stars.

There also are several fields in Argo liberally strewn with 4th-, 5th-, and 6th-magnitude stars, (giving the impression, perhaps, of spray thrown up by the waves through which the ship is cutting). One of these is the Keyhole Nebula region. Another is around the "False Cross" (Epsilon [ε] and Iota [ι] Carinae plus Delta [δ] and Kappa [κ] Velorum). Farther north lie star-rich fields around Gamma (γ) Velorum and between Delta and Lambda Vel. And in Puppis there are good fields around Zeta (ζ) and between Xi (ξ) Puppis and Eta (η) and Tau (τ) Canis Majoris. All these star fields are excellent in the wide fields of 7x binoculars.

Unfortunately, most of Argo lies too far south to be observed from middle northern latitudes. Because Canopus culminates slightly more than 2° above the horizon at latitude 35° north, observers as far north as Chattanooga, Memphis, Albuquerque, and Santa Barbara should be able to glimpse it in binoculars as it crosses the meridian around 9 p.m. local mean time in mid-February. (The night must be very transparent, and of course your southern view has to be unobstructed, right down to the horizon.) However, even from southern Texas and the Florida peninsula the other interesting binocular objects in Carina—open clusters NGC 2516, NGC 3532, IC 2602, and the Keyhole Nebula—are lost in the horizon haze. Therefore, since Puppis is the one part of Argo fairly well seen from even the northern U.S. states and southern Ontario, it is the only section of Argo we'll discuss in detail.

Open clusters M46, M47, and northern Puppis, Map 4. Even for a Milky Way constellation, Puppis is exceptionally rich in open clusters. Most of them are quite distant. Nevertheless, several of Puppis' clusters are good objects for binoculars, two of the best being M46 and M47. These clusters are only about $1\,{}^{1}\!/_{2}°$ apart, M47 being almost due west of M46. They are located about 5° south of Alpha (α) Monocerotis and 8° east of Gamma (γ) Canis Majoris, and are easy to spot because they are large (about 30′ in diameter) and bright. (The integrated apparent magnitude of M46 is 6.7 and that of M47, 5.2.) They have, however, very different appearances. In 10x50s M46 is a hazy patch, unresolved except for couple 10th-magnitude stars on the west side of the cluster and a handful of intermittently visible star-specks sprinkled across its pale disc. M47, on the other hand, resolves even with 7x35 glasses into a coarse, scattered group of a dozen or so stars, the brightest being two 6th-magnitude objects. M47 can be seen with the unaided eye as a small fuzzy spot.

The different binocular appearances of M46 and M47 betray their different intrinsic characters. M46 is very populous with over 500 members, but its brightest stars are A0 objects with absolute magnitudes of only −0.5. M47, though much less populous than M46 (about 60 members), contains several bright blue giant stars. Its two 6th-magnitude stars have B2 and B5 spectra and absolute magnitudes near −3. The difference between the brightest stars in the two clusters is a symptom of their different ages. M46 is old enough that all its high-mass, high-luminosity stars have either gone supernova or fizzled into white dwarfs. M46 is a couple hundred million years old, but M47 is only about 20 or 30 million years old.

M46 and M47 appear side by side but actually M46 is around three times farther away. M47 is estimated to be about 1,700 light-years away and M46 some 5,000 light-years distant. M47 has a true diameter of approximately 16 light-years and an integrated absolute magnitude of at least −3.4 (2000 Suns' luminosity), while M46 is around 45 light-years across and has an absolute magnitude of over −4.2 (over 4000 Suns).

M46 is notable for appearing to contain a planetary nebula, NGC 2438, a tiny smoke-ring 68″ in diameter and of magnitude 11.5, located within the northern edge of the cluster and visible in 6-inch telescopes. (The planetary can also be seen in 4-inch telescopes, but only as a disc.) Planetary nebulae result when stars billions of years old puff off their outer layers. Thus, if a planetary was actually found to be a member of an open cluster like M46, which is only a couple hundred mil-

lion years old, then something would be very wrong. Fortunately for modern astrophysics, NGC 2438 and M46 have different radial velocities: NGC 2438 is receding from us at 47 miles per second whereas M46 is receding at only 25 miles per second. Consequently, the nebula must be physically separate from the cluster. In fact, NGC 2438 seems to be couple thousand light-years closer than M46. By a curious coincidence, an open cluster in neighboring Pyxis, NGC 2818, also has a planetary nebula as an apparent member.

The region around M46 and M47 has several other interesting objects for the binocular observer. About $^{1}\!/_{2}°$ due west of M47 is the beautiful chrome-orange star KQ Puppis, an eclipsing binary consisting of a B2 star orbiting an M2e giant. (The range, magnitude 4.9 to 5.2, is too small to be observed visually.) About $^{2}\!/_{3}°$ north and slightly east from M47 is the 7th-magnitude open cluster NGC 2423, which appears as a faint amorphous area of haze about 12′ across behind a couple 9th-magnitude stars. Two degrees farther north, but still within the same binocular field with M46 and M47, is Mel (for Melotte) 71—an open cluster smaller (8′ in diameter) than NGC 2423 but with the same integrated magnitude (about 7) and therefore appearing as a higher surface brightness patch. Mel 71 is easier to see in binoculars than NGC 2423. Finally, some 9° to the east-northeast is open cluster NGC 2539, a 20′ 8th-magnitude disc of haze on the southeast edge of which is the magnitude 4.5 star 19 Puppis. This star is merely a foreground object, not a true cluster member. In 10x50 binoculars the haze of NGC 2539 has a coarse texture from partial resolution of its 11th-magnitude brightest members.

The Rho-Xi Puppis region, Map 4. The bright Milky Way glow of central and south-central Monoceros continues southeast through Puppis. In binoculars the field from around Rho (ρ) and Xi (ξ) Puppis down to q and r Puppis shows the same beautiful glitter from partial resolution of myriads of momentarily visible stars as the central Monoceros Milky Way. In addition to its fine Milky Way background, the Rho-Xi Puppis vicinity contains several interesting objects for the binocular observer. Because the region does not culminate very high above the horizon for the central and northern United States, it is important to observe it only on dark, transparent nights and when it is near the meridian.

First, Xi Puppis is a G6 Ia supergiant with an apparent magnitude of 3.3 and a fine golden-yellow color. It is about 800 light-years distant and has an absolute magnitude of −4.2. About $1\,{}^{1}\!/_{2}°$ northwest of Xi is the fairly bright (magnitude 6.5) open cluster M93, which has a strange 12′ long crescent, or comma-like, shape. In 10x50 binoculars the haze of M93 shows a coarse tex-

Photograph 3–4. *Open clusters in NW Puppis. Photo by Brian Skiff on Kodak 103a-0 spectroscopic film with the 13-inch Lowell Observatory "Pluto" telescope. In the lower right (SE) corner of the field is the rich cluster M46. Two short lines on the cluster's upper (northern) edge mark the planetary nebula NGC 2438, only an optical member of M46. The loose group of bright stars at bottom center is M47. About ⅔° NNE of M47 is NGC 2423, appearing to be little more than a concentration of field stars but nevertheless a true gravitationally-bound open cluster. Due north of NGC 2423, at the top center of the field, is the much more compact group Melotte 71. The different character of the four clusters in this photo can be discerned easily with most binoculars.*

Identification Chart 3–7. (Overleaf) Star Clusters in the Canis Major, Monoceros, and Puppis Milky Way. *The faintest stars shown are of magnitude 7.5.*

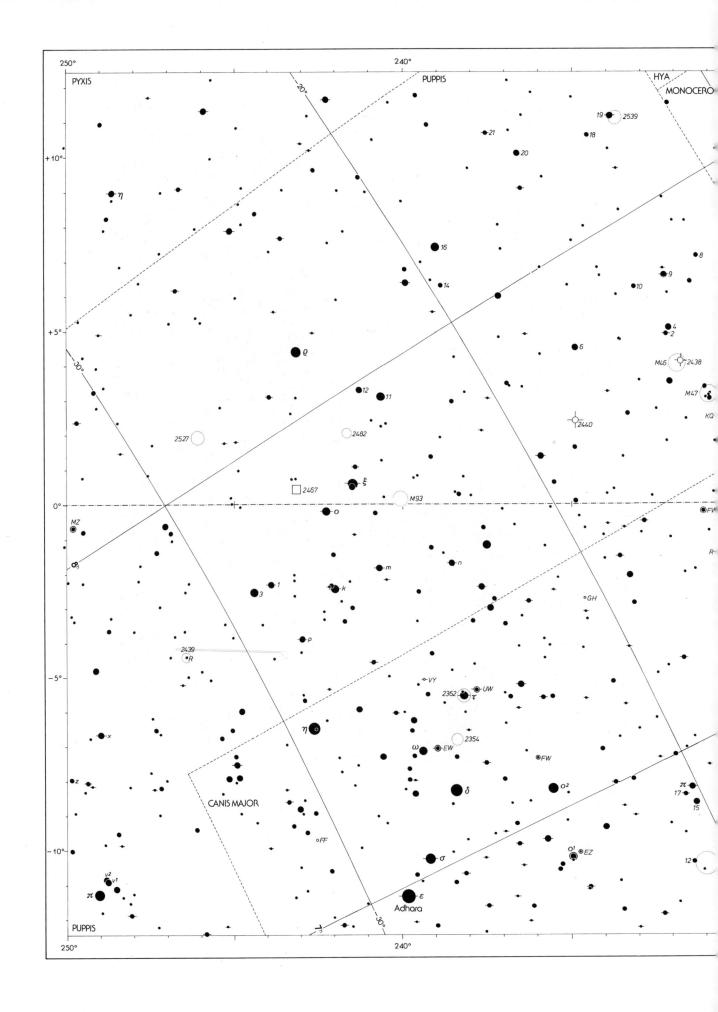

PYXIS

250°

240°

PUPPIS

HYA

MONOCERO

+10°

η

19 ○⋯ 2539

21

18

20

16

8

14

9

10

+5°

4

2

6

ϱ

M46 ⊕ 2438

12

11

M47

2527

2482

2440

KQ

ξ

2467

M93

0°

o

⊙ FV

MZ

R

♋

m

n

GH

1

k

3

p

2439

R

VY

UW

−5°

2362 τ

η

2354

x

ω EW

FW

z

δ

O²

π

17

CANIS MAJOR

15

FF

O¹ ⊕ EZ

−10°

σ

12

v²

v¹

π

ε

Adhara

PUPPIS

−20°

250°

240°

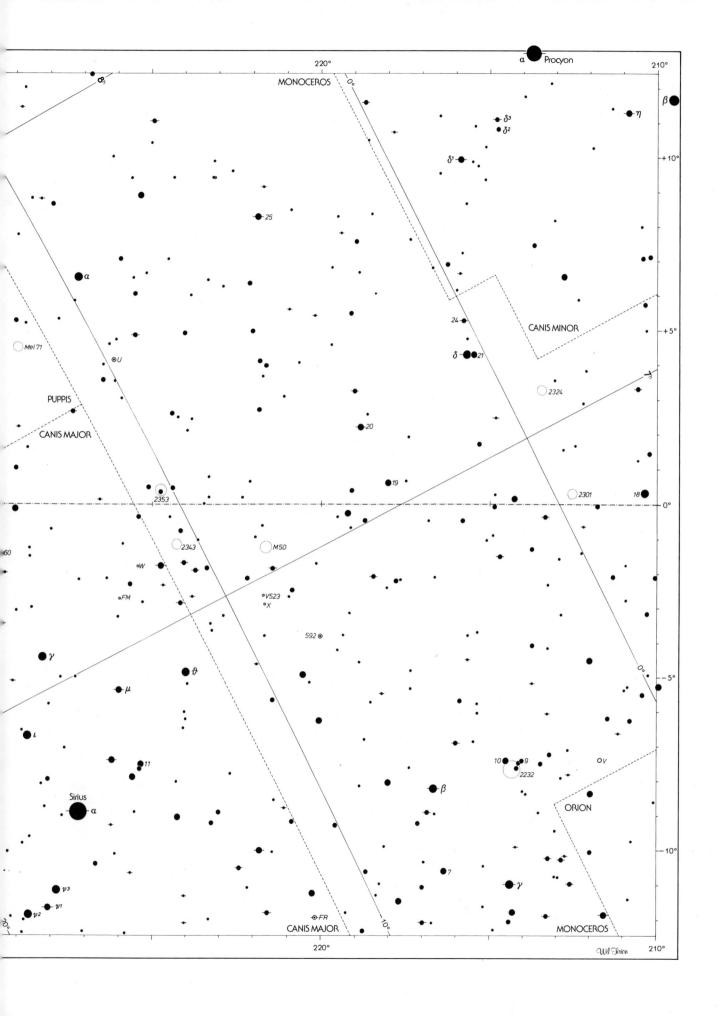

α Procyon

β

η

MONOCEROS

210°

220°

0°

δ³
δ²

+10°

δ¹

25

24

CANIS MINOR

+5°

α

δ 21

Mel 71

U

2324

PUPPIS

20

CANIS MAJOR

19

2301

18

0°

2353

M50

2343

60

W

FM

V523

X

592

γ

ϑ

-5°

μ

0°

ι

11

10 9

V

2232

β

Sirius

ORION

α

-10°

7

v³

γ

v¹

v²

FR

MONOCEROS

20°

CANIS MAJOR

10°

210°

220°

Wil Tirion

ture of half-resolution, particularly on the west side of the crescent. This cluster is around 3,400 light-years away. A much more difficult open cluster (at the limit for 10x50s) is NGC 2482, located about 1° northeast of Xi. NGC 2482 is quite large (18′ in diameter—over half the diameter of the Moon), but its integrated apparent magnitude is only 8.8 and therefore its surface brightness is extremely low. (NGC 2482 covers more area than the notoriously faint NGC 7293, the Helical Nebula, in Aquarius, but is 2.3 magnitudes fainter.) This cluster's structure is loose rather than concentrated, so in binoculars its haze appears clumpy rather than smooth and disc-like. To find NGC 2482, first locate (about midway between Xi and 12 Puppis) a small, thin isosceles triangle of 8th- or 9th-magnitude stars with its vertex pointing toward Xi. The cluster lies in this triangle, near its vertex.

The most interesting object in the Rho-Xi Puppis region is the emission nebula NGC 2467, located almost 2° south-southeast of Xi and about 1° east-southeast of Omicron (o) Puppis. NGC 2467 is less than 6′ across but its integrated apparent magnitude is 7.0, so its surface brightness is quite high—in fact, NGC 2467 is so compact and has such high surface brightness that at first glance, even in 10x binoculars, it is easy to mistake for a star. However, NGC 2467 and other small, high surface brightness objects can be discriminated from stars because their images are hazy-edged and lack the "hardness" of a true stellar point.

In 10x50s a trained eye using averted vision will see an 8th-magnitude star in the center of NGC 2467. This is the hot O6 star whose ultraviolet radiation is fluorescing the gas of the nebula. Just east of the nebula is an 8th-magnitude star and just east of that star are the northwest-southeast pair of 7½-magnitude stars.

NGC 2467 is about 8,200 light-years away. Its true diameter is only about 14 light-years but it is part of a larger nebulous complex that is at least 70 light-years across. This region of nebulosity seems to be isolated and rather thin, however, because long-exposure photographs show four faint galaxies, about ½° west of NGC 2467 and practically right on the galactic equator. In fact, interstellar matter is so sparse here that stars lying on the rim of the Galaxy in this direction (over 20,000 light-years distant) are dimmed by only 4 or 5 magnitudes—a far cry from the *30* magnitudes of obscuration caused by the dust between us and the Galactic Center.

The Zeta (ζ) Puppis region, Maps 4 and 9. If our eyes were sensitive to radiation of all wavelengths, the brightest star in the sky would be Zeta (ζ) Puppis, a super-hot O5 object with a surface temperature of 48,000°K. Because it is so hot Zeta Puppis radiates

mostly ultraviolet light, and therefore although its visual apparent magnitude is only 2.3, its *bolometric* apparent magnitude (the brightness it would have to an "eye" sensitive to all wavelengths of electromagnetic radiation) is −2. Sirius has a visual apparent magnitude of −1.42; but because it is an A1 star with a surface temperature of only 9200°K, most of its radiation is in visual wavelengths and its bolometric apparent magnitude is −1.6, only 0.2 magnitude greater.

Zeta Puppis is one of the most luminous stars known in our Galaxy. It is about 2,400 light-years away, so its visual absolute magnitude is −7.1 and its bolometric absolute magnitude −11.3. Because our Sun's visual and bolometric absolute magnitudes are both around +4.8, Zeta Puppis is 11.9 magnitudes (60,000 times) brighter than the Sun in visual wavelengths but 16.1 magnitudes (2.8 *million* times) brighter over all wavelengths. In the 6000 years since the first constellations were formed, Zeta Puppis has radiated three times as much energy as the Sun has in the entire 5 billion years of its existence! Since even a star like Zeta Puppis probably contains less than 100 times the Sun's mass, it obviously is not going to last very long. Spendthrift blue supergiants are splashy but transient members of a galaxy.

The Zeta Puppis region is one of the several areas in Puppis, Vela, and Carina that are richly scattered with 4th-, 5th-, and 6th-magnitude stars. In addition, there are three good open clusters for binoculars within a few degrees of Zeta. First, about 2½° northeast of Zeta, between two 7th-magnitude stars, is the large (40′) 5th-magnitude cluster NGC 2546, which is about 2,700 light-years distant. Because its brightest stars are 9th- and 10th-magnitude objects, NGC 2546 can be partially resolved in binoculars. The second cluster, about 3½° northwest of Zeta, is the very large (45′) NGC 2451, a loose group of a dozen or so fairly bright stars scattered around the magnitude 3.7 star c Puppis. It is seen better in the wide fields of binoculars than in the small fields of telescopes. NGC 2451 is only about 1,000 light-years away.

Finally, 2° northwest of Zeta and just north of the 4th-magnitude star b Puppis, is NGC 2477, another large (20′ in diameter) cluster, but not as resolvable in binoculars as NGC 2451 because its brightest stars are only 11th-magnitude. (In 10x50s and 50mm zooms a few star specks might be visible glittering in the cluster's softly glowing disc.) In telescopes NGC 2477 can be seen to be a much more populous cluster than either NGC 2451 or NGC 2546. It is also much older. NGC 2546 is perhaps about 8 million years old and NGC 2451 70 million, but NGC 2477 is around the age of the Hyades, 700 million years. It is the farthest of the three clusters, but its precise distance is

Photograph 3–5. *The Milky Way in southern Puppis. The bright star in the lower center of the field is Zeta Puppis. Above and a little to its left (north-northeast) is a loose aggregation of moderately bright stars, the open cluster NGC 2546. The compact and star-rich cluster NGC 2477 is obvious west-northwest of Zeta. (Just southeast of NGC 2477 is the 4th-magnitude star b Puppis.) To the west (right) of NGC 2477 is NGC 2451, a loose scattering of bright stars. The myriads of faint stars in the upper half of the field bears witness to the fact that there is comparatively little dust in that direction through the disc of our Galaxy. Photograph by Georgetown Observatory.*

uncertain; an educated guess would be 7,000 light-years. The integrated apparent magnitudes of NGC 2477 and NGC 2546 (5.5 and 5.0, respectively) imply that for observers far enough south, they are visible to the unaided eye.

Some 8° west-northwest of Zeta Puppis and due south of the Delta-Epsilon-Eta Canis Majoris triangle is the magnitude 2.7 Pi (π) Puppis, a K3 Ib object with an orange color. Within 1° north of Pi is an approximately east-west line of three 5th-magnitude stars, all of which have B3 spectra. In the southern United States, where Pi and its three attendants culminate far enough above the horizon to minimize atmospheric reddening, the bluish tone of these three stars is, in giant binoculars and small telescopes, a fine contrast to Pi's orange. Though the eastern two of Pi's associates, Upsilon 1 (v^1) and 2, are 4′ apart, they probably form a true physical system since their radial velocities and proper motions—and therefore their velocities through space—are nearly the same. They are about 500 light-years away, so their true separation is at least 0.6 light-year—more if one of the stars is slightly farther from us than the other. Pi Puppis, with a distance of 140 light-years, is a foreground object to the Upsilon pair.

Chapter 4

The Constellations of Spring

The one season without a stretch of Milky Way to observe in the first part of the night is the spring. During the early evenings of March the winter Milky Way declines in the west, and it is not until early June that the summer Milky Way is high enough in the east to be clearly observed before midnight.

Though they lie well off the Milky Way, the spring constellations contain quite a few, fairly bright stars. The Big Dipper, for example, consists of six stars of 2nd magnitude and one of 3rd. In the rest of Ursa Major, there are six more 3rd-magnitude stars. Corvus has four stars between magnitude 2.5 and 3.0. Leo includes one 1st-magnitude, two 2nd-magnitude, and five 3rd-magnitude stars. In addition to Leo's Regulus, the spring sky also has the 1st-magnitude Spica in Virgo, and zero-magnitude Arcturus in Boötes. (Arcturus is the brightest star north of the celestial equator.)

Because the spring constellations are formed of so many 1st-, 2nd-, and 3rd-magnitude stars, they are (for the most part) more conspicuous than the southern constellations of autumn. The Water-jar of Aquarius, the Circlet of Pisces, and the Head of Cetus may be visually interesting asterisms, but they are a good deal less striking than the Sickle of Leo, the quadrangle of Corvus, the kite-shape of Boötes, and, of course, the Big Dipper.

The relationship of an area of the sky to the Milky Way determines the types of objects that can be found there. When we look toward the Milky Way we are looking through the star clouds and the thick interstellar matter of a spiral arm of our Galaxy. Thus, Milky Way constellations contain open clusters, bright blue stars, associations, and diffuse and dark nebulae. However, when we look off the Milky Way, we look past comparatively few stars and through little interstellar matter out into intergalactic space. If there are any galaxies in this direction, we should be able to see them—provided only that our instrument is large enough.

And indeed, there are galaxies in the direction of the spring sky. The reader who has the *Sky Atlas 2000.0* or the *Atlas of the Heavens* will notice that there is a long, broad band rich in galaxies running from the area of the Big Dipper down through western Canes Venatici, Coma Berenices, and western Virgo, ending about 10° west of Spica. Several parts of the spring sky adjacent to this region—particularly in Leo and Leo Minor—contain outlying concentrations of galaxies.

The significance of the spring group of galaxies, and the reason that the southern autumn constellations (though also off the Milky Way) are comparatively galaxy-poor, is explained in the last chapter of this book. Also in that chapter are described and discussed most of the surprisingly large number of galaxies that are visible in ordinary binoculars. A few stragglers that don't conveniently fit in any of the larger galaxy groups will be found under their respective constellations. They are for the most part faint, small, and difficult to see in binoculars; so before trying to find them, you should first observe several relatively easy galaxies, such as M31 in Andromeda, M33 in Triangulum, and M81 and M82 in Ursa Major.

The orientation of the Milky Way as observed from mid-northern latitudes in the early evenings of mid-spring is very interesting. During April the autumn Milky Way constellations—Cepheus, Cassiopeia, and Perseus—are strung together over the northern horizon; the farther south your latitude, the nearer the horizon they will be. Because the central line of the Milky Way—the galactic equator—describes a great circle on the celestial sphere, the autumn Milky Way will be above your northern horizon by the same distance that the far southern Milky Way (Carina, Crux, and southern Centaurus) lies below your southern horizon. If you go as far south as latitude 27°30′ north (approximately that of Tampa and Corpus Christi) you'll find that the entire Milky Way will encircle the horizon—considerably dimmed by atmospheric absorption, of course. The autumn Milky Way constellations will lie to the north, those of summer will be rising in the east, the far southern Milky Way will be on the southern horizon, and the winter Milky Way groups are setting in the west. Your horizon marks the galactic equator and straight overhead at the zenith will be the north galactic pole, about 4° due east of the Coma star cluster. If you live close to latitude 27°30′, go outside around 11 p.m. local standard time in late April and see for yourself.

4.1   The Hydra Family of Constellations

Cancer, the Crab, Map 5.

Cancer follows the winter constellations so closely that it is well up in the sky for observation in the early evenings of February. It is the faintest constellation of all in the zodiac. Its brightest star, Beta (β), is only magnitude 3.8 and its constellation-pattern is an untidy jumble of 4th- and 5th-magnitude stars. The body of the Crab is marked by the nearly square quadrilateral of Gamma (γ), Delta (δ), Theta (ϑ), and Eta (η); these enclose the Praesepe star cluster. The creature's legs extend from this central figure southeast to Alpha (α) and Kappa (κ), southwest to Beta, and north to Iota (ι).

Though the constellation lies well out of the Milky Way, the two best objects in Cancer for binoculars or telescopes are open clusters.

Praesepe or the Beehive, M44, Map 5. M44 was one of the handful of fuzzy celestial objects called by the Greeks νεφελοειδήσ (*nepheloeides*), "cloudy spots," and by the Romans *nebulae*, "clouds." The earliest extant reference to M44 is in the astro-poem *Phainomena*, which was written during the early 3rd century B.C. by the Greek poet Aratos, but based upon a prose description of the constellations a century older. Aratos called M44 Φατνε (*Phatne*), "the Manger," which in Latin is Praesepe. The stars just northeast and southeast of M44, Gamma and Delta Cancri, were known to ancient astronomers as the *Aselli*, or "the asses," feeding at the Manger. The origin of M44's other popular name, the Beehive, is unknown. It probably dates only from the early 19th century.

To the unaided eye, M44 usually appears as a north-south elongated patch of dim haze, but in binoculars it resolves into a swarm of stars ("beehive" isn't an inappropriate description of the cluster's binocular appearance), including a dozen bright 6th- and 7th-magnitude objects. M44 is not well concentrated, but in the center and on the north edge of the group are three attractive binocular doubles, each pair involving stars of about equal brightness. Because it is so large (about 80′ in diameter), this is an object well-suited to the wide fields of binoculars. However, M44 is actually at its best at about 40x in a 6- or 8-inch telescope. You won't get all the cluster in the field of view, but the extra aperture makes many of the fainter members visible and brings out the colors of its brightest stars (four are orange and the rest are snow-white or cream-white).

M44 is estimated to lie about 525 light-years away, making it the fifth nearest open cluster to the solar system. Its true diameter is about 13 light-years. From middle northern latitudes during the spring, six of the seven nearest open clusters are simultaneously visible: the Ursa Major Moving Cluster (78 light-years away), the Hyades (150), the Coma Star Cluster (260), the Pleiades (410), Praesepe (525), and the Alpha Persei Cluster (570). The one below the horizon is IC 2391, a loose binocular group centered on the magnitude 3.6 star Omicron Velorum in the far southern Milky Way. IC 2391 is about the same distance as M44.

The bright star population of M44 is very much like that of the Hyades in spectral type and size: its brightest member is an A6 giant (the Hyades' brightest star is an A7 giant), it has four K0 III yellow giants (the Hyades also has four yellow giants), and the rest of M44's brighter stars (like the Hyades') are almost all mid- to late-A subgiants. This remarkable similarity might not be entirely coincidence, for M44 is traveling through the Galaxy with the same speed and direction as the Hyades. At the very least, this indicates both clusters probably formed at about the same time (700 million years ago) from the same cloud of interstellar matter, the original space motion of which is still preserved in the common space motion of the two clusters. Whether or not M44 and the Hyades used to be a gravitationally-connected "double cluster" is more doubtful, especially since at present they are over 450 light-years apart.

Open cluster M67. The open cluster M67 is easily found almost 2° due west of Alpha (α) Cancri. In binoculars it appears as a fairly small, elongated disk of haze, about 12′ across its longer dimension and oriented southwest to northeast. When examined carefully in 10x50s, the cluster's disk can be seen to be coarse and mottled from partial resolution. Just outside the northeast end of the cluster is an 8th-magnitude star, and on the southeast edge can be glimpsed a faint 10th-magnitude object. The first is not a true cluster member; but the second is the cluster's lucida, a blue-white B9 star with an absolute magnitude of about +0.5.

M67 is around 2,500 light-years away. That distance, plus the fact that it is almost 30° away from the galactic equator, means that the cluster must lie about 1,500 light-years away from the plane of our Galaxy. This is unusual, since most open clusters lie near the galactic equator within a few hundred light-years of the galactic plane. (M44 might appear to be even farther from the galactic equator than M67; but because M44 is much closer to us than M67, its true distance from the plane of the Galaxy is actually considerably less.)

The reason for M67's nonconformity is that it is a very old open cluster. Because open clusters form from the great clouds of interstellar gas and dust that strongly concentrate along the plane of the Galaxy, young clusters like NGC 2362 in Canis Major and the Rosette cluster (NGC 2244) in Monoceros lie very near the galactic plane. However, as a cluster orbits the Galactic Center it encounters other open clusters and globular clusters, and passes through or near massive clouds of interstellar matter, and its orbit becomes perturbed out of the galactic plane. Since such encounters are fairly infrequent and the effect of any one encounter is usually not too dramatic, only the oldest open clusters have orbits that take them appreciably above or below the galactic plane. M67 is several billion years old and therefore has had plenty of time to work itself out of the galactic disk.

Hydra, the Water Snake, Maps 5 and 6.

Hydra extends for over 100° across the southern part of the spring sky, its head lying directly south of Cancer and its tail ending below Libra, seven hours of right ascension to the east. Because Procyon is only 15° west of its head and Scorpius 10° east of its tail-tip, Hydra forms something of a link between the winter and the summer constellations. It is the largest of the 88 constellations; within its boundaries, as drawn by modern astronomers, lies an area of 1303 square degrees.

Hydra is a very ancient constellation, going back to the Sumerians of southern Mesopotamia, who called it *Mush*, "the Serpent." Contrary to the assertions of R.H. Allen and virtually every other writer on the history of the constellations, there is absolutely *no* reason to connect Hydra (or Draco or Serpens) with the Babylonian goddess Tiamat, the adversary of the hero-god Marduk in the so-called "Babylonian Epic of Creation." Tiamat, though the goddess of the salt-waters of the sea, is nowhere in the Epic of Creation or in any other Babylonian literature affirmed to be serpentine. However, the Mesopotamian celestial Serpent represented by the star pattern of Hydra was indeed involved in a conflict with a Mesopotamian god. This is proven by a scene carved on two surviving early 1st millennium Assyrian cylinder seals, in which a god is shown running along the back of a serpent whose form—the long extended body, the strange forepaws, and the sharply upraised horned head—precisely matches the constellation-figure of the celestial Snake as it appears on a late Mesopotamian astronomical drawing. This battle between the celestial Serpent and a hero-god is obviously the source of the Greek myth of Hercules and Hydra. (See the section on Hercules for another Mesopotamian representation of a serpent vs. hero-god battle.)

Because Hydra is so long, its head is sinking into the horizon haze in the west by the time its tail has risen

Figure 4–1. *Top Drawing (from W.H. Ward's Seal Cylinders of Western Asia) of the seal impression of a Neo-Assyrian (early 1st millenium B.C.) cylinder seal in the British Museum. A god holding lightning bolts and carrying a quiver of arrows on each shoulder runs along the back of a horned dragon with forepaws. Two other figures, apparently assistants to the god, stand on the dragon's tail. Above the dragon's snout is a crescent moon. Above and between the god's assistants is an 8-pointed star. Both the crescent and the star are common fill-motifs on Mesopotamian cylinder seal designs and by themselves do not necessarily indicate that a scene is astronomical in character. However, the dragon's appearance is exactly the same as that of the Mesopotamian celestial Serpent, the Greek Hydra, as it was drawn on a later tablet. (See below.)*

Bottom illustration shows Leo striding on the back of the celestial Serpent as drawn on a late Mesopotamian astronomical tablet. (Journal of the American Oriental Society Vol. 98.4. [1978], p. 370, fig. 7. The original drawing is on a 3rd cent B.C. clay tablet found at Uruk, the Biblical Erech, and now in the Staatliche Museen, Berlin.) Next to each figure is its original Sumerian name in cuneiform: mul Ur-gu-la ("Constellation of the Lion") and mul Mush ("Constellation of the Snake"). The star figure toward which they face is labelled dingir ("god") Pa-me-gar, one of the many Sumero-Babylonian titles for the planet Jupiter. The dragon here, as the dragon on the Neo-Assyrian seal design above, has horns, forepaws, and a long snout, and is shown with a long, straight body and sharply upraised neck and head—identical to the actual star pattern of Hydra. Notice that the drawing shows the Lion and Serpent facing to the left rather than to the right, as we see them in the sky. It is tempting to suppose that the drawing was made from a Mesopotamian celestial globe, for on a globe the constellations do indeed face the opposite direction from which they are seen to face in the sky (because on a globe the constellations are viewed from "outside" the celestial sphere rather than from "inside," as on the earth's surface).

very high in the southeast. Therefore, it is advisable to study Hydra in two parts, the region from the head to south of Crater during the early evenings of March and the stretch from there to the tail-tip during the early evenings of May. (If you want to study all of Hydra in one night, do it in March. The western part of the constellation culminates in the early evenings and the tail after midnight.) The idea, of course, is simply to observe the objects in Hydra when they are on or near the meridian and therefore as high above the horizon haze as possible. However, you shouldn't neglect the fun of tracing all of Hydra, star-by-star, at one time, even though the head and the tail-tip will both be fairly low. The best time is when Crater is on the meridian, which occurs around 11 p.m. local standard time in April.

Like other off-Milky Way constellations, Hydra is not rich in objects. However, scattered along it are two interesting asterisms, two beautifully colored stars, a bright long-period variable, an open cluster, a planetary nebula, and a galaxy. The galaxy, M83, is one of the easiest for binoculars; it is discussed in the last part of this book and in the section on NGC 6946 in Cepheus. The other Hydra objects are described below in their west-to-east order through the constellation.

Open cluster M48, Map 5. About 12° southwest of the Head of Hydra in the outer fringes of the Milky Way is the 30′ diameter open cluster M48. This cluster resolves well in binoculars, appearing as a rather rich, slightly condensed gathering of over a dozen 9th- and 10th-magnitude stars—the brightest, a magnitude 8.8 object near the cluster center. There are at least 50 cluster members down to the 13th magnitude.

Because its integrated apparent magnitude is 5.2, M48 can be seen with the unaided eye on dark, moonless nights as a fuzzy 5th-magnitude "star." It is not, however, an easy object to find because it lies in a relatively star-poor region. The best way to get to it is from the Head of Hydra. Go about 8° southwest to the 1° long line of three stars, magnitude 4.0 C Hydra flanked by magnitude 5.5 1 and 2 Hydrae, and then scan a farther 3½° to the southwest. You will notice that M48 forms an approximately equilateral triangle with C Hydra and magnitude 4.4 Zeta (ζ) Monocerotis.

Since M48 is about 1,700 light-years away, it has a true diameter of approximately 15 light-years and a luminosity of almost 2,000 Suns. The absolute magnitude of the cluster's white A2 lucida is around +0.2. Because M48's brightest stars are yellow giants and white main sequence objects, it has a bright star population similar in type and age (700 million years) to the Hyades.

The Head of Hydra, Map 5. The Head of Hydra is the conspicuous asterism formed by Delta (δ), Sigma (σ), Eta (η), Rho (ρ), and Epsilon (ϵ) Hydrae plus Zeta (ζ) Hydrae just to the east. It is 5° across and just fits in the field of 10x extra wide-angle binoculars. To the unaided eye, the head of Hydra looks so bright and concentrated that you might assume it to be a sparse but nearby open cluster. However, its stars are all at different distances from us. The brightest star in the asterism is Zeta, a magnitude 3.1 K0 II–III giant with a distance of 220 light-years, an absolute magnitude of −1.1, and a pale orange color. Contrast Zeta with the pale yellow of the magnitude 3.4 Epsilon, a multiple star

system with a G0 III primary and a distance of around 140 light-years.

Alpha (α), Alphard, Map 5. Alphard is Arabic for "The Solitary One." It's a most appropriate name, for there isn't a single star brighter than 3rd magnitude within 20° of Alphard. In fact, at magnitude 2.0 Alphard is the brightest star after Regulus in the huge region of the sky bounded by the Big Dipper on the north; Castor, Pollux, and Procyon on the west; Vela and Centaurus on the south; and Spica and Arcturus to the east. There are actually quite a few 3rd-magnitude stars in that region of the sky, but the only 2nd-magnitude ones are Alphard, Algieba (Gamma [γ] Leonis), and Denebola (Beta [β] Leonis).

Alphard has a K3–4 III spectrum and a beautiful chrome-orange color in binoculars. It is about 95 light-years away and therefore its absolute magnitude is −0.3, a luminosity of 110 Suns.

Planetary nebula NGC 3242, Map 5. Except for such exotic things as supernova remnants and quasars, planetary nebulae are perhaps the most difficult type of object for binoculars. The problem is that the vast majority of planetary nebulae have very small angular diameters. Of the fourteen planetaries of magnitude 9.0 and brighter, only three reveal disks—all the rest are less than 2′ across and consequently look like stars, even in the higher powers of zoom binoculars.

NGC 3242, magnitude 7.8 and 40″ in diameter, is one of the easier of the stellar-appearing planetaries to find, for it is located in a region sparse in field stars and therefore not lost in a clutter. It lies about 1.8° almost due south of the 4th-magnitude Mu (μ) Hydrae, with a 7th-magnitude star just few minutes to its east. At least 10x is necessary to get the planetary out of the glare of its 7th-magnitude neighbor.

The distances of planetary nebulae are not known with much certainty. NGC 3242 is perhaps between 3,000 and 4,000 light-years away, but this estimate is little more than an educated guess. In 8-inch telescopes at high power, NGC 3242 shows a double shell structure: a bright oval inner disk measuring 26″ × 16″ is enclosed within a faint and nearly circular haze about 40″ in diameter. This double shell is probably the result of two distinct ejections of material from the planetary's central star.

Variable star U Hydrae, Map 5. U Hydrae, located about 4° northwest of Nu (ν), is the brightest of the "carbon stars," red-giant variables which have atmospheres rich in carbon molecules. The range of U Hydrae is between magnitudes 4.7 and 6.2, slightly brighter than the more famous Y Canum Venaticorum ("La Superba"), which varies from 4.8 to 6.4. Like many other carbon stars, U Hydrae's variations are irregular.

Carbon stars are the most intensely colored stars in the sky. The poppy red of U Hydrae can be discerned in 50mm glasses even when the star is near minimum brightness. For contrast, compare U's color with the pale orange of the magnitude 3.1 Nu. The remarkable red color of carbon stars is the consequence of the abundance in their atmosphere of the tri-carbon molecule, which is an efficient absorber of blue and violet light.

If it is correct that carbon stars reach an absolute magnitude of around −2 when at maximum, then U Hydrae might be as little as 700 light-years away. In any case, because U Hydrae and Y Canum are the two brightest carbon stars, they are almost certainly also the two nearest.

Variable star R Hydrae, Map 6. R Hydrae, located about 2 1/2° due east of Gamma (γ) Hydrae, was the third of the pulsating long-period variables (LVPs) to be discovered. (The first two were Omicron [o] Ceti and Chi [χ] Cygni.) Because its light ranges between magnitudes 4.0 and 10.0 (though on occasion it exceeds these extremes), R Hydrae is one of the few LVPs that can be followed with binoculars throughout its cycle.

Like all other LVPs, R Hydrae is a red giant. When near maximum its ruddy color is visible in binoculars—for contrast, look at the orange tone of Gamma, which is a magnitude 3.02 G8 III star. R Hydrae is believed to be about 325 light-years away, so it and Chi Cygni (also about 325 light-years distant) are the nearest of the LVPs after Omicron Ceti. R Hydrae ranges in absolute magnitude from about +5 at minimum to around −1 at maximum. At minimum, therefore, it is only about as bright as the Sun, but at maximum it reaches a luminosity some 200 times greater.

Now, as we noted in the section on Omicron Ceti, all LVPs are somewhat erratic in their variations. The neat values for maxima, minima, and periods given in tables are just averages; on any given cycle an LVP might miss its "normal" maximum or minimum by a magnitude or more either way, and the cycle might be a month too long or short. However, over the long run a high maximum will be balanced by a low maximum and a long cycle balanced by a short.

But R Hydrae is different. Since its discovery in 1704, its average period has been decreasing. At first the star's full cycle took about 500 days, but by the early years of this century the period was down to 425 days and is now only 388. Apparently, R Hydrae is undergoing internal changes and practically evolving right before our eyes.

Astronomers think LVPs are solar-mass stars at a very unstable point in their life-history. Their structure is complex: they probably have an inert core of nearly pure carbon surrounded by a shell in which helium is being nucleosynthesized into carbon. Above the

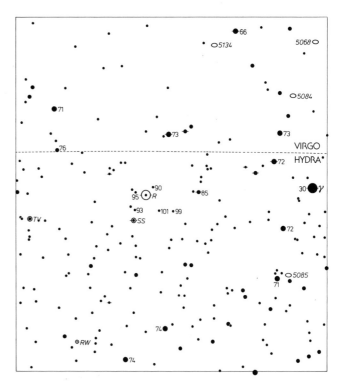

Identification Chart 4–1. R Hydrae. *Stars shown are to 9.5 magnitude. Scale is 18mm per degree. Star brightnesses are to the nearest tenth magnitude, with periods omitted.*

layer of helium is a second energy-producing shell in which the hydrogen of the star's outer envelope is being consumed to form helium. It is the conflict between these two energy-producing shells which probably drives the pulsations and light-variations of long-period, semi-regular, and irregular red variable stars. Small changes in the internal balance of such stars (for example, the distance between the two energy-producing shells) no doubt can induce rapid external changes. R Centauri and R Aquilae are two other LVPs whose periods have decreased since their discovery.

Asterism "Noctua," the Night Owl, Map 6. Perched on the tail-tip of Hydra (58, 59, and 60 Hydrae) is the almost-forgotten asterism of Noctua, the Night Owl, a small group invented around 1800. Noctua lies 3° due west of the 3rd-magnitude Sigma (σ) Librae and consists of the remarkably evenly curved 2° long arc of 54, 55, 56, and 57 Hydrae plus 4 Librae. Like the head of Hydra, Noctua is not a true physical cluster but merely a chance alignment of stars. In binoculars, however, it is a very delicate and attractive little group.

Antlia, the Air Pump, and Sextans, the Sextant, Map 5.

Antlia and Sextans, which are on the opposite sides of the Kappa (κ), Lambda (λ), Mu (μ), and Nu (ν) region of Hydra, are recent inventions. Antlia (originally Antlia Pneumatica, the Air Pump) was the creation of the 18th-century observer of the far southern skies, Abbé Nicolas Louis de Lacaille, who filled unoccupied corners of the southern celestial sphere with an astonishing array of scientific and technical apparatus. Sextans, the Sextant, was formed by Johannes Hevelius, who did for the northern sky in the 17th century what Lacaille was to do for the southern in the 18th—except that Hevelius usually crowded animals instead of scientific instruments into the vacant spaces.

There is no star in either Antlia or Sextans brighter than magnitude 4.4, and for most of the United States, Antlia culminates so near the horizon that binoculars are necessary even to identify its handful of Greeklettered stars. However, Antlia and Sextans each have a galaxy that can be seen with the higher powers of 50mm zoom binoculars. About 8° due east of Alpha (α) Antliae, and $3^{1}/_{2}$° due south of Theta (ϑ) is the spiral galaxy NGC 2997, a fairly difficult low-surface-brightness object. It is decently large, about 6' in diameter, but its integrated apparent magnitude is only 11.0. NGC 2997 has a low surface brightness and a roughly circular shape because it is a loosely-wound Sc spiral galaxy that we are viewing face-on. (M101 in Ursa Major is the same type of object but larger and brighter.) Because of its declination (−31°) and its low surface brightness, NGC 2997 can be seen in binoculars only from the far southern United States—and even there it is an object for a trained eye observing on a very transparent night from a dark-sky site. NGC 2997 is about 45 million light-years distant and is the brightest and largest (in both apparent and absolute terms) of a thin group of galaxies sprinkled over the area extending from about 10° to 25° south of Alphard.

The galaxy in Sextans, NGC 3115, is just north of the midpoint of the line joining Gamma (γ) and Epsilon (ϵ) Sextantis. It is the opposite of NGC 2997, for it is small (4' × 1') and bright (magnitude 9.8) and therefore has high surface brightness. Unless the magnification is high enough, NGC 3115 will merely look like a star. At 15x in even 40mm glasses it can be seen as a tiny, bright sliver of light oriented southwest to northeast. A well-trained eye can glimpse the galaxy's orientation in 10x50's. NGC 3115 is a saucer-shaped S0 object viewed nearly edge-on. It is about 22 million light-years away from us. Though only one-third the size of our Galaxy (its diameter is about 30,000 light-years), NGC 3115 is so compact that its total luminosity is nearly the same— its integrated absolute magnitude is about $-19^{1}/_{2}$ and our Galaxy's is near −20. This high degree of concentration is typical of elliptical and S0 galaxies, in which the stars are compacted together like they are in globular clusters or the central hubs of spiral galaxies.

Crater, the Cup, Map 5, and Corvus, the Crow, Maps 5 and 6.

Antlia and Sextans may be recent inventions, but Crater and Corvus are ancient. In classical mythology they were both associated with Apollo, the god of poetry, music, and prophecy. Greek and Roman writers described Crater and Corvus as sitting on the coils of Hydra and frequently linked the three constellations together in stories involving a Cup, a Raven, and a Serpent. The Greek celestial Raven is very old, for the Sumerians of Mesopotamia had also called this star pattern *Uga*, "the Raven." Therefore, Corvus' history can be traced back at least to the 3rd millennium B.C.

The extreme antiquity of Corvus is no doubt in part due to its conspicuous constellation-pattern, a crude rhombus formed by four 3rd-magnitude stars. This pattern, of course, bears no obvious resemblance to a raven. (A more realistic name was given it by the nomads of Arabia: *al-Hiba*, "the Tent." The outline of Corvus really does have the side-view outline of the black goat's-hair tents still used by the Bedouin.) Crater, on the other hand, actually does look like a thick-stemmed goblet. The bowl is formed by Theta (ϑ), Epsilon (ϵ), Delta (δ), Gamma (γ), Zeta (ζ), and Eta (η), and the base by Alpha (α) and Beta (β) Crateris with Nu (ν) and Chi (χ) Hydrae. Perhaps because it consists only of 4th- and 5th-magnitude stars (except for Nu Hydrae), Crater is a delicate and beautiful constellation. It is harder to make out than Corvus, but very nice when you do trace it.

Unfortunately, Crater has absolutely nothing to look at with binoculars, and it offers even moderately large telescopes only a few routine double stars and a handful of faint distant galaxies. Corvus is a little better, for the colors of the 3rd-magnitude stars at the corners of its quadrilateral contrast nicely with each other:

Table 4–1 The Stars of the Corvus Quadrilateral					
Star	App Mag	Dist (l-y)	Mag	Spectrum	Color
Gamma	2.59	450	−3.1	B8 III	Silver-blue
Beta	2.66	310	−2.3	G5 II	Orange-yellow
Epsilon	3.00	140	−0.2	K3 III	Reddish-orange
Delta A	2.97	124	+0.1	B9.5 V	Silver-blue
B	8.3			+5.4	dK2

To me, Delta has always seemed colorless in binoculars despite its brightness. (Larger instruments, however, bring out its color.) Its 8.3-magnitude companion is 24" from it in a position angle of 214° (south-southwest) and can be seen at about 50x in small telescopes.

4.2 The Galaxy-Rich Constellations of Spring

Leo, the Lion, Map 5.

Leo, the Lion, is one of the oldest of constellations. It was known as lion to all the ancient Mesopotamian cultures and was probably originally formed before 4000 B.C.—perhaps as part of a four-constellation zodiac consisting of a Bull (our Taurus), a Lion, a Scorpion (our Scorpius), and a Fish (Piscis Austrinus). The evidence for this is indirect (cuneiform writing was not developed until nearly 3000 B.C.), but it is fairly good. Early Mesopotamian art repeatedly shows figures of bulls, lions, and scorpions obviously meant as astronomical symbols because on or around them are star images. A recurrent motif is a lion-bull combat with the bull getting the worst of it. This probably is a pictorial allusion to the fact that because Leo is 90° east of Taurus in the zodiac, Taurus sets as Leo crosses the meridian.

Leo's constellation-pattern is conspicuous, but it only marginally resembles a lion: the mane and shoulders are marked by the asterism called the Sickle—Alpha (α), Eta (η), Gamma (γ), Zeta (ζ), Mu (μ), and Epsilon (ϵ)—and the hindquarters by the Beta (β), Delta (δ), Theta (ϑ) triangle. The prehistoric Mesopotamians possibly saw a lion in these stars because during the summer, when the stars of Leo were rising in the morning twilight, the heat would drive the lions (common in the Middle East during ancient times) out of the deserts and hills down to the cool and shady river-flats along the Tigris and Euphrates, a yearly event that could not have been anticipated with pleasure.

Other than Regulus, Leo's best objects for binoculars are galaxies. The M66 and M96 galaxy groups and the galaxies in them visible with binoculars are discussed in the last chapter of this book. Two other binocular galaxies in Leo are discussed below.

Alpha (α) Leonis, Regulus, Map 5.

"Regulus" is Latin for "Little King" and is the name given to this star by Copernicus. Copernicus, however, was merely following the 2nd-century A.D. Greek astronomer Ptolemy, in whose *Syntaxis* (the leading book on astronomy for over a millennium) our Regulus is called *Basiliskos*, or "King." But Ptolemy's name ultimately derives from Mesopotamian astronomy, because the star was called *Kakkab Sarru* by the Babylonians and *Mul Lugal* by the Sumerians, both of which meant "the Star of the King." The association of Regulus with kingship was no doubt because it marked the summer solstice, when the king of heaven—the Sun—was at his highest.

At magnitude 1.4 Regulus is the 21st brightest star in the sky, the second faintest (after Epsilon [ϵ] Canis Majoris) of the 1st-magnitude stars. Because it has a B7 V spectrum and therefore a hot surface temperature, its color in binoculars is a fine silver-blue. For contrast look at the orange of Gamma (γ) Leonis (Algieba), a magnitude 2.0 star located about 9° to the north-northeast in the Sickle and a fine double (with K0 III and G7 III components) at about 100x in small telescopes. Regulus is approximately 85 light-years away, so its absolute magnitude is 0.7, a luminosity of about 160 Suns.

Regulus is a binary star, its companion a dK1 object located 177″ away in position angle 307° (west-northwest). Despite the extremely wide separation, this is not exactly an easy double for binoculars, even using the higher powers of zooms. The companion star is only of magnitude 7.9 and is therefore some 400 times fainter than the primary. The absolute magnitude of the secondary is +5.8, which means that it is only 40% as luminous as the Sun.

Galaxy NGC 2903, Map 5.

NGC 2903 is an Sb/Sc spiral galaxy in extreme east-central Leo. It is fairly bright (magnitude 9.7) and quite large, measuring $11' \times 5'$. Therefore, it isn't at all difficult, as galaxies go, for binoculars with at least 10x. It is easy to find. Exactly 1° due south of magnitude 4.5 Lambda (λ) Leonis are two 7th-magnitude stars about 40′ apart on an east-west line. NGC 2903 lies 20′ due south of the eastern of the two stars.

In 10x50s, the galaxy appears as a small, somewhat bloated streak oriented north-south and pointing directly at the 7th-magnitude star north of it. In 7x50s, unfortunately, the galaxy is merely stellar. NGC 2903 is about 21 million light-years away, so its true diameter is about 75,000 light-years and its integrated absolute magnitude is around −19.5—both values slightly less than our own Galaxy's. It is one of the handful of nearby galaxies that do not seem to belong to any galaxy group.

Galaxy NGC 3521, Map 5.

A much more difficult galaxy is NGC 3521 in extreme southern Leo. This object is only slightly fainter (magnitude 10.2) and smaller ($6' \times 4'$) than NGC 2903. But most of its light comes from a stellar core, so in 10x50 binoculars it appears as a 10th-magnitude "star" embedded in a tiny, very tenuous halo that fades into the sky-background. Averted vision, a transparent night, and a dark-sky observing site are necessary to see this galaxy.

The different binocular appearances of NGC 2903 and NGC 3521 reflect their true structural differences. NGC 2903 appears as a moderately high surface brightness patch because it is loosely-wound with a small central hub and relatively bright inner spiral arms. It is elongated simply because the plane of its spiral arms is tilted to our line of sight. On the other hand, NGC 3521, type Sb, looks like a star embedded in a small hazy glow because it has a bright central hub and relatively faint spiral arms. NGC 3521 illustrates the fact that a significant amount of the light of Sb-type spirals comes from their central hubs. The binocular appearance of the Andromeda Galaxy, another Sb object, confirms this, since the bright circular disk of M31's central hub is much brighter than the faint glow of its tilted spiral plane. NGC 3521 is some 23 million light-years away, exactly ten times the distance of M31.

Because NGC 3521 lies in the star-poor wing of Leo just north of Crater, it is no easier to find than it is to see. Start at Phi (φ) Leonis and go 4° west-northwest to the 5th-magnitude 61 Leo. From 61 Leo go 2° almost due north to a 1° wide north-south pair of 6th-magnitude stars. NGC 3521 is about 1/2° due east of the northern of the two 6th-magnitude stars (62 Leo), with an 8th-magnitude star just to the galaxy's east. The directions sound easier than they actually are, for this region of Leo is cluttered with 5th- and 6th-magnitude stars, and even Phi Leonis isn't all that easy to identify.

Ursa Major, the Greater Bear Maps 1, 2, and 5.

Unquestionably, the most famous of all star patterns is the Big Dipper, which marks the hindquarters and the surrealistic tail of the Great Bear. R.H. Allen's *Star Names: Their Lore and Meaning* spends 18 pages detailing the various titles which Ursa Major (as a whole) and the Big Dipper (in particular) have had in different nations through the millennia.

Because Allen wrote in the 1890's, when Babylonian and Sumerian studies were still new disciplines, he did not know that in Sumeria the Big Dipper was called *Margidda*, "the Wagon." This name was given to it possibly either because the Dipper stars trace arcs that center on the north celestial pole during the course of a night, thus suggesting the rotation of a wheel around an axle, or because the squarish shape of the Dipper's bowl resembles the side view of a wagon. The three stars in the Dipper's handle may well have been considered draught oxen, just as they were thousands of years later in medieval Europe.

The Greeks followed the Mesopotamians, calling the Dipper stars *Hamaxa*, "the Wagon." However, the Greeks also knew the Dipper as part of their larger group *Arctos*, "the Bear." Even in Homer's *Iliad* and *Odyssey*, the stars of the Big Dipper are interchangeably called the Wagon and the Bear. It was certainly natural that a creature of the north, the bear (which in ancient times was very common in the forests of Europe and Asia), should have been placed in the sky as a north circumpolar constellation—but when and where this first occurred is unknown.

Figure 4–2. *Drawing (from W.H. Ward's* Seal Cylinders of Western Asia) *of the impression of an Akkadian (c. 2300 B.C.) cylinder seal now in the Pierpont Morgan Library. It shows the air-god Enlil in the celestial Chariot pulled by the celestial Winged Dragon. His consort Ninlil stands on the dragon's back, grasping lightning bolts in each hand. To the left, a worshipper or priest pours a libation over a stepped altar.*

A Mesopotamian cylinder seal design that probably shows our Big Dipper as a celestial Wagon is illustrated here. It dates from the Akkadian period (*c.* 2300 B.C.). The high-arced pole was characteristic of Sumerian wagons and nicely resembles the arc of the stars in the Big Dipper's handle. The god in the chariot holding the whip is probably Enlil, to whom the stars in the northern sky were sacred. (Assyrian texts assign the northern stars to Enlil, the equatorial stars to the sky-god Anu, and the southern stars to the water-god Enki.) His consort Ninlil stands on the back of the winged lion-eagle that pulls the chariot. These two deities were weather-gods (their names mean "Lord of the Air" and "Lady of the Air," respectively) so we find Ninlil holding lightning bolts in each hand. The winged lion-eagle is very probably the forerunner of the Greek constellation Draco: in the sky the Big Dipper and Draco are so oriented that if the former is thought of as a Wagon, the latter could easily be imagined as the animal pulling it. In Greek mythology the sorceress Medea rode in a chariot drawn by winged dragons, and according to Ovid (*Metamorphoses VII*, 282-3) her chariot was in the sky as our Big Dipper.

The pre-Islamic Arabs knew the bowl of the Dipper as *Al-Na'ash*, "The Bier." The stars of the Dipper's handle were *Al-Banat al-Na'ash*—literally, "The Daughters of the Bier" (in other words "the Mourners"). However, after the Arab conquests in North Africa and southern Europe during the 7th and 8th centuries A.D. had brought them into contact with the remnants of Greek and Roman civilization, the Arabian astronomers in Cairo, Damascus, and Baghdad adopted the Western constellations. Most of our star names come from these Arabian astronomers, who in their star catalogues would refer to a star by its position in the Greek constellation figure. This is well illustrated by the names of the stars in the Big Dipper shown in Table 4–2.

The name for Epsilon, Alioth, shows what has happened to many star names as they passed from scholar to scholar and were translated and transliterated from one language to another over the course of a millennium, often with little real understanding. The case of Mizar is less extreme. Apparently, some scholar called Beta Ursae "Mizar" instead of "Merak" and later another scholar by accident or design transferred the new name to Zeta. "Alcor" is the result of someone's ignorantly combining the Arabic definite article "al" with the Persian name for the star.

Ursa Major has an area of 1,280 square degrees, making it the third largest of the 88 constellations (Hydra and Virgo are larger). The Bear covers most of that area. Its hindquarters and tail are formed by the Big Dipper. A back thigh is marked by Chi (χ), and one back leg goes through Psi (ψ). The two back feet are the Nu (ν)+ Xi (ξ) and Lambda (λ)+ Mu (μ) pairs. The Bear's snout is at Omicron (o) and its shoulders are marked by 23 and Upsilon (υ), with a front leg going from Upsilon through Phi (φ) and Theta (ϑ) to a front foot at Iota (ι)+ Kappa (κ). (The Bear's fourth foot originally was the Alpha [α]-38 Lyncis pair.) The data on the stars of the Big Dipper is shown in Table 4–3.

Mizar and Alcor (Zeta [ζ] and 80) are the famous naked-eye double at the bend in the handle of the Dipper. They appear to form a true physical binary, though Alcor is at least a quarter-light-year away from Mizar. In addition, Alcor and both of the visual components of Mizar are spectroscopic binaries, and there is evidence for a seventh member in this vast and complicated multiple system.

The colors of the Dipper stars are splendid in binoculars. Dubhe (Alpha) is a strong, deep orange—its color resembles the cadmium-barium orange used by painters. Merak, Phecda, Megrez, Alioth, and Mizar are all blue-white—not merely bluish, but in fact having a good strong tint of blue. Alkaid is silver-blue.

The Ursa Major Moving Cluster, Map 1. The fact that five of the seven Dipper stars are all similar objects that lie at comparable distances from us is no accident. Even before 1900 astronomers had discovered that the five central Dipper stars have about the same radial velocity (speed directly toward or away from us) and proper motion (speed and direction perpendicular to the line of sight). This means that these stars are moving through space together and that they are therefore a physically—though not gravitationally—connected group. (They are too scattered to be bound gravitationally.)

The group was named the Ursa Major Moving Cluster and is the nearest star cluster to the solar system, its

Table 4–2 The Names of the Big Dipper Stars		
Star	Present Name	Original Name, with Translation
α	Dubhe (DUBB-hee)	Al-Zahr al-Dubb al-Akbar, "the Back of the Greater Bear"
β	Merak (MEH-rak)	Al-Maraqq al-Dubb al-Akbar, "the Loins of the Greater Bear"
γ	Phecda (FEK-da)	Al-Fakhidh al-Dubb al-Akbar, "the Thigh of the Greater Bear"
δ	Megrez (MEE-grez)	Al-Maghriz al-Dubb al-Akbar, "the Root of the Tail of the Greater Bear"
ϵ	Alioth (AL-ee-oth)	A corrupted form of Al-Ayyuq, "the Goat," the Bedouin name for Alpha Aurigae
ζ	Mizar (MY-zar)	Al-Mi'zar, "the Waist-cloth"
80	Alcor (AL-cor)	Al (Arabic for "the") + Khwar (Persian for "the Friendless One")
η	Alkaid (AL-kade or Benetnasch (be-net-NASH)	Al-Ka'id al-Banat al-Na'ash, "the Leader of the Daughters of the Bier" (i.e., Chief Mourner)

Table 4–3 The Stars of the Big Dipper					
Star	Spectrum	Mag	Dis (l-y)	Abs Mag	Comments
α	K0 II–III	1.81 var?	105	−0.7	very close binary
β	A1 V	2.37	62	+0.7	
γ	A0 V	2.44	80	+0.5	
δ	A3 V	3.30	65	+1.9	
ϵ	A0p	1.79 ± 0.01	70	+0.1	Alpha CVn var
ζ	A2 V, A7 Vp	2.40, 3.96	88	+0.3	wide binary
80	A5 V	4.02	88	+1.9	
η	B3 V	1.87	140	−1.3	

Table 4–4 Other Naked-Eye UMa Cluster Members				
Star	Mag	Dist (l-y)	Abs Mag	Spectrum
21 Leo Minoris	4.5	95	+2.2	A7 V
78 Ursae Majoris	4.9	80	+3.0	F2 V
37 Ursae Majoris	5.2	90	+2.9	F1 V
HD 111456	5.7	90	+3.7	F5 V

center being only about 78 light-years away. The members are moving with a true space velocity of about 9 miles per second in a direction slightly south of due east toward eastern Sagittarius.

As clusters go, the Ursa Major Moving Cluster is not only very scattered but also very sparse, with only 17 recognized members. In addition to the five Dipper stars plus Alcor, the naked-eye UMa Cluster members are shown in Table 4–4. HD 111456 is located about 4° almost due north of Alioth. The other four certain members of the cluster are all G and K yellow dwarf stars. There are also two possible members, one of which is Alpha (α) Coronae Borealis. The UMa Cluster occupies an ellipsoidal volume of space about 30 light-years long and 18 light-years wide.

Scattered around the sky are at least 100 stars which have approximately the same space motion as the Ursa Major Moving Cluster. This Ursa Major Stream is similar to the cluster in that the stream (if it indeed is a true physical entity) and the cluster have comparable ages—on the order of 150 million years. Some of the brightest of the Ursa Major Stream stars (with their spectra and distances) are shown in Table 4–5.

Table 4–5 Brightest Ursa Major Stream Stars		
Name	Spectra	l-y
Sirius	A1 V	8.7
Beta (β) Aurigae	A2 IV-V	90
Delta (δ) Leonis	A4 V	80
Alpha (α) Ophiuchi	A5 III	60
Beta (β) Serpentis	A2 IV	95
Delta (δ) Velorum	A0 V	75

Other nearby open clusters are known to have associated streams. The Taurus Stream of stars that have space motions similar to the Hyades include Capella, Alpha CVn, Delta Cas, Lambda UMa, and Xi Cep.

Galaxies in Ursa Major. M81, M82, and M101, the brightest galaxies in Ursa Major, are discussed in the seventh chapter of this book. There are two other Ursa Major galaxies visible in 10x50 or 50mm zoom binoculars:

NGC 2841, Map 1. Just south of the midpoint of the line joining Theta (ϑ) and 15 UMa is the 6th-magnitude star 37 Lyncis. The Sb spiral galaxy NGC 2841 is located only about $1/3°$ southeast of 37Lyncis. Also, just a few minutes due east of both 37 Lyn and NGC 2841 are faint stars, with the result that 37 Lyn, the two faint stars, and NGC 2841 form a long thin parallelogram, the galaxy occupying the figure's southwest corner.

NGC 2841 is fairly small ($6' \times 2'$) and faint (magnitude 10.3), but its surface brightness is quite good. It appears as a small patch, distinctly elongated north-south, with a rather bright core produced by the glow of its central hub and inner spiral arms. This galaxy's image is very tiny, however, so it is easily mistaken for a star. You'll need averted vision to notice its elongation and the bright core. NGC 2841 is the brightest of a group of half a dozen spiral galaxies scattered over the region west from Theta UMa into central Lynx. The group is about 40 million light-years away.

NGC 3184, Map 1. About $40'$ due west of Mu (μ) UMa and just $10'$ southeast of a 7th-magnitude star is NGC 3184. This galaxy is very faint (magnitude 10.5), quite small ($5.5'$ in diameter), and, because it is a loose-armed Sc spiral that we are viewing face-on, it has an

extremely low surface brightness. In 10x50s the galaxy appears merely as a tiny smudge of haze. It is altogether invisible in 7x50 glasses—7x doesn't magnify the galaxy-disk sufficiently to heighten contrast with its sky background. NGC 3184 is about 31 million light-years distant, so it is one of the more remote galaxies visible in 10x50 binoculars that displays a disk. Its true diameter is over 50,000 light-years and its integrated absolute magnitude is -19.5, only half a magnitude fainter than our own Galaxy's.

After looking at NGC 3184, note the fine color contrast between Lambda and Mu UMa, which conveniently fit in the same binocular field. Lambda is blue-white A2 IV star of magnitude 3.5 and Mu is a magnitude 3.1 object with an M0 III spectrum and a fine reddish-orange color. Their distances are 100 and 170 light-years, respectively.

Canes Venatici, the Hunting Dogs, Maps 1, 2, and 6.

Canes Venatici occupies the area south of the handle of the Big Dipper, east of the Great Bear's hind leg and north of Coma Berenices. Despite the presence of a 3rd-magnitude star (Alpha [α] at magnitude 2.9), this region of the sky was left unformed by the ancients. The idea of providing Boötes with hunting dogs to assist his harassment of the Bear originated early in the 16th century. There are two dogs, and the late 17th-century astronomer Johannes Hevelius named the one marked by Alpha and Beta (β) Canum Venaticorum *Chara*, "Dear," and the other formed by the fine little asterism of 5th- and 6th-magnitude 18, 19, 20, and 23 CVn, *Asterion*, "Starry." Many maps now label Alpha as Cor Caroli, "Charles' Heart" (the title given it by Edmond Halley in 1725) and usually award the name Asterion to Beta alone.

A glance at *Sky Atlas 2000.0* or the *Atlas of the Heavens* shows that the galaxy-richness of the region in and around the Big Dipper's bowl extends southwest through the western half of Canes Venatici. Four of the Canes Venatici galaxies—M51, M63, M94, and NGC 4258—are good binocular objects and are discussed in the last part of this book. But Canes Venatici has two other interesting things to look for:

Y Canum Venaticorum, "La Superba," Map 6. Y CVn, located in a star-poor area 4° northwest of Beta CVn, is one of the two brightest carbon stars. (Carbon stars are intensely red variables with spectra that show them to be rich in carbon. For more on these stars, see the sections on 19 Piscium and U Hydrae.) Y Canum's brightness range is about 4.8 to 6.3 magnitude, so it is slightly fainter than U Hydrae, which varies between magnitudes 4.7 and 6.2. U Hydrae's brightness changes are irregular, but Y Canum goes from minimum to maximum and back to minimum in a period that averages 160 days. Because carbon stars are thought to reach an absolute magnitude of around -2 when they are at maximum light, Y Canum is possibly between 700 and 800 light-years away.

Like other carbon stars Y Canum has a beautiful poppy-red color. Carbon stars are truly red, not the reddish-orange of the so-called "red" giants of spectral type M, such as Betelgeuse and Antares. Its color makes Y Canum easy to spot when it is near maximum, but even when the star is near minimum its color is not difficult to see in 50mm glasses. Though Alpha CVn is rather far from Y ($7\frac{1}{2}°$ to the south-southeast) it is the nearest blue star to use for contrast. Alpha Canum is a blue-white object with a B9.5p spectrum. The "p" stands for "peculiar," which in the case of Alpha Canum's spectrum refers to (1) the presence of absorption lines of such rare metals as chromium and strontium and (2) the periodic changes in these and other lines induced by the star's abnormally strong magnetic field. Alpha Canum is the prototype star of the so-called magnetic spectrum variables.

Globular cluster M3, Map 6. If you've been reading the chapters of this book consecutively, you'll realize that it has been a very long time since we mentioned any globular cluster. After M15 in Pegasus, only NGC 1851 in Columba has been discussed. The skies of late autumn, winter, and early spring are very poor in globular clusters. In the huge region of the celestial sphere between 22 hours right ascension on the west and 12 hours on the east and north of declination $-15°$, Harlow Shapley's catalogue of 93 globular clusters lists only NGC 2419 in Lynx.

The reason for this is that our Galaxy's family of 200+ globular clusters is strongly concentrated toward the center of our Galaxy, which is toward Sagittarius. Therefore, over 40 percent of our Galaxy's globular clusters can be found in Sagittarius, Scorpius, and Ophiuchus; very few are in the opposite region of the sky— Gemini, Taurus, Auriga, Orion, and adjoining constellations.

As a class, globular clusters are so distant (the nearest, M4 in Scorpius, lies about 6,200 light-years away) that they are not very interesting in binoculars. M3 is a better than average specimen, however, appearing as small, bright, glowing disk several minutes of arc across embedded in a large, faint halo best seen with averted vision. The photographic diameter of the cluster is about $18'$ and its integrated apparent magnitude is 6.4. Since M3 lies about 38,000 light-years away, its true diameter is around 220 light-years and its integrated absolute magnitude is about -8.9, corresponding to a total luminosity of over 300,000 Suns. The notable thing about this cluster is that 189 variable stars (183 which are short-period RR Lyrae variables) have been identified in it, more than in any other globular.

M3 is in a very star-poor region and therefore is not particularly easy to find. It lies about 12° north-northwest of Arcturus, just under half-way from Arcturus to Alpha Canum. Probably the best way to get to it is from Coma Berenices. The three stars Alpha, Beta, and Gamma Comae form a large right-angled figure, each leg about 10° long, with Beta Comae at the northeast corner. M3 lies about 6° due east of Beta, approximately the width of field of most binoculars. Put Beta Comae on the western edge of your field and M3 should be near, or just outside, the eastern edge.

Coma Berenices, Berenice's Hair, Map 6.

Despite being such an obvious and beautiful group to the unaided eye, the Coma Star Cluster doesn't seem to have become a separate constellation until late Greek times. The early Greeks perhaps thought of it as the tuft of hair at the end of the Lion's tail—and that, in any case, is what the medieval Arab astronomers called it after they adopted the Greeks' Lion. (The Bedouin of the Arabian Desert, who knew nothing of the Greek constellations but nevertheless had a large zodiacal Lion, also called the Coma cluster "the Tuft.") The first surviving reference to Coma Berenices is by the Greek astronomer Geminos of Rhodes, who wrote an astronomical guide-book in the early 1st century B.C.

The Berenice whose hair is in the sky was an actual person, wife of King Ptolemy III of Egypt (who reigned from 246 to 221 B.C.). The story associating Berenice with the Coma Star Cluster was first related by her contemporary, the Greek poet Callimachus, and survives in a translation by the 1st-century B.C. Roman poet Catullus:

When Ptolemy went on a military expedition to Syria (so the story goes), Berenice vowed her famed amber hair to Aphrodite, the goddess of love, against the king's safe return. In due time Aphrodite came through with her side of the bargain and Berenice had her hair shorn and placed in the goddess' temple at Zephyrium. But the hair disappeared. Conon, the court astronomer (and apparently adept at flattery), told the king and queen that Berenice's offering had been so pleasing to Aphrodite that the goddess had placed it in the heavens. Conon then showed the royal couple the Coma Star Cluster. This story has none of the supernatural machinery of the other Greek star legends and is perhaps therefore the most human and touching of them all. Unfortunately, soon after her husband's death in 221 B.C., the next king—her own son—had Berenice murdered.

The Coma Star Cluster is 250 light-years away, making it the third nearest cluster to the solar system (after the Ursa Major Moving Cluster and the Hyades). Like the Hyades and Pleiades, it is much more attractive in the wide fields of binoculars than in telescopes, which simply magnify it out of all sense of "clusterness." In fact, the Coma Star Cluster is so large (5° across) and so scattered that it is better in 7x than in 10x glasses. 17 Comae is a very attractive double in binoculars, the components being 145″ apart (in position angle 251°) and therefore easy even at 7x. Several of the bright stars in the field—Gamma, 7, and 18 Comae—are not true cluster members. On the other hand, 31 Comae, though 5° east-northeast of the cluster center, has about the same proper motion and radial velocity as the cluster and therefore is probably a true cluster star.

The Coma Star Cluster is in a peculiar location for an object of its type. The vast majority of open clusters lie in the Milky Way, but the Coma cluster is virtually *at* the north galactic pole (which is located less than 1/2° due south of 31 Comae), as far from the galactic equator as it can get. Now, in the case of M67 in Cancer, which is almost 30° from the galactic equator, its large distance off the galactic equator is a result of the cluster's great age (3.2 billion years. See the section on M67 in the discussion on Cancer.). M67 is about 2500 light-years from us and is therefore 1500 light-years from the galactic plane. The Coma cluster, however, is only 250 light-years away, well within the galactic disc. The cluster has a radial velocity of zero and is therefore neither approaching nor receding from us.

Another peculiar thing about the Coma Star Cluster is that it completely lacks any of the low-mass, low-luminosity K and M orange and red dwarfs that are usually the most abundant type of stars in clusters (and indeed in the Galaxy as a whole). Since we have to assume that the Coma cluster started out with them, the problem is to explain where they went. The answer probably lies in the looseness of the cluster. The Coma cluster has a diameter of about 22 light-years but contains less than 100 solar masses, which works out to a density of only one-sixtieth solar mass per cubic light-year, a mere eight times the mass density of the scattering of stars in the solar neighborhood. Indeed, calculations show that the Coma cluster is right on the limit where the mutual gravitational attraction of the cluster members just counterbalances the disrupting gravitational pull of other material in our Galaxy. In short, the Coma cluster is on the verge of falling apart.

Given such a low density, the velocity which low-mass members need to escape from the cluster is quite modest, and such stars will be easily accelerated to escape velocity as the cluster passes near other clusters

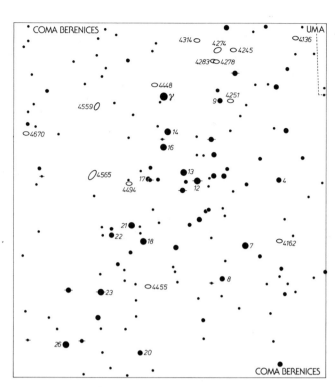

Identification Chart 4–2. Membership for the Coma Star Cluster. *The faintest stars plotted are of magnitude 8.5, and the chart scale is 9mm (=0.35 inch) per degree. North is to the top, east to the left.*

Table 4–6 The Brighter Stars in Coma					
Star	Spectra	Mag	Star	Spectra	Mag
12 Comae	G0 III+A3 V	4.81	17 Comae	A0p	5.29
13	A3 V	5.18	21	A2p	5.46
14	F0p	4.95	22	A4 V	6.29
16	A4 V	5.00	31	G0 IIIp	4.94

or through massive clouds of interstellar matter. Since the Coma Star Cluster is about 500 million years old, and is probably on its third circuit about the Galaxy's center, there has been plenty of time for the low-mass stars to "evaporate" from it. No doubt the Coma cluster will eventually disintegrate completely, its stars joining the rabble of field stars of our Galaxy's disk. Virtually all stars are formed in such clusters or associations and then gradually disperse into the galactic disk as their clusters fall apart. Since our Sun is over five billion years old, the cluster or association of which it originally was a part disintegrated long ago.

Globular cluster M53, Map 6. The constellation of Coma Berenices is of course much larger than the cluster itself, and it contains more than the cluster for binocular observers. About 1° northeast of Alpha (α) Comae is the globular cluster M53. (4.2-magnitude Alpha Comae can be found about halfway between Arcturus and Denebola.) Because it has an integrated apparent magnitude of 7.7 and a photographic diameter of 14′,

M53 appears both fainter and more compact than M3 in Canes Venatici. On a casual look in binoculars it might even seem stellar, but with averted vision you'll see that the tiny disk of a core is surrounded by a fairly extensive but very tenuous halo of light. This halo is, of course, simply the unresolved outer region of the globular.

M53 is quite distant, about 65,000 light-years away. Its true diameter is over 250 light-years and its integrated absolute magnitude is around −8.8. Both values are near those for M3. Since both globulars also show about the same degree of concentration toward their centers, structurally M3 and M53 are nearly twins, and their different binocular appearance is merely a matter of distance.

The Coma-Virgo Supercluster, Map 6. Through Coma Berenices runs a "milky way" of galaxies that begins in and around the bowl of the Big Dipper and extends south-southeast as far as the region just west of Spica. The richest part of this great flattened cloud of galaxies centers on the midpoint of the line joining Beta (β) Leonis (Denebola) and Epsilon (ϵ) Virginis (Vindemiatrix). It covers an area in southwestern Coma and northwestern Virgo about 10° in diameter. This concentration of galaxies, known as the "Realm of the Galaxies," is the core of the huge supergalaxy or supercluster that includes all the galaxies in the region. Our own Milky Way Galaxy is an outlying member of this supercluster. These things are explained more fully in the last chapter of this book.

Most of the galaxies in Coma Berenices that are visible in binoculars are also discussed in the last part of this book. One additional object deserves mention, though it is extremely difficult to see even in 10x50s. NGC 4565, located 1.7° almost due east of 17 Comae, is an almost perfect edge-on spiral galaxy 15′ long and only 1′ wide. Even a 6-inch telescope is sufficient to glimpse the lane of obscuring matter that bisects the image of NGC 4565 along its length—a dust lane like the Great Rift in the Milky Way from Cygnus down to Centaurus. Nothing of this dark lane is visible even in giant binoculars, but NGC 4565 itself can be seen with averted vision in 10x50s or 50mm zooms as needle-like streak oriented approximately northwest-southeast (it points toward Gamma [γ] Comae). However, you must know exactly where to look for the galaxy.

NGC 4565 is about 31 million light-years distant. Thus, it is about 135,000 light-years long, and its integrated apparent magnitude of 10.7 implies an integrated absolute magnitude of −19.2. It appears to be an Sb-type spiral, but with the edge-on orientation it's difficult to be sure. NGC 4565 is a member of the large, rich Coma I galaxy cloud that includes a dozen galaxies of magnitudes 10.5 to 12.0 in north-central and northwest Coma Berenices.

Virgo, the Maiden, Map 6.

Virgo is the second largest constellation. Its 1294½ square degrees is only 8½ square degrees less than Hydra's 1303. Virgo's pattern is sprawling and rather conspicuous, although apart from Spica it contains no particularly bright stars. The western half of the constellation is a large, leaning "Y" formed by Alpha (α), Theta (ϑ), Gamma (γ), Eta (η), Beta (β), Nu (ν), Delta (δ), and Epsilon (ϵ). Its eastern portion is a rough rectangle including Alpha again plus Kappa (κ), Iota (ι), Mu (μ), Zeta (ζ), Tau (τ), and 109.

Needless to say, there's very little resemblance to a human figure in this. However, the Arabs had an even more bizarre conception for the right-angled asterism made by Epsilon, Delta, Gamma, Eta, and Beta Virginis: *Al-Zawiyat al-Awwa*, "the Corner of the Barking Dog." This dog was imagined to be barking at Leo, and the name—after several centuries of distortion by European scholastics—became the present titles for Eta and Beta, Zaniah and Zavijava.

The name for Epsilon Virginis, Vindemiatrix, is Latin for "the (female) Grape-Gatherer." Earlier, the Greeks had called this star *Protrygetor,* "the Forerunner of the Vintage." The reason for these names was that during the first millennium B.C., Epsilon Virginis rose just before the Sun at the beginning of the grape harvest. The Greeks and Romans seem to have had very few names for individual stars. The earliest Greek writer on astronomy whose work has survived, Aratus (early 3rd century B.C.), used only the following star names in his astro-poem *Phaenomena*: Sirius, Procyon, Arcturus, Protrygetor, Aix ("the She-goat," our Capella), and the individual names for the seven Pleiades. In later ancient Greek writings we find Antares, Canopus, Stachys ("Ear of Corn": in Latin, *Spica*), and Basiliskos ("Regal," for our Alpha Leonis). The vast majority of star names now used we owe to the medieval Arabian astronomers who, as a rule, named a star simply after its position in a constellation figure—for instance *Fum al-Hut* (our Fomalhaut), "the Mouth of the Fish."

The "ear of corn" which Spica represents is wheat (not the maize of the New World, which was unknown to the Romans, Greeks, and Mesopotamians). This conception of the star is very old, for the Sumerians called it *Absin*, which also means "Ear of Corn." Spica is a fine silver-blue star that is a spectroscopic binary consisting of a B1 V primary and a B7 companion. Photoelectric measurements have shown that the star is slightly variable, its magnitude range from 0.97 to 1.04. The variation is caused by grazing eclipses of the primary by the cooler, less luminous secondary and by slight pulsations in the primary. Spica's distance is about 275 light-years, so its total absolute magnitude is −3.7, giving a combined luminosity of about 1,740 Suns.

Galaxies in Virgo, Map 6. Other than Spica, the only things in Virgo for the binocular observer are galaxies—and there are a good many visible here in 10x50 or 50mm zoom binoculars. A discussion of the Coma-Virgo Cluster of galaxies and a chart for finding the brightest of them is in Chapter 7 of this book. However, two bright Virgo galaxies lie somewhat away from the core of the Coma-Virgo Cluster (centered between Epsilon Virginis and Beta Leonis). Consequently, they are discussed here: M61 and M104.

On the southern fringes of the Coma-Virgo Cluster, just over 1° north-northeast of 5th-magnitude 16 Virginis, lies the magnitude 10.2, face-on Sbc spiral galaxy **M61**. Like other type Sbc and Sc galaxies turned face on to us, M61 has a very low surface brightness. (The low surface brightness of these types of galaxies reflects their loosely-wound structure.) M61 is only about 6′ in diameter, so 10x50s are the minimum instrument for seeing this galaxy. It will appear as a tiny disk of pale haze, best observed with averted vision. Assuming M61 to be at about the same distance as the core of the Coma-Virgo Cluster (50 million light-years), its true diameter is at least 70,000 light-years and its integrated absolute magnitude is nearly −21, a half-magnitude greater than our own Galaxy's.

In southwestern Virgo about 11½° due west of Spica is **M104**, the so-called Sombrero Galaxy. This object lies in a region that lacks bright stars and therefore is not easy to find. It forms an approximately equilateral triangle with Psi (ψ) and Chi (χ) Virginis, about 4° southwest of Psi and 4° due south of Chi. M104 is not very easy to see even in 10x50 binoculars. It is quite bright (magnitude 8.7) but is so small (6′ × 2′) that it appears merely as a tiny east-west sliver of light. The higher powers of zoom binoculars are very useful on this object—in fact, it is easier at 15x in 40mm zooms than in 10x50s. In 7x glasses, however, the galaxy looks merely stellar.

M104 seems to be slightly farther than the core of the Coma-Virgo Cluster 25° to the north. It is estimated to be about 60 million light-years away and is therefore one of the most distant objects visible in binoculars. M104 is an Sa galaxy oriented only 6° from the edge-on position, which explains why its image is so elongated. A 10-inch telescope shows the lane of dust that makes this galaxy so photogenic and which gives rise to its nickname. M104 is one of the most luminous galaxies known, having an integrated absolute magnitude of an astonishing −22½, a luminosity of nearly 100 billion Suns! Therefore, M104 is about ten times more luminous than our Galaxy.

4.3   The Late Spring Constellations

Boötes, the Herdsman, Maps 2 and 6.

The familiar kite-shape of Boötes (formed by Alpha (α), Epsilon (ε), Delta (δ), Beta (β), Gamma (γ), and the Rho-Sigma (ρ–σ) pair) is one of the landmarks of the northern sky. It is a conspicuous sight as it rises in the northeast during the early evenings of March and sets in the northwest just after twilight in October. Because the northern half of the kite-figure has a more easterly right ascension than the southern part, and therefore "lags behind" as the constellation moves from east to west across the sky, Boötes appears to rise on its side but sets upright as viewed from north-central latitudes. The constellation-figure of Boötes shows almost perfect bilateral symmetry: the shoulders are marked by Gamma and Delta (with the head at Beta), the ends of the waist are the Rho-Sigma and Epsilon-W pairs, and the knees are the Eta-Tau-Upsilon and Omicron-Pi-Zeta trios, which flank Arcturus to the west-southwest and east-southeast, respectively.

The earliest surviving mention of Boötes is in the *Odyssey*. R.H. Allen in *Star Names* says that the name was derived either from an ancient Greek word meaning "clamorous" (in the sense of loud and shouting), or from the two ancient Greek words for "ox" and "to drive." Both possible derivations refer to how Boötes seems to pursue the Big Dipper across the sky during the course of a night. Because the early Greeks knew the Big Dipper as both a Bear and a Wagon, the stars that followed it suggested to them either a bear-keeper goading his bear or a wagoneer shouting at his oxen. It's possible that the early Greeks got the idea of Boötes as wagon-driver from Mesopotamia, for it was from there that they inherited the conception of the Big Dipper as a wagon.

Alpha (α) Boötis, Arcturus, Map 6. Arcturus is so much brighter than any of the other stars in Boötes that probably most of the names for the constellation were originally meant for Arcturus alone. The word "Arcturus" is the transliterated form of the Greek word for "Bear-guard." Its earliest known appearance is in the poet Hesiod (8th century B.C.). The Sumerian name for our Arcturus was *Shupa*, "Hand-staff."

Arcturus, with an apparent magnitude of −0.1, is the fourth brightest star in the sky and the brightest north of the celestial equator. Though Arcturus has a K2III spectrum, it is not as deeply hued as other K-type stars (such as Aldebaran and Pollux). Nevertheless, its golden-white color is attractive in binoculars. Arcturus is 36 light-years distant and therefore has an absolute magnitude of −0.3, which corresponds to a luminosity of 115 Suns.

Most stars in the solar neighborhood have a veloc-

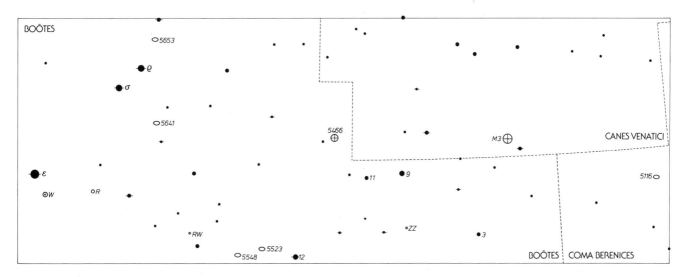

Identification Chart 4–3. NGC 5466. *The faintest stars shown are of magnitude 7.5, and the chart scale is 9mm (0.35 inch) per degree. North is to the top, east to the left.*

ity with respect to the Sun of only around 20 miles per second. But Arcturus' space velocity is 75 mps; therefore, it is one of the appropriately named *high-velocity stars.* Arcturus has a radial velocity of only three mps (approaching), so the largest part of its space velocity is perpendicular to the line of sight. In fact, Arcturus is moving so fast perpendicular to the line of sight that its apparent motion on the celestial sphere is 2.28″ of arc per year (to the south-southwest). Thus, in 6,000 years Arcturus has moved nearly 4°—almost the distance between the pointer stars of the Big Dipper. Among stars of magnitude 3.5 or brighter, Arcturus' proper motion is exceeded only by Alpha Centauri's 3.68″—but because Alpha Centauri is the nearest star to the solar system, only 4.3 light-years away, it would be expected to have a large proper motion anyway.

Arcturus and other high-velocity stars have spectra deficient in absorption lines of elements heavier than helium (called "metals" by astrophysicists). The stars of the vast majority of globular clusters are also "metal-poor." High-velocity and globular cluster stars seem to have been formed early in the history of our Galaxy, before interstellar matter became enriched by heavy elements nucleosynthesized in massive stars and subsequently blasted out into the interstellar medium when such stars went supernova. Arcturus is therefore a very old star, much older even than our 5 billion old (but "metal-rich") Sun.

The speed of high-velocity stars is actually something of an illusion. Our Sun is embedded in the spiral disk of the Galaxy some 30,000 light-years out from the center, around which it is orbiting. Now, the Sun and other stars in the solar neighborhood each have individ-

ual velocities, but their average orbital velocity around the Galactic Center is some 150 miles per second. Thus, it is not Arcturus and the other high-velocity stars that are moving so quickly through the Galaxy, but our own Sun. In fact, Arcturus is receding from the direction of our orbital motion through the Galaxy, and consequently we are passing it, not the other way around.

Arcturus and other high-velocity stars are members of what is called the *halo population* of our Galaxy— very old red and yellow giants and dwarfs distributed in a great sphere with a radius of probably 100,000 light-years (twice the radius of the Galaxy's spiral disk). The density of the halo population is greatest near the Galactic Center (the galactic hub is composed of halo population stars) and falls off very rapidly farther out. This is why, apart from the central hubs, the halo component of spiral galaxies does not usually show up on photographs. M104 in Virgo is an exception, since its central hub is embedded in a very distinct glow of halo stars. Globular clusters and RR Lyrae variables of periods of half a day or more are also part of the galactic halo.

Globular cluster NGC 5466, Map 6. Globular cluster NGC 5466, located about 10° north-northwest of Arcturus, is a low surface brightness object with a visual diameter of about 9′ but an integrated apparent magnitude of only 9.4. It is not particularly easy to spot even in 10x50 binoculars, appearing merely as a vaguely mottled smudge of indistinct haze. Contrast NGC 5466 with the bright globular M3, only about 4½° due west in Canes Venatici. With an apparent diameter of 12′, M3 is only little larger than NGC 5466 but its greater concentration and richness is evidenced by the bright, disk-like core of its binocular image.

M3 and NGC 5466 will just fit in the same field of wide-angle 10x binoculars, and M3 provides the best way to get to its fainter neighbor. Put M3 near the extreme western edge of your binocular's field of view and NGC 5466 will be toward the eastern edge of the field. NGC 5466 can also be found by first locating the 5th-magnitude star 9 Boötis, almost exactly halfway between Epsilon Boötis and Beta Comae Berenices. The cluster is only 2° east-northeast of 9 Boö.

NGC 5466 is about 53,000 light-years distant and therefore has a true diameter of at least 140 light-years and an integrated absolute magnitude of −6.7. As globulars go, it is average in size but well below average in luminosity.

Table 4–7 Double Stars in Boötes Resolvable in Binoculars						
Stars	Mag	Spectra	Abs Mag	Dist (l-y)	Sep (″)	PA (°)
δ A B	3.5 7.8	G8 III G0 V	+0.3 +4.6	140	105	79
μ A B	4.3 6.5	F0 IV dG1	+2.0 +4.2	95	108	171

Double Stars in Boötes. The best double in Boötes is Epsilon, which consists of a yellow-orange K1 II–III star of magnitude 2.5 with a bluish A2 companion of magnitude 5.0. Unfortunately, the pair is only 3″ apart and requires at least 150x to split. There are, however, two doubles in Boötes that can be resolved in 10x binoculars, and both are common proper motion pairs and therefore true physical binaries, though their orbital periods must be tens of thousands of years.

Because the magnitude difference of the Mu pair is less than that of the Delta pair, it is much easier to resolve and can be split with only 7x glasses. The fainter component of the Mu pair is a close telescopic binary consisting of two stars of nearly the same brightness and spectral type, so Mu is actually a triple system.

Libra, the Scale, Map 6.

Our word "zodiac" is derived from the Greek *Kyklos Zodiakos*, or "Circle of Animals." On the face of it Libra, an inanimate object, would therefore be a misfit. However, the early Greeks did not have a zodiacal Scale; they knew the stars of our Libra as the Claws of the Scorpion. (Nevertheless, there were always 12 animals in the zodiac, for Pisces figured as two fish.) The Scale apparently did not enter the Greek zodiac until the 2nd century B.C. Aratos in the early 3rd century had mentioned only the Claws, but 150 years later Hipparchos (who compiled the first star catalog) referred to the stars of Libra both as the Claws and as the Scale.

However, with this change a Scale was merely reappearing in the zodiac, for before the Greeks the Babylonians had a zodiacal Scale (their *Zibanitum*) preceding the Scorpion. This is too much to be a mere coincidence. It seems improbable that the Greek astronomers would unwittingly invent the same name for the same stars as their Mesopotamian predecessors, who had been very un-Greek in temperament, outlook on life, and approach to nature. It therefore seems likely that Hipparchos simply drew on an oral tradition that alluded to a Scale preceding the Scorpion in the zodiac.

Libra represents the classical balance-beam type of scale with Alpha (α) and Beta (β) marking the ends of the balance beam and Gamma (γ) and Iota (ι) the scale trays. Some star charts show the southern scale tray at Sigma (σ) Librae, but that is incorrect; Sigma Librae was originally catalogued as Gamma Scorpii by Bayer early in the 17th century, and only later was the star appropriated by Libra, with the result that Scorpius no longer has a Gamma.

Libra is rather sparse in interesting objects for binoculars or telescopes. Like the other off-Milky Way constellations of the late spring and the summer, it is poor in galaxies. For binoculars, the constellation has two attractively colored stars, a double star, and a loose globular cluster.

Beta (β) and Sigma (σ) Librae, Map 6. Two of Libra's three 3rd-magnitude stars have colors well worth observing in binoculars. Beta Librae is a magnitude 2.6 B8 III star that many early observers like Webb and Olcott reported to be green. Today, however, the star is usually described as blue or bluish; to me it appears silver-blue. The discrepancy is probably due simply to the fact that the refractor telescopes commonly in use then did not correct for chromatic aberration as well as more modern instruments. The only stars that appear unambiguously greenish are B- or A-type secondaries in doubles where the primary is a K- or M-star, and in such situations the green is largely due to color contrast.

The other conspicuously colored star in Libra is Sigma, an M4 III object of apparent magnitude 3.3 and a dull ruddy-orange tone. Compare Sigma to magnitude 3.8 Upsilon (υ) Librae 7° to the east-southeast, a chrome orange K5 star. The colors of Sigma and Upsilon Librae offer a beautiful contrast in binoculars to the silver-blues of Beta, Delta, and Pi (π) Scorpii just to the east.

Beta Librae is 100 light-years away and has an absolute magnitude of −0.1, which corresponds to a luminosity of about 145 Suns. Sigma is about 60 light-years distant and has an absolute magnitude of +2.0, a luminosity of 13 Suns.

Double star Alpha (α) Librae, Map 6. This star is one of the easiest doubles to split—even a small opera-glass can resolve it. The primary is a magnitude 2.8 A3 star; the secondary, 231″ distant in position angle 314° (northwest) has a magnitude of 5.2 and an F5 V spectrum. Despite their wide separation, the two stars have the same proper motion (0.13″ per year); therefore, they probably are a true physical binary. The system is about 65 light-years away, so the actual separation of the stars is at least 120 times the average distance between Pluto and the Sun—more if one of the stars is farther from us than the other. The secondary has an absolute magnitude of +3.6 (a luminosity of 3 Suns) and the primary is +1.2 (25 Suns). The primary is also spectroscopic binary, so Alpha Librae is actually a triple system.

Globular cluster NGC 5897, Map 6. The globular cluster NGC 5897, conveniently located just 1.7° southeast of Iota Librae, is a low surface brightness object difficult even for 10x50 binoculars (particularly from the central and northern United States, where it culminates only some 25° above the southern horizon). It is about 8′ in diameter, but its integrated apparent magnitude is only 9.4 and as a consequence appears merely as a faint smudge of haze in binoculars. For an object like this, 10x glasses are preferable to 7x ones because the higher power darkens the sky background and provides contrast for the faint glow of the globular's disk.

The binocular image of NGC 5897 lacks the bright core of such globular clusters as M5 in Serpens Caput and M3 in Canes Venatici. This is because it is a much looser and less populous cluster. Two similar, loose-structured globulars visible in binoculars are M55 in Sagittarius and NGC 5466 in Boötes, both discussed in some detail under their constellations.

NGC 5897 is about 38,000 light-years distant, so its true diameter is over 90 light-years. Its distance suggests that its integrated absolute magnitude is only −6. However, because the cluster lies only 27° off the galactic plane and behind the periphery of the huge dust cloud in which Antares and the other stars in the head and heart of the Scorpion are embedded, it must be significantly dimmed by interstellar absorption. Thus, its true absolute magnitude is possibly as high as −7.2, a luminosity of 61,000 Suns.

The direction and distance of NGC 5897 imply something rather interesting about its location with respect to our Galaxy. The Galactic Center is about 30,000 light-years away in a direction about 4° west-northwest of Gamma Sagittarii. Therefore, the great spherical central hub of our Galaxy, some 10,000 light-years in diameter, would cover much of western Sagittarius, southeastern Ophiuchus, and Scorpius if the heavy interstellar dust clouds in this direction did not block most of it from our view. Consequently, NGC 5897 must lie straight above the hub of the Galaxy.

Any observers in this cluster would have a magnificent close-up, face-on view of our Galaxy and could see right into the star-dense and (apparently) explosive nucleus of the galactic hub.

Centaurus, the Centaur, Maps 6, 9, and 10.

Centaurus is the ninth largest constellation and is very star-rich, having two 1st-magnitude, four 2nd-magnitude, and seven 3rd-magnitude stars. Unfortunately, it lies between declinations −30° and −65°; consequently, much of it is too far south to be observed from middle northern latitudes. The Alpha (α)-Beta (β) Centauri pair can be seen with the unaided eye from Key West, Florida, where it culminates 5° above the horizon about 11.30 p.m. CDT around June 1. But the southernmost bright star in Centaurus, Lambda (λ), culminates only 2½° above Key West's southern horizon (at about 10 p.m. CDT on May 1) and requires binoculars and a very clear night to see.

Centaurus is a Milky Way constellation. The star fields around Lambda and south of Beta are exceptionally brilliant. (Between Lambda and Beta Centauri lie Crux and the Coal Sack.) Unfortunately, the Centaurus Milky Way cannot be observed even from Key West. However, one of the best binocular open clusters in Centaurus is also one of the farthest north: NGC 5460, a loose group 30′ in diameter, has a declination of about −48° (it lies some 2° east-southeast of Zeta [ζ] Centauri) and should be visible in binoculars on dark, transparent nights from Florida, the Gulf Coast, and southern Texas.

Northern Centaurus is outside the Milky Way and this region of the constellation contains one of the nearest galaxy clusters, the intriguing Centaurus Galaxy Group, centered only about 13 million light-years away. The Centaurus Group extends in a 30° long south-to-north chain from NGC 4945, which lies within the northern fringes of the Centaurus Milky Way, up through NGC 5128, NGC 5102, NGC 5253, and M83 in Hydra, ending at NGC 5068 in extreme southern Virgo. The Centaurus Group is discussed in more detail in Chapter 7 of this book. NGC 5128, with an integrated apparent magnitude of 7.2, is the second-brightest galaxy in the southern hemisphere, excluding the Magellanic Clouds. Because its declination (2000) is −43°01′, NGC 5128 culminates high enough to be spotted with binoculars (as a fuzzy disk about 10′ in diameter) from as far north as 35°—roughly the latitude of Chattanooga, Memphis, Albuquerque, and Santa Barbara.

Alpha (α) and Beta (β) Centauri, Map 10. Unfortunately for observers in North America and Europe the most concentrated group of 1st-magnitude stars in the entire sky lies in the extreme southern Milky Way. Both the Alpha-Beta Cen and Alpha-Beta Crucis pairs are separated by only about 4° and therefore fit the same field of view in most binoculars—they are the only 1st-magnitude pairs in the sky that do so.

Alpha and Beta Centauri have a nice color contrast: Alpha is yellowish, Beta is bluish. At magnitude −0.3, Alpha Centauri is the third brightest star in the sky; Beta is the tenth brightest. The Beta double is separated by only 1.3″ and therefore is difficult even in fairly large telescopes. However, the Alpha pair has a highly elongated orbit and the apparent separation between the two stars reached the maximum of 22″ in 1980; in 2000 their separation will still be 15″, the secondary lying to the southwest of the primary (See Table 4–8).

The Alpha Centauri system is the nearest to the Sun. However, the nearest star of the system is not the bright pair, but an 11th-magnitude red dwarf located about 2° to the south-southwest and orbiting them in a period that must be hundreds of thousands of years long. This star, called Proxima (Latin for "nearest") Centauri, has a parallax of 0.762″ and therefore is 4.2 light-years from us. (The parallax of the bright pair is 0.751″, 4.3 light-years.) It is almost a fifth of a light-year from the primary pair, but its physical connection with them is certain because it shares their proper motion (3.68″ per year in PA 281°). See Table 4–9.

Proxima Centauri is a representative of a type of red dwarf variable called a flare star. At unpredictable intervals the star will suddenly brighten by as much as a full magnitude and then fade to normal within a half hour. These flares seem to be identical with the familiar solar flares, which occur on the Sun at sites of intense magnetic fields. A flare does not perceptibly increase the Sun's brilliance, but on a dim red dwarf like Proxima Centauri, less than $1/10,000$ as luminous as the Sun, a flare is a major event. (The flare star UV Ceti once brightened by five magnitudes!)

Globular cluster Omega (ω) Centauri, Maps 6 and 10. The great Omega Centauri cluster (NGC 5139) is, in both apparent and real terms, the largest and brightest of the approximately 200+ globular clusters known to be associated with our Galaxy. Omega Centauri's integrated apparent magnitude is 3.7 and its visual diameter in binoculars exceeds the 30′ apparent diameter of the Moon. Its photographic diameter is twice as great, about 65′. Because globular clusters gradually thin with increasing distance from their centers, it is almost impossible to assign specific diameters to them. A globular's photographic diameter varies with the length of the exposure, and its visual diameter depends upon the size of the telescope used to observe it and on the darkness of the sky at the observing site. But even if we could explore a glob-

Table 4–8 Alpha and Beta Centauri					
Star	Total App Mag	Sep App Mag	Spectra	Dist (l-y)	Abs Mag
Alpha Cen	−0.27			4.34	
A		−0.01	G2 V		+4.4
B		1.40	K4 V		+5.8
Beta Cen	0.63			490	
A		0.7	B1 III		−5.2
B		3.9	?		−2.0

Table 4–9 The Alpha Centauri System						
Comp	Spectrum	App Mag	Abs Mag	Lum (× Sun)	Radius (× Sun)	Mass (× Sun)
A	G2 V	−0.01	+4.4	1.45	1.07	1.10
B	K4 V	1.40	+5.8	0.40	1.22	0.85
C	dM5e	10.7(var)	+15.1	0.00008	0.05	0.1

ular cluster with a starship, we would be hard put to say exactly where it ends and where the general star field in which it is embedded begins.

Because the distance of Omega Centauri is about 15,000 light-years, its 30′ visual diameter corresponds to 130 light-years and its 65′ photographic diameter, to 280 light-years. The cluster's true diameter is probably well over 400 light-years. Its integrated absolute magnitude is −10.4, a luminosity of 1.2 million Suns. A globular of this luminosity contains well over a million stars and at least a million solar masses. (All the mass of a globular cluster lies in its stars, for whatever interstellar gas and dust it originally contained was swept out billions of years ago during its early orbital passes through the Galaxy's central hub.)

The declination (2000) of Omega Centauri is −47°29′, so it culminates about 10° above the horizon (around 11:00 p.m. local mean time in late April and early May) at Savannah, Montgomery, Dallas-Ft. Worth, Phoenix, and San Diego, and can be seen in binoculars as a bright hazy patch from dark-sky sites along the latitude of those cities. Look for it about 4° due west of Zeta (ζ) Centauri. On moonless, transparent nights from the Florida peninsula, the Gulf Coast, and southern Texas, the cluster is actually visible to the unaided eye as a fuzzy 4th-magnitude "star."

Several other globular clusters are visible to the unaided eye. Unfortunately the easiest of them, the second largest and brightest globular in the sky, is even farther south than Omega Centauri. 47 Tucanae (NGC 104) has an apparent magnitude of 4.4, a visual diameter of 25′, but a declination (2000) of −72°05′. Therefore, even at the equator, it never gets as high as 20° above the horizon. 47 Tucanae is 16,000 light-years distant, so its integrated absolute magnitude is around −9.5—a luminosity of 500,000 Suns—and its 44′ photographic diameter corresponds to a true diameter of about 200 light-years. It is of particular interest to astrophysicists because its stars have a greater abundance of elements heavier than helium than the stars of most globular clusters. This implies that 47 Tucanae was formed after the interstellar matter from which stars condense had begun to be enriched by heavy elements nucleosynthesized in stellar interiors and blasted out in supernova explosions.

Centaurus-Lupus Maps, 6, 9, and 10.

The constellations of Centaurus and Lupus are related in a couple of interesting ways. First, they have a mythological connection that probably predates the Greeks and goes back to early Mesopotamia. The Greeks described Centaurus as carrying the "Beast" (it became a Wolf only during the Middle Ages) to Ara the Altar as a sacrifice. This scenario, plus the presence of the ship Argo immediately to the west of Centaurus, reminded at least one 19th-century scholar of the Biblical story of the Flood. And in this region of the sky there is even a celestial representation of the raven Noah sent out after the rain stopped, for our Corvus originally represented a raven.

However, if anybody consciously placed the main figures of the Flood in the sky, it was not the Hebrews, for they did not originate the story but received it from Mesopotamia. According to Genesis 11:31 Abraham came to Palestine from "Ur of the Chaldees," which lay on the southern Euphrates, and he naturally would have brought Mesopotamian myths with him. Indeed, the earliest surviving version of the Flood story (similar to the Biblical version even in detail) is on an early Babylonian fragment dated about 1700 B.C. The fragment is written in Sumerian, which implies the story originated with these people, who had developed a high civilization before 3000 B.C. However, the Sumerians also created many of our constellations, including Centaurus (which they called *En-te-na Mash-lum*), Lupus (which they knew as *Ur-idim*, "the Mad Dog"), and Corvus (their *Uga*, "the Raven"). (It is not known whether or not they had a celestial ship that later became our Argo.) Thus, the Sumerians originated both the Flood story and a number of constellations in the same region of the sky which represent figures that appear in the story. Therefore, it is possible that they consciously placed the main figures of the Flood story in the sky and that the Greek association of Lupus with Centaurus is a survival of Sumerian astro-mythology.

The Scorpio-Centaurus Association

There is, however, more than just a historical connection between Centaurus and Lupus: early this century it was discovered that many of the bright stars in Centaurus, Lupus, Crux, and Scorpius have similar proper motions and radial velocities and therefore are moving through space together. The brightest Scorpio-Centaurus Association stars are plotted on the accompanying chart—pages 102–3. (The total membership of the association is probably in the hundreds.) It will be seen that they are distributed in an elongated area stretching from Crux and Musca on the southwest up to Scorpius on the northeast. The center of the association is about 550 light-years away in a direction between Alpha (α) Lupi and Zeta (ζ) Centauri. There is one red supergiant star in the group, Antares, but almost all the rest of its bright members are hot B0, B1, and B2 giant and main sequence stars.

The Scorpio-Centaurus Association's space velocity with respect to the Sun is about 15 miles per second, and the direction of its motion is toward the southwest. If the directions of motion of the individual stars of the association were extended, the lines would converge at a point near Beta (β) Columbae. Since this is the approximate direction of the solar antapex (the direction from which the Sun and the Solar System are moving), the Sco-Cen Association must be falling behind the Sun. In fact, the association's velocity with respect to the Sun (that is, its velocity measured assuming the Sun to be stationary), 15 miles per second, is very near the velocity by which the Sun exceeds the theoretical speed of revolution of the solar neighborhood around the center of the Galaxy. In other words, the Sco-Cen Association is revolving around the center of our Galaxy at the "correct" orbital velocity for this region of the Galaxy, but it is being passed by the slightly faster Sun.

The Scorpio-Centaurus Association is part of the Local Star Cloud, a sub-unit of the Orion Spiral Arm of our Galaxy. Because the Galactic Center is toward southwestern Sagittarius (about 4° WNW of Gamma [γ] Sagittarii), the Sco-Cen Association must be slightly nearer the Galactic Center than we are—it can be taken to mark the inner edge of the Orion Arm in the solar neighborhood. And because the direction of revolution around the Center of the Galaxy of the solar neighborhood is approximately toward Deneb in Cygnus but the Sco-Cen Association extends about 60° from the direction toward the Galactic Center *back* to Crux, the association must lie somewhat *behind* us. (Though all this can be seen on a star chart, the best way to get this sort of "galactic depth perspective" is from direct observation of the night sky.)

The stars in associations are not gravitationally connected—they are simply too far apart: they move together because they were formed in the same cloud of interstellar matter and they "remember" the motion of their parent cloud. Because associations are

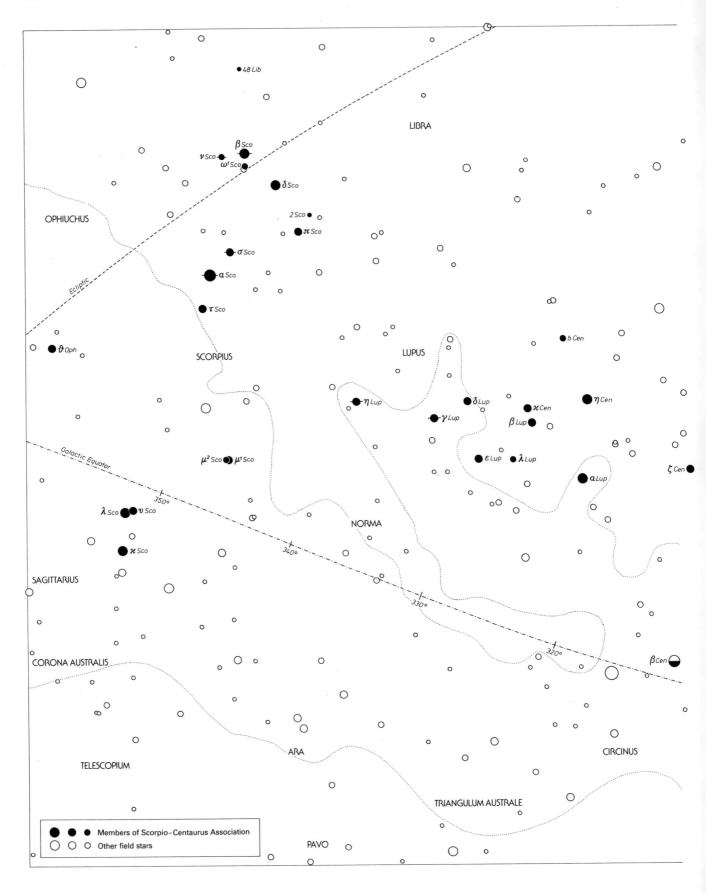

48 Lib

LIBRA

β Sco
ν Sco
ω¹ Sco

OPHIUCHUS

δ Sco

2 Sco
π Sco

σ Sco

α Sco

Ecliptic

τ Sco

ϑ Oph

SCORPIUS

LUPUS

b Cen

η Lup

δ Lup

κ Cen

η Cen

γ Lup

β Lup

Galactic Equator

ε Lup

λ Lup

ζ Cen

μ² Sco   μ¹ Sco

α Lup

350°

λ Sco   ν Sco

NORMA

κ Sco

340°

SAGITTARIUS

330°

320°

CORONA AUSTRALIS

β Cen

ARA

CIRCINUS

TELESCOPIUM

TRIANGULUM AUSTRALE

● ● ● Members of Scorpio - Centaurus Association
○ ○ ○ Other field stars

PAVO

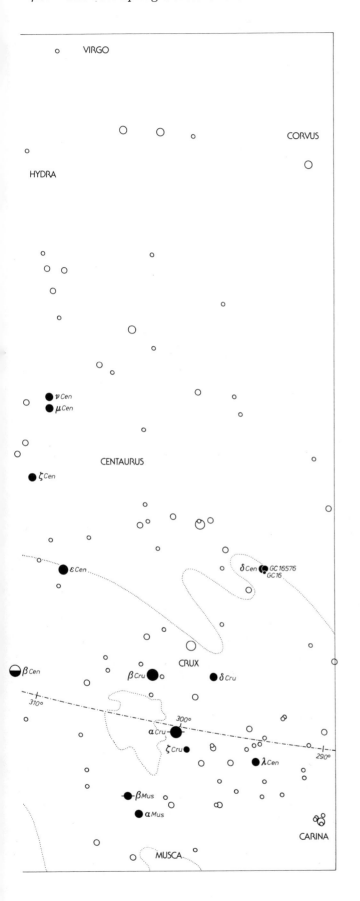

Table 4–10 Brightest Members of the Scorpio-Centaurus Association					
Star	App Mag	Spectrum	Dist (l-y)	Abs Mag	Remarks
α Mus	2.66–2.73	B2 IV–V	430	−2.9	
β Mus	3.06		470	−2.1	close bin
A	3.58	B2.5 V		−1.5	
B	4.10			−1.2	
α Cru A	0.87		510	−5.1	
A₁	1.39	B0.5 IV		−4.6	} 4.4″ PA 115°
A₂	1.86	B1 V		−4.1	
α Cru B	4.90	B3	510	−1.1	90″ PA 202°
β Cru	1.25–1.31	B0.5 III	490	−4.6	β CMa var
δ Cru	2.78–2.84	B2 IV	570	−3.4	
δ Cen	2.56–2.62	B2 IVne	370	−2.7	shell star
GC 16575	6.4	B9	370	+1.1	2.5′ S of δ
GC 16576	4.5	B6	370	−0.8	3.7′ N of δ
ε Cen	2.33(var)	B1 III	570	−3.9	β CMa var
ζ Cen	2.56	B2.5 IV	520	−3.4	spec bin
η Cen	2.33–2.45	B1.5 Vne+A2	390	−3	
κ Cen	3.15	B2 V	320	−1.9	
λ Cen	3.15	B9 III	370	−2.1	
μ Cen	3.08–3.17	B2 Vpne	470	−2.7	
ν Cen	3.40(var?)	B2 IV	750	−3.4	
α Lup	2.23–2.31	B1.5 III	580	−4.1	β CMa var
β Lup	2.69	B2 IV	540	−3.4	
γ Lup	2.80	B2 IVn	650	−3.4	
A	3.55			−2.7	} close bin
B	3.75			−2.6	
δ Lup	3.21(var)	B2 IV	680	−3.4	β CMa var
ε Lup	3.36	B2 IV–V	510	−2.6	
η Lup	3.45	B2 V	570	−2.7	
A	3.47			−2.7	} 15″ PA 21°
B	7.70			+1.6	
α Sco A	0.86–1.06	M1.5 Iab	520	−5.1	} 3″ PA 275°
B	5.07	B2.5 V		−0.6	
β Sco	2.65	B0.5 V	650	−3.7	A–C: 14″ PA 23°
A	2.78			−3.6	
B	5.04			−1.3	
C	4.93			−1.4	
δ Sco	2.34	B0 V	590	−4.0	
κ Sco	2.39–2.42	B1.5 III	650	−4.2	β CMa var
λ Sco	1.59–1.65	B1.5 IV	310	−3.3	β CMa var
μ₁ Sco	2.80–3.09	B1.5 V+B6 V	520	−3.0	ecl bin
μ₂ Sco	3.56	B2 IV	520	−2.4	346″ from μ₁
ν Sco A	4.0	B2 IV	400	−1.4	} 41″ PA 336°
B	6.23	A0 IV		+0.8	
π Sco	2.92	B1 V+B2 V	570	−3.3	
σ Sco A	2.82–2.90	B1 III	570	−4.4	A=β CMa var
B	8.49	B9		+1.3	20″ PA 273°
τ Sco	2.85	B0 V	750	−4.0	
υ Sco	2.71	B2 IV	540	−3.4	
ϑ Oph	3.23–3.27	B2 IV	710	−3.4	β CMa var
Minor: Stars:					
ζ Cru	4.3	B3			
b Cen	4.1	B3			
λ Lup	5.1	B3			
48 Lib	4.8	B3			
2 Sco	4.7	B3			
ω₁ Sco	4.1	B2			

Spica (α Virginis) and β Centauri are possible Sco-Cen members.

not gravitationally bound like open or globular clusters, they tend to disperse fairly soon (by astronomical standards) after their stars form. Their disintegration is caused principally by two effects. First, because of turbulence in the original cloud of interstellar matter from which they condensed, the stars of associations do not move exactly parallel, but have slight velocities away from each other. Thus, associations gradually expand. The rate of expansion of the Scorpio-Centaurus Association (determined from extremely careful measurements of the radial velocities and proper motions of its members) indicates that it could not have been formed more than 20 million years ago. It is, however, considerably older than the Orion Association (the oldest stars of which are about 10 million years old) and the Zeta (ζ) Persei Association (1.3 million years old). The greater age of the Sco-Cen Association is confirmed by the presence of the red supergiant Antares: neither the Orion nor the Zeta Persei associations contain stars that have yet evolved to the red supergiant stage.

The second thing that disrupts associations is the "differential rotation" of our Galaxy's disc. The disc of the Galaxy is not rotating like a solid body: stars farther from the Center of the Galaxy fall behind those nearer the Center. Therefore, more remote stars in associations lag behind as the association revolves around the Center of the Galaxy, and with time the association elongates. This obviously has already happened to the Sco-Cen Association, which is strongly elongated in a direction roughly parallel to the galactic equator. Differential rotation and the slow expansion of the group eventually will completely destroy the Sco-Cen Association, leaving its members scattered along the galactic plane. Our Sun seems to be passing through the remnants of at least two associations in advanced states of decay, the Ursa Major and Taurus "streams." (See Ursa Major.)

Chapter 5

The Constellations of Summer

The summer Milky Way is the brightest and most visually interesting stretch of the Milky Way visible from the United States, Canada, and Europe. Scattered along it are bright clouds—the Great Sagittarius Star Cloud, the Small Sagittarius Star Cloud, the Scutum Star Cloud, the Cygnus Star Cloud—and it is bisected by the obscuring lane called the Great Rift, which extends from Deneb in Cygnus southwest all the way to Centaurus.

The eastern branch of the summer Milky Way includes the Great and Small Sagittarius Star Clouds and the Scutum Star Cloud and extends up through Aquila, Sagitta, central Vulpecula, and into southeastern Cygnus. The western branch is brightest at the Cygnus Star Cloud and is fairly bright down through western Vulpecula, western Sagitta, and northwest Aquila. However, it fizzles out after it passes through the Taurus Poniatovii asterism in northeast Ophiuchus, reappearing, much fainter, in the Eta (η) Ophiuchi region 20° to the southwest.

The Great Rift consists of clouds of interstellar dust that block the light of the star clouds beyond. It is therefore the same kind of feature as the obscuring lanes seen on photographs of such edge-on spiral galaxies as NGC 4565 in Coma Berenices and NGC 891 in Andromeda. We lie in the spiral disk of our Galaxy well over halfway out from the center, and therefore when we look toward the central regions of our Galaxy—which are in the direction of the summer Milky Way—we are in effect looking at a spiral galaxy edge-on and very close up.

The summer Milky Way, particularly the sections in Scorpius, Sagittarius, and Cygnus, is the richest region of the sky for binoculars or telescopes with its abundance of open and globular clusters, emission nebulae, and interesting Milky Way fields. In fact, the finest Milky Way field visible from middle northern latitudes is the Deneb region of Cygnus: in binoculars it is a sight surpassed only by the Pleiades. The one respect in which the summer sky is inferior to the winter is in 1st-magnitude stars, of which it has only four (compared to winter's eight): Antares in Scorpius, Vega in Lyra, Al-

tair in Aquila, and Deneb in Cygnus. (Arcturus almost counts as a 1st-magnitude star of summer, for during the early evenings it still lingers high in the west.)

The summer constellations have perhaps the most distinctive and interesting star patterns of any of the seasonal groups. Even the summer's non-Milky Way constellations (Ursa Minor, Draco, Hercules, Corona Borealis, Serpens Caput, and Ophiuchus) contain an abundance of 2nd and 3rd-magnitude stars and have well delineated forms. Most of the summer constellations actually resemble what they are named after. Scorpius, Corona Borealis, Sagitta, and Delphinus look like a scorpion, a laurel wreath, an arrow, and a dolphin—and to see flying birds in Aquila and Cygnus, serpents in Draco and Serpens, and a kneeling man in Hercules requires only a modest imagination. Perhaps the most beautiful summer constellation, however, is the exquisite little Lyra, jewelled by the blue-white Vega, the "sapphire of the summer."

5.1 The Off-Milky Way Constellations of Summer

Ursa Minor, the Lesser Bear, Maps 1 and 2.

By a strange coincidence there are two distinctly dipper-shaped star patterns near the north celestial pole. The Little Dipper, formed by Alpha (α), Delta (δ), Epsilon (ϵ), Zeta (ζ), Eta (η), Gamma (γ), and Beta (β) Ursae Minoris, differs from the Big Dipper only in its handle, which curves upward instead of down, thus giving the figure a ladle-like appearance. The ridiculous conception of this star pattern as a Bear seems to have been the responsibility of the Greeks. Because only one celestial Bear, the one corresponding to our Ursa Major, is mentioned in the *Iliad* and the *Odyssey* (first written down in the 8th century B.C.), the Little Bear was no doubt an afterthought. A Greek tradition recorded by the poet Callimachus in the late 3rd century B.C. credits the invention of the Little Bear to the semi-legendary philosopher Thales, who lived (if indeed he was a real person) around 600 B.C.

The Arabs, before they adopted the Greek constellations, called the two Dippers' bowls *Al-Na'ash al-Kubra* and *Al-Na'ash al-Kughra*, "the Greater Bier" and "the Lesser Bier," respectively. The three stars in each Dipper handle were *Al-Banat al-Na'ash*, "the Daughters of the Bier"—in other words, the Mourners.

The north celestial pole lies in Ursa Minor, less than 1° from Alpha Ursae Minoris, Polaris. In 1990 the pole was about 3/4° from Polaris, approximately on the line toward Beta UMi. The distance is decreasing and will reach a minimum of 27′31″ (slightly less than the apparent diameter of the Moon) about 2102 A.D.

The reason for the change in position of the north celestial pole is the phenomenon called *precession*. Because of precession the celestial equator and poles slowly change location with respect to the stars: the two points where the celestial equator intersects the ecliptic (the vernal and autumnal equinoxes) gradually slide westward, and the poles trace circles 23 1/2° in radius on the celestial sphere. The period it takes the poles to return to the same position is about 25,800 years. Consequently, in the past different stars have been the Pole Star. During the first millennium B.C., the nearest bright star to the north celestial pole was Beta Ursa Minoris, whose present name (Kochab) is from the Arabic *Al-Kaukab al-Shamaliyy*, "the Star of the North," and is therefore a survivor of its reign as North Star. Around 3000 B.C. the North Star was Thuban, Alpha Draconis. When the earliest constellations were created about 4000 B.C., the north celestial pole was a bit closer to Iota (ι) Draconis than to Thuban.

The south celestial pole is, of course, invisible north of the equator. At present it lies in the star-poor reaches of Octans the Octant, where there is no true "south star." (The magnitude 5.5 star Sigma [σ] Octantis lies closest.) The Greeks and Romans were aware of the existence of the south celestial pole. The Roman architect Vitruvius (1st century B.C.) wrote:

> Just as the Bears turn round the pivot of the axis without ever setting or sinking under the Earth, there are likewise stars that keep turning round the southern pivot, which on account of the inclination of the firmament lies always under the Earth, and, being hidden there, they never rise and emerge above the Earth...The star Canopus proves this. Unknown in our vicinity, we have reports of it from merchants who have been to the distant parts of Egypt.

In most observing guides, Ursa Minor is listed as a circumpolar constellation. And so it is, even from as far south as latitude 20° north. However, circumpolar constellations are best observed when they lie between the pole and the zenith. For Ursa Minor this happens in the early evenings of summer. Unfortunately, there is very little for binoculars or even telescopes in Ursa Minor. Polaris is interesting for its location, and small telescopes at moderate powers will reveal that it is a binary, the magnitude 8.2 F3 V secondary lying about 18″ in position angle 218°. The bright primary is an F8 Ib supergiant and a Population II Cepheid variable, though its range (1.99 ± 0.02) is too slight to be followed visually. The Polaris system is about 820 light-years away so the primary has an absolute magnitude of −5.1 and the secondary +1.2 (luminosities of 9000 and 28 Suns, respectively).

The most interesting thing for binoculars in Ursa Minor is the color contrast between Beta and Gamma: Beta is a chrome-orange K4 III star of magnitude 2.1, and Gamma is a blue-white A3 III magnitude 3.0 object. Beta lies about 83 light-years away and its absolute magnitude is −0.2; the distance of Gamma is 110 light-years and its absolute magnitude is +0.4. The two stars are only about 3° apart and therefore easily fit together in the same binocular field of view.

Draco, the Dragon, Maps 1 and 2.

Wrapped in a huge reverse-S around half the north celestial pole is Draco the Dragon. The Head of Draco is the Beta (β)-Gamma (γ)-Nu (ν)-Xi (ξ) Draconis asterism; the Dragon's first fold is formed by Delta (δ), Epsilon (ε), and Tau (τ) and its second fold, which curves around the bowl of the Little Dipper, goes through Zeta (ζ), Eta (η), Theta (ϑ), Iota (ι), Alpha (α), and Kappa (κ). Its tail-tip lies at Lambda (λ), just east of the line from the Pointers of the Big Dipper to Polaris. While most of the bright stars in this region of the sky are claimed by the two Dippers, the remainder form this serpent-pattern that is fairly conspicuous in a dark sky.

Four serpents inhabit the sky: Draco, Hydra, Serpens, and in the south circumpolar region, Hydrus. Hydrus was introduced by Johannes Bayer in 1603. However, the other three serpent-constellations are extremely ancient, possibly dating to Sumerian times. Draco is almost certainly that old, because during the 4th millennium B.C. the north celestial pole was in central Draco, approximately between Alpha and Iota, and consequently the Dragon would have been a very striking celestial figure as it wheeled each night around a point nearly at its center.

Most of Draco lies well off the Milky Way and therefore is rather poor in interesting objects. However, it has three excellent double stars for binoculars (Table 5–1).

Table 5–1
Double Stars in Draco for Binoculars

Star	App Mag	Sep	PA	Spectra	Dist (l-y)	Abs Mag
16 + 17	5.2 5.2	90″	194°	A0 A2	300	+0.4 +0.4
Nu (ν)	4.9 5.0	62″	312°	A5p A5p	120	+2.1 +2.2
Psi (ψ)	4.9 6.1	30″	150°	F5 F8	70	+3.3 +4.5

All three of these doubles are easy in 10x binoculars—even the close Psi pair—and 7x resolves 16+17 and Nu without difficulty. The visually attractive thing about these three doubles is that the components of each have similar brightness. All three systems are common proper motion pairs and therefore must be true physical binaries—not just chance alignments.

Hercules, the Kneeler, Maps 2 and 7.

The star pattern we call Hercules was known to the earliest Greeks merely as "the Kneeler." Even Aratus, writing (in his *Phaenomena*) as late as the 3rd century B.C., referred to it only by that name. Not until Roman times did the identification of this constellation with the mythological hero Hercules become general. The Greek Kneeler was figured exactly the way Hercules is drawn on modern star charts, with the head at Alpha (α), the shoulders at Beta (β) and Delta (δ), and the waist at Zeta (ζ) and Epsilon (ϵ). One arm stretches out toward Lyra, the kneeling leg is marked by Eta (η), Sigma (σ), Tau (τ), Upsilon (υ)-Phi (φ), and Chi (χ), and the foot of the other leg at Iota (ι) is planted on the Head of Draco.

The Kneeler was inherited by the Greeks from Mesopotamia, but somewhere in the transition its Mesopotamian name and mythological significance were lost. (Aratus wrote apropos the Kneeler, "No one can speak of it clearly, nor to what toil he is attached.")

Writers on the history of astronomical mythology continue to claim that the Mesopotamian hero Gilgamesh was figured in the stars of our Hercules. There is absolutely no evidence for this. Indeed, the fact that the celestial Kneeler has his foot planted so rudely on the head of Draco is an argument against the Gilgamesh identification, for in the Babylonian "Epic of Gilgamesh" and in the older Sumerian stories about him, he is never portrayed as a serpent-slayer (except for one minor incident in one of the Sumerian tales). The Greek mythological hero Hercules *did* in part derive from the Sumero-Babylonian hero Gilgamesh; but as was earlier stated, Hercules was not even identified with the star pattern of the Kneeler until Roman times.

Figure 5–1. *(Top) An Old Babylonian era (c. 1700 B.C.) cylinder seal design. (Drawing from W.H. Ward, Seal Cylinder of Western Asia.) To the left a Kneeler is attacked by a standing Winged Dragon. To the right a rampant lion attacks a seated Goat. This rather common Old Babylonian seal scene includes three adjacent Mesopotamian constellations: the Kneeler (Hercules), the Winged Dragon (Draco and Cygnus + Cepheus), and the goat (Lyra). On this particular seal a second rampant lion stands between the two groups. Behind this second lion, as fill motifs, there are a small lion (below) and a turtle (above).*

(Bottom) Drawing of a Sumerian seal impression on a fragment of clay dated (on stratigraphic considerations) to c. 2500 B.C. (From Henri Frankfort, Stratified Cylinder Seals from the Diyala Region, *University of Chicago Oriental Institute Publications Vol. 72, 1955, no. 497.) A Heroic Kneeler battles a Hydra. Behind is a human-headed lion of a type seen on other late 3rd millennium B.C. Mesopotamian cylinder seals with astronomical themes. Presumably the numerous scorpions on this seal design are allusions to the celestial Scorpion.*

The Mesopotamian celestial Kneeler can be recognized on cylinder seal designs. One type of design that was very common during the Old Babylonian period (*c.* 1700 B.C.) shows both the Kneeler being attacked by a winged lion-eagle and a seated goat attacked by a lion. This scene is unquestionably astronomical because it involves not just the constellation of the Kneeler but two other Mesopotamian star groups in the same area of the sky, the Winged Lion-Eagle (probably represented in both Draco and the stars of Cygnus + Cepheus) and the Goat (our Lyra). A lion rather than a second lion-eagle appears on these seals simply to avoid repetition in the seal design. (Cylinder seals, after all, were not intended to be scientific documents, and aesthetic criteria meant more to the seal-carvers than strict accuracy.)

The Old Babylonian celestial Kneeler is shown as the Vanquished. However, nearly a thousand years earlier Sumerian cylinder seals portray the Kneeler instead as the Vanquisher. The most stunning and astonishing of the series, surviving only as an impression on a fragment of clay, pictures the Heroic Kneeler in combat with, of all things, a *seven-headed snake*. (Two of the serpent's heads appear as already severed.) Here clearly is the very origin of the myth of Hercules and the Hydra. The Kneeler on this seal design can identified: he is the Sumerian god of war and agriculture, Ninurta, who according to several surviving Sumerian texts killed a seven-headed serpent. Therefore, the earliest mythological association of the stars of the celestial Kneeler was unquestionably *not* with Gilgamesh. Ninurta, by the way, was also pictured in the stars of Sagittarius, which are not far to the south of the Hercules region of the sky.

Hercules contains only three interesting binocular objects. In fact, despite its relatively large area, Hercules is poor in sights, even for telescopes. And this whole region of the sky—Ursa Minor, Draco, Hercules, Corona Borealis, Boötes, Ophiuchus, Serpens Caput, and Libra—is notably poor in bright (mag 12.0 or brighter) galaxies.

Alpha (α) Herculis, Ras Algethi. Alpha Herculis is an M5 II star with a fine orange color. For contrast compare it to the nearby Alpha Ophiuchi, a snow-white object of magnitude 2.1. (Both stars fit in the same field in 7x binoculars.) Like many other red giants, Alpha Herculis is a semi-regular variable, its period being roughly 90 days and its extremes reaching 3.1 and 3.9 magnitude. This range is great enough to be followed with the unaided eye. For comparison stars use Iota (ι) and Kappa (κ) Ophiuchi, which lie about $6\frac{1}{2}°$ to the southwest of Alpha Her and have apparent magnitudes of 4.3 and 3.2, respectively.

Alpha Herculis is about 410 light-years distant. Its absolute magnitude varies between magnitudes -2.4 and -1.6, which correspond to luminosities of 760 Suns at maximum brightness and 360 Suns at minimum. This star is an excellent binary at 100x in small telescopes, the secondary having an apparent magnitude of 5.4 (implying an absolute magnitude of about -0.1) and lying 4.6″ from the primary in position angle 110° (east-southeast). The secondary is a spectroscopic binary consisting of G5 III and F2 components and appears greenish by contrast with the deep orange of the primary.

Globular clusters M13 and M92, Map 7. M13 and M92 are two of the largest and brightest globular clusters visible from middle northern latitudes—indeed, M13 is the largest and brightest globular cluster north of the celestial equator. M13 is easy to locate. It lies about 2° due south of Eta (η) Herculis, approximately $\frac{1}{3}$ the distance from Eta to Zeta (ζ). (The quadrilateral of Eta, Zeta, Epsilon [ϵ], and Pi [π] Hercules is usually called "the Keystone.") M92 however, is a bit more difficult to find because it is in a rather star-poor area about 4° southwest of Iota (ι) Herculis. Look for it just over $\frac{1}{3}$ the way from Iota to Eta Her.

The vital statistics of M13 and M92 are given in Table 5–2. The "true diameters" quoted are based on the clusters' photographic diameters but must be understood to be minimum estimates: globular clusters thin gradually with increasing distance from their center and therefore have no distinct outer boundaries even on photographs.

Table 5–2 Globular Clusters in Hercules						
	App Mag	Vis Dia	Photo Dia	Dist (l-y)	Abs Mag	True Dia (l-y)
M13	5.7	14′	23.2′	21,000	−8.7	140
M92	6.5	8′	12.2′	35,000	−9.1	125

Globular clusters in general are too distant to be good objects for binoculars—even M13 appears only as a fuzzy disk. M92 is so small and compact that it is easy to mistake for a star (especially in 7x glasses) and you have to look carefully to discern its tiny, bright, hazy-edge disk. On clear, moonless nights at a dark-sky observing site, M13 can be seen with the unaided eye as a 6th-magnitude "star."

Corona Borealis, the Northern Crown, Maps 6 and 7.

The early Greeks had only one celestial Crown, the present Corona Borealis. The Southern Crown, Corona Australis, does not seem to have been formed until the 3rd or 2nd century B.C. The Greek name for Corona, *Stephanos*, actually translates as "Wreath" and refers to the laurel wreath given to honor courage in war or distinction in poetry or athletics. Corona Borealis is one of the few star patterns that actually looks like what it's named for.

This constellation does not offer much to the binocular observer. Its two brightest stars are rather attractive blue-white objects: Gamma (γ) is an A0 IV object and has a distance of 140 light-years; Alpha (α) is an eclipsing binary with A0 V and dG6 components and the very slight range of 2.23 to 2.34 magnitude. Alpha CrB is 75 light-years away and shares the space motion of the Ursa Major Moving Group (see the Ursa Major section), of which it might be an outlying member. For 50mm glasses two other nicely colored stars are Nu (ν) 1 and Nu 2 Coronae in the northeastern part of the constellation some 4° northwest of Zeta (ζ) Herculis. Both are deep orange, with the magnitude 5.4 M-type Nu 1 being slightly more so than the magnitude 5.3 K5 Nu 2. They are not a true binary pair.

Corona Borealis also has two exceptionally interesting variable stars. R CrB, conveniently situated about 2° northeast of Gamma and the same distance northwest of Epsilon (ϵ), is the prototype of the rare and peculiar "reverse novae." R CrB will remain near its maximum of magnitude 5.8 for months or even years at a time, but then suddenly and rapidly fade. On occasion it will sink all the way down to 14th-magnitude. The star has been as faint as magnitude 14.8, which is 9,000 times fainter than its normal brightness.

The spectrum of R Cor Bor shows strong carbon absorption bands, and the star's atmosphere might be as much as two-thirds carbon. Its dramatic fading probably occurs when some instability in the star puffs off a layer or ring of its outer atmosphere. As the ejected gas expands into space, it cools until its carbon condenses into soot, obscuring the star. R Cor Bor can be seen with the unaided eye when it is at its 6th-magnitude maximum. (There is a magnitude 7.2 star just 22′ northwest of the variable that might be confused for it in binoculars.) The distance of R Cor Bor type stars are uncertain. The spectrum of the star suggests that it is a supergiant with a peak absolute magnitude of −4 or −5, implying that its distance is around 3,000 or 4,000 light-years.

The other remarkable variable in Corona Borealis is T CrB, located almost exactly 1° south-southeast of Epsilon. T Cor Bor, nicknamed the Blaze Star, is a representative of a rare type of variable, the recurrent nova. T Cor Bor normally stays at about 10th magnitude, with small fluctuations that become more pronounced just before an outburst. In 1866 it suddenly rose to magnitude 2.0, and in February 1946 it again flared up to 2nd magnitude. (On both occasions, it faded back below 9th magnitude within a month.) While you will probably never see any changes in this star, whenever Corona Borealis is in the sky it's worth a glance to see if it has exploded again.

There are a relatively small number of recurrent novae known, one of which—T Pyxidis—has undergone five observed outbursts. Recurrent novae usually brighten by 7 or 8 magnitudes, whereas "normal" or classical novae have amplitudes of 10 or 12 magnitudes. Nevertheless, both phenomena appear to be caused by the same mechanism. Most recurrent novae and a large number of normal novae are known to be extremely close binary systems consisting of a red or yellow dwarf or giant star coupled with a bluish dwarf or subdwarf. Astronomers suspect that the outburst occurs when matter lost from the bloated red or yellow star falls onto its small, dense companion and becomes explosively unstable.

Serpens Caput, the Snake's Head, Map 6.

The only constellation that is in two separate sections is Serpens the Snake, held by Ophiuchus ("the Serpent-Bearer"). The western part of the constellation, Serpens Caput, contains the Serpent's head and neck (*caput* is Latin for "head"). The head itself is the Iota (ι), Kappa (κ), Gamma (γ), Beta (β) asterism, and the neck goes down through Delta (δ), Lambda (λ), Alpha (α), Epsilon (ϵ), and Mu (μ). From there it angles over to Delta (δ) and Epsilon (ϵ) Ophiuchi, the two stars that mark one of the hands of Ophiuchus.

Globular cluster M5, Map 6. Serpens Caput lies well off the Milky Way and has only one object of interest for binocular observers, the globular cluster M5. With an apparent magnitude of 6.0 and a visual diameter of about 12′, M5 is the second largest and brightest globular north of the celestial equator—only M13 in nearby Hercules is superior. Though it lies in an area of the sky poor in bright stars, M5 is not difficult to find. Look about 4° due east of 110 Virginis and just 20′ northwest of the 5th-magnitude star 5 Serpentis. (109 and 110 Virginis and 5 Serpentis are spaced at about 4° intervals on an east-west line.) In binoculars M5 appears as a bright, fuzzy-edged disk embedded in a faint halo. It is a spectacular, well-resolved cluster in telescopes of 6-inches aperture or larger.

M5 is about 26,000 light-years distant and has an integrated absolute magnitude of about −8.5, corresponding to a luminosity of nearly a quarter million Suns. The globular's photographic diameter is about 20′, so it has a true diameter of at least 150 light-years. Like M13, M5 is moderately concentrated. About 100 variables have been identified in it, most being RR Lyrae short-period pulsating stars, but one is an SS Cygni cataclysmic variable.

Ophiuchus, the Serpent-Bearer, Map 7.

The vast figure of Ophiuchus lies half in and half out of the Milky Way. The area enclosed by its boundaries makes Ophiuchus only the 11th largest constellation, but it has one of the largest star patterns. The head of the figure is at Alpha (α). (The name of this star, Rasalhague, is from the Arabic *al-Ra's al-Hawwa*, "the Head of the Serpent Collector.") The shoulders are marked by the Iota (ι)-Kappa (κ) and Beta (β)-Gamma (γ) pairs; one knee is at Theta (ϑ). Ophiuchus grasps the Serpent's tail at Nu (ν) and its neck at the Delta (δ)-Epsilon (ϵ) pair. The names for these last two, Yed Prior and Yed Posterior, are composites of the Arabic word for hand, *al-Yad*, with the Latin *prior*, "preceding," and *posterior*, "following." Eta (η), Zeta (ζ), and Lambda (λ) complete the figure's outline.

In Greek mythology Ophiuchus was identified with Aesculapius, a son of Apollo and the inventor of medicine. Aesculapius was the surgeon aboard the *Argo* during the quest for the Golden Fleece. Classical writers associated a surprisingly large number of constellations, particularly in the spring and summer skies, with the Argonautic expedition. Because some of these constellations had been formed around 3000 B.C. by the Sumerians, this suggests that at an early stage in its development the Argonaut legend was adjusted to conform to what was already in the sky. In addition to Ophiuchus, the Argonautic constellations include Aries (the ram with the Golden Fleece), Hydra (the dragon that guarded the Fleece), Hercules and Castor and Pollux (all of whom were on the quest), Lyra (the lyre of Orpheus, also an Argonaut) and Centaurus (the benign and educated Chiron, tutor of both Aesculapius and Jason himself). The constellations that represent parts of the ship *Argo* are a feature of the winter sky and lie southeast of Orion.

Globular clusters in Ophiuchus. We know of about 200+ globular clusters associated with our Galaxy. They are distributed in a sphere about 100,000 light-years in radius centered upon the galactic core. Because the number of globular clusters increases dramatically toward the center of the Galaxy, almost half of the known globular clusters lie in the three constellations around the direction of the Galactic Center—Scorpius, Sagittarius, and Ophiuchus.

The six Messier globulars in Ophiuchus all can be seen as small, fuzzy disks in 10x binoculars. M10 and M12 are the best of them. In binoculars these appear as small, fairly low surface brightness discs surrounded by diffuse, very faint halos. Their low surface brightness reflects the fact that they are loosely-structured. M10 and M12 are just over 3° apart and therefore fit together in the same binocular field. The best way to locate these two clusters is to start at the Delta-Epsilon Oph pair and sweep due east 8° to 10°. Their hazy disks make them quite easy to spot.

Of the four lesser Messier globulars in Ophiuchus, M19 and M62 are the best and even in 7x binoculars can be seen as tiny, fuzzy-edged disks. They are, however, in the rather star-poor region between Theta Ophiuchi and Scorpius and are somewhat difficult to locate. M19 is about 7° due east of Antares and 2° just north of due west of the magnitude 4 star 36 Ophiuchi. M62 lies about 4° north-northeast of Epsilon Scorpii and 1° south of the midpoint of the line joining 45 Ophiuchi and Tau Scorpii.

The last two Messier globulars in Ophiuchus, M9 and M14, are too faint and small to be seen as disks at powers less than 10x. They also lie in star-poor regions. M9 is about 3° southeast of Eta Ophiuchi and 2° just

west of due north from Xi (ξ) Oph. M14 is slightly over 3° northeast of the 4th-magnitude star 47 Ophiuchi. The distances of M9 and M19 imply that they are either in or on the outer fringes of the great central hub of our Galaxy. The galactic hub, about 30,000 light-years away, has a diameter of about 10,000 light-years and would cover much of western Sagittarius, eastern Scorpius, and the Theta Ophiuchi region if it were not obscured by interstellar matter. The distance and direction of M14 means that it lies beyond the central hub and over the far part of our Galaxy's spiral disk.

Table 5–3 Messier Globulars in Ophiuchus				
	App Mag	Visual Diam (')	Dist (l-y)	Abs Mag
M9	7.3	4	30,000	−8.5
M10	6.7	8	14,000	−6.5
M12	6.6	10	19,000	−7.2
M14	7.7	5	45,000	−9.0
M19	6.6	6	33,000	−9.4
M62	6.5	6	20,000	−8.5

Asterism "Taurus Poniatovii," Map 7. Taurus Poniatovii, "Poniatovski's Bull," is an obsolete constellation in northeast Ophiuchus formed in 1777 by Abbe Poszobut to honor King Stanislaus II Poniatowski of Poland. It lies just east of Beta and Gamma Ophiuchi and consists of 66, 67, 68, 70, and 73 Ophiuchi, which form a 3° tall "V" pattern reminiscent of the Hyades. The figure fits in the field of 7x and 10x wide-angle glasses. Taurus Poniatovii is a rather attractive asterism with a nice background because the western branch of the summer Milky Way extends into this region from the northeast. In binoculars the Milky Way glow behind Taurus Poniatovii is rather faint, but the field is richly strewn with 7th- to 10th-magnitude stars. 67 and 70 Ophiuchi, only about 1° apart, show a fine color contrast in 50mm glasses (smaller apertures don't bring out the colors): 67 is a mag 4.0 star with a B5 Ib spectrum and a silver-blue tone, and 70 is a rather close binary whose K0 V and dK6 components have a combined magnitude of 4.0 and a composite yellow-orange color.

There are three large open clusters in the Taurus Poniatovii region, all of which can be seen with the unaided eye as small patches of haze when the sky is dark and transparent. In binoculars the best of them is IC 4765, about 8° east-northeast of Taurus Poniatovii in Serpens Cauda. (See the section on Serpens Cauda for a discussion of this cluster.) About 3° northwest of IC 4765, but just within Ophiuchus, is NGC 6633, a fairly loose cluster 20′ long with an integrated apparent magnitude of 4.9. NGC 6633 appears merely as a concentration of 7th- and 8th-magnitude stars in this

$\alpha = 17^h 8^m .8 - 27°.4$

Photograph 5–1. *The Pipe Nebula and globular clusters in the Ophiuchus Milky Way on an E.E. Barnard photo. The Pipe Nebula extends from the center to the left edge, the "pipe-stem" oriented virtually due east-west. In the star field west of the "pipe-bowl" is the over-exposed image of the 3rd-magnitude star Theta Ophiuchi. Near the lower right of the photo is the small disc of the globular cluster M62, which lies right on the Ophiuchus-Scorpius border. Nearly 2° WNW of the end of the pipe-stem is the globular M19. Both M62 and M19 are not difficult to see as small hazy spots in 10x50 glasses. Two globulars suitable for small telescopes at about 50x also appear in this field: NGC 6293 is the small disc at the NW corner of the pipe-stem; and 2° south of the western segment of the pipe-stem, embedded in a rich little star cloud, is NGC 6304.*

region's rich star field and is therefore better in 10x glasses than it is at the higher powers of zoom binoculars, which spread it out too much. The cluster has an interesting shape. The southwest half consists of about eight 7th- and 8th-magnitude stars crowded into a 10′ long triangle out of which extends, another 10′ to the northeast, a rectangular scattering of cluster members. A magnitude 6 star is located just 1/4° southeast of the cluster.

A much looser cluster than even NGC 6633 is IC 4665, which lies only about 1° northeast of Beta Ophiuchi. This group is 55′ in diameter—almost twice the apparent diameter of the Moon—and has an integrated apparent magnitude of 5.9. However, in binoculars it appears to consist of only 10 or 12 stars ranging from magnitude 6½ to magnitude 8 and is best in 7x glasses. IC 4665 is about 1100 light-years away and therefore has a true diameter of nearly 20 light-years but a total luminosity of only about 400 Suns.

The Pipe Nebula. As mentioned in the section on Ophiuchus' globular clusters, the great central hub of our Galaxy would cover much of eastern Scorpius, western Sagittarius, and southwest Ophiuchus if thick clouds of obscuring matter did not block it from view. However, interstellar matter has one redeeming feature: sometimes relatively nearby dark masses of it are silhouetted against distant Milky Way star clouds to beautiful effect. The Great Rift in the Milky Way from Deneb in Cygnus to Alpha Centauri is this kind of thing. Even more famous, though too far south to be seen from the United States and Europe, is the Coal Sack in the Southern Cross, a single dark cloud of dust placed on a very bright Milky Way background.

Next to the Great Rift and the "northern coal sack" in Cygnus, the most conspicuous obscuring feature visible from mid-northern latitudes is the "Pipe Nebula," a 7° long chain of dark clouds on the Milky Way south and southeast of Theta Ophiuchi. The stem of the Pipe is about 1° thick and extends for about 4° on a west-to-east line from 3° southwest to 2° south-southeast of Theta. The Pipe's bowl is a single dark cloud about 2° in diameter and centered 3° east-southeast of Theta. The clouds in the pipe-stem are catalogued from west to east as B (for E.E. Barnard, their cataloguer) 59, 65, 66, and 67. The pipe-bowl is B78. The Pipe Nebula is visible to the unaided eye even from the northern United States and southern Ontario, but binoculars brighten its Milky Way background and therefore bring it out better. Because this nebula must be nearer than the star clouds of the Carina-Sagittarius spiral arm, it is at most 5,000 or 6,000 light-years away. If so, its true length is about 600 light-years, but probably it is somewhat nearer and smaller.

5.2   The Southern Summer Milky Way

Scorpius, the Scorpion, Map 7.

The stars of Scorpius certainly look like a scorpion, so it's not surprising that Scorpius is one of the oldest of the constellations. It seems to have been formed before 4000 B.C. by the neolithic peasants of Mesopotamia. The Sumerians, who inherited the prehistoric Scorpion (*Gir-tab* in Sumerian), called our Antares "the heart of the Scorpion" (*Gab Gir-tab*). The Bedouin also knew Antares as the Heart of the Scorpion (*Al-Kalb al-'Akrab*), and they called the curve of Beta (β), Delta (δ), and Pi (π) Scorpii "the Crown of the Scorpion" (*Al-Iklil al-'Akrab*) and the Lambda (λ)-Upsilon (υ) pair "the Sting" (*Al-Shaula*).

All this implies that Scorpius has been figured exactly the same way for at least 6000 years. Originally, however, the creature's claws were marked by the stars of our Libra. The Sumerians were the first to form a zodiacal scale from our Alpha (α), Beta, Gamma (γ), and Iota (ι) Librae, but they probably thought of it as being enclosed by the Scorpions claws. The early Greeks apparently did not adopt the Mesopotamian scales, for they knew our Libra only as the Claws; not until the 2nd century B.C. did a Scale reappear in the zodiac.

The celestial Scorpion appears on a large number of Mesopotamian cylinder seals. One from Ur dated to the early 2nd millennium B.C. shows two scorpions, opposed claw-to-claw, with a very large multi-pointed star- (or planet-) figure between them. Even older (mid 3rd millennium) and more remarkable is a seal with a design that illustrates a bearded deity (in flowing skirt and the multi-horned crown of divinity) seated in a boat with a prow in the shape of the upper half of a human body. The prow-figure is likewise bearded and crowned, and propels the boat with a punting pole. Behind the seated god is a bearded lion. Over the back of the lion is a jar, and above the lion's head is a Mesopotamian plow of a type still used on the Euphrates into the early decades of our century. Behind the lion is a scorpion-man. Now, the best interpretation of this scene (which appears, with variations, on a rather large number of Sumerian and Akkadian cylinder seals of the mid to late 3rd millennium B.C.) is that it symbolizes the sun-god in his celestial boat, the other figures being some of the constellations of the zodiac: the lion is Leo, the jar is the Water-jar of Aquarius, the plow is the Sumerian *Mul Apin* ("Constellation of the Plow," our Triangulum plus Gamma Andromedae), and the scorpion-man is, of course, Scorpius. Even the boat in which the sun-god sits was a Sumerian ecliptic constellation, for before they were a Goat-fish the stars of Capricornus represented a Sumerian goat-prowed *magur*-boat. The seal shows two dots within the curve of the scorpion-man's

Photograph 5–2. *Another Barnard view of the Pipe Nebula. Centered in this field is the dust cloud, catalogued as B (=Barnard) 78, which forms the "pipe-bowl." Theta Ophiuchi is the overexposed star image in the star field west of B78. About $1\frac{1}{2}°$ due north and slightly east of Theta Oph is the small, but aptly named, "S" Nebula (B72), an object unfortunately visible only in moderately large amateur telescopes. The direction toward the Center of our Galaxy is very near the bottom left corner of this photo.*

tail and a crescent at his tail-tip: probably two planets and the moon.

The galactic equator cuts through the tail of Scorpius. Because it is therefore a Milky Way constellation, Scorpius is rich in open clusters and contains two of the best for binoculars, M6 and M7. And because the Galactic Center is in this direction (4° west-northwest of Gamma [γ] Sagittari, to be precise), Scorpius is well-populated with globular clusters, including one of the largest and brightest, M4. But for both the amateur and the professional astronomer, the most interesting aspect about Scorpius is the physical connection of most of its bright stars.

The Scorpio-Centaurus Association, Map 6. Like Orion, the star pattern of Scorpius is not entirely a chance alignment of stars. Most of the bright stars of Scorpius are moving through space together and are part of a large moving group of hot main-sequence and subgiant stars scattered from Scorpius on the northeast down through Lupus and Centaurus to Crux and Musca on the southwest. This group, the Scorpio-Centaurus Association, is also discussed in the final section on the spring constellations. In Scorpius the major association stars are Antares (the only evolved red supergiant in the group), Beta (β), Delta (δ), Pi (π), Sigma (σ), Tau (τ), the Mu (μ) pair, Kappa (κ), Lambda (λ), and Upsilon (υ).

Unlike the very young Orion Association, in which star formation is still occurring, the Sco-Cen Association contains little interstellar matter. Antares is embedded in a very faint reflection nebula some five light-years across and faint emission glow surrounds Sigma, but none of the other bright stars of the association have nebulous halos. The dim nebulae around Antares and Sigma Scorpii are on the southern fringe of a large complex of bright and dark nebulosity that surrounds 5th-magnitude Rho (ρ) Ophiuchi and extends eastward as far as the Theta (ϑ) Ophiuchi region. This cloud of interstellar matter lies only about 600 to 700 light-years away.

The Head of Scorpius, Map 7. The arc of Beta (β), Delta (δ), and Pi (π) Scorpii is the summer sky's answer to the Belt of Orion, for all three stars fit together in the same binocular field, have beautiful silver-blue colors and are embedded in a region rich in 4th-, 5th-, and 6th-magnitude stars.

About 1° south-southeast of Beta Scorpii is the wide naked-eye double, Omega (ω) l and Omega 2 Sco. This attractive pair is, however, only an optical double, a chance alignment of a distant star with one much nearer. The magnitude 4.1 Omega 1, the northwest star of the pair, is a Sco-Cen star and therefore shows a small proper motion to the southeast. However, the magnitude 4.6 Omega 2 has a large proper motion to the

southwest. This indicates that it is neither a binary star with Omega 1, nor in fact a Sco-Cen member at all. Omega 1 is a bluish B2 star and Omega 2 is a yellow-white G0 object: they are therefore a good color-contrast pair for small telescopes.

About $1\frac{1}{2}$° east-northeast of Beta is the multiple star Nu (ν) Scorpii—unlike the Omega pair, a true physical system of gravitationally-bound stars. It is a "double-double" resembling the more famous Epsilon Lyrae, for it consists of a wide pair, each component of which is a very close binary. The wide pair, of magnitudes 4.0 and 6.2, is separated by 41″ (in P.A. 336°) and can be split (when the atmosphere is stable) in 10x glasses. The true separation of the wide pair is at least 0.08 light-year—nearly 6000 times the distance between the Sun and the Earth. Telescopes at high power are necessary to resolve these two stars into their close components.

The Heart of Scorpius, Map 7. By a happy coincidence the star marking the heart of the Scorpion, Antares, is a red supergiant—an M1 Ib object with a ruddy-orange color. ("Red" giants and supergiants seldom appear truly *red*.) The name Antares is transliterated from the Greek and means "rival of Mars," presumably because of the similarity in color. The earliest known use of the name is in the *Syntaxis* of Ptolemy, written in the early 2nd century A.D.

Antares and Betelgeuse, both about 520 light-years away, are the nearest red supergiants to the solar system. Both are near enough and large enough that their diameters can be directly measured. Betelgeuse pulsates between extreme apparent diameters of 0.034″ and 0.054″, and Antares (which pulsates with smaller amplitude) has a maximum apparent diameter of about 0.041″. At these stars' estimated distances, the apparent diameters imply maximum true diameters of about 750 million miles for Betelgeuse and 570 million miles for Antares.

Antares' apparent diameter can be measured a second way, too. Because the star lies close to the ecliptic, it is occasionally occulted by the Moon. When this occurs, the star does not disappear instantaneously, as it would if it were a point source, but fades out over a small but measurable interval. Since the motion of the Moon is known, the apparent diameter of Antares is easy to calculate. Occultation studies have confirmed the 0.041″ apparent diameter of Antares and also seem to indicate that the star is highly flattened, with a polar diameter of only about 0.026″.

The stars Sigma (σ) and Tau (τ) Scorpii were called *Al-Niyat*, "the Outworks" (of the Heart—in other words, "the Pericardium") by Arabian astronomers. They both are early B-type stars (B1 III and B0 V) with fine silver-blue colors that provide a stunning contrast

Photograph 5–3. *Northern Scorpius, from a plate in the Ross-Calvert Atlas of the Northern Milky Way. The shallow curve of the three bright stars in the Head of the Scorpion, Beta-Delta-Pi Scorpii, are near the upper right (northwest) corner of the field. Near the field's top edge, just left and slightly above Beta Sco, is the 4th-magnitude Nu Scorpii, veiled with a tenuous nebula that is invisible to the eye even in large telescopes. Just above and slightly left of the center of the field is the shallow arc of (from northwest to southeast) Sigma-Alpha (Antares)-Tau Sco, the first two embedded in nebulous halos (also too faint to be seen even in telescopes). Antares appears spuriously faint because the photo was taken on blue-sensitive film. Immediately to the right (west) of Antares, at the vertex of an isosceles triangle with Antares and Sigma Sco, is the partially-resolved disc of the globular cluster M4. The bright nebulae north of Antares and Sigma Scorpii surround the stars 22 Sco and Rho Ophiuchi. Other dramatic dust clouds are in the southeast (lower left) of the field.*

to Anatres' ruddy-orange. All three stars fit in the same binocular field of the Scorpio-Centaurus Association.

Due west of Antares and in the same binocular field is the globular cluster M4. With an apparent magnitude of 6.4 and a visual diameter of 14', M4 is one of the largest and brightest of the globular clusters. From the southern half of the United States it can be detected with the unaided eye on dark transparent nights. In binoculars the cluster appears as a large, fairly low surface brightness disk of haze, slightly brighter toward its center but lacking the bright core that globulars like M13 in Hercules and M3 in Canes Venatici have. M4's binocular appearance reflects its rather loose structure.

M4 may be the nearest globular cluster to the solar system. Usually, the distances of globulars can be estimated with good accuracy because their RR Lyrae variable stars have known brightnesses. Unfortunately, M4 lies behind the southwestern fringe of the Rho Ophiuchi nebulosity and therefore is dimmed by an uncertain amount. In any case, at a probable 6,200 light-years, M4 seems to be closer to us than its rival NGC 6397 in Ara for that honor, thought to be about 8,000 light-years away.

Assuming it to be 6,200 light-years distant and dimmed by one magnitude, M4 has an integrated absolute magnitude of −6 (a luminosity of 21,000 Suns). Its 23' photographic diameter, then, implies a true diameter of not much over 40 light-years. Thus, M4 is well below the average globular cluster in both size and luminosity. If the great Omega (ω) Centauri cluster lay at the same distance from us as M4, it would have an apparent magnitude of around 2.0 and a diameter nearly three times the Moon's!

The Tail of Scorpius, Map 7. The Tail of the Scorpion is one of the richest regions of the Milky Way for binoculars and telescopes. Unfortunately, it is so far south that for most of the United States it does not culminate very far above the horizon, and consequently atmospheric thickness somewhat diminishes its glory. However, this region offers the binocular observer two wide doubles, several interesting star color contrasts, and over a half dozen open clusters including two of the best for binoculars, M6 and M7.

The Scorpio-Centaurus Association members in the Tail of Scorpius are Kappa, Lambda, Upsilon, and the Mu pair. They all have beautiful silver-blue colors. For contrast compare the blues of Kappa, Lambda, and Upsilon with the yellow-orange of the magnitude 3.2 K2III star G Scorpii, located almost 3° due east of Lambda. And compare the bluish Mu pair to the mag 2.3 K2.5III star Epsilon (ϵ) Sco 3½° to its north, another orange-toned star. (For observers in the northern half of the United States atmospheric thickness will deepen the or-

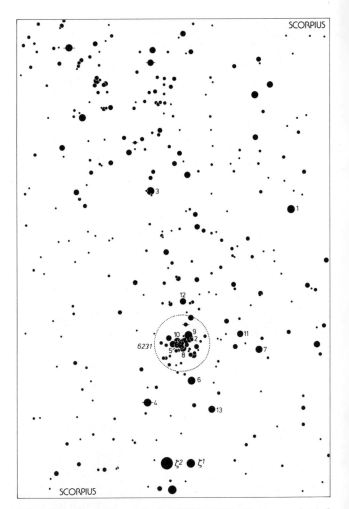

Identification Chart 5–1. NGC 6231. *Stars are plotted to magnitude 11.0, and the chart scale is 60mm (=2.36 inch) per degree. North is to the top, east to the left.*

Table 5–4 The Spectra of Brighter Stars in NGC 6231 (Stars as labeled in Chart 5–1 immediately above.)					
Star	Spectra	Mag	Star	Spectra	Mag
ζ^1Sco	B1.5 Ia⁺	4.77	7	WN 7	6.53
1	O8 Iaf	5.22	8	OC 9.5 Iab	6.48
2	B0.5 Ia	6.09	9	O6 IIIf	6.56
3	O8 Iafpe	5.77	10	WC7	6.70
4	OC9.7 Ia	6.35	11	O9.7 Iab	7.03
5	O7 Ib	6.14	12	O9.5 II–III	7.18
6	B0.5 Ia	6.30	13	O9.7 Ib	7.31

ange of G and Epsilon but wash out the blue of Kappa, Lambda, Upsilon, and the Mu's.)

The Mu pair is 346″ apart in an east-west direction and can be resolved with the unaided eye. The components must be physically related because they are both Scorpio-Centaurus stars and have the same proper motion. However, it seems improbable that they are actually orbiting around each other because their projected separation is 0.87 light-year.

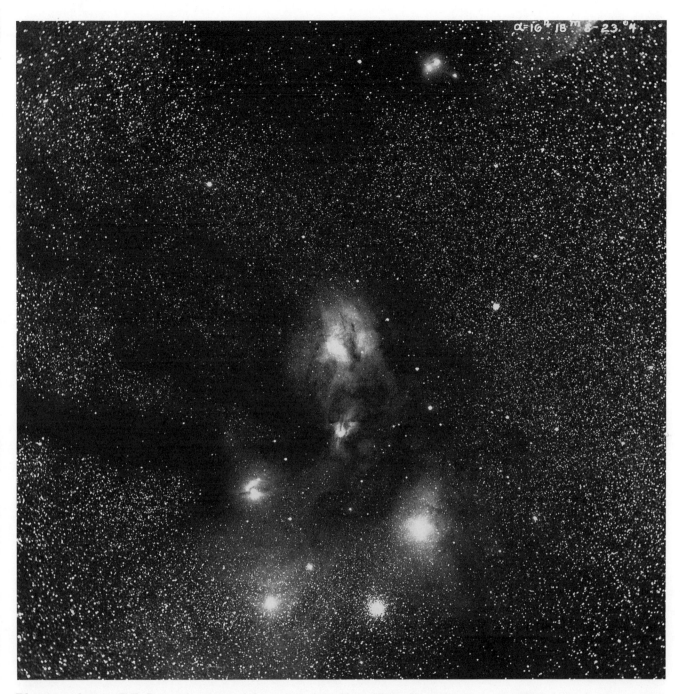

Photograph 5–4. *E.E. Barnard's photo of the region of the Heart of the Scorpion. The pair of discs in the lower center are Antares (to the left) and the globular cluster M4 (to the right–due west of Antares). M4 is a very large, loose globular, so its edges are partly resolved. NW of M4 is Sigma Scorpii, a blue giant star much overexposed on this blue-sensitive photo (which is the reason its image appears larger than that of red Antares). The obscuration of distant stars by the large dark cloud of interstellar matter north of Antares and Sigma Sco can be noticed in binoculars, but the three patches of glowing gas embedded in the obscuration north of Antares are beyond all but large telescopes. About 2° WNW of Rho Oph (the star embedded within the northernmost patch of nebulosity), out in the star field, is the disc of M80, a globular cluster some 36,000 light-years distant that can be glimpsed in 10x50 binoculars as a tiny 8th-mag speck of haze. Another globular in this field, but suitable only for telescopes, is NGC 6144, a 10th-mag object whose tiny, granular disc can be seen just NW of Antares.*

Photograph 5–5. *A field of open clusters in the Tail of the Scorpion. To the upper left of center is the wide unaided-eye double star Mu Scorpii, whose components are of nearly equal brightness and lie approximately on an east-west line. Due east (to the right in this photo) of Mu is the small open cluster NGC 6281; SSE, and slightly closer to Mu, is somewhat richer cluster NGC 6242. (Both NGC 6242 and NGC 6281 can be observed in binoculars, and this photo gives a good idea of how they actually appear.) Due south of Mu, near the lower edge of the field, lies the compact but well-populated open cluster NGC 6231. The loose scattering of fairly bright stars about midway between NGC 6231 and NGC 6242 is catalogued as cluster H (=Harvard) 12. This, however, is not a true gravitationally-bound group, but merely the richest section of the association Scorpius OB1, which includes H-12, NGC 6231, and Zeta-one Scorpii (the western of the pair of east-west star-dots $\frac{1}{2}°$ due south of NGC 6231.) Notice the NE-SW elongation of Sco OB1: this flattening is parallel to the galactic equator and implies the group is rotating. The whisp of nebulosity in the NE part of H-12 is beyond the reach of the eye even in large telescopes. From E.E. Barnard's Atlas of Selected Regions of the Milky Way.*

The stars Sigma (σ) and Tau (τ) Scorpii were called *Al-Niyat*, "the Outworks" (of the Heart—in other words, "the Pericardium") by Arabian astronomers. They both are early B-type stars (B1 III and B0 V) with fine silver-blue colors that provide a stunning contrast to Antares' ruddy-orange. All three stars fit in the same binocular field of view. Both Sigma and Tau Sco are members of the Scorpio-Centaurus Association.

About 4° south of Mu are Zeta (ζ) 1 and Zeta 2 Scorpii, which are more than 400″ apart (also in an east-west direction) and therefore another naked-eye double. These, however, are not physically related. The magnitude 3.6 K5 III Zeta 2 is about 155 light-years from us, but the magnitude 4.8 Zeta 1 is a B1.5 Ia$^+$ supergiant some 6200 light-years distant. In fact, Zeta 1 Scorpii is the most luminous member of the extremely young Scorpius OB1 association. Involved in the association is the open cluster NGC 6231, centered just $1/2$° north of Zeta 1.

NGC 6231 is one of the most astrophysically interesting open clusters that can be resolved in binoculars. It is rich in extremely hot, high-luminosity, young giant and supergiant stars. Such stars have formed from clouds of interstellar matter only recently, and NGC 6231 is estimated to be only 3 million years old. Zeta 1 Scorpii, with an absolute magnitude of -8.7 (a luminosity of 250,000 Suns), is one of the most brilliant stars known in our Galaxy. Its *bolometric* absolute magnitude (its brightness if observed by an "eye" sensitive to all wavelengths of radiation and not merely to visible light alone) is -10.8, which is 15.6 magnitudes greater than the Sun's bolometric absolute magnitude of $+4.8$. Zeta 1 Sco therefore radiates each second as much energy as 1.7 *million* Suns!

NGC 6231 is also notable for containing two of the rare Wolf-Rayet stars. Wolf-Rayet stars have spectra that show strong emission bands from various ionized elements: in "WN" Wolf-Rayets bands of ionized nitrogen are abundant, and in "WC" stars ionized carbon predominates. The spectra indicate that these stars are embedded in luminous and turbulent shells or rings, which are being blasted outward at velocities of as much as 1,800 miles per second. This is like the expansion velocities of novae, but in Wolf-Rayet stars the explosion is ongoing, with the star's shell or ring being continuously fed with matter from its main body. Wolf-Rayet stars also differ from novae in being very young objects, for they are usually found in young clusters and associations.

The magnitude 6.5 WN7 member of NGC 6231 is perhaps the easiest individual Wolf-Rayet star to identify in binoculars. It lies almost $1/2$° due west of the crowded main body of the cluster and can be picked out even in 7x glasses. The other Wolf-Rayet member of NGC 6231, a magnitude 6.7 WC7 object, is in the center of the cluster and is resolvable only in the higher powers of zoom instruments.

Centered about 1° north and slightly east of the core of NGC 6231 is a loose scattering of 6th-, 7th-, 8th-, and 9th-magnitude stars covering an area about 40′ across. This group is catalogued as open cluster H (for Harvard) 12 or Tr (Trumpler) 24. However, it is not a true gravitationally-bound cluster, but simply the richest outlying part of Scorpius OB1.

A line drawn from Zeta 1 through the core of NGC 6231 and up to the center of H12 roughly parallels the galactic equator. Scorpius OB1 is therefore elongated in the galactic plane—probably because the cloud of interstellar matter from which it formed was rotating and consequently somewhat flattened. The 2° distance from Zeta 1 to the extreme northeastern edge of H12 corresponds to a true distance of about 220 light-years, but the full size of the association is perhaps twice that. Long exposure photographs show that Scorpius OB1 is enclosed in a huge ring of faint nebulosity some 4° in extent.

A couple other open clusters in this area of Scorpius can be seen with binoculars. About $1^1/_2$° south-southeast of the Mu Scorpii double is NGC 6242, a compact cluster which in 10x glasses appears as a 10′ patch of haze with two or three of the group's brightest members (8th-magnitude stars) resolved in the cluster-glow. Slightly over 2° due east of the Mu pair is NGC 6281, a cluster about the same size as NGC 6242, but with a coarser and more mottled appearance. As its binocular image suggests, NGC 6281 is a less populous and more scattered cluster than NGC 6242.

Open clusters M6 and M7, Map 7. Above the Stinger of the Scorpion lie two of the brightest open clusters in the sky, M6 and M7. Both clusters can be seen with the unaided eye as small shreds of haze. In fact, M6 and M7 were two of the handful of nebulous objects known to the Greeks and Romans. (The others were the Perseus Double Cluster, the Orion Nebula, the Praesepe Cluster in Cancer, and the Lagoon Nebula in Sagittarius.) The Bedouin called M6 and M7 *Al-Humah al-Akrab*, "the Venom of the Scorpion."

M7 falls 2° north and slightly east of G Scorpii and 5° due west of Epsilon (ϵ) Sagittarii; M6 is about $3^1/_2$° northwest of M7. Both clusters will fit in the same field of view in most binoculars. Detailed studies have identified outlying members of both clusters, increasing the apparent diameter of M6 to 54′ and of M7 to 72′; their full diameters are therefore about 24 and 17 light-years, respectively.

M6 and M7 both resolve well in binoculars. The lucida of M6, BM Scorpii, is a semi-regular yellow variable with a period of about 850 days; its variations can be easily followed in binoculars by using the other cluster members as comparison stars. BM Scorpii has such a long period that if you catch the star at maximum one summer, you will probably have to wait over the winter to see it at its subsequent minimum.

Two small but interesting open clusters lie in the vicinity of M6. Just $1\frac{1}{4}°$ west-southwest is the magnitude 5.5 O-type star h 4962, the brightest member of the tight and rather poor cluster NGC 6383. (10x50 binoculars show only a half-dozen 8th- and 9th-magnitude cluster stars grouped just west—barely out of the glare—of h 4962). NGC 6383 is only about 10 million years old. Almost 3° northeast of M6, and the same distance west of Gamma Sagittarii, is NGC 6451, a 6′ long, north-south patch of mottled haze in a fairly rich star field. NGC 6451 is located only about $1\frac{1}{2}°$ southeast of the direction to the Center of the Galaxy.

Table 5–5 Open Clusters M6 and M7						
	App Mag	Vis Diam	Dist (l-y)	Abs Mag	Lum (× Sun)	True Dia (l-y)	Age (×10⁶ yrs)
M6	5.3	26′	1500	−2.8	1100	11	40
M7	4.1	50′	800	−2.9	1200	12	70

Sagittarius, the Archer, Map 7.

The single most important fact about Sagittarius is that within its borders is the direction toward the Center of our Galaxy. The Galactic Center is at Right Ascension 17^h42^m, declination $-28°59'$. The chapter on studying galactic structure with binoculars will say more about the hub and the nucleus of our Galaxy.

Because it contains the Galactic Center and its Milky Way is therefore a part of the star- and matter-rich interior of our Galaxy, Sagittarius is abundant in objects for binoculars and telescopes. Most of Sagittarius' objects are in the western half of the constellation. Its eastern half, where it borders on Capricornus and Microscopium, lies off the Milky Way and is poor in stars and binocular and telescopic objects.

Since most of our Galaxy's globular clusters concentrate near the Galactic Center, Sagittarius is rich in globular clusters, three of which—M22, M28, and M55—are good binocular objects. And like most other Milky Way constellations, Sagittarius is well-populated with open clusters, the two best for binoculars being M23 and M25. However, the outstanding objects for binoculars and telescopes in Sagittarius are its Milky Way fields, particularly the Great and Small Sagittarius Star Clouds, and the Lagoon, Swan, and Trifid Nebulae (M8, M17, and M20).

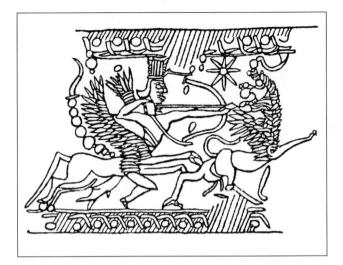

Figure 5–2. *Drawing (from W.H. Ward's Seal Cylinders of Western Asia) of the design on a Neo-Assyrian cylinder seal in the Pierpont Morgan Library. Shown is Sagittarius shooting at a fleeing winged lion. The Centaur-Archer has a feather crown, wears a quiver over his shoulder, and is represented with both a scorpion-tail (rooted just behind his wings) and a normal horse-tail. The scorpion-tail is likely an allusion to the fact that the Scorpion's Tail immediately precedes the Centaur-Archer in the zodiac. Beneath the Archer's stomach is a fish, a standard motif on seals with this theme and perhaps a reference to the proximity of the Sumerian celestial Fish (our Piscis Austrinus) to the zodiacal Archer. Above, on either side of the fleeing lion's back-turned head, are a crescent and an eight-pointed star. The design's field is bordered above and below by an ornamental pattern.*

Before discussing the astronomical objects in Sagittarius, a few words about its history are necessary to correct some false notions that keep popping up in discussions of constellation mythology. The concept of a centaur—a composite creature with horse body and human head, arms, and upper torso—was another of the many monsters Greek art inherited from Mesopotamia. Centaurs were fairly common in Mesopotamian gyptic of the late 2nd millennium B.C., but one appears on a cylinder seal dated to about 2200 B.C. Now, the magnificent Dendera Circular Zodiac, carved for a temple ceiling in Egypt in the 1st century B.C., shows Sagittarius as a winged centaur. Other Hellenistic representations give him a scorpion-tail. The design above, an impression of an Assyrian cylinder seal of the early 1st millennium. B.C., depicts a centaur-archer that is *both* winged *and* with scorpion- and horse-tails—proof enough of where the Greeks got their conception of Sagittarius. That this Assyrian centaur-archer corresponded to the star pattern of Sagittarius is proven by other Assyrian cylinder seals in which a human-archer shoots the same kind of winged lion (also turned about to face his attacker), but with a bow that is studded with stars. The Mesopotamian deity figured in this celestial human- or archer-centaur can be identified. As-

Photograph 5–6. The Sagittarius Milky Way. *Photo by Jack Marling on hypered 2415 film with a 50mm lens at f/2.8 and a hydrogen-alpha pass filter. The bright patch near the center is the Lagoon Nebula, M8. Directly below (south) of it is the Great Sagittarius Star Cloud. The bright spot just above and to the right of M8 is the Trifid Nebula, M20. The north-south pair of bright patches in the upper center are M16 (above) and M17 (below). Due south of them is the distinctive "bent-rectangle" form of the Small Sagittarius Star Cloud, M24.*

syrian texts that list the star patterns "in the path of the moon" (i.e., in the zodiac) catalogue *Pabilsag* after the Scorpion and before the Goat-fish. Pabilsag was one of the epithets of the old Sumerian god of war, Ninurta. A relief from the Assyrian temple to Ninurta at Nimrud in northern Iraq shows the god (holding thunderbolts rather than a bow-and-arrow) attacking a winged lion-eagle which is upreared and backward-looking like the one on the seal design in Figure 5–2. As has been mentioned earlier, Ninurta also seems to have been represented by our constellation Hercules. Since one of the emblems of Ninurta was the eagle, figured in the stars of the Graeco-Roman Aquila, it would seem that this whole region of the sky had been sacred to Ninurta.

The bright stars of Sagittarius offer the binocular observer some good color contrasts. The most striking is between Epsilon and Eta Sagittarii, conveniently located only about 2½° apart. (See Table 5–6.)

The stars of the Milk Dipper's bowl are also a good color contrast group. (See Table 5–7.) The Milk Dipper's bowl fits in the field of wide-angle glasses of 10x or less.

Globular clusters in Sagittarius. The total number of globular clusters in Sagittarius exceeds two dozen. Many are distant clusters heavily obscured by interstellar dust and therefore visible only in large telescopes, but three are good binocular subjects. M22 and M28 are very easy to find—M22 is 2.3° northeast and M28 just 0.8° northwest of Lambda (λ) Sagittarii. M22 is so large and bright that from dark-sky observing sites in the southern two-thirds of the United States it can be seen with the unaided eye. In binoculars it appears as a large, hazy disk, slightly brighter in its center. M28 is much more compact than M22 and a casual glance in 7x glasses might mistake it for a star. However, with careful observing you will be able to identify its bright, hazy-edged spot. M55 lies in the star-poor region of east-central Sagittarius and therefore is more difficult to locate than M22 and M28. Fortunately, its large, low surface brightness disk is fairly obvious in 50mm binoculars and the globular can be found by simply sweeping 7° east and slightly south from Zeta Sagittarii. Also, a line from Sigma to Tau Sagittarii points to M55.

The different binocular appearances of M22, M28, and M55 are the consequences of differences in their structure. The compact, high surface brightness M28 is fairly concentrated, whereas M22 is moderately concentrated and the low surface brightness M55 is very loose. Nowhere else in the sky are three contrasting globulars so well situated for comparison. And because M55 is almost as large as M22 in apparent size, the contrast of image brightness between the two is especially striking. (See Table 5–8.)

Table 5–6 Epsilon and Eta Sagittarii			
Star	Mag	Spectra	Color
Epsilon (ε)	1.8	B9.5 III	bluish
Eta (η)	3.1	M3.5 III	reddish-orange

Table 5–7 Color Contrast of the Stars in Milk Dipper's Bowl			
Star	Mag	Spectra	Color
Sigma (σ)	2.1	B2 V	silver-blue
Phi (φ)	3.2	B8 III	silver-blue
Zeta (ζ)	2.6	A2 III+A2 V	bluish-white
Tau (τ)	3.3	K1 III	orange

Table 5–8 The Brightest Globular Clusters in Sagittarius						
	App Mag	Vis Diam	Dist (l-y)	Abs Mag	Lum (× Sun)	Photo Diam	True Diam (l-y)
M22	5.9	18′	10,000	−8.2	160,000	26′	75
M28	7.1	6′	15,000	−7.9	120,000	15′	65
M55	6.3	15′	20,000	−7.7	100,000	21′	120

Another good globular for binoculars in Sagittarius is NGC 6723, a 7th-magnitude cluster about 7′ in diameter located only about half a degree northeast of the 5th-magnitude star Epsilon (ε) Coronae Australis. Unfortunately, this globular's declination is −36°38′ (2000), so it does not culminate very far above the horizon for observers in the northern half of the United States. NGC 6723 is about 34,000 light-years distant and is notable for the high abundance of elements heavier than hydrogen and helium in its stars, suggesting that this is one of the youngest of our Galaxy's globular clusters.

This is perhaps the best place to mention a few things about the minor constellation Corona Australis, which lies on the eastern edge of the Milky Way due south of the Milk Dipper of Sagittarius. Because Corona Australis is so far south (−37° to −45° declination), it is almost lost in the horizon haze for observers in the northern United States and southern Ontario. (Observing from Minnesota, I find binoculars necessary to discern most of its Greek-lettered stars.)

The constellation's pattern is similar to that of Corona Borealis, but it did not become known as the Southern Wreath until the 2nd century B.C. Corona Australis offers binocular observers in the southern United States one good object, the globular cluster NGC 6541, a 6th-magnitude cluster about 6′ in diameter which appears as a compact, very high surface brightness, fuzzy-edged disk. NGC 6541 is not difficult to find—extend a line through Lambda (λ), Kappa (κ), and Iota (ι) 1 Scorpii to the southeast for a distance slightly more than that between Lambda (λ) and Iota

Photograph 5–7. *The Sagittarius Milky Way on a Ross-Calvert Plate. This is a somewhat enlarged view of the region shown on the preceding photograph. The Great Sagittarius Star Cloud occupies the center of the field, with the bright patch of M8, the Lagoon Nebula, just above it. North and slightly west of M8 is the small bright patch of M20, the Trifid nebula. On the upper edge of the field is the southwest-to-northeast rectangle of the Small Sagittarius Star Cloud, with the open clusters M23 and M25 at equal distances to its right (west) and left, respectively. The bright star southeast of the Great Star Cloud is Epsilon Sagittarii (Kaus Australis). Northeast of the Great Star Cloud and due east of M8 is the disc of the globular cluster M22. Near the lower right (southwest) corner of the photo is Lambda Scorpii in the Sting of the Scorpion. Various other stars and clusters can be identified with the assistance of Map 7 at the back of this book.*

Photograph 5–8. *The northwestern region of the Sagittarius Milky Way. The field extends from the Lagoon Nebula, M8 (the bright patch on the bottom right side of the photo), NE up to the Small Sagittarius Star Cloud, M24 (in the upper left corner). The northern-most billows of the Large Sagittarius Star Cloud are in the lower left corner. About 1½° NNW of M8 is the somewhat smaller Trifid Nebula, M20. (The length of the exposure has washed out the internal details of both nebulae.) The rich field of faint stars NNE of M8 and SE of M20 can be seen in 10x50 binoculars as a small hazy low-surface-brightness Milky Way star cloud. In the upper right corner of the field is the very large, populous, but poorly concentrated open cluster M23, which, as this photo suggests, can be resolved even in small binoculars. From E.E. Barnard's Atlas of Selected Regions of the Milky Way.*

1. This brings you to a 5th-magnitude star lying just to the northwest of the cluster. NGC 6541 is a concentrated globular only about 13,000 light-years away. Its true diameter is at least 90 light-years, and its true luminosity is over 65,000 Suns.

The Great Sagittarius Star Cloud, Map 7. The Great Sagittarius Star Cloud occupies an irregular area several degrees across immediately north of Gamma and Delta Sagittarii. It is beautiful in binoculars—a bright glow scattered over with faintly twinkling star-specks. To the southeast the Star Cloud fades imperceptibly. On its northwest it is bordered by the Great Rift, the dust clouds of which make large bays into its bright glow.

The Great Sagittarius Star Cloud is the one part of our Galaxy's central hub that is not blocked from our view by the thick masses of interstellar matter that lie in the interior spiral arms of the Galaxy. The Star Cloud therefore is 30,000 light-years away and composed of Population II stars: red and yellow dwarf stars and modest-luminosity giants that are known to be the oldest stellar members of our Galaxy. It is possible that some of the faintest stars visible in binoculars in the glow of the Star Cloud are not merely dim foreground objects but much more luminous ones actually embedded in it: the brightest type of Population II stars are RV Tauri variables, which are thought to achieve peak absolute magnitudes near −5 and at the distance of the Great Sagittarius star cloud would have peak apparent magnitudes of around 10—visible in 50 mm glasses.

The Lagoon Nebula and its Region, Map 7. One of the handful of emission nebulae visible to the unaided eye is M8, the Lagoon Nebula. It has an apparent magnitude of 5.0 and in binoculars covers an area about 40′ × 25′. Exactly how extensive the Lagoon will appear to you depends on the darkness of the sky at your viewing site, the transparency of the night, the type of binoculars you are using (10x50s, for example, show more nebula-glow than 7x50s), and the altitude of the nebula when you observe it. Look at it when it is near the meridian and use averted vision to see its faint outlying regions. Unfortunately, the 2′ wide curved rift of obscuring matter that bisects the nebula, from which it gets its name, is visible only in telescopes.

In 10x binoculars several stars in and around M8 can be resolved. The magnitude 5.5 star just outside the western edge of the nebula is 7 Sagittarii, a foreground object between us and M8. East of 7 Sgr, in the western half of the Lagoon's glow, is a 3′ wide pair of stars, both of which are actually involved with the nebula. The fainter star to the northeast is a magnitude 7.1 O9 III–IV object with an absolute magnitude of −4.9; and the southwest star is the mag 6.0 9 Sagittarii, which has an O4V spectrum and an absolute mag-

nitude of −6.1. 9 Sagittarii's spectrum implies that its surface temperature is 50,000°K, which means the star radiates mostly ultraviolet light. If our eyes were sensitive to light of all wavelengths, 9Sagittarii would appear 4.6 magnitudes—69 times—brighter to us and therefore would be a 1st-magnitude object. 9 Sagittarii is one of the most luminous stars known in our Galaxy, each second radiating as much energy as 1.6 million Suns. This star is the primary source of the ultraviolet radiation that is exciting the hydrogen gas of the nebula to glow, and even in binoculars it can be seen that the nebula is the brightest in its vicinity.

Just 3′ southwest of 9 Sagittarii is a "star" of approximately 9th magnitude. Actually, this star combines a hot O7 magnitude 9½ star and the 30″ tall Hourglass Nebula just to its east, the brightest patch of M8. The star is obviously fluorescing the nebula. The Hourglass (which requires a telescope to be separated from its exciting star) is bright because it is dense—so dense that the gas in it is at higher pressure than the surrounding gas and therefore must be expanding. In fact, one researcher calculated that the Hourglass would dissipate only 10,000 years after it formed. Thus, the O7 star must have started shining no more than 10,000 years ago.

In 10x binoculars a small knot of perhaps a half-dozen stars can be seen in the eastern part of M8. This is the open cluster NGC 6530, which is physically associated with the nebula. The brightest star in the cluster is a magnitude 6.9 object with an O6.5 V spectrum. It has a surface temperature of about 37,500°K and therefore must contribute significant ultraviolet light toward making M8 glow. The second brightest star in NGC 6530 has an apparent magnitude of 7.5 and a B0 spectrum. The absolute magnitude of both stars is about −5.1.

The Lagoon Nebula is estimated to be about 5,200 light-years distant. The nebula's 40′ × 25′ visual size therefore corresponds to its true dimensions of 60 × 38 light-years. Photographs show faint outlying streamers that about double the nebula's extent, so its full size is around 120 light-years.

As the extreme youth of the Hourglass Nebula and its O7 star implies, the Lagoon region is a site where star formation is presently occurring. Photographs show scattered around the Lagoon many small, dark "Bok globules," thought to be proto-stars at an early stage in their contraction. And like the Orion Nebula, the Lagoon is the heart of an association, Sagittarius OB1, which includes the open cluster M21 and the B8 Ia supergiant eclipsing binary Mu (μ) Sagittarii.

It isn't clear, however, if the Lagoon's neighbor, M20, the Trifid Nebula, also belongs in the association. Recent estimates place it about 1,500 light-years beyond the Lagoon. If it is actually involved, the Trifid must be embedded in the same great cloud of interstellar matter as the Lagoon. In any case, the Trifid is located only about $1\,1/2°$ north and slightly west of the center of the Lagoon. In binoculars it appears as a very dim haze, perhaps $15'$ in diameter, around a magnitude $6\,1/2$ central star. 10x50 glasses reveal that the nebular glow of the Trifid is distinctly elongated north-south. (The three obscuring lanes from which M20 has been named require a 6-inch telescope at about 100x to be seen.) The $6\,1/2$-magnitude central star is actually embedded in the nebula: it is the telescopic multiple HN 40, whose O7 primary component is the principal source of the ultraviolet radiation that is fluorescing the nebula.

On color photographs the Trifid appears red because its excited hydrogen gas emits radiation at 6563 Ångströms wavelength, the red hydrogen alpha (Hα) line. (The same mechanism also gives the Lagoon its reddish tone on photographs.) However, the photographs also show a slightly smaller blue nebulosity surrounding the magnitude $7\,1/2$ star just north of the Trifid proper. This is a reflection nebula—the magnitude $7\,1/2$ star (which can be discerned in 10x glasses) is not hot enough to ionize the hydrogen gas in the interstellar matter around it, but the dusty material nearby is just the right size to scatter the star's blue light. The north-south elongation of the Trifid's image as seen in binoculars comes from your eye picking up the reflection nebula. There aren't many reflection nebulae visible in binoculars.

The full photographic diameter of the Trifid (excluding the blue reflection nebula) is about $25'$. If it is 6,700 light-years distant, its true diameter is therefore nearly 50 light-years. HN 40 has an absolute magnitude of about -6.

About $1/3°$ northwest of the Trifid is one of the more luminous members of the Sagittarius OB1 association, the magnitude 5.8 double star HD 164402, a B0 Ib supergiant with an absolute magnitude of about -6. As mentioned earlier, the open cluster M21, only about $3/4°$ northeast of the Trifid, is also involved in Sagittarius OB1. M21 is a very compact cluster, only about $10'$ in diameter. It contains about 50 members between magnitudes 7 and 12, but in 10x50 binoculars the cluster appears only as a tight knot of four or five stars. M21's brightest member is a B0.5 III star with an apparent magnitude of 6.7 and an absolute magnitude of -5.0; its second brightest star is a magnitude 7.3 B0 V object. Including outliers, M21 has a full diameter of $12'$. Assuming it to be about 5,000 light-years distant, its true diameter is therefore around 17 light-years. The cluster's total luminosity is over 10,000 Suns.

With careful looking in 10x50 or giant binoculars, a pale glow about $1°$ across can be seen due north of the Lagoon equidistant from the Lagoon and the Trifid. Photographs show that this is a field of distant and faint Milky Way stars over which is spread a thin sheen of nebulosity. This must be a direction where the clouds of interstellar matter in which the Lagoon and Trifid nebulae are embedded are thinner. The glow visible in binoculars is from the tenuous nebulosity as well as Milky Way starlight.

The Small Sagittarius Star Cloud, M24, Map 7.
One of the very best sights in binoculars or richest-field telescopes is the Small Sagittarius Star Cloud, a roughly rectangular Milky Way cloud measuring about $2° \times 1°$, located about $2°$ north and slightly east of Mu (μ) Sagittarii. It is so bright that its rectangular shape is obvious even to the unaided eye. The thing that makes the Small Sagittarius Star Cloud so remarkable in binoculars is the profusion of stars scattered across and embedded in its glow, both bright 7th- and 8th-magnitude stars and faint, momentarily resolved star-specks. The Great Sagittarius Star Cloud has higher surface brightness, but lacks this embellishment of star-gems.

This difference in appearance between the two star clouds is the result of, firstly, their difference in distance. The Small Star Cloud is only about half as distant as the Great Cloud (16,000 compared to 30,000 light-years). Second, the Great Star Cloud is a portion of the hub of our Galaxy and is composed of Population II stars, the brightest of which have absolute magnitudes of only -5; but the Small Sagittarius Cloud is a portion of an inner spiral arm of the Galaxy and therefore contains Population I stars, including blue and red supergiants with absolute magnitudes of -7 and -8. Consequently, because it is both nearer and contains intrinsically brighter stars, the Small Sagittarius Star Cloud resolves better. Of course, many of the stars visible on the glow of both Clouds are merely foreground objects. The Small Cloud has more of these because it lies only $1°$ off the galactic equator, and our line of sight to it therefore runs along the galactic plane, toward which are concentrated luminous super-giant stars.

The key to observing the Small Sagittarius Star Cloud and similar Milky Way fields is to keep your eyes at your binoculars for a couple of minutes at a time. This allows your eyes to become more sensitive to the marginally or momentarily resolved star-specks embedded in the Cloud. This observing technique also adjusts your eyes to the subtle difference between the glow of the Star Cloud and the relatively dark masses of interstellar dust that surround it ("frame it" might be more accurate to say, because the star cloud is more remote— probably twice as far—as the surrounding dust clouds).

With this sort of careful viewing the Cloud's basic

Photograph 5–9. *Barnard's photo of the Small Sagittarius Star Cloud, M24, and its field. The distinctive bent-rectangle shape of M24 is easily seen in any binocular. More difficult are the two dark dust clouds on the NW side of the star cloud, catalogued as B92 and B93 (west-to-east), which require 10x50s and a very transparent and dark sky. The bright patch NNE of M24 near the top of the field is the Swan Nebula, M17, an easy binocular object (though it will not appear as large relative to M24 as it does in this photograph). The tight knot of stars midway between M17 and the very northern corner of M24 is the open cluster M18. Due north of M24 and west of M17 is an extensive star cloud which, though fainter than M24, can be glimpsed as a faint haze in 10x50 glasses.*

shape will appear exactly as it does on photographs—pinched in the middle, with the northeastern half bent a little toward the east out of the line of symmetry of the southwestern half. The southeast long side of the Star Cloud has a fairly sharp border and the dark region in that direction extends just over 1° to the east, where it ends at the faint Milky Way glow of the M25 region. In 10x50 binoculars two small circular dark nebulae can be seen at about the midpoint of the cloud's northwest side. They are 1/2° apart (center to center) in a southwest to northeast direction, an 8th-magnitude star between them. Both nebulae are about 1/4° across with the southwest one, B92, being slightly larger than its neighbor, B93. Southwest from B92 runs a channel of obscuration, very difficult even in 10x50s because it is not as opaque as B92 and B93. This channel separates the bright southern half of the Star Cloud from the fainter amorphous Milky Way glow just to its west.

Objects in the Region of the Small Sagittarius Star Cloud, Map 7.

Open cluster M23. About 5° due west of the Small Sagittarius Star Cloud is M23, a large (27′ diameter) and fairly bright (magnitude 6.0) open cluster. M23 is populous—it has 150 stars of 9th magnitude and fainter. 10x50 binoculars can partially resolve it, giving perhaps a dozen star-specks on a grainy background. The cluster is about 2,200 light-years away, so its true size is about 17 light-years and its absolute magnitude is −3.2. M23's brightest stars are B9 main-sequence objects and G-type yellow giants, which suggest that the cluster is 150 to 200 million years old.

Open cluster M25. Only 2° due east of the Small Sagittarius Star Cloud is another large open cluster, M25. Though it is even larger than M23 (its diameter is 35′), M25 is a less populous and therefore appears looser in structure. Thus, it is easily resolved in binoculars: in fact, even in 7x glasses M25 shows no hint of background of unresolved stars. M25 is about 2,000 light-years distant and has a true diameter of 20 light-years. Its integrated absolute magnitude is about −4.

The brightest member of M25, located right in the center of the cluster, is the Cepheid variable U Sagittarii, which ranges from magnitude 6.3 to 7.1 in a period of 6.745 days. There are only nine open clusters in our Galaxy known to contain Cepheid variables. (NGC 7790 in Cassiopeia has four.) None of the nine clusters is young, which confirms the theoretical prediction that Cepheid-type pulsations occur only in large stars when they are at least 20 million years old. M25 is estimated to be about that age. U Sagittarii's spectral range is F5 Ib to G1 Ib, and its peak absolute magnitude is about −3.6. Its variations can be followed in binoculars by using the other bright cluster members as comparison stars.

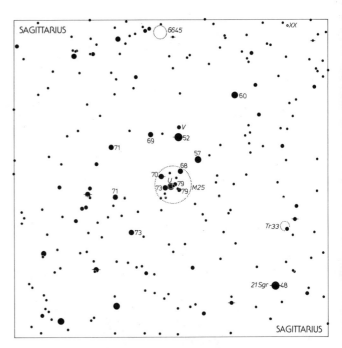

Identification Chart 5–2. U Sagittarii. *The faintest stars shown are of magnitude 9.5, and the chart scale is 18mm (=0.71 inch) per degree. North is to the top, east to the left. Comparison star brightnesses are to the nearest tenth magnitude, with periods omitted.*

Open cluster M18. The least impressive of the three Messier open clusters in the vicinity of the Small Sagittarius Star Cloud is M18, located about 1° due north of the Small Cloud's northeast side. M18 is only 7′ in diameter and has an integrated apparent magnitude of just 8.0. Even in 10x and zoom binoculars it appears merely as a tight knot of three or four stars in a tiny patch of haze. (The haze, coming from the cluster's unresolved members, makes it a bit easier to identify.) Telescopes show that M18 consists of only about a dozen 9th-, 10th-, and 11th-magnitude stars. The cluster is around 4,900 light-years away and therefore has a true diameter of approximately 10 light-years and an integrated absolute magnitude of −4.3, a luminosity of 4,400 Suns.

The Swan Nebula, M17, Map 7.
About 1° due north of M18 (and 2 1/2° southwest of magnitude 4.7 Gamma [γ] Scuti) is the emission nebula M17, variously called the Swan, Horseshoe, or Omega Nebula. The core of this nebula—the 7′ long east-west bar that forms the body of the "swan"—has exceptionally high surface brightness and is visible (though very small) even in 7x35 binoculars. In 10x50s a "prong" can be seen extending south from the west end of the bar. This is the arc which in telescopes appears to be the curved neck of the swan, and which has suggested to some observers the shape of a horseshoe or a Greek capital omega (Ω). Dark masses obscure the outlying portions of the nebula to the north and west, which makes the north and

west edges of M17 quite distinct, even in binoculars. But to the southeast there is no foreground obscuration and in that direction the nebula fades out gradually. Photographs of M17 show a network of faint filaments and tendrils of luminosity that cover an area of $45' \times 35'$. Because the nebula is estimated to lie about 5,700 light-years away, its full size is therefore about 75×60 light-years. (The body of the swan-figure, however, is only about 12 light-years long.) Unlike those of the Lagoon and the Trifid, the chief illuminating stars of the Swan Nebula lie behind thick clouds of obscuring matter and are not visible to us.

Just 1° due west of M17 is the eastern edge of a fine Milky Way star cloud. This cloud, about $2\frac{1}{2}$° in diameter, is fainter than the Small Sagittarius Star Cloud and lacks the bright 8th- and 9th-magnitude stars of its magnificent neighbor. But it has the same star-speckled texture of intermittently resolved star-sparks.

Serpens Cauda, the Snake's Tail, Map 7.

The tail of the Serpent held by Ophiuchus extends northeast up the Great Rift, passing through Nu (ν), Xi (ξ), and Omicron (o) Serpentis, Nu (ν) Ophiuchi (which marks one of the Serpent-bearer's hands), Zeta (ζ) and Eta (η) Serpentis, and ending at Theta (ϑ) Ser, the only bright star between Aquila and the "Taurus Poniatovii" region of Ophiuchus. Serpens Cauda has more Great Rift than the Milky Way, but it offers binocular observers a fairly easy emission nebula and a large and rich open cluster. It also contains one of the closest and most beautiful double stars resolvable in 10x glasses.

The Star Queen Nebula, M16, Map 7. The large emission nebula M16 lies in a region of the Milky Way that is poor in bright stars. It is some $2\frac{1}{2}$° north of M17 in Sagittarius and the same distance west-northwest of magnitude 4.7 Gamma (γ) Scuti. (M16, M17, and Gamma Scu form an equilateral triangle.) However, the nebula's fairly large, hazy patch is not difficult to spot, though its surface brightness is significantly less than M17's. In binoculars (using averted vision) the nebula-glow can be seen to cover an area about 15' across, extending from the tight cluster on the nebula's northwest edge (in 10x glasses the cluster appears as a knot of a half dozen stars) down to the 5' wide east-west pair of 8th-magnitude stars on the nebula's south. The full photographic dimensions of M16 are $35' \times 30'$.

The cluster and most of the other 8th-, 9th-, and 10th-magnitude stars scattered in and near M16 are physically associated with it. The brightest M16 stars are all hot, luminous O and early B-type objects. (The magnitude 8.3 star at the southwestern corner of the nebula is a foreground object.) Such stars are known to be extremely young. A star like the O4 V lucida of

the M16 cluster probably contains only about 100 times the Sun's mass, but is radiating over a million times as much energy per second and therefore is consuming the hydrogen in its interior so fast that it is necessarily short-lived.

The average age of the stars of M16 is only about 800,000 years. In fact, the M16 complex shows all the evidences that star formation is still occurring in it. First, some stars in the cluster show evidence they are still deriving energy from gravitational contraction. Second, the M16 complex contains many T Tauri variables, infant stars just appearing within the clouds of matter from which they have formed. And third, scattered around M16 are the small, dark Bok globules present in other regions of star formation and thought to be proto-stars in the initial stages of gravitational contraction.

M16 is estimated to lie about 7,100 light-years away; its true size is therefore around 70 light-years. The name Star Queen Nebula, introduced by Burnham, was inspired by the complicated dust formation that projects into the cluster's center from its SE corner. The traditional name for M16, the Eagle Nebula, is not as evocative—or even as faithful to the object's true appearance on photographs—as Burnham's new name is.

Double star Theta (ϑ) Serpentis, Map 7. At magnitude 4.5, Theta Serpentis, lying at the very tip of the Serpent's tail, is a splendid double star consisting of two A5 stars of magnitudes 4.6 and 5.0 separated by 22″ in position angle 104°. It is resolvable at 10x and is an easy split at 15x. Its two stars have surprisingly strong bluish tints—mid-A stars generally appear simply white. Theta Serpentis is about 130 light-years distant, so its components have absolute magnitudes of +1.6 and +2.0. This is a true gravitationally-connected binary, but the actual distance between the components is so great (at least 80 billion miles) that the orbital period of the system is thousands of years long. The separation and position angle of the two stars have not changed since they were first measured in 1830.

Open cluster IC 4756, Map 7. Although IC 4756, located only about 4° west-northwest of Theta Serpentis, is not one of the more famous open clusters, it is certainly one of the most beautiful in binoculars. It consists of a circular frame of a half dozen stars of magnitudes 6 and $6\frac{1}{2}$ within which is a rich and crowded swarm of 7th-, 8th-, and 9th-magnitude objects. IC 4756 is much better in binoculars than it is in a telescope, for it is extremely large—70′ in diameter (over twice the apparent diameter of the Moon)—and its 80 stars are pretty evenly scattered over the area. The low powers of binoculars are necessary to preserve the cluster-appearance of this object. Because the integrated apparent magnitude of IC 4756 is 4.5, it can be seen by the unaided eye (when sky conditions are good) as a smudge of haze.

IC 4756 is about 1,400 light-years away. It therefore has a true diameter of almost 30 light-years and an integrated absolute magnitude of about −3.7. This is one of the older open clusters, with an age estimated to be around a billion years.

Scutum, the Shield, Map 7.

Scutum is not an ancient constellation. It was introduced in 1690 by the Danzig astronomer Johannes Hevelius under the name Scutum Sobiescianum, "Sobieski's Shield." Hevelius formed it in honor of John III Sobieski, King of Poland. In 1683, Sobieski defeated the Turks near Vienna in a battle that not only prevented central Europe from becoming an Islamic state, but initiated the decline of Turkish influence over the Balkan nations and the Ukraine. (In the classic storybook manner, Sobieski himself led the decisive cavalry charge.)

Scutum has no true star pattern. It is an area $9\frac{1}{2}°$ wide by 12° tall in which are scattered one 4th-magnitude and eight 5th-magnitude stars. Nevertheless, Scutum lies in the heart of the summer Milky Way and it offers the binocular observer three interesting open clusters, two beautiful star clouds, and an important variable star.

Open clusters in Scutum, Map 7. There are two Messier open clusters in Scutum, M11 and M26. The least impressive of the two is **M26**—which is, however, only 1° east-southeast of Delta (δ) Scuti and is therefore very easy to locate. M26 is rather small (9′ in diameter) and has an integrated apparent magnitude of only 9.3. In binoculars it is merely a small, hazy spot. At first glance it may appear virtually stellar, but with careful looking it will be seen to be surrounded by a tight, dim, fuzzy halo. M26 is around 4,900 light-years away.

M11 is by far the best cluster in Scutum for binoculars or telescopes. It is only a bit larger than M26—12′ in diameter—but is much brighter, having an integrated apparent magnitude 6.3. To find the cluster, begin at Lambda (λ) Aquilae and go $1\frac{1}{2}°$ southwest to 12 Aql and then another 1° west to the magnitude 5.0 Eta (η) Scuti: M11 is located $1\frac{1}{2}°$ west-southwest of Eta Scu. In binoculars M11 appears as a compact, high surface brightness disk and actually looks more like a globular than an open cluster. Its binocular appearance is not entirely misleading, for M11 is one of the most populous and concentrated of the open clusters. One researcher found 870 members in M11 down to magnitude 16.5 and computed a total mass for the cluster of 2900 solar masses, both unusually high figures for an open clus-

ter. The central star density of M11 is 2.4 stars per cubic light-year, a value comparable to the central densities of looser globular clusters. A sphere having the central star density of M11 and a radius equal to the distance between the Sun and Alpha Centauri would contain about 820 stars! M11 is estimated to lie 5,500 light-years away, implying a true cluster diameter of about 20 light-years and an integrated absolute magnitude of −5.1.

The third interesting binocular cluster in Scutum is **NGC 6664**, located only about $\frac{1}{2}°$ due east of Alpha Scuti. This cluster is 18′ in diameter but its integrated apparent magnitude is only about 9, and in binoculars it appears merely as an amorphous, very low surface brightness patch of haze. The proximity of the comparatively bright Alpha, at magnitude 4.2, makes spotting NGC 6664 difficult in 7x binoculars—10x or more is necessary to get the cluster away from Alpha's glare. As the cluster's low surface brightness suggests, it is a fairly loose and poor group, with only about three dozen stars down to 13th magnitude scattered around its 18′ area. However, two members of NGC 6664 are Cepheid variables: only eight other open clusters in our Galaxy are known to contain Cepheids (one being M25 in Sagittarius). NGC 6664 is well over 10,000 light-years away.

Star clouds in Scutum, Map 7. Scutum's Milky Way is hardly inferior to Sagittarius'. In fact, because it culminates higher in the sky, the Scutum Milky Way is even better than the Sagittarius Milky Way for observers in the northern United States, Canada, and Europe. There are two good star clouds in Scutum, one in the southwest corner of the constellation and the other in the northeast, both easily visible to the unaided eye.

The fainter of these two star clouds is the one in southwest Scutum. This cloud is centered about 3° due east of M16 and measures about 3° across. The magnitude 4.7 star Gamma (γ) Scuti is located within the star cloud near its southwest corner. On its northeast and northwest, the cloud is bordered by obscuring lanes of dust, both about 3° long and $\frac{2}{3}°$ wide. These give the star cloud a triangular shape. Outside each obscuring lane is a thin streak of pale Milky Way glow and then a parallel obscuring lane. Naturally, it is not easy to see all this detail even in 10x50 binoculars. When observing this star cloud (and similar low surface brightness objects), it's essential that you keep your eyes at the oculars for a minute or two at a time, which allows them to adjust to the subtle difference between the faint glow of the star cloud and the darker (but not completely black) obscuring lanes. Also, remember to look with averted vision rather than directly.

In the northeast quadrant of Scutum, occupying the region between the Alpha (α)-Delta (δ)-Epsilon (ϵ)

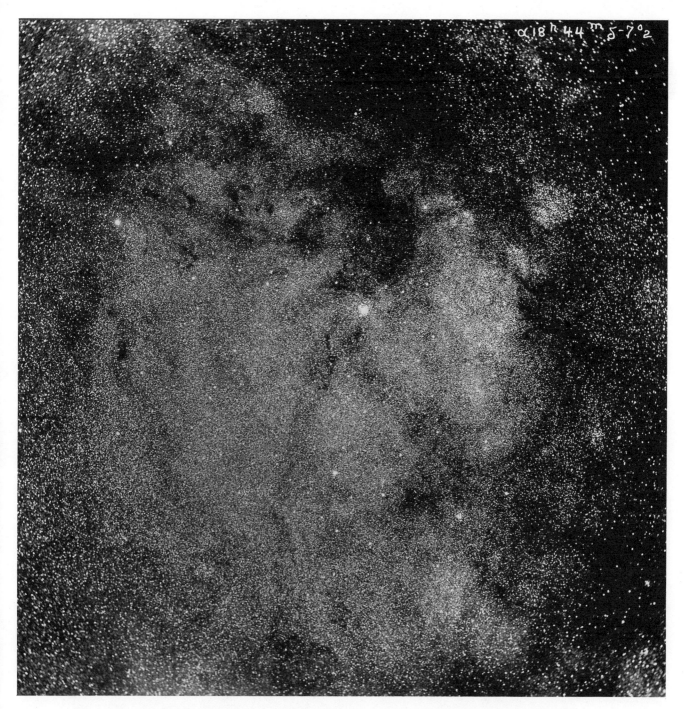

Photograph 5–10. *The Scutum Star Cloud on a Barnard photo. The brightest (north-western) section of the Cloud is right of center. At center, near the southern edge of a large dark "bay" of obscuring matter, is the rich open cluster M11. The dust clouds of the Great Rift are at the right (west) and top (north). Northwest of the brightest lobe of the Scutum Cloud, out in the Great Rift, is a nearly circular little cloud: it can be observed in binoculars. The star disc at the extreme NE tip of the Scutum Star Cloud, not far from the left edge of the field, is Lambda Aquilae. The region of heavy dust lanes NW of Lambda Aql can be seen in 10x50 glasses as a mixture of dark and bright Milky Way masses.*

Scuti triangle to the southwest and Beta (β) and Eta (η) Scuti to the north and northeast, is the Scutum Star Cloud, a magnificent object in any size binoculars. In 10x50s the Scutum Star Cloud will seem alive with glittering, momentarily resolved stars. On the northeast edge of the Cloud is the bright disk of M11. (The cluster is considerably nearer to us than the star cloud.) Note the dark obscuring patch between M11 and Beta Scuti. Another thickly obscured region lies to the west of the southern two-thirds of the star cloud. Two semidetached sections of the Scutum Cloud are to its northwest, cut off from the main cloud by parallel channels of translucent, semi-obscuring dust lanes. The outer, detached section is larger but a bit dimmer than the inner one. All these details can be made out in the higher powers of 40mm zooms, but small aperture binoculars lose the glittering partial resolution that makes the Scutum Cloud such a beautiful sight in 10x50s.

Northeast of the Scutum Star Cloud, in the area between Beta Scuti and Lambda Aquilae, is a fine region of mixed bright and dark Milky Way clouds. It is rather like the North America Nebula region in Cygnus, though here the star clouds are not so bright nor the obscuring masses so dark.

Variable star R Scuti, Map 7. On the northern edge of the Scutum Star Cloud, about 1° northwest of M11 and the same distance south of Beta (β) Scuti, is R Scuti, the brightest of the RV Tauri pulsating variables. R Scuti has an extreme range of magnitude, 4.9 to 8.2 (a deep minimum occurs only every fourth or fifth cycle), and therefore can be followed throughout its 140-day period in any size binoculars. R Scuti has the longest period of any RV Tauri star and its range is above average as well. Like other RV Tau stars, the spectra of R Scuti changes with its light changes. As it approaches maximum brightness, the star becomes hotter and hydrogen emission lines appear in its spectra, but near minimum light, the star is cooler and has spectral features typically found in M-type red-giants. The spectral range is G0e to K0p according to some sources, G8 to M3 according to others—the difference is merely a matter of how the star's spectrum is interpreted.

RV Tauri stars usually show secondary cycles in their variations (R Scuti's periodic deep minima are the result of a secondary cycle) which indicates that their atmospheres are undergoing complex pulsations, with some layers expanding while others contract. These variables are thought to be massive supergiants with peak absolute magnitudes of near −5. If R Scuti indeed does get this bright, it must lie about 2,500 light-years away.

The distribution of RV Tauri stars, Cepheids, and long-period variables (LPVs) in our Galaxy indicates that the three types of variable have significantly dif-

ferent ages. Because Cepheids are associated with the spiral arms of the Galaxy, they must be comparatively young. LPVs, however, are scattered throughout the galactic disk between, and above and below, the spiral arms; therefore, they are older. But RV Tauri stars are found *everywhere*—in and around the spiral arms, in the central hub, throughout the halo, even in the very old globular clusters. Consequently, they must be ancient objects. R Scuti itself is located near the galactic plane between two spiral arms, our Orion Arm and the next one in toward the Galaxy's center, the Sagittarius-Carina Arm.

5.3   The Northern Summer Milky Way

Aquila, the Eagle, Maps 7 and 8.

Aquila is one of the most beautiful constellations. Its attractiveness comes partly from how it appears to be flying northeast up the Milky Way and partly from the symmetry of its pattern. The Eagle's head is at Alpha (α), its shoulders are at Beta (β) and Gamma (γ), one wing tip is marked by the Epsilon (ϵ)-Zeta (ζ) pair and the opposite by the Theta (ϑ)-Eta (η) pair, the center of the body is at Delta (δ), and the tip of the tail is the Lambda (λ)-12 pair.

Aquila is one of the many constellations the Greeks got from the earlier civilizations of Mesopotamia. It is possible that the Sumerian Eagle consisted only of the Alpha-Beta-Gamma trio. The Bedouin included only the Alpha-Beta-Gamma group in their asterism *Al-Nasr al-Tair*, "the Flying Eagle." The ancient Greek celestial Eagle was pictured flying perpendicular to the Milky Way, with its head at Eta-Theta Aql, its tail at the Epsilon-Zeta pair, one wing marked by the Alpha-Beta-Gamma line, and the other by Delta.

Aquila occupies a fairly large area, and the bright eastern branch of the summer Milky Way passes southwest to northeast through it. However, Aquila is not as rich in interesting and attractive objects as the neighboring Milky Way constellations. It is especially poor in open clusters. Aquila occupies six times as much area as Scutum to its south and two times as much as Vulpecula to its north, but Burnham credits Scutum with five open clusters, Vulpecula with nine, and Aquila with only three (none being binocular objects).

For binoculars Aquila offers two things—a splendid Milky Way field and the Alpha-Beta-Gamma group. The Alpha-Beta-Gamma trio is a 5° long line that fits in most binocular fields of view. The name for Alpha, Altair, comes from the Bedouin title for the whole group. Alshain (Beta) and Tarazed (Gamma) are corrupted from the Persian *Shahini Tarazad*, "the Plundering Falcon." Altair and Gamma are a striking color

Photograph 5–11. *The Milky Way in Aquila NW of Altair, the large overexposed star disc near the lower left. The upper right quarter of the field is occupied by the Great Rift. Notice the abruptness of the boundary between the obscuring dust of the Great Rift and the rich star cloud in the center: this can be seen nicely in a scan with binoculars. Just to the left of center are two small, very dark dust patches superimposed on the bright star cloud. The double-pronged northern cloud is B143, and the crescent-shaped southern cloud B142. They are both easy binocular objects. They seem to be joined by a thin loop that arcs to the east (left) nearly as far as Gamma Aquilae, a 3rd-mag orange star that appears only as a dot on this blue-sensitive plate from E.E. Barnard's Atlas of Selected Regions of the Milky Way.*

contrast pair: Altair has an A7 IV–V spectrum and a blue-tinted white color; Gamma is ruddy-orange K3 II object. Their apparent magnitudes are 0.8 and 2.7, respectively. Altair is only 16.5 light-years away and is notable for its rapid rotational velocity. The star is spinning so fast—160 miles per second at the equator—that its equatorial diameter must be about twice its polar diameter.

The Milky Way in Aquila, Map 7. The Great Rift is most distinct in Aquila and the best scan across it is from Gamma Aquilae in the eastern branch of the Milky Way to the Zeta-Epsilon Aql pair in the western. Where the eastern edge of the Great Rift meets the bright, billowy, and star-speckled Gamma Aquilae region, the transition is so abrupt that it makes the Rift seem to be not just a starless region, but a mass in the foreground obscuring the view beyond—which is precisely what it is.

Immediately west of Gamma Aquilae, silhouetted on the bright Milky Way background, lie two small dark nebulae. The northern one, catalogued as B (for Barnard) 143, is a strangely-shaped object slightly over 30′ in diameter with two short (15′ long) extensions pointing west. The southern obscuring patch, B142, is elongated east-west and measures about 30′ × 15′. The center-to-center separation of the two nebulae is slightly less than 1°. Photographs show them connected by a long thin loop of dark matter that arcs east almost back to Gamma. B142 and B143 are not difficult to spot even in 7x35s when sky conditions are dark, and the two prongs of B143 can be seen in 10x50s and 50mm zooms. Use averted vision.

Minor Constellations of the Summer Milky Way

Sagitta, the Arrow, Map 7. The small arrow of Alpha (α), Beta (β), Delta (δ), Gamma (γ), and Eta (η) Sagittae is about 7° long and will just fit in the field of view of 7x wide-angle binoculars. It lies in the bright eastern branch of the Milky Way, a beautiful area to sweep with binoculars. The Sagitta Milky Way is fainter than the neighboring Gamma Aquilae region and lacks that region's scintillating partial resolution of star-specks, but its pale, clumpy background glow is scattered with a multitude of 7th-, 8th-, 9th-, and 10th-magnitude foreground stars. The edge of the Great Rift runs just west of Alpha and Beta Sagittae and is very distinct in binoculars.

Slightly south of the midpoint of the line between Gamma and Delta Sagittae is the globular cluster M71, a magnitude 8.3 object 6′ in diameter appearing as a small, fuzzy disk. As the low surface brightness of its binocular image suggests, M71 is one of the loosest globulars. In fact, for many years astronomers were uncer-

tain whether M71 was a very poor globular or a very rich open cluster. Its distance is about 12,000 light-years, so its true diameter is slightly over 20 light-years and its integrated absolute magnitude is −5.5—both very small values for a globular cluster. While you are in the M71 field, note the fine colors of Gamma and Delta Sagittae: Gamma is a yellow-orange magnitude 3.7 K5 star and Delta an orange magnitude 3.8 object with a composite M+A0 spectrum.

Delphinus, the Dolphin, Map 8. One of the most beautiful constellations is Delphinus, which takes no imagination at all to see as a dolphin leaping out of the stream of the Milky Way. Chances are that Delphinus was invented either by one of the early Mediterranean maritime nations (Minoans or Phoenicians) or by the early Greeks themselves, who would have seen plenty of dolphins playing around the islands of the Aegean.

Delphinus is about 6° long and fits the field of view of most 7x binoculars. (At 10x the Dolphin's star pattern is too spread out to make its best impression.) Because the constellation lies on the eastern edge of the Milky Way, it has a fairly rich background of 8th-, 9th-, and 10th-magnitude stars. Despite the compactness of the figure, the stars of Delphinus do not comprise a true physical cluster but lie at different distances from us. The data on Delphinus' brightest stars are given in the accompanying table. 50mm glasses are the smallest that can bring out the star colors listed. Delta Delphini is a short-period Delta Scuti-type pulsating variable. Gamma Delphini is a good double at moderate powers in small telescopes, the components being separated by 10″ in an east-west direction.

Table 5–9 The Brightest Stars of Delphinus					
Star	App Mag	Spectrum	Dist (l-y)	Abs Mag	Color
Alpha	3.8	B9 V	180	0.0	blue-white
Beta	3.8	F5 III–IV	125	+0.9	off-white
Gamma	3.9		100		yellow-orange
A	4.3	K2 IV		+1.8	
B	5.1	F8 V		+2.6	
Delta	4.4-4.5	F0 IVp	100 (?)	+2 (?)	white
Epsilon	4.0	B6 III	950	−3.3	silver-blue

Equuleus, the Foal, Map 8. Just southeast of Delphinus and outside the Milky Way is the small and inconspicuous constellation Equuleus. Consisting only of five faint stars (its brightest is magnitude 4.1 Alpha), Equuleus was formed by the Greeks, probably during the 2nd century B.C. It is one of the poorest constellations in the whole sky, having no clusters or nebulae and only one galaxy as bright as magnitude 13.0. The only thing in it for binoculars is the Gamma (γ)-6 Equulei double, a mere optical pair 6′ apart and of magnitudes

4.6 and 6.0, respectively. In small telescopes at about 50x, Epsilon (ϵ) is an attractive double star of magnitudes 5.3 and 7.2, separated by 11″ in position angle 70°. Epsilon is a true physical binary.

Vulpecula, the Little Fox, Maps 7 and 8. The narrow rectangle of Milky Way between Cygnus on the north and Sagitta and Delphinus on the south was called *Vulpecula cum Ansere*, "the Little Fox with the Goose," by the imaginative Johannes Hevelius. He justified his innovation by noting that foxes have the same rapacious greedy character as the neighboring birds, Aquila and Vultur Cadens. (Vultur Cadens was a common name for our Lyra in the 17th century. It means "the Plunging Vulture.")

Vulpecula contains no star brighter than magnitude 4.5, but because of its fine Milky Way fields, its abundance of open clusters, and the planetary nebula M27, it is a splendid constellation for the binocular observer. The Cygnus Star Cloud extends south of Albireo (Beta [β] Cygni) into northwest Vulpecula. Therefore, the Milky Way between Albireo and Alpha (α) Vulpecula is bright with multitudes of momentary visible star-specks embedded in its glow. An especially rich little field of 8th-, 9th-, and 10th-magnitude stars lies about 4° due east of Albireo.

Southeast of the Albireo-Alpha Vul star clouds lies the Great Rift, which in this region lacks the unbroken opaqueness it has in Aquila. Here it is in strangely shaped masses with faint channels of Milky Way light in-between. The eastern branch of the Milky Way in Vulpecula, across the Great Rift, has no very bright background glow, but like the adjoining Sagitta Milky Way it is rich in 8th-, 9th-, and 10th-magnitude foreground stars.

Four of Vulpecula's open clusters are good binocular objects. The largest is the coarse, loose group catalogued as **Collinder 399**, visible to the unaided eye as a hazy little patch about 4° northwest of Alpha Sagittae. In binoculars Collinder 399 has a strange appearance. It consists of a 45′ diameter circle of five stars of magnitudes 5 to 7, the northern one of which is also part of a 100′ long east-west line of six 6th- and 7th-magnitude stars. The cluster resembles a wire coat hanger and has been nicknamed "the Coat Hanger." It is so large and sparse that you'll see it best at 10x or less—more power simply spreads it out too much.

A more orthodox cluster is **NGC 6800**, located in a star-rich Milky Way field only 30′ northwest of Alpha Vul. In 10x50s NGC 6800 appears as a low surface brightness patch of haze with a granular texture from partial resolution of its brightest stars. The cluster is about 15′ in diameter.

The best open clusters for binoculars in Vulpecula are NGC 6885 and NGC 6940. **NGC 6885** is about 20′ in diameter and consists of 6th-magnitude 20 Vulpeculae with a scattering of some three dozen stars of magnitudes 8 to 11. 20 Vul lies in the center of the cluster and in 10x50 binoculars you can see a tight group of 8th- and 9th-magnitude stars just west and south of it, a couple more stars to the east, and a small patch of unresolved star-haze to the northwest.

NGC 6940, the other good Vulpecula cluster, is also about 20′ in diameter (noticeably elongated north-south) but is an intrinsically richer cluster than NGC 6885, with hundreds of stars of the 9th-magnitude and fainter. In 7x35s the cluster appears grainy with partial resolution, but in 10x50s the background is scattered with the glitter of resolved cluster members. NGC 6885 and NGC 6940 are in an area poor in bright stars and therefore aren't easy to find. Start at Epsilon (ϵ) Cygni and go 3° due south to the magnitude 4.3 star 52 Cygni. NGC 6940 is $3\frac{1}{2}°$ southwest of 52 Cyg. Then from NGC 6940 go 4° due west to the 1° wide pair of 5th-magnitude stars 21 and 23 Vulpeculae. NGC 6885 lies about 1° to the southwest of the southern star of the pair, 23 Vul.

But the outstanding object for binoculars and telescopes in Vulpecula is **M27**, the Dumbbell Nebula. With a size of $8' \times 5'$ and an integrated apparent magnitude of 7.6, M27 is the second largest and brightest of all planetary nebulae. (Only NGC 7293 in Aquarius is its superior.) M27 can be tricky to pick out in this jumble of 5th- and 6th-magnitude stars, especially in 7x glasses. Since it lies 3.3° due north of Gamma (γ) Sagittae, put this star at the southern edge of your binocular field and estimate how far toward the northern edge M27 should be. The distances of planetary nebulae are not known with good accuracy. However, several studies independently estimate a distance for M27 of around 900 light-years, which would make its true diameter just over 2 light-years and its integrated absolute magnitude at least +0.4.

Lyra, the Lyre, Map 7.

Though the Greeks got most of their constellations from Mesopotamia, a Lyre was probably not one of them. The earliest Mesopotamians knew the stars of our Lyra (or possibly Vega alone) as *Uza*, "the Goat." The desert Arabs of the 1st millennium A.D. called the Alpha (α)-Epsilon (ϵ)-Zeta (ζ) Lyrae triangle *Al-Nasr al-Waki*, "the Plunging Eagle" (This was corrupted into our "Vega.") European astronomers late in the Renaissance adopted the Arabs' Plunging Eagle for the whole of Lyra, but used the Latin name *Vultur Cadens*, "the Plunging Vulture."

Lyra lies on the western edge of the summer Milky Way. Its best Milky Way field is in the extreme eastern part of the constellation, the region around and south of Eta (η) and Theta (ϑ) Lyrae. The Milky Way background here is fairly faint but has an interesting fine-grained texture and is jewelled with multitude of star-specks and many bright 7th- to 9th-magnitude stars. (Eta and Theta are a nice color contrast pair in 10x50 glasses, Eta a sky-blue B3 star and Theta an orange-red K0 object.) Another nice field is the loose scattering of 5th-, 6th-, 7th-, and 8th-magnitude stars around the bluish 3rd-magnitude Beta (β) and Gamma (γ) Lyrae.

Despite its relatively small area, Lyra is rich in interesting objects for binoculars:

Alpha (α) Lyrae, Vega, Map 7. The beautiful blue-white magnitude 0.0 Vega is the second brightest star north of the celestial equator (Arcturus at magnitude -0.1 is the brightest). Vega has an A0 V spectrum, which means that it is slightly hotter—and therefore slightly bluer—than A2 Deneb in Cygnus; the color difference is perceptible in good quality binoculars on transparent nights when both stars are near the zenith. The closest reasonably bright-red star to contrast Vega's color with is R Lyrae, about 6° to the north-northeast. R Lyr is a red-orange M5 semiregular variable with a range of 3.9 to 5.0 magnitude and a period averaging 46 days.

Vega is 26.5 light-years away from us and therefore has an absolute magnitude of $+0.5$ (a luminosity of 53 Suns). It is estimated to be 2.7 million miles in diameter and to contain about 3 solar masses.

Variable star Beta (β) Lyrae, Map 7. Beta Lyrae, one of the most-studied variables in the sky, is the prototype of a special class of eclipsing binary star. It ranges between magnitudes 3.4 and 4.4 over a period of 12.9079 days; the star's variations can be followed with the unaided eye or binoculars by comparing it to the magnitude 3.3 Gamma Lyrae, which lies only 1.7° to the east-southeast. In binoculars Beta Lyrae has a distinctly bluish tint.

The distinguishing characteristic of Beta Lyrae type eclipsing variables is their light curve. Usually, an eclipsing binary, like Algol in Perseus, will show a light curve with a flat maximum (when both stars are visible to us), a flat minimum (when one star is behind the other), and a straight-line decline to minimum and ascent to maximum. Beta Lyrae stars, however, have light curves that are sinusoidal (wave-shaped). This happens because in such systems, the two stars are so close together that their mutual gravitational attraction distorts them into ellipsoids. Thus, as they revolve around each other they present a continually changing surface area.

The Beta Lyrae system consists of a large B8 II–III primary and a smaller and cooler late A or early F companion. Minimum occurs when the cooler star partially

eclipses the B8 primary. There is a second minimum (which reaches mag 3.8) when the B8 primary totally eclipses the cooler star. The spectrum of Beta Lyrae is extremely complicated and difficult to interpret (which is why the exact spectral type of the smaller star is uncertain). It seems to show that gas is streaming between the two stars (the B star apparently losing matter to its companion) and that there is a large turbulent and expanding spiral of matter around the system. This mass-exchange between the stars affects their evolution in unpredictable ways.

Because of its spectral peculiarities, astronomers find it difficult to estimate the true brightness of Beta Lyrae and, therefore, its distance. However, it has four visual companions, two of which might be true physical associates. The brightest is a mag 7.8 B7 V star. B7 V stars usually have absolute magnitudes around -0.6, which implies a distance to the B7 V companion of Beta Lyrae—and therefore to Beta Lyrae itself if the B7 star is actually associated with it—of about 1500 light-years. Some authorities give Beta Lyrae's distance as about 900 light-years. Until the star is better understood, however, no estimate of Beta Lyrae's distance will be very reliable.

Double stars Epsilon (ϵ) and Zeta (ζ) Lyrae, Map 7. Just $1\frac{1}{2}$° northeast of Vega is one of the finest doubles in the sky, Epsilon Lyrae, the famous Double-Double. Epsilon 1 and Epsilon 2 are 208″ apart in position angle 173° (almost due north-south, with Epsilon 1 the northern of the two). It can be resolved with the unaided eye if your eyesight is keen enough. (Mine isn't; I find the glare of nearby Vega interferes.) At about 100x in small telescopes, Epsilon 1 and Epsilon 2 both split into two components each, thus making Epsilon Lyrae a quadruple star.

Table 5–10 The Epsilon Lyrae Double Stars							
Star	Tot App Mag	Comp App Mag	Spectra	Abs Mag	Sep (″) (1982)	PA (°) (1982)	Orbital Period (yrs)
ϵ^1	5.1						
A		5.4	A2	+1.7	}2.7	355	1200
B		6.5	A4	+2.8			
ϵ^2	4.4						
A		5.1	A3	+1.4	}2.3	83	600
B		5.3	A5	+1.6			

Because all four stars of Epsilon Lyrae share the same proper motion, the entire group must be a true gravitationally-connected multiple. However, orbital motion has been observed only in the two close pairs. This is not surprising, because at the 180 light-years distance of the system, the true separation between Epsilon 1 and Epsilon 2 is $\frac{1}{5}$ light-year (more if one star is significantly nearer to us than the other) and their orbital period must be extremely long.

About 1½° southeast of Vega lies another splendid double, Zeta (ζ) Lyrae. The magnitude 4.3 and 5.9 components of Zeta Lyr are separated by 44″ in position angle 150° and can be split even in 7x glasses. Because its components are tighter, Zeta Lyrae is actually an even more attractive sight in binoculars than Epsilon. Like the components of Epsilon, the two stars of Zeta have the same proper motion and therefore must be a true physical binary. The magnitude 4.3 star's spectrum is A0, and its magnitude 5.9 companion's is F0. The distance to Zeta Lyrae is 135 light-years, so the main star's absolute magnitude is +1.2 and the other's is +2.8.

The Delta (δ) Lyrae cluster, Map 7. Delta Lyrae is a 10′ wide naked-eye double. In 50mm binoculars the pair has a noticeable color contrast: Delta 1, the western star, is a magnitude 5.5 bluish object, and Delta 2 is a ruddy-orange variable with a range between magnitudes 4.5 and 5.0. Their spectra are B3 V and M4 II, respectively. In 10x glasses a small knot of half a dozen stars can be seen just east of Delta 1, the higher powers of zooms being very useful on this tiny group. This seems to be a sparse star cluster physically associated with the Delta pair. The distance of the Delta Lyrae cluster is around 800 light-years, so the absolute magnitudes of Delta 1 and Delta 2 are about −2 and −3. The Delta Lyrae cluster has approximately the same space motion as the Pleiades and might therefore be part of a Pleiades stream similar to the Hyades and the Ursa Major Streams.

The Ring Nebula, M57, Map 7. No doubt the most famous planetary nebula is the Ring Nebula, M57. At apparent magnitude 8.8, it is one of the brightest planetaries. But since it measures only 85″ × 62″, it appears merely as a star in the low powers of binoculars. Use the finder chart to pick out M57's star-like image from the clutter of field stars. Note that the nebula lies at the south vertex of an isosceles triangle formed by the planetary and two stars. This triangle has a base about 10′ and sides 7′ long and is fairly easy to spot in binoculars midway between Beta and Gamma Lyrae.

The central "hole" in the Ring Nebula can be seen with averted vision at about 100x in telescopes of 4-inch aperture, but lies far beyond the grasp of any binoculars. The only planetary nebulae that show disks at 10x are NGC 7293 in Aquarius (the Helical Nebula), NGC 246 in Cetus, M27 in Vulpecula (the Dumbbell Nebula), and NGC 1360 in Fornax. These are discussed under their respective constellations.

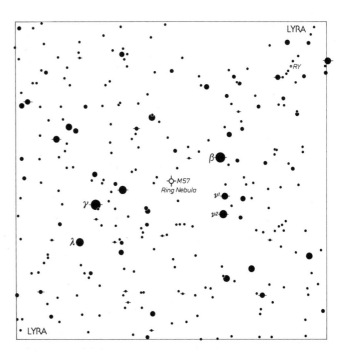

Identification Chart 5-3. M57. *Stars are plotted to magnitude 9.5, and the chart scale is 18mm (=0.35 inch) per degree. North is to the top, and east to the left.*

Cygnus, the Swan, Maps 2, 7, and 8.

The brightest stretch of the Milky Way north of the celestial equator is in Cygnus. The brightest section of the Cygnus Milky Way is the Cygnus Star Cloud between Beta (β) and Gamma (γ) Cygni. Because Cygnus culminates at the zenith for observers in middle northern latitudes, its Milky Way fields can be viewed with the darkest possible sky background. The best sections of the Cygnus Milky Way are discussed in detail below, beginning with the southwest end of the Cygnus Star Cloud and working northeast through the constellation.

However, there is more in Cygnus for binoculars than Milky Way fields. The constellation also contains three fine binocular doubles, a large open cluster (M39), two emission nebulae (both described in the Deneb section), and a supernova remnant.

The Veil Nebula, NGC 6992, Map 8. You would think binoculars to be very unpromising instruments with which to search for supernova remnants. However, two of the most famous supernova remnants are not difficult binocular objects. One is the Crab Nebula (M1) in Taurus; the other is the NGC 6992 section of the Veil Nebula in Cygnus. The latter can be unmistakably discerned in even 8x40s as a fishhook-shaped condensation of Milky Way about 78′ long and 8′ wide. Because NGC 6992 lies in a grainy-textured region of the Milky Way, the trick is to pick it out from the many knots and patches of Milky Way in the area. The nebula's distinctive shape will help you spot it, and you can confirm your sighting by its southeast-to-northwest orientation. (The "hook" lies to the southeast and the "shaft" points toward Epsilon [ε] Cygni, 3° to the northwest.) NGC 6992 is approximately at the right angle of a triangle with Epsilon and 52 Cygni.

NGC 6992 is actually just the northeast segment of the Veil Nebula. The whole Veil consists of a group of nebulous fragments, all with filamentary structure, spread over an area 3.5° × 2.7° and centered about 3° south-southeast of Epsilon Cygni. The other bright section of the Veil, NGC 6960, lies adjacent to 52 Cygni (which is merely a foreground star and not actually involved with the nebula). The filamentary structure of both NGC 6992 and NGC 6960 and their curvature—in photographs they resemble opposing parenthesis marks—make it obvious that they are simply different parts of the same structure. This bubble appearance is why the Veil Nebula is sometimes called the Cygnus Loop.

The Veil Nebula is estimated to be around 2,000 light-years away and therefore is about 100 light-years in diameter. It is expanding by about 0.06″ per year. At this rate, the time required for it to reach its present size would be about 160,000 years. However, the expanding gas shells of a supernova outburst sweep up the interstellar matter they encounter and therefore are decelerated. (The Veil has unquestionably swept up matter as it expanded, for on photographs there are more faint, distant stars visible within than outside the arcs of the nebula.) No doubt the Veil was originally expanding at a much faster rate, and the time that has elapsed since the supernova explosion that formed it may possibly be only 30,000 years.

Binocular Doubles in Cygnus

Beta (β) Cygni, Albireo, Map 7. One of the most famous doubles in the sky is the star marking the head of the Swan, Albireo (Beta [β] Cygni). It consists of a magnitude 3.1 K3 II primary with magnitude 5.1 B8 Ve companion 34″ distant in position angle 54° (northeast). Albireo can be split with difficulty in 10x50s, but is decidedly easier in 10x40s—the smaller aperture decreases the glare of the 3rd-magnitude primary. (This is one situation where less offers more!) The beautiful orange-yellow and bluish color contrast of the components can be glimpsed in 50mm binoculars but is best appreciated in telescopes at about 100x. Albireo lies around 410 light-years away, so its primary's absolute magnitude is −2.4 and its secondary's is −0.4 (luminosities of 760 and 120 Suns). The primary is a spectroscopic binary, and Albireo therefore is actually a triple system.

Table 5–11 The Stars of 61 Cygni						
Star	Spectrum	App Mag	Abs Mag	Luminosity (× Sun)	Radius (× Sun)	Mass (× Sun)
61 Cygni A	K5 Ve	5.22	+7.6	0.08	0.48	0.6
61 Cygni B	K7 Ve	6.08	+8.4	0.04	0.45	0.5

61 Cygni, Maps 2 and 8. Although the two stars of 61 Cygni are only 29″ apart (closer than the Albireo pair), 61 Cygni is decidedly easier to resolve; 7x glasses will do it easily. The reason for this is that the magnitude difference of the 61 Cygni pair is only 0.8, significantly less than the two-magnitude difference of the Albireo double. 61 Cygni is just 11.2 light-years away, the 12th nearest star to the solar system. The components of 61 Cygni both have a striking chrome orange-red color; this color and the tightness of its stars make 61 Cygni one of the two or three most beautiful binocular doubles.

61 Cygni also is one of the few binocular doubles in which orbital motion has been observed. The first measurement of the separation and position angle of the system was made in 1830. Since then, the secondary has moved through about one-fifth of its apparent orbit around the primary. The estimated orbital period is 650 years, with maximum separation (34″) predicted to occur around 2100 A.D. Some years ago astronomers believed they had evidence for a planet-size third body in the 61 Cygni system, but this idea has now been abandoned.

Omicron (o) 1 Cygni, Maps 2 and 8. Omicron 1 and Omicron 2 Cygni are a 1° wide north-south pair of 4th-magnitude stars located about 4 1/2° west-northwest of Deneb (Omicron 1 is the southern of the pair). Both stars have a nice chrome-orange color and both are also eclipsing binaries. Omicron 1 has a range of 3.8–4.2 and a spectrum of K2 II+B3 V; Omicron 2's spectrum is K3 Ib+A3 V and its range is 3.9 to 4.2. (These ranges are too small to be obvious visually.) Because the bluish component of Omicron 1 is almost as luminous as its primary, Omicron 1 shines a noticeably paler orange than Omicron 2. The periods of Omicron 1 and Omicron 2 Cygni are 10.42 and 3.15 years, respectively. The light decreases occur when the K-type primaries eclipse the blue secondaries. Omicron 1 is about 350 and Omicron 2 550 light-years distant.

Omicron 1 Cygni is also a visual triple: 338″ away to the northwest is a magnitude 5.0 A3 star, and 107″ due south is a magnitude 6.9 B5 object. The first star's sky-blue color can be discerned in 50mm glasses and provides a nice contrast to Omicron 1's orange. These stars, however, are probably not actually physically associated with Omicron 1.

Photograph 5–12. The Cygnus Milky Way. *Photograph by Tom Eby on hypered 2415 film with a 50mm lens at f/2 and a hydrogen-alpha pass filter. The North America Nebula, NGC 7000, is conspicuous in the upper left (NE) corner of the field. Just west of it is the much fainter Pelican Nebula, IC 5067, the brightest section of which can be glimpsed in 10x50 or larger binoculars. Further west is Deneb. Around Gamma Cygni in the upper center of the field are several patches of diffuse nebulosity, all catalogued as IC 1318: the two immediately east, and the one twice as far to the NW, of Gamma are visible in large binoculars. Toward the lower left of the field are the two arcs of the Veil Nebula, NGC 6960 to the west and the much brighter NGC 6992 to the east. The appearance of the latter in this photo is similar to its appearance in 10x50 binoculars.*

The Cygnus Star Cloud, Maps 7 and 8.

The Cygnus Star Cloud is the most conspicuous Milky Way cloud north of the celestial equator. It extends in a 16° long ellipse from the region of Albireo northeast to the area of Gamma (γ) Cygni. In binoculars the appearance of the Cygnus Star Cloud changes as you sweep northeast. Around Albireo the Milky Way is a billowy haze, with myriads of momentarily resolved star-specks embedded in it. (Make sure your eyes are well dark-adapted and keep your eyes at the oculars for a couple minutes at a time.) Near the Great Rift (in the Albireo section of the Cygnus Cloud) are heavy, strangely-shaped obscuring patches. Northeast of Albireo, around Eta (η) Cygni, is an area where fine dust lanes snake through the Milky Way background glow. Farther northeast, between Eta and Gamma Cygni, the background glow becomes fainter, but the loss is made up by an abundance of bright 5th-, 6th-, 7th-, and 8th-magnitude foreground stars.

The best part of the Cygnus Star Cloud, however, is around Gamma Cygni, where broad and very dark obscuring channels cut through the background glow. One particularly notable channel extends in a 45′ long west-to-east line immediately south of Gamma. 1° east-southeast of Gamma this channel bends toward the northeast, where it is flanked by two small, relatively star-rich patches. These are actually two emission nebulae, part of the IC 1318 complex. In binoculars these nebulae are defined as much by the stars overlying them as by their own pale luminescence. Another emission nebula, 2.3° across, can be detected in 10x50 binoculars about 2° north-northwest of Gamma. This patch is another section of IC 1318.

About 1.7° south-southeast of Gamma Cygni, appearing in the higher powers of zoom binoculars as a small (5′ in diameter) knot of a half dozen 9th- and 10th-magnitude stars, is the open cluster M29. (In 10x glasses M29 is very tight, but identifiable to a practiced eye.) This is not one of the more striking Messier objects even in telescopes, but its brightest stars are all highly luminous B0 giants. M29 is some 6000 light-years away. About 1° west-southwest of M29 is the peculiar variable P Cygni, a star that at present is almost constant at magnitude 4.9 (photoelectric measurements indicate that it varies by a couple tenths of a magnitude) but which during the 17th century brightened to 3rd-magnitude. P Cygni is a very distant and highly luminous star, perhaps 7,000 light-years away and with an absolute magnitude of nearly −9. Its spectrum is classified as B1 eq, the "eq" referring to broad emission bands bordered on their violet side by sharp absorption lines, which indicates that the star is surrounded by a large expanding envelope and is therefore ejecting mat-

ter into space. Stars with P Cygni spectra are usually found in very young clusters and associations.

The Deneb Region, Maps 2 and 8. At magnitude 1.3, Deneb is the 19th brightest star in the sky. It is an A2 Ia supergiant about 1,600 light-years away, making it the most distant 1st-magnitude star. Its absolute magnitude is −7.1, equal to Rigel's. In binoculars the star looks merely white, not blue-white like Vega and Sirius. Deneb is the brightest member of a rather scattered association, Cygnus OB7, which includes magnitude 4.8 B3 Ia 55 Cygni, magnitude 5.0 O7.5 III 68 Cygni, and several fainter blue and white stars in this region.

The Great Rift begins at Deneb. The large area of obscuration between Deneb and Gamma (γ) Cygni is sometimes called the "Northern Coal Sack," but the name is perhaps as appropriate for the darker obscuring cloud centered about midway between Deneb and Alpha (α) Cephei.

Extending for several degrees east and northeast from Deneb is the most beautiful region of the Milky Way north of the celestial equator. In binoculars and rich-field telescopes it is a breathtaking mixture of dark and bright Milky Way masses, the bright clouds unusually brilliant and the dark clouds virtually black. The bright cloud centered 3° east and slightly south of Deneb is NGC 7000, the North America Nebula. Its basic "North America" outline is evident in any size binoculars, but 10x50s show the nebula's *entire* photographic extent—including the narrow "isthmus of Panama." By a strange coincidence the nebula is oriented on the celestial sphere just like a map, with Canada upward (to the north). NGC 7000 can be seen with the unaided eye as an amorphous patch of Milky Way glow. The nebula measures about 100′ east-west and 120′ north-south, and its integrated apparent magnitude is 4.5.

There are several interesting things to notice in and around the North America Nebula. Bordering the nebula on the east is perhaps the most opaque obscuring channel of the region, in the center of which (off the "California coast") is the magnitude 3.9 Xi (ξ) Cygni, a K5 star with a beautiful chrome-orange color. In the west-central part of NGC 7000 (its "Appalachian" region) is the tiny, granular patch of the loose open cluster NGC 6997, an object only 8′ in diameter with an integrated apparent magnitude of just 10.0. It is not certain that NGC 6997 is actually involved with the nebula, or even if the object is a true cluster. Out in the "Atlantic" from "Florida" are the 5th-magnitude stars 56 and 57 Cygni, separated by about ⅔°. In most binoculars an amorphous, very pale glow can be detected around 56 Cygni, the southwest star of the pair. This glow is the emission nebula IC 5067, the Pelican Nebula, which is simply another illuminated section of the cloud

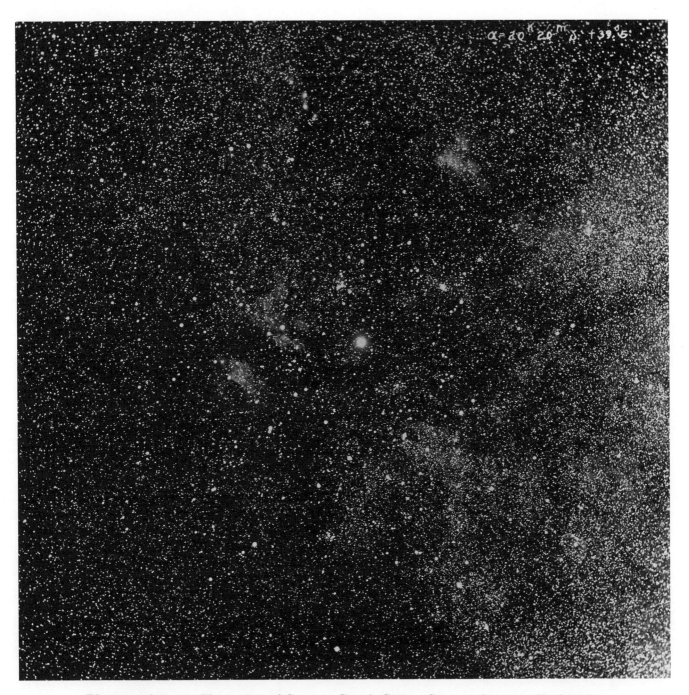

Photograph 5–13. The region of Gamma Cygni. *Gamma Cyg is at the center. To the right (west) and lower right (southwest) are the northeasternmost billows of the Cygnus Star Cloud. Near the lower right, in the Star Cloud, can be seen the little arc of NGC 6888, a possible supernova remnant which can be glimpsed in richest-field telescopes and giant binoculars (under excellent observing conditions). Normal binoculars reveal the heavy lanes of obscuring matter superimposed on the Milky Way glow west and south of Gamma Cyg. Immediately south of the star is a broad obscuring channel oriented due east-west. At its east end, about $^3/_4°$ ESE of Gamma, it turns NE and is flanked by two patches of stars mingled with pale nebulosity—segments of the scattered diffuse nebula IC 1318. Another fragment of IC 1318 visible in 10x50 and larger binoculars is the triangular nebulosity 2° NW of Gamma Cygni. Photo by E.E. Barnard.*

Photograph 5–14. *The North America Nebula, NGC 7000, from E.E. Barnard's Photographic Atlas of the Milky Way. To its west (right) are the dim whisps of the Pelican Nebula, IC 5067, which extends north-to-south between the 4th-magnitude stars 56 and 57 Cygni. The isolated bright star off the "Pacific coast" is Xi Cygni, an orange star that appears relatively fainter than it really is on this blue-sensitive photograph. The size of this field is comparable to that of wide-angle 10x binoculars.*

of interstellar gas that also contains the North America Nebula itself.

The North America Nebula is thought to be involved with the Cygnus OB7 association and therefore is probably the same distance as Deneb, 1,600 light-years. Its true dimensions are about 60 × 50 light-years.

The M39 Region, Maps 2 and 8. About 9° east-northeast of Deneb is the 30′ diameter, very loose open cluster M39. It contains only about two dozen stars between magnitudes 7 and 10.5, arranged in a rough triangle. M39's brightest members are so scattered that the cluster is better in 7x binoculars than in telescopes. (Even the higher powers of zoom binoculars magnify it too much). The cluster's integrated apparent magnitude is 4.6, meaning that under good sky conditions (a dark, transparent night at a site far from city lights) it can be seen with the unaided eye as a small fuzzy patch. M39 is about 800 light-years away, so its true diameter is about 7 light-years and its integrated absolute magnitude is around −2.4, a luminosity of 760 Suns.

The Milky Way in the M39 region is only slightly less spectacular than the Milky Way east and northeast of Deneb. The background glow here is very bright and embedded in it are myriads of momentarily resolved stars. With careful looking, dark channels can be glimpsed on the star clouds. Just under 2° south of Pi (π) 2 Cygni is a very striking, 2° long streak of obscuration, one of the easiest individual dust features visible anywhere in the Milky Way. It lies midway between M39 and NGC 7209 in Lacerta and is oriented along the line joining the two clusters.

From the bright star clouds around M39 and Pi 2 Cygni, sweep slowly due north. As you near the Mu (μ) Cephei region, the star clouds abruptly disappear behind the dust of the IC 1396 complex. The effect is so dramatic, and the irregular outlines of the IC 1396 obscuring clouds so easy to discern in most binoculars, that even if you knew nothing about interstellar matter you would assume that you had scanned into a region where relatively nearby opaque material blocks the light of the star fields beyond.

Chapter 6

The Structure of Our Galaxy

On the face of it, you'd think it hopeless for a backyard astronomer, armed only with binoculars or a small telescope, to see anything of the structure of our Galaxy. But such pessimism is unjustified. The details of the spiral structure of the Galaxy in the solar neighborhood—out to some 6,000 or 8,000 light-years—can be traced with binoculars and the unaided eye quite easily. Admittedly, these features aren't so obvious that you could have discovered them with binoculars on your own. But once you know the details of local spiral structure, they make perfect visual sense in terms of where the brightest star clouds of the Milky Way are and how the familiar diffuse nebulae and open clusters are distributed. The only tricky part in getting "galactic perspective" is learning to think of the night sky in terms of the Milky Way.

The Milky Way slashes across the dome of the sky with no regard for the equatorial coordinate system, cutting the celestial equator at an angle of about 63°. Astronomers therefore have established a galactic coordinate system based upon the central line of the Milky Way (the galactic equator) which, like the celestial equator itself, describes a great circle on the celestial sphere. Galactic longitude is measured along the galactic equator from 0° to 360°. The zero point (which lies in Sagittarius) is the direction toward the center of the Galaxy, 90° (in Cygnus) is the direction the solar neighborhood is moving toward as it orbits the center of the Galaxy, 180° (in Auriga) is the direction away from the Galactic Center (this is called the anticenter), and 270° (in Vela) is the direction from which the solar neighborhood is moving. Galactic latitude is measured from 0° to 90° (just like declination and terrestrial latitude). It gives a celestial object's height above or below the galactic equator. The two galactic poles are 90° away from the galactic equator. The north galactic pole is in Coma Berenices, some 4° due east of the central region of the Coma Star Cluster, and the south galactic pole is in the star-poor spaces of Sculptor, about 9° almost due south of Beta (β) Ceti.

The first step in acquiring galactic perspective is to think of the celestial sphere in terms of the galactic co-ordinate system and particularly in terms of the galactic equator and its four cardinal points. This sounds difficult, but when you are actually standing under the Milky Way outside at night, and know where galactic longitudes 0°, 90°, 180°, and 270° are with respect to familiar bright stars, then things in fact are pretty straightforward. For observers in the middle northern latitudes, the best times to study the structure of the Milky Way are in the early autumn and the early spring, when first the Galactic Center and then the galactic anticenter are favorably placed during the early evening hours.

The basic statistics of the Milky Way Galaxy are these: the disk is about 100,000 light-years in diameter, with the Sun being about 30,000 light-years out from the Galactic Center. The edge-on thickness of the spiral arms is less than 1000 light-years, but the great spherical central hub is some 10,000 light-years in diameter. (Like globular clusters, the central hubs of spiral galaxies gradually thin with increasing distance from their centers, and therefore a specific figure for hub diameter is a bit misleading.) In structure the Milky Way System seems to lie between spiral classes Sb and Sc, with fairly loosely wound spiral arms and a relatively small central hub. (Viewed face-on, our Galaxy might resemble M51, the Whirlpool Galaxy, in Canes Venatici.) Its stellar population numbers in the hundreds of billions. The mass is uncertain, but a minimum estimate would be 200 billion solar masses, half in stars, half in interstellar gas and dust. The total luminosity of Galaxy is on the order of 10 billion times the Sun's, corresponding to an integrated absolute magnitude of −20 or −20.5. In comparison with other galaxies, the Milky Way is well above average in size, mass, and luminosity.

6.1   The Autumn Milky Way

In the early evenings of late August and September, the Milky Way is at its most spectacular for observers in mid-northern latitudes. It sweeps in a broad, glowing path from Sagittarius in the south-southwest up

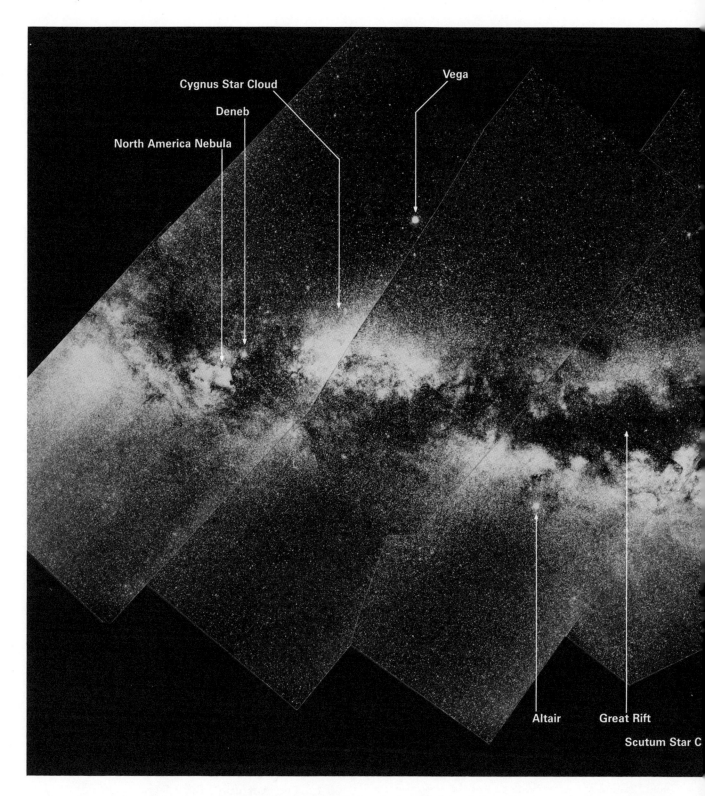

A Milky Way mosaic of the summer Milky Way photographed and assembled by Robert Reeves, each plate a 30-minute exposure on Kodak Technical Pan film with a 50mm f/2.8 lens. The Milky Way is here shown from northern Centaurus, Lupus, Norma, and Ara up to Lacerta and southern Cepheus—an extent of about 130° in galactic longitude. This mosaic resembles photos of such nearby edge-on spiral galaxies as NGC 4565 in Coma Berneces and NGC 891 in Andromeda, and therefore dramatically illustrates the fact that our Solar System lies on an outer arm of a fairly large spiral galaxy. Despite the heavy dust clouds in that direction, the shape of the great spherical central hub of our Galaxy can be plainly discerned in the Sagittarius-Scorpius region near the lower edge of the mosaic.

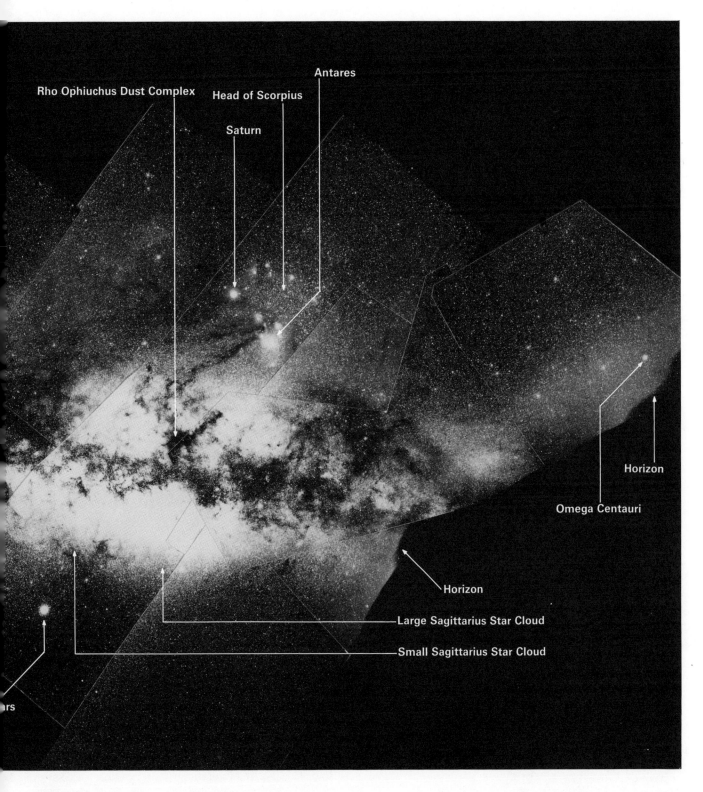

Some of the more prominent features and objects visible in the mosaic are labelled on the chart. A good many more can be identified with the assistance of the star maps in the back of this book. One final point: Notice that the central line of the Great Rift from Cygnus to Scutum is tilted with respect to the central line of the Milky Way itself. In Cygnus the brightest part of the Milky Way is NW of the Great Rift, but in Aquila and Scutum it is SE. This is because the dark clouds of the Great Rift are relatively close, by galactic standards, and are involved in the chain of nearby associations, young star clusters, and emission nebulae and hot blue stars named Gould's Belt, a feature of galactic structure discussed in the text that is tilted with respect to the galactic plane.

through Scutum, Aquila, Sagitta, and Vulpecula to Cygnus, which is nearly overhead. From Cygnus it descends through southern Cepheus and northern Lacerta, Cassiopeia, and Perseus toward the northeastern horizon. The brightest of the Milky Way star clouds are in Sagittarius because that is the direction toward the Galactic Center. Radio astronomy studies have established that the precise position of the Galactic Center is R.A. $17^h07^m39^s$ and declination $-29°03'14''$ (equinox 2000), a visually unremarkable spot about 4° west-northwest of Gamma (γ) Sagittarii.

Galactic longitude 90°, the direction of revolution of our region of the Galaxy around the Galactic Center, lies in Cygnus just 5° northeast of Deneb. (The Sun's individual motion through space is carrying it not directly toward galactic longitude 90°, but somewhat off the galactic plane in the general direction of Vega.) For observers in mid-northern latitudes, galactic longitude 90° is nearly straight overhead during early autumn evenings. Imagine yourself standing outside at that time of year and facing west. When you look overhead toward Deneb and longitude 90°, you are looking *into* the direction of orbital motion of the Galaxy. The Galactic Center will lie to your left, in the Milky Way just above the southwest horizon, and the galactic anticenter will be on your right, below the northeast horizon.

The Great Rift, Maps 7, 8, and 10. The most striking naked-eye feature of the early autumn Milky Way is the Great Rift, which divides the Milky Way southwest from Deneb into two more or less parallel streams. (The western stream fades out in northern Ophiuchus, blocked by a large dust cloud that covers much of the eastern section of that constellation, but reappears some 20° farther on in the region of Eta [η] Ophiuchi.) The Great Rift extends beyond Sagittarius, through the Tail of Scorpius and far along the deep southern Milky Way, finally ending at Alpha (α) Centauri.

Wide-angle photos of the Milky Way from Cygnus to Centaurus are remarkably similar to photos of edge-on spiral galaxies like NGC 891 in Andromeda and NGC 4565 in Coma Berenices. This is because the Great Rift of our Galaxy and the dark lanes of other galaxies are caused by the same phenomenon—clouds of interstellar gas and dust obscuring the light of stars beyond. The true nature of the Great Rift is best appreciated by sweeping between the two streams of the autumn Milky Way with binoculars. Particularly fine scans across the Great Rift are in Cygnus and Aquila. From the billowy star clouds around Albireo (Beta [β] Cygni) scan slowly southeast toward the tip of Sagitta. And from the sparkling star field west of Gamma (γ) Aquilae sweep west to the Epsilon (ϵ)-Zeta (ζ) Aquilae

pair. The abrupt fall into darkness of the Great Rift in both of these scans would suggest to you, even if you knew nothing about interstellar matter, that the Great Rift consists of huge billows of obscuring dust.

Sagittarius: toward the Center of the Galaxy, Map 7. Because it contains the Galactic Center, the logical place to begin study of galactic structure is Sagittarius. Despite the dust clouds of the Great Rift, which are particularly thick toward the Galactic Center, we can see at least four layers of the Galaxy's structure in the direction of Sagittarius. The most distant is the Great Sagittarius Star Cloud north of Gamma (γ) and Delta (δ) Sagittarii—in fact, it is the most distant structural feature visible with the unaided eye or binoculars anywhere along the Milky Way. This brilliant star cloud is actually a section of our Galaxy's spherical central hub. Because the Galactic Center is some 30,000 light-years distant and the hub is about 10,000 light-years in diameter, the stars of the Great Sagittarius Star Cloud must lie between about 25,000 and 35,000 light-years from us.

The actual nucleus of the galactic hub, which contains the Galactic Center, is thought to be something like a super-globular cluster crowding perhaps 10,000,000 stars into a sphere 25 light-years in radius. (By contrast, there are only about 250 stars within 25 light-years of the Sun!) The density of mass at the Galactic Center—including both stars and gas—is millions of times as great as in the solar neighborhood. The galactic nucleus can be studied only at radio, microwave, and infrared wavelengths because the dust of the Great Rift and the interior spiral arms blocks all shorter-wavelength radiation. Astronomers have estimated that visible light from the galactic nucleus is obscured 27 magnitudes by the intervening interstellar matter. If a supernova exploded at the Galactic Center and became as bright as the whole rest of the Galaxy combined, it nevertheless would have an apparent magnitude of only about 22—barely detectable with the 200-inch Hale telescope!

Most of our Galaxy's central hub is obscured by interstellar matter. If all of it could be seen, it would cover virtually the entire area between Nunki (Sigma [σ] Sgr) on the east and Antares on the west, and Eta (η) Ophiuchi to the north and Theta (ϑ) Scorpii to the south. The Great Sagittarius Star Cloud section of the galactic hub is visible only because of a "window" through the interstellar matter. There are several such windows through which we can see relatively large distances across the spiral arms of our Galaxy. These windows exist because the interstellar medium is not evenly distributed in the plane of the Galaxy, but has coagulated into large and small clouds. (One famous example of a nearby cloud of interstellar dust is the Coal

Sack in Crux, the Southern Cross.)

Another window in the interstellar matter lets us view the second most distant feature of galactic structure in Sagittarius, the Small Sagittarius Star Cloud. The estimated distance to the Small Sagittarius Star Cloud, 16,000 light-years, implies that it is a section of one of the interior spiral arms of the Galaxy—possibly of the Inner Arm itself, the first spiral feature outside the galactic hub. (For more on the two Sagittarius star clouds, see the section on Sagittarius in Chapter 5.)

The dark interstellar matter framing the distant Small Sagittarius Star Cloud is associated with the third galactic structure visible in Sagittarius, the Sagittarius-Carina Spiral Arm, the next arm in from the Sun's. It is so-named because most of the major emission nebulae and open clusters from northeast Carina through Sagittarius are embedded in it. Objects in Sagittarius belonging to the arm include the emission nebulae M8 (the Lagoon), M20 (the Trifid), and M17 (the Swan), and open clusters M21 and M18—all of which are discussed in the Sagittarius section of the book. These objects range in distance from about 5,000 light-years for M18 to almost 7,000 light-years for the Trifid. The figures suggest the distance and minimum width of the Sagittarius-Carina Arm. (Major spiral arms are typically 3,000 to 4,000 light-years wide.)

The fourth galactic structure visible in Sagittarius is, of course, our own spiral arm, represented by the bright 2nd- and 3rd-magnitude stars that form the traditional constellation pattern of the Archer, and by the open clusters M23 and M25. The distances to the bright stars of Sagittarius fall between 70 light-years (for Lambda [λ]) and 600 (for Phi [φ]). M23 and M25 are both just over 2,000 light-years away. (Many extremely faint stars that are part of our spiral arm also lie in this direction, but their cumulate light output is negligible.) It may strike you as trivial to consider these scattered stars and isolated open clusters as a feature of galactic structure, but the very skimpiness of objects in Sagittarius that belong to our spiral arm demonstrates an important fact about our location in the Galaxy: the Solar System lies near the inside edge of its spiral arm. Therefore, if we wish to see the major associations, open clusters, and emission nebulae of our own spiral arm, we must look opposite Sagittarius toward the galactic anticenter, which is in the direction of Auriga.

To summarize, then, when we look toward Sagittarius, we are looking past a scattering of foreground stars and open clusters across an interarm void to the Sagittarius-Carina Arm, which is rich in open clusters and bright and dark nebulae. A window through the gas and dust of the Sagittarius-Carina Arm allows us to see the Small Sagittarius Star Cloud, a large section of a spiral arm that lies well interior of us. Finally,

just over the Sagittarius-Carina Arm we see the Great Sagittarius Star Cloud, part of the galactic hub itself.

Scutum: The edge of an interior spiral arm, Map 7. Southwest from Sagittarius, the Sagittarius-Carina Arm extends along the southern Milky Way as far as the northeast corner of Carina. Its course is traced by such notable southern Milky Way objects as the open cluster NGC 6231 and its surrounding association in Scorpius (discussed in the section on that constellation), the NGC 6193 open cluster in Ara (4,500 light-years away), the famed Jewel Box Cluster, NGC 4755, in Crux (8,200 light-years away), and the Keyhole Nebula, NGC 3372, in Carina (about 7,000 light-years distant). The star clouds around the Keyhole Nebula are exceptionally brilliant. In that direction we are looking lengthwise down the Sagittarius-Carina Arm where it curves around the central regions of the Galaxy. A profusion of very distant star clusters and star clouds crowds the view.

Northeast of Sagittarius the Sagittarius-Carina Arm includes the Star Queen Nebula, M16 (discussed in the section on Serpens Cauda), and extends as far as the Scutum Star Cloud. The open clusters M11 and M26, though quite distant (about 5,500 and 4,900 light-years away, respectively) lie just outside the Sagittarius-Carina Arm and are therefore actually foreground to the Scutum Cloud. The Scutum Star Cloud is exceptionally bright because it marks the other edge of the Sagittarius-Carina Arm, and therefore toward it we again look down, not merely across, the Arm. Notice that the Scutum Cloud lies only about 25° along the galactic equator from galactic longitude 0°, whereas the star clouds around the Keyhole Nebula at the other extremity of the Sgr-Car Arm are about 75° from galactic longitude 0°. The reason for this asymmetry is that toward Scutum, the Sagittarius-Carina Arm arcs inward toward the central regions of the Galaxy; whereas toward Carina, it arcs outward. In other words, the Galaxy's spiral arms are "wound up" in the direction of Scutum and the late summer Milky Way, and "trail outward" in the direction of Carina, Vela, and far southern Milky Way. Remember that we are rotating approximately toward Deneb in Cygnus; consequently, in our Galaxy, as in other spiral galaxies, the spiral arms are wound up in the direction of rotation.

The Scutum Star Cloud is only a small section of the edge of the Sagittarius-Carina Spiral Arm. The rest of the edge of that Arm is blocked from our sight by the obscuring clouds in the section of the Great Rift around Eta (η) Serpentis.

Cygnus: looking down our spiral arm, Maps 2, 7, and 8. The next bright star cloud northeast along the Milky Way from the Scutum Cloud is the Cygnus Star Cloud. In the direction of the Cygnus Star Cloud we are again looking lengthwise down a spiral arm, but in this case it is our own Orion Arm. There is an abundance of distant open clusters and stellar associations in the Cygnus Star Cloud and in the neighboring parts of Vulpecula. However, the Aquila Milky Way (between Vulpecula and Scutum) is very poor in open clusters—Burnham lists five open clusters in Scutum, nine in Vulpecula, but only three in the very much larger Aquila. This is because toward Aquila is the interarm region between our own spiral arm and the Sagittarius Carina Arm. Thus, toward Aquila we look past a sprinkling of bright foreground stars and down the long, relatively empty interarm area toward very distant star clouds. When we scan the autumn Milky Way from Scutum to Cygnus, we look first at the edge of the Sagittarius-Carina Arm, then at the interarm space (of which we have a particularly clear view, since we are on the inner edge of our arm), and finally down our own spiral arm.

Because we are on the inside edge of our spiral arm, the first relatively nearby stellar associations northeast of Sagittarius do not appear until the Cygnus-Cepheus stretch of the Milky Way. They are: Cygnus OB7, which includes Deneb and the North America Nebula and lies about 1,700 light-years distant; Cepheus OB2, involving Mu (μ) Cephei and IC 1396 and centered some 2,700 light-years away; and small Lacerta OBl, scattered over the southern half of that constellation, about 2,000 light-years from us. (All three associations are discussed under their respective constellations.) Notice that these three associations lie at or beyond galactic longitude 90°. The Cygnus Star Cloud itself, however, lies between galactic longitudes 60° and 80° in other words, a bit inward toward the interior of the Galaxy. This is because the spiral arms of our Galaxy wind up in this direction, the direction of galactic rotation. Thus the Cygnus Star Cloud is actually our view of the Orion Arm's arc toward the interior of the Galaxy. In the opposite part of the Milky Way, around galactic longitude 270° (Puppis-Vela), we see where our arm trails outward from the galactic interior. Toward Cygnus-Vulpecula our spiral arm is somewhat nearer the Galactic Center than we are, toward Puppis-Vela it is somewhat farther.

Cassiopeia: a window out to an exterior arm, Maps 1 and 2. By November (or after midnight in September) the Milky Way constellations that follow Cepheus—Cassiopeia and Perseus—approach the zenith of mid-northern latitudes. You will observe that the Milky Way in Perseus is much thinner and fainter than the Milky Way in Cassiopeia: a scan with binoculars shows that the star fields of Perseus (except for the region of the glorious Double Cluster) are much poorer than those of Cassiopeia. The reason is that toward Perseus the interstellar gas and dust of our own spiral

arm are especially thick, whereas toward Cassiopeia a window though our arm—a gap between the dust clouds of Cepheus and Perseus—opens up, through which we look at the next spiral feature outward from ours.

To get a better galactic perspective on this, look up toward Deneb and the approximate direction of galactic longitude 90°. Stand as before, with the Galactic Center (Sagittarius) on your left and the direction of the galactic anticenter (Auriga-Gemini) on your right. You now see that Cassiopeia lies somewhat to the right of 90°, about a third of the way from 90° back toward the galactic anticenter. Therefore, toward Cassiopeia we are looking *ahead* (in the direction of galactic rotation, that is) but at an angle back into our spiral arm (because we are on the inside of our arm). However, since there is a window in the interstellar matter in this direction, what we see toward Cassiopeia are not the associations, clusters, and nebulae of our own arm, but those of the next arm outward from us.

The Cassiopeia window extends from just east of the famous variable Delta (δ) Cephei through Cassiopeia to the Perseus Double Cluster. The spiral feature visible to us through this window is called the Perseus Arm because of the Double Cluster, one of its major sub-units. Embedded in the Perseus Arm are most of Cassiopeia's many open clusters, including M52, M103, NGC 457, NGC 663, and NGC 7789, which lie from about 5,000 to 9,000 light-years away.

NGC 7789 lies in the Perseus Arm, but in the astrophysical sense does not belong to it. It is a very old open cluster, born elsewhere, that merely strayed into the Perseus Arm. (In just this same sense, our Sun lies in, but not *of*, the Orion Arm.) The emission nebula IC 1848 (in Cassiopeia) is also part of the Perseus Spiral Arm. IC 1848 and the Double Cluster are at about the same distance (slightly over 7,000 light-years) and a line between them is perpendicular to the galactic equator. Therefore, their projected separation, 600 light-years, is the minimum width of the Perseus Arm. Of course, the stars that form the "W" of Cassiopeia are foreground objects that belong to our own spiral arm. A foreground open cluster is the large, loose group Stock 2, mentioned in the section on the Double Cluster.

6.2 The Winter Milky Way

Just after twilight during the mild evenings of early spring, observers in the middle northern latitudes can see the Milky Way as a great bow arching over the western horizon. It sweeps out of Cepheus, low in the north, up through Cassiopeia and Perseus in the northwest to crest in Auriga, still high in the west. From Auriga, the winter Milky Way descends between Gemini and Orion, goes down through Monoceros, then sweeps over the back of Canis Major in the southwest; finally, it is lost from view in the spaces of Puppis, low in the south.

The Milky Way of winter looks different from the late summer/early autumn Milky Way. Its glow is uniform, lacking the bright star clouds and obscuring features like the Great Rift. It is also not as bright as the summer Milky Way. The reason for the difference is that toward the winter Milky Way we look out of our Galaxy, away from the dust and star-rich interior. The galactic anticenter is located $3\frac{1}{2}°$ due east of El Nath (Beta [β] Tauri), almost exactly on the Taurus-Auriga border. During early spring evenings this point will be high in the west for mid-northern observers. Consequently, if you stand facing west and looking up at El Nath, galactic longitude 90° will be on your right (at just about at the north point of the horizon) and galactic longitude 270° will be on your left, near the south point of the horizon. (The precise locations of longitudes 90° and 270° with respect to the horizon will depend on your exact latitude and time of night. However, the preceding is a useful way for observers over most of the United States and southern Canada to keep track of galactic longitudes 90° and 270° during the early spring.)

Because galactic longitude 90° is the direction of galactic rotation, along the Milky Way from El Nath to the north point of the horizon we are looking ahead (that is, in the direction of our motion through the Galaxy) but out of the Galaxy. And from El Nath to the south point of the horizon, we look behind and out.

The foreground of the Orion Arm, Map 4. Because we lie on the inner edge of our spiral arm, when we look at the winter Milky Way (away from the interior of the Galaxy) we are looking back into our own spiral arm, the Orion Arm. This is confirmed by all the relatively nearby open clusters, associations, and emission nebulae in the constellations from Perseus to Canis Major. Beginning with Perseus (which is in the northwest in the early spring) we find the Alpha (α) Persei Cluster, 570 light-years away, and the Zeta (ζ) Persei Association, 1,200 light-years distant. In Taurus over the west-northwest horizon are the Pleiades and the Hyades clusters, 410 and 150 light-years from us, respectively. To the west-southwest is the mighty Orion Association, centered some 1,600 light-years away and the aggregation from which our spiral arm has been named. Low in the southwest stands the Canis Major Association, 2,500 light-years distant.

The clusters and associations just mentioned (except the Alpha [α] Persei Cluster) lie well below the bright stream of the Milky Way proper. Consequently, as you look at the arch of the early spring Milky Way, the Zeta Persei Association, the Pleiades and Hyades, and the Orion and Canis Major Associations seem pendant

from it. The effect is quite beautiful.

The arrangement of the nearby clusters and associations in the winter Milky Way is part of a larger structure: The chain of clusters and associations from Perseus down to Canis Major lie on the south galactic pole (Sculptor) side of the Milky Way. However, the nearest association to us, the sprawling Scorpio-Centaurus Association which extends from Crux up to Scorpius more or less on the opposite part of the Milky Way from the Perseus to Canis Major stretch, is on the *north* galactic pole (Coma Berenices) side of the Milky Way. On star charts that show the two hemispheres of the celestial sphere, you will see that as you draw a line among the clusters and associations of the winter Milky Way and extend it into the southern Milky Way, it will go along the central axis of the elongated Sco-Cen Association. (If extended beyond Scorpius the line will approximately follow the Great Rift. It crosses the galactic equator in Crux and in Cassiopeia.) This line of bright objects defines what is known as *Gould's Belt* and is comprised of nearby clusters, associations, and dark nebulae. Gould's Belt tilts at an angle of about 16° to the galactic equator. It is apparently a local feature in the Orion Arm, because the more distant clusters and associations of our arm do not follow the Belt but are distributed along the galactic equator.

Careful studies have shown that the objects in Gould's Belt are moving outward from their common center at a rate of about 6 miles per second. This, along with the fact that the diameter of Gould's Belt is about 3,200 light-years, suggests that the expansion started about 60 million years ago—which agrees with the estimated age of the oldest stars in the Belt. Apparently something, possibly a supernova explosion, initiated star formation in our part of the Galaxy some 60 million years ago and the process is continuing. (The Hyades, by the way, are technically not part of Gould's Belt because they are about 700 million years old.)

The core of the Orion Arm, Map 4. As the preceding suggests, the winter Milky Way itself actually lies behind a series of relatively nearby clusters and associations. Thus, when we look at it, we are looking past foreground objects deep into the core of our spiral arm. Consequently, beyond the Zeta (ζ) Persei Association and the Hyades and Pleiades lie the great open clusters M36, M37, and M38 (all about 4,200 light-years away) in Auriga. And over and beyond the Orion Association are the open clusters M35 in Gemini (2,200 light-years) and NGC 2264 in Monoceros (2,300 light-years), the Rosette Nebula, NGC 2237, in Monoceros (4,900 light-years), and the Gemini OB1 association (centered about 5000 light-years away). (Gem OB1 is discussed under NGC 2174 in Orion.)

The galactic longitude of the Canis Major Association in the southern winter Milky Way is about 240°, almost opposite the direction of galactic rotation, so toward it we are looking lengthwise down our spiral arm. Consequently, this is a direction abundant in open clusters, many very distant. M41 (2,350 light-years), M47 (1,700 light-years), and M93 (3,400 light-years) all lie more or less as far away as the CMa Association, but in the background are NGC 2362 (4,900 light-years), M46 (5,000 light-years), and the emission nebula NGC 2467 (8,200 light-years). Interstellar dust is fairly thin in this direction, so with telescopes it's possible to see extremely remote open clusters. For example, about 4° southeast of Eta (η) Canis Majoris is NGC 2439, perhaps 14,000 light-years away—so distant that it might even lie in the Perseus Spiral Arm rather than in ours.

Toward the rim of the Galaxy, Map 4. Because of the gas and dust of our spiral arm, very little of the Perseus Arm can be seen in the Milky Way from Perseus to Monoceros. Perhaps the only Perseus Arm object available to binoculars is the open cluster NGC 1893 in Auriga, which is about 10,000 light-years distant. However, from beyond even the Perseus Arm shines NGC 2158, the very remote open cluster that lies just $1/2$° southwest of M35 in Gemini. At a distance of about 16,000 light-years, NGC 2158 is at least seven times farther from us than its more famous neighbor. Because NGC 2158 is only a few degrees from the galactic anticenter, in which direction the rim of the Galaxy is probably no more than 20,000 light-years away, this cluster must lie almost at the Galaxy's rim.

Chapter 7

Galaxies and Galaxy Groups for Binoculars

Binoculars, with their modest light-gathering power and small magnifications, are obviously not the ideal galaxy-search instrument. Nevertheless, several dozen galaxies can be identified in a good pair of 10x50 binoculars. Many will appear virtually stellar (so you will need a finder chart to identify them), but over two dozen are distinctly and unambiguously disks or patches of haze. These patches may be visually unspectacular, but to be able to see objects that are millions—even tens of millions—of light-years distant with nothing more than a pair of binoculars is a satisfying experience for an observer. It is something of a Promethean defiance of the limitations of aperture.

7.1 The Requirements

Of course, searching for galaxies in binoculars is not easy. First you need a moonless night at a site well away from city lights. We see galaxies at all only because the glow of their disks is brighter than the surrounding sky-glow; moonlight or city light brightens the sky and lessens the contrast between galaxy and sky. However, the night does not have to be perfectly transparent—a bit of atmospheric humidity and turbulence actually helps somewhat. The reason for this strange fact is that a thick atmosphere scatters light and therefore smears out the tiny galactic disks, making them somewhat less star-like and therefore easier to spot. A night that would be poor for splitting close double stars or looking at planets can be excellent for galaxy-observing in binoculars or a telescope.

The second thing you need for galaxy-searching in binoculars is a trained eye. Most galaxies visible in binoculars appear either as small, low surface brightness patches or as "stars" surrounded by tiny faint haloes. If you don't have some idea of what you are looking for, either type of galaxy image will elude you. The place to start training your eyes is with the Andromeda Galaxy, M31 (Map 3). The tenuous glow of the extreme edges of

the elongated disk of M31 will show you the meaning of the phrase "low surface brightness." Then look at the Triangulum Galaxy, M33 (14° southeast of M31) to get some idea of what an extended low surface brightness object looks like. But keep in mind that M33 is actually a very large galaxy in terms of apparent size (it is larger even than the Moon). Most galaxies visible in binoculars as disks or patches have only a small percent of M33's surface area. To prepare your eye for the other type of galaxy image, a halo-surrounded star-speck (like the enigmatic galaxy M87), study the binocular appearance of the globular clusters M15 (Map 8) in Pegasus, M3 (Map 6) in Canes Venatici, and M5 (Map 6) in Serpens Caput. The haloes that surround the small, bright disks of these globulars are very much like the ghostlike, tenuous haloes around the star-speck cores of galaxies such as M87 and M49 in Virgo, M96 in Leo and M94 in Canes Venatici.

The third thing you need for galaxy-searching in binoculars is, obviously, a good pair of binoculars. As I said in the preface, this book is written for normal garden-variety binoculars. Probably most of the galaxies in this section can be glimpsed with 7x50 glasses. However, 7x neither darkens the sky background nor magnifies a galaxy image as much as 10x, consequently many galaxies that distinctly appear as disks or patches in 10x50s will be merely stellar in 7x50s—and perhaps altogether invisible in 7x35s, which gather only half as much light as 50mm binoculars. Since 10x50s are perhaps the best binoculars for astronomy and most of my own binocular observing has been done with glasses of that type, this section is unabashedly slanted to 10x50s.

Several observing techniques are worth bearing in mind while you search for a faint galaxy or study the image of a galaxy you have found. First, keep your eyes well dark-adapted. Second, remember to use averted vision—the retina is most sensitive just off the center of the eye's focus. Third, do not keep the binoculars rock-solid steady (as if that's possible anyway!). If you allow the field to jiggle a little, the contrast between the galaxy-glow and the sky-background will be easier to detect. Fourth, it is imperative that you keep your eyes at the oculars for a minute and a half or two minutes at a time. This gives your eyes a chance to acclimatize to the light conditions in the field of view and they will sense better the subtle difference between the galaxy light and the sky. (Don't stare, however—blink as you feel the need.) To be sure that you have sighted a faint galaxy, it's a good idea to search for it with only a general idea of its location. Then later, after you think you have spotted the galaxy and have noted its location with respect to field stars, you can compare your observation with the galaxy's actual position as plotted on star charts.

7.2   Galaxy Groups

Few galaxies are truly isolated. In general, galaxies cluster in gravitationally-bound groups containing anywhere from a handful to many dozens of members. The Milky Way and Andromeda galaxies are the two brightest of a modest little cluster of at least 30 galaxies, most of which are dwarf galaxies, called the Local Group. Galaxy groups, in turn, gather into huge aggregations called superclusters. You might think that all this is as relevant to binocular observing as thermonuclear fusion is to toasting marshmallows. However, there are some fine pairs and triplets of galaxies for binoculars that are the bright members of galaxy groups. And the core of our supercluster, the famous Realm of the Galaxies in northwestern Virgo and southern Coma Berenices, is a fascinating (though difficult) galaxy field for binoculars or small telescopes.

7.3   The Galaxies of Autumn

M31 and the Local Group, Map 3. The place to begin any study of galaxies is with the Great Andromeda Galaxy, M31. This giant Sb-type spiral, relatively near (as such things go) at a distance of 2.2 million light-years, is the only galaxy other than the special case of our two Magellanic satellites in which binoculars reveal structural detail. You will see a pale circular glow, 20′ in diameter and brighter toward its center, within a very hazy, much elongated oval of indistinct extent. (Use indirect vision to see as much of the elusive extremities of the oval as possible.)

The large circular glow (which has an apparent diameter two-thirds that of the Moon) is the great spherical central hub of M31, and in reality is some 12,000 light-years across. The tenuous oval envelope, which in good binoculars can be traced perhaps 4°, is the spiral disk of the galaxy and appears elongated merely

because M31 is tilted only about 15° from the edge-on position for us. The true diameter of M31's spiral disk is over 150,000 light-years. This is quite large—our Milky Way, itself a fairly sizeable galaxy, is 100,000 light-years across.

If you look carefully, you can perhaps see that the northwest side of M31 is somewhat less ambiguously bordered than the southeast side. It almost has a distinct edge. This is because the northwest side of the galaxy is the nearest to us and (as photographs show) contains long, thick lanes of obscuring dust that block most of the light from that side of the galaxy's spiral disk. (The inner dust lane can be glimpsed under good sky conditions in 11x80 binoculars.) At the very center of M31's inner circular feature you will see a tiny, bright, nearly stellar image. This is the nucleus of M31's central hub. It seems to be extremely concentrated, with perhaps 10 million stars crowded into a volume with a radius of only 25 light-years. A sphere with the star density of the nucleus of M31 and a diameter equal to the distance between the Sun and Alpha (α) Centauri, would contain over 6000 stars!

At such high star densities the possibility of collisions between stars is not negligible, and the explosion resulting from such a collision would send out an intense shock wave of matter and energy that could trigger a chain reaction of stellar explosions in the densely populated nucleus. There is evidence that some great explosion—possibly caused in this way—occurred in the nucleus of our own Galaxy some 10 million years ago. Unfortunately, the nucleus of our Galaxy is blocked from optical wavelengths by interstellar dust, but even with mere binoculars we can look directly into the nucleus of M31.

The Andromeda Galaxy has eight satellite galaxies gravitationally bound to it, all small elliptical systems. Two can be seen in 10x50 binoculars. M32 is rather bright (its apparent magnitude is 9.5), but so compact that it looks stellar. It is the farther of the two 9th-magnitude star images directly south of the M31 hub. NGC 205, located only about 35′ northwest of the M31 hub, is highly elongated—measuring about 8′ × 3′—and can be easily seen as a fuzzy little ellipse even though its integrated apparent magnitude is only 10.8. M32 is visible in 7x binoculars. Unfortunately, even in 7x50s NGC 205 cannot be seen, since 7x does not sufficiently magnify its image or darken its sky background.

As was mentioned earlier, the Milky Way and M31 are the largest and brightest members of the Local Group of galaxies. The Local Group has a binary structure, with our Galaxy and its two Magellanic satellites at one end and the Andromeda Galaxy, its satellites, and the Triangulum Galaxy, M33, at the other. M33 is not as large as M31, but with an apparent diameter that

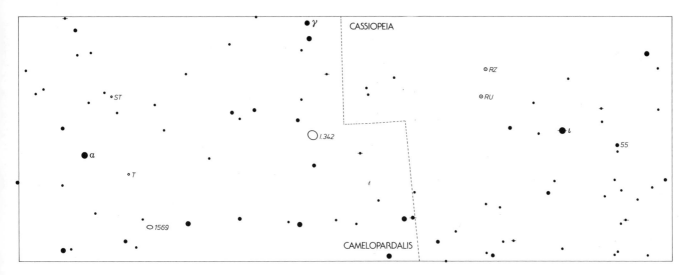

Identification Chart 7–1. IC 342 *The faintest stars shown are of magnitude 7.5, and the chart scale is 9mm (=0.35 inch) per degree. North is to the top, east to the left.*

is just a little more than the Moon's, it is plenty large for a galaxy and is a fine binocular object. In fact, when sky conditions are excellent and it is near the zenith, M33 can be glimpsed with the unaided eye—though I have never been able to do so with certainty. This means that it is the most distant object visible to the unaided eye, for it seems to be somewhat farther than M31, with a distance of about 2.9 million light-years.

M33 is an almost face-on, loose-armed Sc spiral. This is reflected in the nearly circular shape and the extremely low surface brightness of the galaxy's binocular and telescopic appearance. There are several other face-on Sc spirals visible in binoculars and all have this same general appearance—a roughly circular low surface brightness disk—though all but a couple are much smaller than M33. In binoculars, M33 shows none of the structural detail that M31 does, but you will be able to see that its disk is a little brighter toward the center and that it has a slightly oval shape (oriented north-northeast to south-southwest), reminiscent of the galaxy's photographic appearance.

The Milky Way and M31 are giant spirals, M33 is an average spiral, but the more than two dozen other members of the Local Group are all either dwarf ellipticals or dwarf irregulars. Other than M32, NGC 205, and the Magellanic Clouds, the only binocular object in the Local Group—and a marginal one at that—is the irregular system NGC 6822 (Barnard's Galaxy) in extreme northeastern Sagittarius. It lies around 2 million light-years away. Under extremely good observing conditions a well-trained eye using 10x50 binoculars might be able to see NGC 6822 as a small smudge elongated almost due north-south; it is slightly larger than NGC 205, but has even lower surface brightness. A line drawn from

55 Sagittarii northeast through the magnitude 5½ star ⅔° away from 55 Sgr, and extended another ⅔°, ends at NGC 6822.

The Sculptor Group, Map 3. Sculptor and Fornax, the constellations south of Cetus, are perhaps the faintest, most star-poor, in the sky. They are, however, rich in galaxies. Two of Sculptor's galaxies are easy even in 7x35 binoculars. About 7½° south of Beta (β) Ceti is the almost edge-on spiral NGC 253, which in binoculars appears as a skinny gash of light, over 20′ long (remember that the Moon's apparent diameter is just over 30′) and oriented northeast-southwest. Near its southern tip you can see the close pair of relatively bright (about magnitude 8.5) field stars that are so conspicuous on photographs of the galaxy. With an integrated apparent magnitude of 7.0, NGC 253 is one of the brightest galaxies in the sky. In fact, after the Magellanic Clouds, it is the brightest galaxy in the southern celestial hemisphere.

NGC 253 is far enough north that it can be observed from all of the mainland U.S. and from southern Canada. However, the other bright galaxy in Sculptor, NGC 55, can be well observed only from the southern half of the U.S. It is located about 3° north-northwest from Alpha (α) Phoenicis. Because my latitude is 45°N, I have never seen NGC 55, but my impression from the usually reliable statistics in Burnham (who gives NGC 55's size as 25′ × 4′ and its integrated apparent magnitude as 7.8) is that it should be seen fairly easily even in small binoculars as a streak of light as long as NGC 253, but decidedly thinner.

NGC 253 and NGC 55 are the brightest members of the Sculptor Galaxy Group, which at a distance estimated to be about 8 million light-years is probably the nearest to our Local Group. Other members of the Sculptor Group are NGC 45 and NGC 247 in southwest Cetus, and NGC 300 and NGC 7793 in Sculptor. All the Sculptor Group galaxies are extremely loose Sc or Sd spirals—except for NGC 55, which seems to be an irregular galaxy with incipient spiral structure that we view edge-on. The Sculptor Group is distributed in a large ring some 20° in diameter. This peculiar structure suggests that these galaxies were formed from the same huge primordial gas cloud and have been expanding outward ever since. The ring of Sculptor Group galaxies seems to be rotating; the galaxies in the southern part of the ring, NGC 55 and NGC 300, have only half the corrected recessional velocity of the galaxies in the northern part of the ring. There are several other galaxy groups with structures similar to the Sculptor Group's.

Of the fainter Sculptor Group members, NGC 7793 should be visible in 10x50 binoculars (to an observer in the southern U.S.) as a small, oval smudge of light. It is fairly bright, with a magnitude of 9.7, but measures only 6′ × 4′. NGC 247, which has had an extremely low surface brightness—its size is 18′ × 5′ but its integrated apparent magnitude is only 10.7—is a good object for giant binoculars, being right at the limit of visibility in 10x50s.

7.4   Galaxies of the Spring

The Ursa Major Group, Map 1. One of the best galaxy pairs for binoculars or a small telescope is the M81/M82 pair, situated 40′ apart in northern Ursa Major. Both are fairly bright, with integrated apparent magnitudes of 8.0 and 9.2 respectively. M81 appears as a small oval core surrounded by a diffuse aura or halo and is elongated north-south (it measures 18′ × 10′). M82 is a thin (8′ × 3′) east-west spindle. (7x binoculars show the different orientations of the two galaxies, but higher powers are necessary to see the different character of their images.)

Both galaxies are abnormal. M81 is a large Sa or Sb spiral with an unusually extensive and star-dense central hub. (The hub is the oval interior of the galaxy's binocular image.) And M82 is undergoing either an explosive ejection of matter from its center or an intensive burst of star formation. The outburst in M82 is not as violent as the cataclysm that is occurring in the core of the Seyfert galaxy M77 in Cetus, but nevertheless several million solar masses are involved, and M82—like M77—is a strong emitter in radio frequencies.

M81 and M82 are the heart of the Ursa Major Galaxy Group, the second nearest group to us with an estimated distance of slightly over 8 million light-years. (Because extragalactic distance finding is still anything

but an exact science, there is an outside chance that the Ursa Major Group is actually nearer than the Sculptor Group.) Ursa Major Group galaxies scatter over a large oval area that extends from Kappa (κ) Draconis on the east through northern Ursa Major and west into Camelopardalis. (It may even run all the way through Camelopardalis if IC 342 is an outlying member of the Ursa Major Group rather than one of the Local Group.)

A third Ursa Major Group galaxy for binoculars is the Sc spiral NGC 2403, which is about 14° west-southwest of the M81/M82 pair in the star-poor wastes of eastern Camelopardalis. NGC 2403 is reasonably bright (magnitude 8.8) and quite large (16′ × 10′), but because of its isolation it is not easy to locate, especially in 7x binoculars. In higher power glasses you will see this galaxy as a small, bright, highly-elongated core embedded in a compact, elliptical halo. NGC 2403 is about 2 million light-years from the M81/M82 pair, comparable to the distance between the Milky Way and Andromeda galaxies. As this suggests, the Ursa Major Group has a binary structure similar to the Local Group's, with the M81/M82 pair and NGC 2403 the brightest galaxies of two small sub-groups.

A possible Ursa Major Group member that is an interesting and fairly easy object for 10x50 or larger binoculars is the face-on Scd spiral IC 342, located in extreme west-central Camelopardalis, about 3° due south of Gamma (γ) Camelopardalis. IC 342 is rather large (15′ across) and not at all as faint as the magnitude 12.0 given for it by Burnham. In fact, its integrated apparent magnitude is 8.5. But IC 342 is tricky to find because there are no nearby bright stars—you have to "star-hop" to the galaxy from Gamma (γ) Cam. IC 342 lies within the outer fringes of the Milky Way and can be easily mistaken for a small, dim Milky Way cloud, especially since there are a few faint foreground stars from our own Galaxy sprinkled over its disk. It will appear perhaps slightly elongated north-south.

Because we are viewing it through the edges of the Milky Way, IC 342 is subject to an uncertain amount of dimming by the dust of our own Galaxy, which makes its distance difficult to fix. According to early estimates it was 3.3 million light-years away and an outlying member of the Local Group. But now it is thought to be 13 million light-years distant and an outlying member of the Ursa Major Galaxy Group.

The M101 Galaxy Group, Maps 1 and 2. One of the largest galaxies in the heavens in terms of surface area is M101, a face-on, very loose Scd system some 20′ in diameter. M101 forms an isosceles triangle with the two end stars in the handle of the Big Dipper, Eta (η) and Zeta (ζ) Ursae Majoris: it lies 5° east of Zeta and the same distance north-northeast of Eta. Because it is such a loosely-wound spiral, M101's surface brightness is extremely low. Despite its size, it has an integrated apparent magnitude of only 7.7. M33 is considered a low surface brightness object, but M101 has 40% of M33's area with only about 15% of that galaxy's total brightness! M101 can be a problem to spot in 7x binoculars because this magnification does not darken the sky background very much. Keep in mind as you look for M101 that you are searching for an object with a diameter two-thirds the Moon's, but with a surface brightness not much greater than that of the night sky itself. Zoom binoculars are nice to have for an object like this because you can use 12x or 15x to get the sky background dark and thereby increase its contrast with the galaxy's tenuous glow.

M101 is 15 or 20 million light-years distant and its true diameter is probably well over 100,000 light-years. Its integrated absolute magnitude is around −20.5, the same as our Galaxy's. M101 is one of the bright members of large galaxy group scattered loosely around the region of the handle of the Big Dipper and down into northern Canes Venatici. A possible member of the group is M63, a highly-tilted Sb spiral about 1° due north of the small asterism called "Asterion" (18, 19, 20, and 23 Canum Venaticorum). M63 is at magnitude 9.8, measures about $9' \times 4'$, and in 10x50 binoculars appears as a very thin east-northeast to west-southwest streak. If you study it carefully, you will notice that there is an 8th-magnitude star near its northwest extremity, and that the galaxy's center is stellar. (This is its central hub: if M31 was as far away as M63, its central hub would also look stellar in binoculars.)

The premier member of the M101 Galaxy Group, however, is the Whirlpool Galaxy (M51) located about 3° southwest of Eta (η) Ursae Majoris. M51 is not especially large, measuring $10' \times 5'$, but it is quite bright (magnitude 8.7). It has good surface brightness and even 7x glasses are sufficient to see its small disk. In 10x50s M51 looks pear-shaped. The larger southern part, which has a stellar core marking its central hub, is the main Sc galaxy and the small northern lobe is the companion system, NGC 5195. In high-power binoculars, therefore, M51 looks like (and is) a binary galaxy. The Large Magellanic Cloud is so large that it and the Milky Way also form a binary system. However, the Large Magellanic Cloud seems for the present to be rather innocuously orbiting us, whereas the Whirlpool spiral and its companion apparently underwent a grazing encounter several millions of years ago that has left the structure of both distorted. (See Timothy Ferris' *Galaxies* for a fascinating account of this.)

The Canes Venatici I Galaxy Cloud, Map 6. The M101 Galaxy Group, centered 15 or 20 million light-years away, seems to be the fifth nearest galaxy group

to our Local Group. The third nearest (after the Sculptor and Ursa Major groups) is probably the Canes Venatici I Galaxy Cloud, estimated to be 12 or 13 million light-years distant. It includes M94, M106 (NGC 4253) in Canes Venatici, and possibly M64 down in central Coma Berenices. M94 is a nearly face-on Sa or Sb spiral that is quite bright (magnitude 8.9) and not too small ($5' \times 3'$), but which appears stellar even in 10x50 binoculars because most of its light comes from its central hub and inner spiral arms. On a good night you might be able to detect around its stellar core a fairly large but extremely faint halo—the higher powers available in zoom binoculars would darken the sky background and make this halo somewhat easier to see. M64, another Sa or Sb galaxy, is a better binocular object than M94 because it shows a rather bright (magnitude 8.6) and distinctly elongated ($7' \times 3'$) disk in 10x glasses. M64 is very easy to find because it is located only 1° east-northeast of the 5th-magnitude star 35 Comae.

But the best galaxy for binoculars in the Canes Venatici I Cloud is M106. It is reasonably bright (magnitude 9.0), very large ($19' \times 6'$), and can be easily seen as a northwest-southeast spindle even in 7x instruments. The one drawback of this galaxy is its rather star-poor field, which makes it somewhat difficult to locate. M106 is about 4° almost due east of the 4th-magnitude Chi (χ) Ursae Majoris. Try finding it by putting Chi UMa on the west edge of your binocular field and estimating how far across the field the galaxy will lie.

The Centaurus Galaxy Group, Map 6. The fourth nearest galaxy group to us is the Centaurus Group, a 30° long chain of half a dozen galaxies that begins about 10° south of Spica and extends down across the tail of Hydra and into central Centaurus, ending only about 10° north-northeast of Crux. The Centaurus Group galaxies are (from north to south): NGC 5068 in extreme southern Virgo, M83 in Hydra, and NGCs 5253, 5102, 5128, and 4945 in Centaurus. The members of this intriguing galaxy-chain seem to be an average of about 13 million light-years distant from us, which implies the chain is at least 7 million light-years long.

Three of the Centaurus Group galaxies are abnormal: M83 has had five supernovae in the past sixty years (more than has been observed in our Galaxy in the last 1,000 years); NGC 5253 has a peculiar structure—a smooth elliptical outer profile with a roughly rectangular inner region of huge emission nebulae and has had two unusually brilliant supernovae in the past century; and NGC 5128 apparently is undergoing an extensive explosion in its interior—it is a strong radio source and most of the radio energy comes from a broad band of obscuring matter that slashes across the galaxy's disk.

The Centaurus Galaxy Group is obviously not well situated for observers in Canada and most of the United

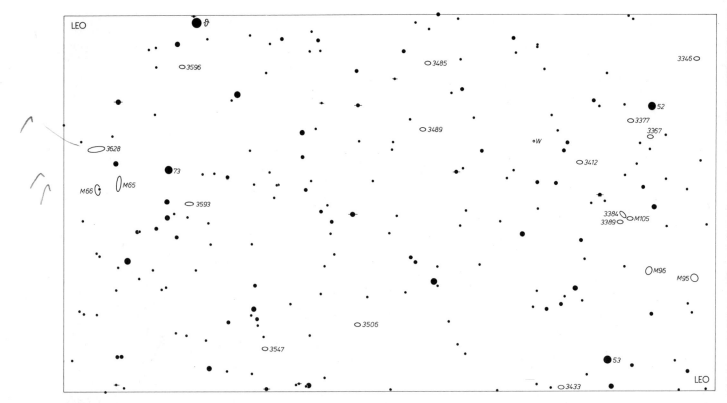

Identification Chart 7–2. M66 and M96 galaxy groups. *Stars are plotted down to magnitude 9.5, and the chart scale is 18mm (=0.71 inch) per degree. North is to the top and east to the left.*

States. However, M83 is at declination −30° and consequently culminates at least 20° above the horizon over all the "lower 48" and southern Ontario. It is an excellent object in any size binoculars and will appear as a fairly large (10′ × 8′) and quite bright (magnitude 8.0) oval patch similar in shape and surface brightness to M33 in Triangulum. As good a binocular galaxy as M83 is, NGC 5128 (magnitude 7.2, size 10′) is even better; however, it culminates 20° above the horizon only for observers in the Florida peninsula and southern Texas.

The Leo Galaxy Cloud, Map 5. A galaxy pair that rivals M81 and M82 are M65 and M66. These are 21′ apart (northwest-southeast) and located about 2 1/2° south-southeast of Theta (ϑ) Leonis. M66 is an Sb system measuring about 8′ × 2′ and has an integrated magnitude of 9.7. M65, an Sa galaxy, is 8′ × 1′ and at magnitude 10.3. In 7x50 binoculars M66 can be clearly seen as a tiny patch elongated roughly northwest-southeast, but it takes 10x50s to see M65's approximately north-south orientation. Under excellent observing conditions a well-trained eye with 10x50 glasses can just glimpse a small, ambiguously-shaped patch of haze 35′ due north of M66—the edge-on Sb spiral NGC 3628. This galaxy is as bright as M65 (magnitude 10.3), but its extreme elongation (12′ × 2′) makes it very challenging. For-

tunately, its location is well marked: about 20′ north-northeast of M65 is a 7th-magnitude star, another 20′ northeast of which is the elusive NGC 3628.

The M65/M66/NGC 3628 trio is the heart of a cluster of about a dozen galaxies spread between Theta and Iota (ι) Leonis and centered approximately 25 million light-years away. This cluster is, however, just the eastern half of the Leo I Galaxy Cloud. The western cluster of the Leo I Cloud lies in the region midway between Regulus on the west and Theta and Iota Leonis on the east. It has at least 20 members, including M95, M96, and M105 (NGC 3379). This cluster is better suited for giant binoculars or richest-field telescopes than small binoculars, but in 10x50s M96 can be seen as a tiny, fuzzy spot (it is an Sa galaxy, magnitude 10.2, size 6′ × 4′). M95, M105, NGC 3377, and NGC 3384 can be glimpsed as stellar objects if you study the field carefully. Use the accompanying star chart. The M96 cluster, which seems to be centered a few million light-years beyond the M66 cluster, is of particular interest because two of its members, M105 and NGC 3377, are probably the nearest of the supermassive, superpopulous giant elliptical type of galaxy that is so numerous in the center of our supergalaxy.

Photograph 7–1. The M65–M66 Galaxy Group in Leo. *Photo by David Healy with an 8-inch Schmidt-Cassegrain telescope. In the center of the field are M65 (right=west) and the slightly wider M66 (left). Toward the right edge of the field is the magnitude 5.5 star 73 Leonis, which helps in the identification of the two galaxies. North of M66 is the nearly edge-on spiral NGC 3628: it is a challenging object for 10x50 glasses, but can be found with the help of the mag 7 star 20′ NNE of M65 that forms a flattened isosceles triangle with M65 and NGC 3628. This field is very easy to locate, for M65 and M66 lie exactly halfway between Theta and Iota Leonis. A fourth galaxy can be seen on this photo, near the lower right edge SW of 73 Leo: it is the magnitude 12.0 SO/Sa NGC 3593, an object suitable only for moderately large telescopes.*

The Core of our Supercluster, Map 6. By now it will be obvious that there are a good many galaxy groups in the spring sky. There was, you may recall, only one in the autumn—the Sculptor Group. This reflects an important fact. Our Local Group is near the outside edge of a supercluster. The inner regions of our supercluster (called, of course, the Local Supercluster) are in the direction of the spring sky—specifically toward southern Coma Berenices and western Virgo, the "Realm of the Galaxies."

If you examine the distribution of galaxies in the spring sky on the *Atlas of the Heavens* or the *Sky Atlas 2000.0*, you will notice that there is something of a "milky way" of galaxies that begins at the Big Dipper and sweeps down through Canes Venatici, Coma Berenices, and western Virgo, to end west of Spica. The density of galaxies falls off quickly as you move perpendicularly off this axis. There are some aggregations of galaxies in eastern Leo, in Leo Minor, and in the area of 109 and 110 Virginis, but only a poor scattering of galaxies populate the other spring constellations.

Notice also that the Ursa Major and Centaurus galaxy groups lie on the same axis as the galaxy stream from the Big Dipper through western Virgo. This elongation implies that our supercluster has a flattened

Photograph 7–2. The M96 galaxy cluster in Leo. *Photo by Jack Marling on hypered 2415 film with an 8-inch f/4.5 telescope. M96 is the bright, large galaxy in the lower left (SE) quadrant of the field. Toward the lower right corner, WSW of M96, is the SBb barred spiral M95, which measures 4′ × 3′ and has an apparent magnitude of 11.0—an object suitable only for giant binoculars. North of M96 in the upper left (NE) area of the field is a small triangle of galaxies. The brightest is the E1 giant elliptical M105 (NGC 3379), 0.75° due N of M96. M105 measures only about 2″ of arc across, but its apparent magnitude is 10.6 so it should be visible as a hazy-edged "star" in 50mm zooms and giant binoculars. Its companions are, to the NE, NGC 3384, a magnitude 11.0 E7/S0 object, and NGC 3389, a faint (magnitude 12.2) Sc spiral due east. To the west of the M105–NGC 3389 triangle is a 7th-magnitude star, the brightest in the field. To find this field, first locate the magnitude 5.5 star 52 Leonis, which is just over halfway from Regulus to Theta Leonis. (See Chart 5 at the back of this book.) About 4° SSE of 52 Leo is 53 Leo, another magnitude 5.5 star. (They are not difficult to identify because they have no competition in the star-poor spaces of central Leo.) M105 is almost exactly halfway from 52 to 53 Leo, and M96 is almost two thirds along, and slightly west, of the line joining 52 and 53.*

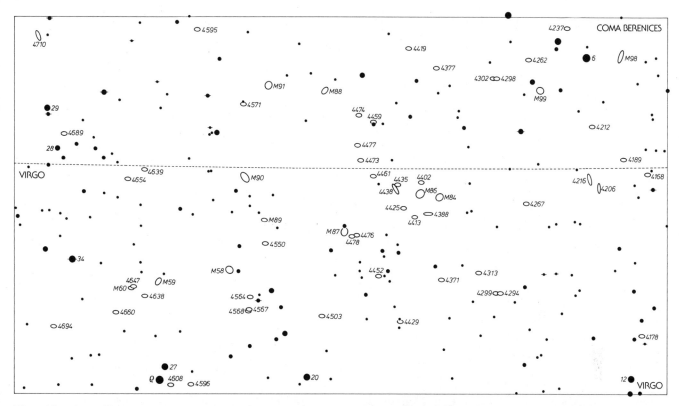

Identification Chart 7–3. Galaxies in the center of the Coma-Virgo Supercluster. *Stars are plotted down to magnitude 9.5, and the chart scale is 18mm (=0.71 inch) per degree. North is to the top and east to the left.*

structure. Since flattening implies rotation, the Local Group and other galaxy groups in the supercluster must be revolving around the supercluster core in southern Coma/northwestern Virgo in periods hundreds of millions of years long. The diameter of our supercluster is probably well over 100 million light-years.

Before we venture into the core of our supercluster, let's take one last look back out of the supercluster. The *Atlas of the Heavens* or *Sky Atlas 2000.0* will show you that the autumn constellations are generally very galaxy-poor, particularly the western autumn constellations. (Capricornus, for example, occupies a fairly large area but has only one galaxy brighter than magnitude 13.0.) However, you will see that in the southern constellations of late autumn there is a faint and scattered imitation of spring's "milky way" of galaxies. Two tight galaxy groups lie in eastern Cetus (the M77 group and, 8° south of it, the NGC 1052 group). Also around the nine Tau (τ) Eridani stars is a reasonably galaxy-rich region, and in southeastern Fornax is the compact but populous Fornax Galaxy Cluster. This line of galaxy groups continues into the far south, with a group in northeastern Horologium and two loose clusters in Dorado. The line of galaxy groups from Cetus down through Dorado seems to be the outlines of a neighboring supercluster that we are viewing edge-on. The distance of these groups averages 50 or 60

million light-years. Because we are near the edge of our supercluster, that value can be taken as the approximate separation between the Local Supercluster and its Cetus-Eridanus-Fornax-Dorado neighbor. Notice also that this other supercluster is oriented in space differently from ours. Its plane cuts across the celestial sphere from Cetus to Dorado in a north-northwest to south-southeast direction, but the plane of our supercluster (if you extend it from the spring sky) runs north-northeast to south-southwest through the Sculptor Group.

The heart of our supercluster is the great Coma-Virgo Galaxy Cluster, centered about midway between Denebola (Beta [β] Leonis) and Epsilon (ε) Virginis and about 10° in diameter. This cluster, roughly 50 million light-years distant, is rich in intrinsically large and luminous galaxies, including the spirals M58, M88, M90, M98, M99, and M100 and the giant ellipticals M49, M59, M60, M61, M84, M85, M86, M87, and M89. Even though the Messier galaxies of the Coma-Virgo Cluster are intrinsically huge and bright, they are so distant that they are hardly good binocular objects. 7x35s and 7x50s are simply inadequate for this field—10x50s are the minimum instrument and even in these, most of the galaxies appear simply as stellar points. However, the finder chart of the central region of the Coma-Virgo Cluster that accompanies this section will help you identify a surprising number of Coma-Virgo galaxies. (In my 10x50s I have seen twenty, including all the Messier galaxies.)

But even with a good finder chart the Coma-Virgo Cluster gives up its treasures reluctantly. The problem is the lack of bright field stars. My approach was to begin at 6th-magnitude 6 Comae, which is about 7° due east of Denebola. About 50′ southeast of 6 Comae (and some 20′ southwest of a 6th-magnitude star) is the face-on Sc galaxy M99. This is 4′ in diameter and is one of the few Coma-Virgo galaxies that shows a disk (albeit a very tiny one) at 10x. After finding M99, follow the loose chain of 8th- and 9th-magnitude stars that goes first east and then south from M99. (You have three stars in a 1° line due east from M99, then four stars in a 2/3° north-south line.) This takes you to a loose group of four faint stars slightly west of the M84/M86 pair. M84 and M86 are only about 20′ apart on an east-west line and are both magnitude 9.3 objects. When I first studied this field in binoculars, they looked merely stellar to me, but a couple years later, when I examined the Coma-Virgo Cluster a second time, they appeared to have perceptible disks—by then my eyes had learned to distinguish the subtle difference between a true star-point and a "stellar" galaxy image. The stellar-looking galaxy image will have less intensity—less "hardness" or sharpness—than a true star point of the same magnitude.

M84 and M86 are giant ellipticals, both with integrated absolute magnitudes of at least −21.5. M86 is remarkable for having a blue shift instead of a red shift—it is overriding the general cosmological expansion and is actually approaching us at 257 miles per second. Over a dozen of the Coma-Virgo Cluster galaxies have blue shifts.

From the M84/M86 pair, the place to go in exploring the Coma-Virgo Cluster is about 1 1/2° southeast to M87, another giant elliptical system. M87 is slightly brighter than M84 and M86, with an apparent magnitude of 9.2, and you therefore have a better chance of seeing it as nonstellar. It is of particular interest because it is a strong source of both radio and x-ray emission, and photographs show a jet of ionized matter being shot at high velocity from the galaxy's nucleus. What is occurring in galaxies like this is simply not known, though the presently-favored speculation is that there are supermassive black holes at the centers of these galaxies. The intense energy and the jets are blasting out of clouds of matter as they vortex into the black holes.

The rest of the Coma-Virgo Cluster I leave to the interested observer. A few more of the Coma-Virgo galaxies have distinct (but very small) disks in 10x50 binoculars, the easiest being those of the giant elliptical M49 (which is at apparent magnitude 8.6, implying an absolute magnitude of −22.5) and the nearly face-on Sc spiral M100 (magnitude 10.5 size 5′) in Coma Berenices.

Appendix A

The History of the Constellations

The Greek and Roman star myths have been retold in countless books and articles. (See especially Percy M. Proctor's *Star Myths and Stories* and Ian Ridpath's *Star Tales*.) However, few of them go into any detail about the Mesopotamian origins of the classical constellations and star myths and those that do usually simply follow R.H. Allen's *Star Names: Their Lore and Meaning*—a book first published in 1899. Scholarly research on the great civilizations of ancient Mesopotamia—the Assyrians, the Babylonians, the Akkadians, and, most ancient of all, the Sumerians—has come a very long way from where it was in 1899. For the past several years I have been studying the technical archaeological reports from excavations in Mesopotamia and reading translations of Assyrian, Babylonian, and Sumerian tablets, searching for whatever information I could find. Some of my conclusions are given in this book. Indeed, most of what I say about the pre-Greek history of the constellations seems never before to have appeared in the literature of popular astronomy.

The purpose of this appendix is to put into historical perspective the discussions of the Mesopotamian star groups, star names, and star myths that are scattered throughout the main body of this book. To make this survey complete, I will also briefly narrate the invention during the 16th to 18th centuries A.D. of the far southern and the "filler" constellations.

A.1 The Ancient Greek Constellations

There are 88 officially recognized constellations. (To the modern astronomer a "constellation" is not a star pattern, but merely an area on the celestial sphere.) We have inherited 51 of those 88 constellations from the ancient Greeks. The actual total of the classical constellations is only 49, but last century astronomers divided the huge celestial ship Argo, the largest of the ancient constellations, into Puppis the Stern, Vela the Sails, and Carina the Keel. The 49 Greek constellations, here presented in the three groups by which the ancients classified them, are found in Table A–1.

Table A–1
The Classical Constellations

Northern

Andromeda	Equuleus
Aquila	Kneeler (=Hercules)
Auriga	Lyra
Boötes	Ophiuchus
Cassiopeia	Pegasus
Cepheus	Perseus
Coma Berenices	Sagitta
Corona Borealis	Serpens
Cycnus (=Cygnus)	Triangulum
Delphinus	Ursa Major
Draco	Ursa Minor

Zodiacal

Aquarius	Libra
Aries	Pisces
Cancer	Sagittarius
Capricornus	Scorpius
Gemini	Taurus
Leo	Virgo

Southern

Ara	Crater
Argo	Eridanus
Canis Major	Hydra
Canis Minor	Lepus
Centaurus	Orion
Cetus	Piscis Austrinus
Corona Australis	Therion ("Beast"=Lupus)
Corvus	

All the classical constellations but Coma Berenices were catalogued by the Greek-Alexandrian astronomer Claudius Ptolemaeus (now usually referred to simply as "Ptolemy") in his monumental *Syntaxis* ("System"), a book written before A.D. 150 but the foremost astronomical text until the Enlightenment. (By this time it had picked up the Arabic name *Almagest*. Ptolemy, incidentally, *did* mention Coma: not as a separate constellation, but merely among the "unformed" stars outside the star pattern of Leo.) Ptolemy's list was derived from earlier Greek constellation catalogues, the oldest surviving of which is a poetical description of the heav-

163

ens titled *Phaenomena*, composed about 270 B.C. by
the Greek Aratos of Soli but based upon a prose work
of the same name written a century earlier by the astronomer Eudoxos. Aratos listed 48 constellations (49 if
you count the Pleiades, to which he devoted 14 lines of
his poem). Of the classical 49, he omitted only Coma
Berenices and Equuleus, both of which reliable tradi-
tions have dated after him. Aratos' 48th group is *Hy-
dor*, the "Water" pouring from Aquarius' Jar, which
two centuries later Geminos of Rhodes still catalogued
as a separate southern constellation.

Thus, almost all the ancient 49 constellations can
be traced with confidence back to the early 4th century
B.C., when Eudoxos wrote the original prose *Phaenomena*. That many, or most, of the star groups in the
Aratos-Eudoxos canon were already very old cannot be
doubted, for there are references to several of them in
early Greek literature. The playwright Aeschylus, who
lived from about 525 to 456 B.C., related the story of
the Pleiades and mentioned Sirius under the name of
the "Dog Star." The poet Hesiod, in his agricultural
manual *Works and Days* (composed in the last half of
the 8th century B.C.), mentioned Orion, the Pleiades
and Hyades, and Arcturus and Sirius. The *Iliad* and
the *Odyssey* (which date from about the same period
as Hesiod), referred to all these plus the Bear (Ursa
Major).

The Greeks seem to have invented quite a number of the ancient 49 constellations themselves. Canis Minor, Coma Berenices, Corona Australis, Equuleus, and Ursa Minor are certainly Greek innovations,
and Corona Borealis, Crater, Cygnus, Delphinus, Lyra,
and Triangulum probably are. It is also likely that
the Perseus group of constellations (Andromeda, Cassiopeia, Cepheus, Cetus, Pegasus, and Perseus) were
introduced to the heavens by the Greeks. However, the
majority of the classical constellations, about 30 of them
in all, originally came to Greece from the great civilizations of Mesopotamia.

A.2   The Ancient Mesopotamian Constellations

There is not, of course, an abundance of sources surviving that specify the Mesopotamian star and constellation names, fewer still that enable us to identify the
particular stars and star patterns to which these names
applied. Hundreds of astronomical texts, written in
cuneiform on clay tablets, have been unearthed at various sites in modern Iraq (ancient Mesopotamia), but
they nearly all deal with lunar and planetary positions
and were written at a very late period (last centuries
of the 1st millennium B.C.). There are, however, about
a half dozen dating from around 1000 B.C. that treat

particularly of the stars and constellations. The most
important of these is one of a two-tablet series titled
Mul Apin, "Constellation of the Plow." (The agrarian
Mesopotamians likened the path of the Sun through the
stars (the ecliptic) to a plow-furrow. See the discussion
of this under Aries earlier in this book.) *Mul Apin* was
written down about 700 B.C., but research has shown
that the observations recorded in it must have been
made 400 or 500 years earlier. Because *Mul Apin* contains statements about the heliacal rising of the stars
and star groups, about stars and star groups that rose
and set simultaneously, and even about the orientations
of star groups with respect to each other, scholars have
been able to identify nearly all of the Mesopotamian
constellations named in it.

Mul Apin is not impressively old: it was written
roughly contemporaneously with Hesiod and the leg-
endary Homer, *c.* 700 B.C. But there is a very peculiar thing about *Mul Apin*: it was written by the Assyrians, but the star and constellation-names that appear in it are Sumerian. The Sumerians were the first
great civilization in Mesopotamia. In the 4th millennium B.C. they founded a loose confederation of agricultural city-states strung along the lower Tigris and
Euphrates rivers. The Sumerians invented the plow,
the 2- and 4-wheeled wagons, monumental construction
in brick, large-scale irrigation, sculpture in stone, and,
before 3000 B.C., writing. However, during the late
3rd millennium they began to lose their pre-eminence
in Mesopotamia, and by the reign of Hammurabi the
Great of Babylon in the 18th century B.C., they had
been ethnically and politically absorbed by the Babylonians.

The Babylonians (and their Assyrian successors)
were a Semitic people speaking a language related to
Hebrew and Arabic. The Sumerians, however, had
been non-Semitic and spoke a language unrelated to
any other, living or dead. Nevertheless, the Babylonians not only absorbed Sumeria politically, they absorbed Sumeria culturally: they adopted Sumerian religion and mythology, Sumerian literature, Sumerian
architecture, Sumerian *mores* and *Weltanschauung*—
Sumerian everything. They even used Sumerian as a
technical language (just as today we use another dead
language—Latin—in science, law, and religion). Thus,
around 1000 B.C. Assyro-Babylonian scribes were still
writing Sumerian star and constellation names in *Mul
Apin* and other astronomical works. That these names
had actually been used more than a millennium earlier
by the Sumerians themselves is proved by two extant ar-
chaic astronomical name-lists, one dated to 1700 B.C.
and the other to around 2100 B.C., both of which item-
ize many Sumerian star titles that appear in the later
Assyrian tablets.

Table A–2		
Selected Constellation Names		
Sumerian Predecessors of the Greek Constellations		
Modern Latin Name	Ancient Greek Name	Sumerian Name
Aquila = Eagle	Aetos = Eagle	A = Eagle
Auriga = Charioteer	Heniochos = Charioteer	Gigir = Chariot
Capricornus = Horned Goat	Aegoceros = Horned Goat	Suhurmash = Goat-fish
Corvus = Crow	Corax = Raven	Uga = Raven
Gemini = Twins	Didymoi = Twins	Mastabba Galgal = Great Twins
Hydra = Water-serpent	Hydra = Water-serpent	Mush = Serpent
Leo = Lion	Leon = Lion	Urgula = Lion
Libra = Scales	Zygos = Balance-beam	Rin = Scales
Orion = Hunter	Orion = Hunter	Sibzianna = True Shepherd of Heaven
Piscis Austrinus = Southern Fish	Ichthues Notios = Southern Fish	Ka = Fish (probably Alpha PsA alone)
Sagittarius = Archer	Toxeuter = Archer	Pabilsag = (an epithet of the war-god Ninurta)
Scorpius = Scorpion	Scorpios = Scorpion	Girtab = Scorpion
Taurus = Bull	Tauros = Bull	Guanna = Bull of Heaven
Lupus = Wolf	Therion = Beast	Ur-idim = Wild Dog
Ursa Major = Great Bear	Arctos = Bear / Hamaxa = Wagon (Dipper only)	Margidda = Wagon (Dipper only)
Regulus = Little King	Basiliskos = Regal	Mul Lugal = Star of the King
Spica = Ear of Corn	Stachys = Ear of Corn	Absin = Ear of Corn

Table A–2 is a partial catalogue of the Sumerian constellations and star names which from *Mul Apin* we know corresponded to identical Greek constellations and star names.

A.3 Arabian Star Names and Renaissance Constellation Invention

Ptolemy's *Syntaxis* was the unrivaled work on astronomy for over 1200 years. After the Islamic conquest of North Africa and the Middle East during the 7th and 8th centuries A.D., Arabian astronomers discovered classical astronomy and translated the *Syntaxis* into Arabic (calling it *Al Kitab al Mijisti, The Greatest Book*, which later was shortened to *Almagest*, the name by which it is usually referred to even today.) Arabian astronomers absorbed Ptolemaic astronomy as completely as the Babylonians before them had absorbed Sumerian astronomy, to the point of abandoning the constellations of their ancestors, the nomads of the Arabian Desert. Fortunately, some of the Arabian astronomers preserved the Bedouin star and constellation names—most particularly Al Sufi (903–986 A.D.) in his *Book on the Fixed Stars* and Al Biruni (973–1048) in the *Book of Instruction on the Art of Astrology*. (Most of the Arab star names mentioned in the present book are from a 1934 translation of Al Biruni.) Some of the Bedouin constellations and star names are identical with the Greek ones (the nomads had a zodiacal Lion and Scorpion, and knew Capella as a Goat and Altair as an Eagle), no doubt because they too inherited con-

stellations from Mesopotamia (though because of their proximity to Mesopotamia they probably learned the Sumero-Babylonian constellations directly, not through intermediaries). When Europeans began penetrating the Arabian peninsula in the 19th and early 20th centuries, they found the nomads still using the Arab star names recorded by Al Sufi and Al Biruni—which should not be surprising, because before this century and its oil wealth, the Bedouin way of life had not substantially changed since the beginning of the widespread use of the camel in the late 2nd millennium B.C.

In Europe astronomy lay dormant until the Renaissance, and then it picked up where it had left off—with Ptolemy. However, the Arabian influence was felt, particularly through translations into Latin of the *Almagest* and of such original Arabian astronomical works as the *Alphonsine Tables*, which had been compiled by Moorish astronomers in Spain in the mid-13th century under the patronage of King Alphonso X "the Wise," and the *Tables* of Ulug Beg, published in 1437 in the Islamic central Asian city of Samarkhand. The Arabic names we still use for most of the bright stars are the legacy of the influence of Arabian upon Renaissance European astronomy.

The first significant addition to the Ptolemaic constellations occurred after European mariners sailed into the South Atlantic and saw the south circumpolar stars, which of course had been invisible to the Greeks and Mesopotamians. In 1603 the German astronomer Johannes Bayer published, in his *Uranometria*, drawings of 12 south circumpolar groups. (In the *Uranometria*

| Table A–3 |
The Bayer Constellations
Apis: Bee (later in the 17th century changed to the present Musca, the Fly) **Avis Indica:** Indian Bird (now Apus, the Bird of Paradise) **Chamaeleon** **Dorado:** Goldfish (referring not to the small aquarium species but to the large tropical dolphin) **Grus:** Crane **Hydrus:** Water-snake (the masculine form of the Greek "hydra") **Indus:** (American) Indian **Pavo:** Peacock **Phoenix** **Piscis Volans:** Flying Fish (now simply Volans) **Toucan:** (later Latinized to the present Tucana) **Triangulum Australae:** Southern Triangle

| Table A–4 |
The Hevelius "Northern Filler" Constellations
Canes Venatici: Hunting Dogs. (This group, though always credited to Hevelius, in fact appears first on a planisphere published in 1536 by Petrus Apianus.) **Lacerta:** Lizard **Leo Minor:** Small Lion **Lynx** **Scutum Sobiescianum:** Sobieski's Shield (now simply Scutum) **Sextans Uraniae:** Sextant (now simply Sextans) **Vulpecula cum Ansere:** Little Fox with the Goose (now simply Vulpecula)

| Table A–5 |
The Lacaille "Southern Filler" Constellations
Antlia Pneumatica: Air Pump (now Antlia) **l'Atelier du Sculpteur:** Sculptor's Workshop (now Sculptor) **Caelum:** Chisel **Circinus:** Compasses **Equuleus Pictoris:** Painter's Easel (now simply Pictor) **Fornax Chemica:** Chemical Furnace (now Fornax) **Horologium Oscillatorium:** Pendulum Clock (now Horologium) **Microscopium:** Microscope **Mons Mensae:** Table Mountain (in back of Cape Town where Lacaille did his observing; now Mensa) **Norma et Regula:** Level and Square (now Norma) **Octans Hadleianus:** Hadley's Octant (formed in honor of John Hadley, inventor of the octant; now Octans) **Pyxis Nautica:** Mariner's Compass (now Pyxis) **Reticulum Rhomboidalis:** Rhomboidal Reticle (now Reticulum. Lacaille's reticle had a rhombus-shaped cut-out in the center of its field.) **Telescopium:** Telescope

Bayer also introduced the use of Greek letters for designating stars.) Despite the fact that these groups (shown in Table A–3) are still known as the "Bayer constellations," Bayer never even saw the southern sky: he based his drawings on the reports of the mariners who had sailed in the South Atlantic, Indian, and Pacific oceans.

Most of the "Bayer" constellations seem, in fact, to have been actually invented by a Dutch navigator named Peter Theodore.

The stars of our Crux, the Southern Cross, had been included by the ancients in Centaurus. On his chart Bayer showed them in Centaurus, but he also traced a cross over them and in his text referred to them as "the modern cross, Ptolemy's feet of the Centaur." However, these four stars had already been called the Cross for a century by mariners.

After Bayer the only significant constellation-invention that remained to be done involved merely the filling-in of unoccupied spaces. The largest blank regions between the ancient constellations were filled by the introduction of Columba Noae, "Noah's Dove" (now simply Columba), south of Lepus, Monoceros the Unicorn east of Orion, and Camelopardalis the Giraffe north of Perseus and Auriga. All three were invented during the last decades of the 16th century. A hundred years later the Polish astronomer Johannes Hoevelke (usually referred to by the Latin form of his name, "Hevelius") squeezed several small constellations between the older groups in the northern sky (they were published in 1690 after their inventor's death). The ones that were accepted and remain in the sky are listed in Table A–4.

Many of the classical constellations have a reasonable resemblance to the objects they are named for. However, with Bayer and Hevelius all pretence of verisimilitude has obviously been abandoned. The height of imagination was reached in the mid-18th century by Nicolas Louis de Lacaille, a French astronomer who observed from Cape Town (South Africa) and crowded 14 new constellations among the Bayer and southernmost Greek constellations. These are listed in Table A–5. Europe in the 18th century was mad about mechanical gadgets, and Lacaille proved that he was a true child of his time by naming all (but one) of his constellations after implements of science and art.

The ancient 51 with Bayer's 12, Hevelius' 7, Lacaille's 14, and Crux, Columba, Monoceros, and Camelopardalis add up to the presently accepted 88 constellations. From the late 17th to the early 19th centuries many minor constellations were introduced that never caught on. A couple, such as Taurus Poniatovii (see Ophiuchus) and Noctua (see Hydra), really were visually logical, but most were squeezed in merely to flatter some monarch or to satisfy the inventor's whimsicality.

In the modern scientific sense a constellation is not a star pattern but simply a region of the celestial sphere. The present boundaries between the constellations were established by the International Astronomical Union in 1928 and published two years later.

Appendix B

Star Basics

This section is designed primarily as a refresher for readers who have already had some contact with star magnitudes, stellar spectral types, and the H-R diagram. Those who are coming to these subjects for the first time might find this section a bit challenging in places, but should be able to absorb enough to understand the material in this book easily. A fairly detailed summary of stellar evolution concludes this appendix.

B.1 Star Brightness

The two visible qualities of starlight are brightness and color.

The relative brightness of stars is measured by the magnitude system, which has its roots in the astronomy of the ancient Greeks. The Greeks divided the stars into "magnitudes," 1st magnitude being the brightest and 6th magnitude, the faintest.

Precise modern light-measuring instruments show that the typical 1st-magnitude star is about 100 times brighter than the typical 6th-magnitude star. Therefore, astronomers defined the magnitude system so that an interval of five magnitudes corresponds to a true brightness ratio of 1:100, and consequently the brightness ratio corresponding to a difference of one magnitude is the fifth root of 100, which turns out to be 2.512. A 1st-magnitude star, therefore, is about 2.5 times brighter than a 2nd-magnitude star, 6.3 (2.5×2.5) times brighter than a 3rd-magnitude star, 16 (2.5 × 2.5 × 2.5) times brighter than a 4th-magnitude star, and 40 (2.5 × 2.5 × 2.5 × 2.5) times brighter than a 5th-magnitude star.

Because of the way the Greeks set up the system, stars with the smaller numerical magnitudes are the brighter. The brightest stars of all even have negative magnitudes. (Sirius, for example, has a magnitude of −1.4 and Arcturus, of −0.1.) On this scale the Sun's magnitude is −26.8, the Full Moon's is about −12.6, and Venus' (at its brightest) is −4.4. The faintest stars that have been photographed by the 200-inch Hale telescope are 23rd-magnitude—a hundred million trillion times fainter than the Sun. Trained variable star observers can discern brightness differences of 0.1 magnitude, but photoelectric photometers measure differences of a mere 0.001 magnitude.

The brightness of a star (or planet) as seen from Earth is called its apparent magnitude. However, because stars lie at different distances from us, their apparent magnitudes tell us little about their true luminosity. Rigel, for instance, appears 1.5 magnitudes (4 times) fainter than Sirius but in reality is 100 times farther away and therefore actually 2,500 times brighter. To measure true luminosity astronomers use absolute magnitude, which is the apparent magnitude an object would have if it were 32.6 light-years away from us. Rigel's absolute magnitude is about −7.1, Sirius' +1.4, and the Sun's is only +4.8.

Integrated magnitude is the brightness that an extended object like diffuse nebula, a star cluster, or a galaxy would have if all of its light were concentrated into a single stellar point. The integrated apparent magnitude of the Pleiades, for example, is 1.4, equivalent to the apparent brightness of Regulus. The Pleiades' integrated absolute magnitude—their magnitude if all of their light were concentrated at a stellar point 32.6 light-years away—is about −4.1. This is almost nine magnitudes (3,600 times) brighter than the Sun's absolute magnitude but still three magnitudes fainter than Rigel. (This says something about how luminous Rigel really is.)

Integrated absolute magnitudes are a useful way of expressing the total luminosity of a cluster or a galaxy—though it is rather awesome imagining all the light of a galaxy concentrated in one stellar point only 32.6 light-years away! The integrated absolute magnitude of our own Milky Way Galaxy is estimated to be −20.5. This is about 25 magnitudes, or 10 billion times, brighter than the Sun.

B.2 Star Colors and Spectral Types

The differences in color you see among stars in your binoculars correspond to actual differences in surface temperature. Blue stars are hotter than white stars,

			Table B–1 Spectral Types	
Type	Temperature (°K)	Color	Examples	Spectral Features (Absorption Lines)
O	Over 25,000	Bluish	ζ (Zeta) Puppis (O5), ι (Iota) Orionis (O9)	Ionized Helium; hydrogen weak; doubly or triply ionized metals.
B	25,000 to 11,000	Bluish	Spica (B1), Rigel (B8)	No ionized helium; neutral helium strong; hydrogen stronger; fewer ionized metals.
A	11,000 to 7,600	Blue-white to white	Sirius (A1), Altair (A7)	Helium absent; hydrogen strong (strongest at A0); Calcium II present but weak; other singly ionized metals strong.
F	7,600 to 6,000	Yellowish-white	Canopus (F0), Procyon (F5)	Hydrogen weaker; calcium II stronger; at F0 singly ionized metals as strong as neutral metals, but in later F neutral metals predominate.
G	6,000 to 4,500	Yellow	Sun (G2), Capella (G8)	Hydrogen weak; calcium II at maximum; many lines of neutral metals; lines of molecules CH and CN appear and become stronger toward late G.
K	5,100 to 3,200	Orange	Arcturus (K2), Aldebraran (K5)	Hydrogen faint; neutral metals very strong; CH and CN stronger.
M	Less than 3,700	Orange-red	Antares (M1), Betelgeuse (M2), Mira (M5e-M9e)	Neutral metals and CH & CN strong; titanium oxide (TiO) appears and becomes stronger toward late M; "Me" stars have hydrogen emission lines.
C	Same as K and M	Red	19 Psc (C6), Y CVn (C5)	"Carbon stars": strong lines of such carbon molecules as C_2, CN, CO; TiO absent.
S	Same as K and M	Orange-red	[None discussed in this book.]	Resembles type-M but with oxides of such exotic elements as zirconium and ytterbium replacing TiO.
WN, WC	Above 50,000	Bluish	γ (Gamma) Velorum (WC8)	"Wolf-Rayet" stars. [See the discussion on NGC 6231 in Scorpius.]

which are hotter than yellow stars, which are hotter than red stars.

Astronomers class stars by temperature and call the result the star's *spectral type*. From hottest to coolest, the spectral types run O, B, A, F, G, K, M. Each spectral type is subdivided into 10 subclasses, numbered 0 to 9. Thus, you see spectral types given as A0, M5, F3, and so on. The Sun is in spectral class G2.

If all stars were of the same size, hotter stars would be more luminous than cooler stars simply because they radiate more energy per unit of surface area. However, stars are not all of the same size. Some very large red stars are more luminous than many blue stars simply because they are very much larger than the blue stars. If you have a group of stars of the same spectral type (i.e., temperature and color) but of different luminosities, the stars must be of different sizes.

That stars can have the same color but much different luminosities became clear earlier this century. After astronomers began to get reliable estimates of the distances and therefore absolute magnitudes of stars,

they made diagrams plotting stars' absolute magnitudes against their spectral types. This diagram has been called the Hertzsprung-Russell or H-R diagram, named for Einar Hertzsprung and Henry Norris Russell, the first two astronomers to publish plots of magnitude vs. spectral type.

The majority of stars fall in a relatively narrow band that extends diagonally across the H-R diagram from faint, cool stars on the lower right to hot, luminous stars on the upper left. (See Figure B–1, page 170.) This band is called the main sequence. Above and below the main sequence, however, lie three other distinct concentrations of stars. In the lower left is a scattering of hot but low-luminosity B- and A-type stars, the white dwarfs. Above the G-K-M region of the main sequence the red giants form a fairly well-populated group slanted slightly upward toward the red. And across the upper part of the H-R diagram are sprinkled the highly luminous supergiants. Because the luminosity of a star is the product of its surface area and the amount of energy being radiated per unit of its surface area, the

Table B–2 Luminosity Classes		
Ia$^+$ or Ia-0	Extreme Supergiants	ζ^1 (Zeta-1) Scorpii (B5 Ia$^+$)
Ia	Luminous Supergiants	Rigel (B8 Ia), μ (Mu) Cephei (M2 Ia)
Ib	Less Luminous Supergiants	Antares (M1 Ib)
II	Bright Giants	β (Beta) Canis Majoris (B1 II)
III	Normal Giants	Arcturus (K2 III)
IV	Subgiants	Procyon (F5 IV or V)
V	Main-Sequence stars	Sun (G2 V), Sirius (A1 V)
D	White Dwarfs	Companion to Sirius (DA)

basic difference between main-sequence, giant, and supergiant stars of a given spectral type (and therefore temperature) must be size.

The *luminosity class* of a star is the zone of the H-R diagram into which it falls and is expressed by a Roman numeral (except for white dwarfs, which are indicated only by a "D" preceding their spectral type): supergiants are luminosity class I, giants luminosity class III, and main-sequence stars luminosity class V. There are also intermediate luminosity classes, called bright-giants and subgiants.

Thus, the spectral type and luminosity class of a star together give its precise location on the H-R diagram, and stars are usually described by these two parameters. Rigel, for example, is a B8 Ia star, and our Sun is a G2 V object. Occasionally, the luminosity class is indicated only by a lowercase letter preceding the spectral type: "c" stands for supergiant, "g" for giant, "d" for main-sequence or dwarf, and "sd" for subdwarf (a star that falls just below the main sequence). Other lowercase letters are sometimes given that indicate notable features in a star's spectrum: "e" means that the spectrum has emission features, "n" that the spectral lines are widened, "f" that ionized helium is present, and "m" that lines of metals are in the spectrum. A simple "p" refers to other spectral peculiarities.

B.3 The Formation and Evolution of Stars

The Great Rift that divides the summer Milky Way is a conglomeration of great clouds of cold interstellar matter that obscures the light of the stars beyond. A relatively close and very conspicuous cloud of interstellar matter is the famous Coal Sack in the far southern Milky Way, which is about 550 light-years away and 60 or 70 light-years in diameter. It is from such clouds of matter that stars form. One evidence for this is that all highly luminous supergiant stars—which must have been only recently (by astronomical time scales) formed because they contain only a few dozen times as much mass as the Sun but are radiating energy hundreds of thousands times faster—are associated with complexes of bright and dark nebulae.

The first stage in star formation is the gravitational contraction of a cloud of interstellar matter. For this to occur, the cloud must have sufficient density to overcome such factors as its own internal turbulence and the sheer produced because the part of the cloud nearest to the galactic center has a different angular velocity from the part farthest from the galactic center. The initial compression that causes a cloud to reach the density necessary for gravitational contraction could occur from the shock wave of a nearby supernova explosion. Some astronomers also think that spiral-shaped gravity fields rotate in the planes of spiral galaxies, causing the matter which passes through them to compress—the result being the familiar spiral arms of such galaxies, which are known to consist of newly-formed clusters, associations, and star clouds.

In any case, as a cloud of interstellar matter gravitationally contracts, internal turbulence and local density enhancements cause it to fragment, at first into smaller clouds containing a few thousand solar masses (approximately the amount of matter observed in large open clusters like M11 in Scutum and NGC 869 and NGC 884 of the Perseus Double Cluster), then into *protostars*. The Coal Sack, which has a size comparable to the extreme diameters of many open clusters and contains some very opaque, oval spots, could be a "proto-cluster" just beginning to fragment into protostars. The small dark "Bok globules" that can be seen on photographs of such emission nebulae as the Rosette Nebula in Monoceros and the Lagoon Nebula in Sagittarius are generally assumed to be protostars in an early stage of their gravitational contraction.

The gravitational energy released as a protostar contracts increases its temperature. Because its interior contracts much faster than its outer regions, the protostar develops a relatively hot core surrounded by a cool, opaque envelope. The core continues to contract (very rapidly in its final phases) and to increase in temperature until radiation pressure and stellar winds (streams

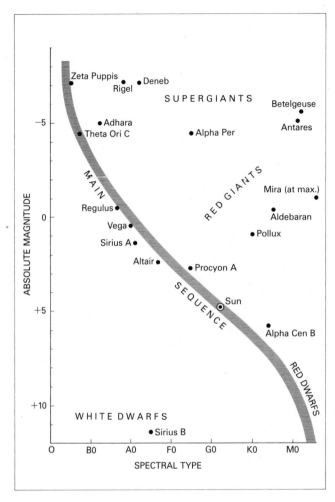

Figure B–1. *The Hertzsprung-Russell (H-R) Diagram, with the various stellar classes.*

of particles from the star accelerated by radiation pressure and other forces) disperse the envelope and reveal the infant star.

When the central temperature of the contracting young star reaches 20 million degrees Kelvin, thermonuclear fusion of hydrogen into helium becomes possible (four hydrogen nuclei—protons—are brought together to form one helium nucleus—two protons plus two neutrons—with a net release of energy. The high temperature is necessary to overcome the mutual repulsion of the positively charged protons.). The energy now being generated in the star's interior halts contraction, and the star achieves "hydrostatic equilibrium" in which internal radiation and gas pressures counterbalance gravity. It is at this point that the star settles into the main sequence, where it will spend most of its life.

The place in the main sequence where a star settles depends only on its mass: a star of 10 solar masses will be a B1 V object with a surface temperature of about 25,000°K and an absolute magnitude of around −3.9; but a star of only 0.1 solar mass will be an M6 V red dwarf with a surface temperature of just 2800°K and an absolute magnitude of a mere +15.5. As this implies, the main sequence is a *mass* sequence, with the lightest stars on the lower right and the heavier stars to the upper left. (The width of the main sequence is the result of the slightly variable composition of the stars: if two stars have the same mass, but one contains more "metals"—elements heavier than helium—then the metal-rich star will be the slightly more luminous and lie directly over the other star in the main sequence.) Now, the total energy output of a B1 V star is 33,000 times that of the Sun. Obviously, such stars will run out of their nuclear fuel long before the Sun and consequently will have relatively short main-sequence lifetimes (roughly 20 million years compared to the Sun's 10 *billion* years). On the other hand, a star of only 0.1 solar mass has an energy output of just 0.0001 times the Sun's and will stay on the main sequence for perhaps hundreds of billions of years—assuming the universe lasts that long.

There are limits to stellar masses. Theoretical calculations predict that a protostar of over 100 solar masses would develop internal instabilities and disrupt before reaching the main sequence. The most massive stars—those with about 100 solar masses—are O3 supergiants with surface temperatures of 55,000°K and total energy outputs of around two million times the Sun's. The lower limits of stellar masses depend on exactly how one defines "star." If you choose to make the determining factor whether or not thermonuclear fusion is occurring (or in the case of a contracting object, *will* occur) in a body's interior, then objects of less than 0.08 solar mass are not stars, because during gravitational contraction they do not develop sufficiently high internal temperatures to ignite their hydrogen. On the other hand, enough energy is released by the gravitational contractions of such bodies that they become self-luminous, appearing on the H-R diagram as extreme red dwarfs of late-M spectral types. However, if you take self-luminosity to be the basic criterion defining what shall be considered a star, you still have a problem: some bodies are so light (and therefore can derive so little energy from gravitational contraction) that they end up radiating only at infrared or radio wavelengths. Jupiter, which contains just 0.001 solar mass, is technically self-luminous because it weakly radiates radio waves, but it hardly seems proper to consider it a "star."

The post-main-sequence evolution of high-mass and of low-mass stars are quite different and therefore will be discussed separately. Extremely low-mass M dwarfs simply radiate away the energy they accumulated from gravitational contraction, gradually (over a period of hundreds of billions of years) fading into *black dwarfs*, objects with a surface temperature equal to that of interstellar space itself.

Post-Main-Sequence Evolution of Solar-Mass Stars

In a solar-type star the nucleosynthesis of hydrogen into helium takes place over a rather large part of the interior. Eventually, however, a small core of inert (but very hot) helium is built up at the very center of the star, around which hydrogen-burning continues in a thick shell. As helium is added to the core, it gravitationally contracts. This releases energy, which stimulates the rate of hydrogen-burning in the shell and therefore increases the star's overall luminosity. The increased flow of radiation from the star's interior expands and cools its envelope. Consequently, during core contraction the star evolves toward the right and off the main

sequence and up the red giant branch.

During the approximately 300 million years the star evolves up the giant branch, the hydrogen-burning shell continues to add helium to the contracting helium core. At the tip of the giant branch, the energy released by core contraction and by the increasing rate of hydrogen-burning in the shell, has finally raised core temperature to 80 million degrees Kelvin, the point at which the nucleosynthesis of helium into carbon can take place. After core helium-burning settles down to a sustainable rate, the star evolves rapidly off the tip of the giant branch down to the *horizontal branch*, where it will be for about 60 million years. The horizontal branch is a conspicuous feature of the H-R diagrams of most globular clusters, which are very old and therefore contain highly evolved stars. Horizontal-branch stars have A and F spectral types and absolute magnitudes of between +0.5 and +2. Because of the mass loss that occurs while a star is a bloated red giant (matter from the upper atmosphere of red giants is blown off by radiation pressure and becomes a strong stellar wind of particles), horizontal-branch stars contain only about 0.6 to 0.8 solar mass (the A-type stars being the less massive). There is a narrow instability strip in the horizontal branch which contains the RR Lyrae short-period pulsating variable stars that are so useful for estimating globular cluster distances. The pulsations of RR Lyrae variables originate in an ionization zone near their surface and therefore involve only their outer layers.

While on the horizontal branch, a star has two energy sources—a helium-burning core and a hydrogen-burning shell (a residual of its main-sequence life). Both contribute about the same amount of energy to the star's total luminosity. After a time the helium at the center of the core is exhausted and helium-burning can continue only in a shell surrounding a gradually enlarging core of pure carbon. This has the same result as when shell-burning (of hydrogen) began in a main-sequence star: the rate of energy generation in the interior of the star increases, which forces the star's outer layers to expand and cool, increasing its luminosity. Thus, the star evolves up the red giant branch for a second time. Stars leaving the horizontal branch follow a slightly different path up the giant branch than stars leaving the main sequence; but because both tracks approach each other near their tips, the path of horizontal-branch stars is called the *asymptotic giant branch.*

As the now very old star nears the tip of the giant branch for a second time, its inner helium-burning shell approaches its outer hydrogen-burning shell. This creates a strong instability within the star, which is manifested by the Mira-type regular, semiregular, or irregular pulsations that are observed in many red giants. By the time the star reaches the tip of the giant branch, the pulsations of its outer layers have become so extreme that they actually reach escape velocity and are ejected out into space as a planetary nebula. The multi-ring structure of many planetaries suggests that the outer layers of a planetary-forming star can be shed in more than one stage.

The remaining planetary nebula central star consists of a helium-burning shell enclosing a small core of pure carbon. Initially, it is very luminous—several thousand times more luminous than the Sun—but the helium fuel of the shell is very quickly exhausted. When it is, there is nothing left to sustain interior pressure, and the star (perhaps it would be more precise to say "stellar remnant") begins to contract. Because it contains only a few tenths solar mass of matter and therefore cannot derive enough energy from gravitational contraction to initiate carbon-burning in its interior, the star simply contacts into a *white dwarf*. It is now incredibly dense (the density of the white dwarf companion of Sirius is 125,000 times that of water), but it shines only by the energy left over from its gravitational contraction. White dwarfs are so small (they average about the size of the earth) that they have very little radiating surface and it takes them billions of years to cool down from hot type DB to cool type DM objects. After billions of years more a white dwarf radiates away all of its residual energy and becomes a black dwarf.

White dwarfs occupy the very bottom of the H-R diagram in a slanting sequence, with the relatively more luminous DB and DA white dwarfs on its upper left and the faint DK and DM "white" dwarfs on its lower right. The range of white dwarf absolute magnitudes is between +9 and +16.

Post-Main-Sequence Evolution of High-Mass Stars

Like solar-type stars, the early post-main-sequence evolution of massive stars involves the exhaustion of hydrogen in the star's center, the establishment of a hydrogen-burning shell around an inert helium core, and the expansion and cooling of the star's outer layers as the core contracts. Unlike solar-type stars, the luminosity of massive stars in their red giant phase is about the same as it was when they were on the main sequence.

Gradually, however, the rate of core helium-burning increases, increasing the luminosity of the star. At the same time the star undergoes an overall contraction, with the concomitant rise in surface temperature. The net result is that the star leaves the red giant region and heads to the left and slightly up across the H-R diagram. It is during this phase of their evolution, and in subsequent passes through this area of the H-R diagram, that stars of more than three solar masses experience the instabilities in their envelopes which result in Cepheid-variable pulsations.

When the helium-burning core becomes its predominant energy source, the star begins evolving back toward the red giant region. On the way, helium is exhausted in the very center of the star, and helium-burning continues at an increased rate in a shell, with the consequence that the star enters the red giant region with a somewhat higher luminosity than it had during its earlier red giant stage.

Stars of more than 10 solar masses will have an outer shell where hydrogen is being nucleosynthesized into helium, an inner shell where helium is being nucleosynthesized into carbon, and a core where carbon is being nucleosynthesized into oxygen. (Between each nuclear-burning region is a shell of inert material, carbon above the carbon-burning core and helium above the helium-burning shell. Above the hydrogen-burning shell is the hydrogen-rich outer envelope of the star.) Eventually, a pure oxygen core will be built up, which in its turn will contract and achieve a high enough temperature to nucleosynthesize neon. A massive supergiant star will thus develop an "onion-shell" structure with several nuclear shell sources burning at once and successively higher atomic weight nuclei being constructed at its center.

But the sequence dead-ends at iron. The synthesis of iron nuclei occurs with a net release of energy and is therefore self-sustaining, but the amount of energy required to synthesize trans-iron nuclei is greater than the amount of energy released. Therefore, as the iron core of the supergiant star contracts, the exotic nuclear-burning processes that occur simply *absorb* energy and accelerate the contraction. When the core's contraction has pushed its temperature to 5 billion degrees Kelvin, the iron nuclei photodisintegrate into helium nuclei and free neutrons. Since this process requires huge amounts of energy, the bottom literally drops out from under core temperature and pressure.

But now there is nothing at all resisting gravity. The core violently implodes, at the same time (in a manner not yet understood) blasting the star's outer layers away in a supernova explosion. The collapse of the core literally crushes its electrons and protons together into neutrons. If the core mass is less than about 2 solar masses (the exact value is still a matter of debate among astrophysicists), the pressure of the degenerate neutrons (neutrons as compacted together as the exclusion principle of quantum mechanics allows) can halt the implosion and a *neutron star* will be left at the center of the supernova's expanding debris cloud. If, however, the core's mass is more than 2 solar masses, gravity overwhelms even the neutrons themselves, and the result is a body so dense that not even light can escape its gravitational pull—it has become a *black hole*.

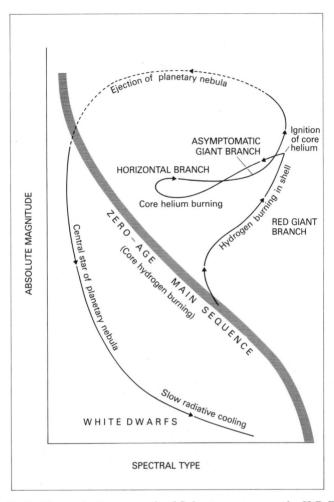

Figure B–2. *The evolutionary track of Solar-type stars on the H-R Diagram.*

Appendix C

Bibliography

C.1 Basic Observing Guides

Any of the following inexpensive handbooks will provide you with the basic knowledge that you need to use this book.

Stars, Herbert S. Zim and R.H. Baker, Golden Press, various printings. This is one of the Golden Nature Guide series and is particularly good as an introduction to the constellations. Also has a brief but very clear explanation of the magnitude system, stellar spectral types, double and variable stars, clusters, and nebulae.

Stars and Planets, Robin Kerrod, Arco Publishing Co., 1984. Another introductory guide to astronomy, but has more detailed star charts than *Stars* and discusses more individual constellations.

Skyguide, Mark R. Chartrand and H.K. Wimmer, Golden Press, 1982. The heart of this introductory guide is a constellation-by-constellation survey of the sky. Each of the 88 constellations is individually discussed with a chart of the constellation on the facing page. In general, the selection of objects recommended for viewing with binoculars or a small telescope is excellent.

The Sky Observer's Guide, R. Newton Mayall, M. Mayall, and J. Wychoff, Golden Press, 1977. A basic introduction to the practicalities of amateur astronomy: telescope types, telescope care, observing techniques, the celestial sphere, how to read star charts, time, etc. Also has brief sections on the Sun, the Moon, comets, meteors, stars, and nebulae. Although there is no section on constellation identification, the star charts at the end of the book are so uncluttered and well-designed that they should be sufficient to help any beginner find their way around the sky.

Seasonal Star Charts, James B. Sweeney, Jr., Hubbard Scientific Co., 1972. An excellent basic star atlas. Its eight charts cover the sky down to declination $-50°$ and plot about 3,000 stars (to magnitude 5.75) and 170 deep sky objects. This atlas is particularly good for beginning observers because it clearly marks the basic constellation figures. The majority of the constellations are discussed in some detail in the accompanying text.

The book is spiral-bound for convenience in the field and the pages are plastic-coated to protect them from night moisture.

C.2 For the Advanced Amateur

Burnham's Celestial Handbook, Robert Burnham, Jr., Dover, 1978 (3 volumes). This constellation-by-constellation guide to the sky, perhaps the single most important work in amateur astronomy published this century, is an almost inexhaustible source of interesting reading and new astronomical data. For each of the 88 constellations it presents three lists: double and multiple stars; variables; and clusters, nebulae, and galaxies. Following the lists, the more interesting objects are given extended discussions, often with photographs and finder charts. Included in these descriptive notes are numerous essays on such topics as globular clusters, emission nebulae, planetary nebulae, white dwarfs, supernovae, etc.

Sky Atlas 2000.0, Wil Tirion, Sky Publishing and Cambridge University Press, 1981. The perfect complement to *Burnham's Celestial Handbook*. Has 26 charts covering the whole sky, with 43,000 stars (to magnitude 8.0) and 2,500 deep-sky objects. It is available in three formats: a large-scale (and expensive) six-color deluxe edition; smaller black-on-white and white-on-black desk and field editions; and loose-leaf monochrome desk and field editions at reduced size.

Observing Handbook and Catalogue of Deep-Sky Objects, Christian B. Luginbuhl and Brian A. Skiff, Cambridge University Press, 1990. This observing guide is indispensable for owners of large telescopes (8 inches or more in aperture) and fills a long-standing gap in the literature of amateur astronomy. In it the visual appearances as seen in various-sized astronomical instruments are described for over 2000 objects, including some galaxies as faint as the 15th magnitude. Twenty-seven full-page finder charts (many of the former being photographs) are included as well as numerous small ones, and constellations down to Declination $-50°$ are covered. This guidebook can be used in association with either *Sky Atlas 2000.0* or, better yet, *Uranometria 2000.0* (2 vol.; Wil Tirion, Barry Rappaport, George Lovi; Willmann-Bell, Inc., 1987).

Amateur Astronomer's Handbook and *Observational Astronomy for Amateurs*, J.B. Sidgewick, Dover, 1980 (reprints the 3rd edition of l971; both books also exist in 4th editions from Enslow Press, 1980, for considerably more money). These two volumes are technical and delve into the specifics of equipment and technique for observing. *A.A.H.* describes telescopes, optical systems, vision, etc., while *O.A.A.* explains how to methodically observe the Sun, Moon, planets, etc. Both use math wherever necessary.

Planetary Nebulae, Steven J. Hynes, Willmann-Bell, Inc., 1991. A semi-technical, but non-mathematical, handbook. Separate chapters discuss the history of planetary nebula discovery and research, the astrophysics of planetaries, and how to observe these elusive but fascinating objects. The book has a catalogue of virtually all of the planetary nebulae known in our Galaxy (complete as of May 1990), with their locations and vital statistics, and detailed discussions of 33 specific planetaries. At the back are 82 pages of finder charts for dozens of individual nebulae.

C.3   Astronomy Texts

There is an abundance of good college-level astronomy texts, each with specific strengths and weaknesses. My personal favorite is William K. Hartmann's *Astronomy: the Cosmic Journey* (Wadsworth Publishing Co., 1979 and later editions). It gives especially clear explanations of such topics as star formation, evolution, and stellar populations.

Three good books on astronomy written for general audiences are:

1. *Beyond the Moon*, Paolo Maffei, Avon Books, 1980. This surveys most of the same material as a college astronomy text, but does it at a popular level. Deep-space topics are handled very well. Adequately illustrated for a small format book.

2. *Stars and Clusters*, Cecilia Payne-Gaposchkin, Harvard University Press, 1979. A non-mathematical presentation of stellar evolution in terms of star clusters—of how the stages of stellar evolution are represented in the different types of star groupings. The photos are mediocre, but there are dozens of interesting tables, graphs, and charts.

3. *Colours of the Stars*, David Malin and Paul Murdin, Cambridge University Press, 1984. A book with splendid color illustrations and photos coupled to a well-written, non-mathematical explanation of the astrophysics of stars and nebulae.

C.4   For Aesthetic Enjoyment

No small part of astronomy's pleasure comes from the beauty of astrophotographs. Besides *Colours of the Stars* (above), try:

Galaxies, Timothy Ferris; Stewart, Tabori, and Chang, 1982.

Catalogue of the Universe, Paul Murdin and David Allen, Crown, 1979.

The Illustrated Encyclopedia of the Universe, Richard S. Lewis and others, Harmony Books, 1983.

These three books also have very interesting and well-written texts.

C.5   Periodicals

The two major monthly magazines for amateur astronomers are *Sky & Telescope* (49 Bay State Rd., Cambridge, MA 02138) and *Astronomy* (21027 Crossroads Circle, P.O. Box 1612, Waukesha, WI 53187). Both publish articles on all aspects of astronomy, but *Astronomy* devotes more space to astrophotos and to departments and features about what to observe, while *Sky & Telescope* tends to run more stories on specific observatories and astronomers, about the history of astronomy, and about professional and amateur meetings.

A periodical for advanced amateurs is the *Webb Society Quarterly Journal* (England), the North American Secretary of which is Ron Morales (1440 South Marmora Avenue, Tuscon, AZ, 85713-1015), who can supply membership/subscription information.

An inexpensive annual is the *Observer's Handbook* of the Royal Astronomical Society of Canada (136 Dupont St., Toronto, Ontario, M4S 2Z2, Canada). This gives a wealth of astronomical data for the coming year—daily sunset and sunrise times, moonrise and moonset times, locations of the planets each month, and special events (eclipses, occultations, oppositions, etc.). In addition, it has tables of data on the solar system and deep-sky objects. (The table of data on stars brighter than 3.55 magnitude near the back of the annual is one of the best of its type that I have seen anywhere.)

Indices

THE BRIGHTEST STARS

(Data mostly from RASC's *Observer's Handbook*, 1991)

Star	Proper Name	Magnitude	Spectrum	Distance (l-y)	Text
α CMa	Sirius	−1.46	A1 V	8.6	21–22, 66–68, 92
α Car	Canopus	−0.72	A9 II	74	22, 75
α Cen	Rigel Kentaurus	−0.27	G2 V+K1 V	4.34	99–100
α Boö	Arcturus	−0.04	K2 III	34	10, 96–97
α Lyr	Vega	0.03	A0 V	25	12, 135–136
α Aur	Capella	0.08	G6 III+G2 III	41	21, 69
β Ori	Rigel	0.08(var)	B8 Ia	900	20, 62–63
α CMi	Procyon	0.38	F5 IV-V	11.4	21, 57
α Eri	Achernar	0.46	B3 V	69	20, 56
β Cen	Hadar	0.63(var)	B1 III	320	99–100
α Ori	Betelgeuse	0.7(var)	M2 Iab	520	20, 66
α Aql	Altair	0.77	A7 V	16.5	12, 14, 132–133
α Tau	Aldebaran	0.86(var)	K5 III	60	21, 58
α Cru	Acrux	0.87	B0.5 IV+B1 V	510	103
α Sco	Antares	0.92(var)	M1 Iab	520	13, 114–116
α Vir	Spica	1.00(var)	B1 V+B3	220	10, 95–96
β Gem	Pollux	1.14	K0 III	35	21, 71
α PsA	Fomalhaut	1.16	A3 V	22	17, 32–33
α Cyg	Deneb	1.25	A1 Ia	1500	12, 13, 140
β Cru	Becrux	1.28(var)	B0.5 III	460	103
α Leo	Regulus	1.35	B7 V	69	9, 89
ε CMa	Adhara	1.49	B2 II	570	67
α Gem	Castor	1.59	A2 V+A5 V	49	21, 71
λ Sco	Shaula	1.62(var)	B1 IVV	330	103, 112, 116
γ Cru	Gacrux	1.63	M3 III	120	
γ Ori	Bellatrix	1.64	B2 III	470	63
β Tau	El Nath	1.65	B7 III	138	70
β Car	Miaplacidus	1.68	A1 III	64	
ε Ori	Alnilam	1.70	B0 Ia	1600	63, 65
γ Vel	Al Suhail	1.7(var)	WC8+O9, B3	1500	22
α Gru	Al Na'ir	1.74	B7 V	57	33
ζ Ori	Alnitak	1.79	O9/B0 Ib+B0 III	1600	63, 65
ε UMa	Alioth	1.79(var)	A0p IV	65	91
α Per	Mirfak	1.79	F5 Ib	630	48–49
α UMa	Dubhe	1.79	K0 III	100	91
δ CMa	Wesen	1.84	F8 Ia	2500	67
ε Sgr	Kaus Australis	1.85	A0 II	76	14, 122
ε Car	Avior	1.86	K3 III+B2 V	79	
η UMa	Alkaid	1.86	B3 V	138	91
θ Sco	Sargas	1.87	F1 III	200	
β Aur	Menkalinan	1.90(var)	A1 IV	55	92
α TrA	Atria	1.92	K2 II–III	110	
γ Gem	Alhena	1.93	A1 IV	57	71
α Pav		1.94	B3 V	150	
δ Vel		1.96	A1 V	64	
α Hya	Alphard	1.98	K3 II–III	110	10, 86
β CMa	Murzim	1.98(var)	B1 II–III	750	22
γ Leo	Algeiba	1.98	K1 III+G7 III	76	89
α UMi	Polaris	1.99(var)	F5–8 Ib	820	8, 106
α Ari	Hamal	2.00	K2 III	78	51
σ Sgr	Nunki	2.02	B3 IV	170	122
β Cet	Deneb Kaitos	2.04	K0 III	53	52

SELECTED VARIABLE STARS

Star	Variable Type	Magnitude Range	Period	Spectrum	Text
Eta Aquilae	Cepheid	3.7 – 4.5	7.2 days	F6-G4 Ib	
Epsilon Aurigae	Uncertain	3.0 – 3.8	27.06 yrs	F0 Ia	
Alpha Canum Venaticorum*	Magnetic spectrum var	2.9 – 2.95	5.74 days	B9.5p	93
Y Canum Venaticorum	Carbon star	4.8 – 6.4	≈158 days	C5	92–93
Gamma Cassiopeiae	Uncertain	1.6 – 3.0	Irregular	B0 IVep	43
Delta Cephei*	Cepheid	3.6 – 4.3	5.37 days	F5-G3 Ib	8, 40
Mu Cephei	Semi-regular red giant	3.7 – 5.0	Semi-reg	M2 Ia	40–41
Mira (Omicron Ceti)*	Long-period variable	2.5 – 9.5	333 days	gM6e-M9	18, 52–53
R Coronae Borealis*	R CrB "reverse nova"	5.8 – 14.8	Irregular	F8 Iap	109
T Coronae Borealis	Recurrent nova	2.0 – 10…	Irregular	gM+B	109
Chi Cygni	Long-period variable	3.5 – 14.2	407 days	gM6ep	
P Cygni*	P Cygni "permanent nova"	3.0 – 5…	Irregular	B1eq	140
Eta Geminorum	Semi-regular red giant	3.1 – 3.9	≈230 days	M3 III	71
Alpha Herculis	Semi-regular red giant	3.1 – 3.9	≈90 days	M5 II	108
R Hydrae	Long-period variable	4.0 – 10.0	386 days	gM7e	87
U Hydrae	Carbon star	4.7 – 6.2	Irregular	N2	86–87
Beta Lyrae*	Lyrid eclipsing binary	3.4 – 4.3	12.91 days	B8II-III+A	12, 136
R Lyrae	Semi-regular red giant	4.1 – 5.0	≈46 days	gM6	136
RR Lyrae*	Cluster variable	7.1 – 8.0	0.57 days	A8-F7	
Alpha Orionis	Semi-regular red giant	0.2 – 1.3	Uncertain	M2 Iab	66
Beta Pegasi	Irregular red giant	2.1 – 3.0	Irregular	M2 II-III	36
Algol (Beta Persei)*	Eclipsing binary	2.1 – 3.4	2.867 days	B8V+K0IV	47–48
Rho Persei	Semi-regular red giant	3.3 – 4.0	≈40 days	gM4	48
TX=19 Piscium	Carbon star	5.2 – 6.0	Irregular	C6	51–52
L-2 Puppis	Semi-regular red giant	3.0 – 6.0	≈140 days	gM5e-gM6e	
U Sagittarii	Cepheid	6.3 – 7.1	6.74 days	F5-G1 Ib	128
R Scuti	RV Tauri variable	4.8 – 8.2	140 days	G0eIa-K0pIb	132

*indicates stars that are prototypes of their variable class.

BINOCULAR DOUBLE STARS

Star	Text
Delta [δ] Boötis	98
Mu [μ] Boötis	98
Alpha [α] Capricorni	17, 32
Beta [β] Capricorni	32
Delta [δ] Cephei	40
Beta [β] Cygni	138
Omicron [o] Cygni	138
61 Cygni	138
Nu [ν] Draconis	107
Psi [ψ] Draconis	107
16+17 Draconis	107
Gamma [γ] Leporis	56
Alpha [α] Librae	98–99
Delta [δ] Lyrae	137
Epsilon [ε] Lyrae	136
Zeta [ζ] Lyrae	136–137
Delta [δ] Orionis	63
Sigma [σ] Orionis	63
Theta [θ] Orionis	64
Σ747 (Orion)	65
Upsilon [v] Puppis	82
Mu [μ] Scorpii	13, 116
Nu [ν] Scorpii	114
Theta [θ] Serpentis	129
Zeta [ζ] Piscium	52
Psi-one [ψ¹] Piscium	52
Theta [θ] Tauri	61
Zeta [ζ] + 80 Ursae Majoris	6, 91

ASSOCIATIONS

Association	Text
Canis Major	67, 69, 151–152
Cepheus OB2	40, 150
Cygnus OB7	140, 150
Gemini OB1	65–66, 151
Lacerta OB1	41, 150
Orion	62–65, 104, 151
Perseus OB2	49, 104, 151
Sagittarius OB1	125–126
Scorpio-Centaurus	101–104, 114, 116, 151
Scorpius OB1	119
Ursa Major Stream	92

GLOBULAR CLUSTERS

Cluster	Constellation	Text
M2	Aquarius	35
M3	Canes Venatici	93
M4	Scorpius	116
M5	Serpens	109
M9	Ophiuchus	110
M10	Ophiuchus	110
M12	Ophiuchus	110
M13	Hercules	108
M14	Ophiuchus	110
M15	Pegasus	36
M19	Ophiuchus	110
M22	Sagittarius	122
M28	Sagittarius	122
M53	Coma Berenices	94–95
M55	Sagittarius	122
M62	Ophiuchus	110
M71	Sagitta	134
M92	Hercules	108
NGC 1851	Columba	56
NGC 5466	Boötes	97–98
NGC 5897	Libra	99
NGC 6541	Corona Australis	122
NGC 6723	Sagittarius	122
Omega Centauri	Centaurus	100
47 Tucanae	Tucana	100–101

OPEN CLUSTERS

Cluster	Constellation	Text
M6	Scorpius	13, 119–120
M7	Scorpius	13, 119–120
M11	Scutum	130, 149
M18	Sagittarius	128, 149
M21	Sagittarius	126, 149
M23	Sagittarius	128, 149
M25	Sagittarius	128, 149
M26	Scutum	130, 149
M29	Cygnus	140
M34	Perseus	49
M35	Gemini	21, 71, 151, 152
M36	Auriga	70, 151
M37	Auriga	70, 151
M38	Auriga	70, 151
M39	Cygnus	143
M41	Canis Major	69, 152
M44	Cancer	9, 84
M45	Taurus	21, 59–61, 151
M46	Puppis	76, 152
M47	Puppis	76, 152
M48	Hydra	86
M50	Monoceros	73
M52	Cassiopeia	43, 150
M67	Cancer	84–85
M93	Puppis	80, 152
M103	Cassiopeia	43, 150
Alpha Persei Moving Cluster		18, 46, 49, 151
Coma Berenices Star Cluster		10, 50, 93–94
Delta Lyrae Cluster		137
Hyades	Taurus	20–21, 57–58, 60, 84, 151
Pleiades	Taurus	21, 59–61, 151
Praesepe	Cancer	9, 84
Ursa Major Moving Group		91–92
NGC 457	Cassiopeia	43, 45, 150
NGC 663	Cassiopeia	43, 45, 150
NGC 752	Andromeda	50
NGC 869+884	Perseus	18, 48, 150
NGC 1647	Taurus	60
NGC 1893	Auriga	71, 152
NGC 1907	Auriga	70
NGC 1981	Orion	65
NGC 2158	Gemini	71, 152
NGC 2232	Monoceros	75
NGC 2244	Monoceros	73–74
NGC 2264	Monoceros	74–75, 151
NGC 2301	Monoceros	75
NGC 2324	Monoceros	75
NGC 2353	Monoceros	75
NGC 2354	Canis Major	69
NGC 2360	Canis Major	69
NGC 2362	Canis Major	69, 152
NGC 2423	Puppis	76
NGC 2439	Puppis	152
NGC 2451	Puppis	80
NGC 2477	Puppis	80, 82
NGC 2482	Puppis	80
NGC 2506	Monoceros	75
NGC 2539	Puppis	80
NGC 2546	Puppis	80
NGC 4755	Crux	149
NGC 5460	Centaurus	99
NGC 6193	Ara	149
NGC 6231	Scorpius	116, 119, 149
NGC 6242	Scorpius	119
NGC 6281	Scorpius	119
NGC 6383	Scorpius	120
NGC 6451	Scorpius	120
NGC 6530	Sagittarius	125
NGC 6633	Ophiuchus	110, 112
NGC 6664	Scutum	130
NGC 6800	Vulpecula	135
NGC 6885	Vulpecula	135
NGC 6939	Cepheus	41
NGC 6940	Vulpecula	135
NGC 7209	Lacerta	41
NGC 7243	Lacerta	41
NGC 7789	Cassiopeia	43, 45–46, 150
IC 4665	Ophiuchus	112
IC 4756	Serpens	129
Collinder 399	Vulpecula	135
Melotte 71	Puppis	76
Stock 2	Cassiopeia	43, 48, 150

BRIGHT NEBULAE

Nebula	Name	Type	Constellation	Text
M1	Crab	Supernova Remnant	Taurus	61–62
M8	Lagoon	Diffuse	Sagittarius	14, 16, 125, 149
M16	Star Queen	Diffuse	Scutum	129, 149
M17	Swan	Diffuse	Sagittarius	128–129, 149
M20	Trifid	Diffuse	Sagittarius	125–126, 149
M27	Dumb-bell	Planetary	Vulpecula	135
M42	Great Nebula	Diffuse	Orion	20, 63–65
M43		Diffuse	Orion	65
M57	Ring	Planetary	Lyra	137
M78		Reflection	Orion	65
NGC 246		Planetary	Cetus	53
NGC 1360		Planetary	Fornax	54
NGC 1435	Merope	Reflection	Taurus	61
NGC 1499	California	Diffuse	Perseus	49
NGC 1931		Diffuse	Auriga	70
NGC 1977		Diffuse	Orion	65
NGC 2024		Diffuse	Orion	65
NGC 2070	Tarantula	Diffuse	Dorado	63
NGC 2174		Diffuse	Orion	65–66
NGC 2237	Rosette	Diffuse	Monoceros	73–74, 151
NGC 2438		Planetary	Puppis	76
NGC 2467		Diffuse	Puppis	80, 152
NGC 3242		Planetary	Hydra	86
NGC 3372	Keyhole	Diffuse	Carina	149
NGC 6992	Veil	Supernova Remnant	Cygnus	137–138
NGC 7000	North America	Diffuse	Cygnus	14, 140
NGC 7009	Saturn	Planetary	Aquarius	35
NGC 7293	Helix	Planetary	Aquarius	34–35
IC 410		Diffuse	Auriga	71
IC 1318		Diffuse	Cygnus	140
IC 1396		Diffuse	Cepheus	40
IC 1848		Diffuse	Cassiopeia	43, 46, 150
IC 5076	Pelican	Diffuse	Cygnus	140

GALAXIES

Galaxy	Constellation	Text
M31	Andromeda	16, 154–155
M32	Andromeda	154
M33	Triangulum	16, 154–155
M49	Virgo	161–162
M51	Canes Venatici	157
M61	Virgo	96, 161
M63	Canes Venatici	157
M64	Coma Berenices	157
M65+66	Leo	158
M74	Pisces	52
M77	Cetus	53, 156, 161
M81+82	Ursa Major	156
M83	Hydra	41, 157–158
M84+86	Virgo	161–162
M87	Virgo	161–162
M94	Canes Venatici	157
M95+96	Leo	158
M99	Coma Berenices	161–162
M100	Coma Berenices	161–162
M101	Ursa Major	156–157
M104	Virgo	96
M105	Leo	158
M106	Canes Venatici	157
NGC 55	Sculptor	156
NGC 205	Andromeda	154
NGC 247	Sculptor	156
NGC 253	Sculptor	156
NGC 2403	Camelopardalis	156
NGC 2683	Lynx	57
NGC 2841	Ursa Major	92
NGC 2903	Leo	89
NGC 2997	Antlia	88
NGC 3115	Sextans	88
NGC 3184	Ursa Major	92
NGC 3521	Leo	89–90
NGC 3628	Leo	158
NGC 4564	Coma Berenices	95
NGC 5128	Centaurus	157–158
NGC 6822	Sagittarius	155
NGC 6946	Cepheus	41
NGC 7793	Sculptor	156
IC 342	Camelopardalis	155
Scl System	Sculptor	54
For System	Fornax	54

THE CONSTELLATIONS

Constellation	Possessive Form	Abbr.	Meaning	Maps	Text
Andromeda*	Andromedae	And	The Chained Lady	1, 3, 8	8, 16, 22, 49–50
Antlia	Antliae	Ant	Air Pump	5	87–88
Apus	Apodis	Aps	Bird of Paradise	10	166
Aquarius	Aquarii	Aqr	Water-pourer	8	17, 33–35
Aquila	Aquilae	Aql	Eagle	7	14, 132–134
Ara	Arae	Ara	Altar	10	149
Aries	Arietis	Ari	Ram	3	18, 22, 50–51
Auriga	Aurigae	Aur	Charioteer	4	21, 69–71
Boötes	Boötis	Boo	Herdsman	2, 6	10, 96–98
Caelum	Caeli	Cae	Chisel	9	166
Camelopardalis	Camelopardali	Cam	Giraffe	1	9, 57, 166
Cancer	Cancri	Can	Crab	5	9, 84–85
Canes Venatici	Canum Venaticorum	CVn	Hunting Dogs	1, 2, 6	10, 92–93, 166
Canis Major	Canis Majoris	CMa	Great Dog	4	21, 22, 66–69
Canis Minor	Canis Minoris	CMi	Little Dog	4	21, 56–57
Capricornus	Capricorni	Cap	Goat-fish	8	17, 31–32
Carina	Carinae	Car	Keel	9, 10	22, 25, 49, 75–76
Cassiopeia*	Cassiopeiae	Cas	The Queen	1, 2	8, 41–46
Centaurus	Centauri	Cen	Centaur	6, 9, 10	12, 22, 99–101
Cepheus*	Cephei	Cep	The King	1, 2	8, 36–41
Cetus	Ceti	Cet	Sea-monster	3	8, 18, 52–53
Chamaeleon	Chamaeleontis	Cha	Chamaeleon	9, 10	166
Circinus	Circini	Cir	Drafting Compass	10	166
Columba	Columbae	Col	Dove	4	20, 56, 166
Coma Berenices	Comae Berenices	Com	Berenice's Hair	6	10, 93–95
Corona Australis	Coronae Australis	CrA	Southern Crown	7	16, 122
Corona Borealis	Coronae Borealis	CrB	Northern Crown	6, 7	10, 12, 108–109
Corvus	Corvi	Cor	Crow	5, 6	12, 88
Crater	Crateris	Cra	Cup	5	10, 88
Crux	Crucis	Cru	Cross	9, 10	166
Cygnus	Cygni	Cyg	Swan	2, 7, 8	13–14, 137–143
Delphinus	Delphini	Del	Dolphin	8	14, 134
Dorado	Doradus	Dor	Golden Dolphin	9	166
Draco	Draconis	Dra	Dragon	1, 2	8–9, 106–107
Equuleus	Equulei	Eql	Foal	8	14, 134
Eridanus*	Eridani	Eri	The River	3, 4, 9	18, 20, 56
Fornax	Fornacis	For	Furnace	3	18, 53–54, 166
Gemini	Geminorum	Gem	Twins	4	21, 71–72
Grus	Gruis	Gru	Crane	8, 10	17, 33, 166
Hercules*	Herculis	Her	The Kneeler	2, 7	12–13, 22, 107–108
Horologium	Horologii	Hor	Clock	9	166
Hydra	Hydrae	Hya	Water-serpent	5, 6	9–10, 85–87
Hydrus	Hydri	Hyi	Water-serpent	9, 10	166
Indus	Indi	Ind	Indian	10	166
Lacerta	Lacertae	Lac	Lizard	2, 8	16, 36, 41, 166
Leo	Leonis	Leo	Lion	5	9, 89–90
Leo Minor	Leonis Minoris	LMi	Little Lion	5	10, 166
Lepus	Leporis	Lep	Hare	4	20, 56
Libra	Librae	Lib	Scales	6	12, 98–99
Lupus	Lupi	Lup	Wolf	6, 10	12, 99
Lynx	Lyncis	Lyn	Lynx	1, 5	9, 57, 166
Lyra	Lyrae	Lyr	Lyre	7	12, 22, 135–137
Mensa	Mensae	Men	Table (Mountain)	9, 10	166
Microscopium	Microscopii	Mic	Microscope	8, 10	32, 166
Monoceros	Monoceroti	Mon	Unicorn	4	21, 71, 73–75, 166
Musca	Muscae	Mus	Fly	9, 10	166
Norma	Normae	Nor	Level	10	166
Octans	Octantis	Oct	Octant	9, 10	166
Ophiuchus	Ophiuchi	Oph	Serpent-bearer	7	13, 22, 109–112
Orion*	Orionis	Ori	The Hunter	4	20, 62–66
Pavo	Pavonis	Pav	Peacock	10	166
Pegasus*	Pegasi	Peg	The Winged Horse	8	16, 36
Perseus*	Persei	Per	The Hero	1, 3, 4	8, 18, 22, 46–49
Phoenix	Phoenicis	Phe	Phoenix	9, 10	17, 166
Pictor	Pictoris	Pic	Painter	9	166
Pisces	Piscium	Pis	Fishes	3, 8	17, 51–52
Piscis Austrinus	Piscis Austrini	PsA	Southern Fish	8	17, 32–33
Puppis	Puppis	Pup	Stern	4, 9	22, 75–82
Pyxis	Pyxidis	Pyx	Mariner's Compass	5	49, 166
Reticulum	Reticuli	Ret	Net	9	166
Sagitta	Sagittae	Sag	Arrow	7	14, 134
Sagittarius	Sagittarii	Sgr	Archer	7	14, 16, 120–129
Scorpius	Scorpii	Sco	Scorpion	7	13, 112, 114–120
Sculptor	Sculptoris	Scl	Sculptor	3, 8	18, 53–54, 166
Scutum	Scuti	Sct	Shield	7	14, 130–132, 166
Serpens	Serpentis	Ser	Serpent	6, 7	13, 109, 129
Sextans	Sextantis	Sex	Sextant	5	10, 87–88, 166
Taurus	Tauri	Tau	Bull	3, 4	20–21, 57–62
Telescopium	Telescopii	Tel	Telescope	10	166
Triangulum	Triangle	Tri	Triangle	3	18, 50
Triangulum Australe	Trianguli Australis	TrA	Southern Triangle	10	166
Tucana	Tucanae	Tuc	Toucan	9, 10	166
Ursa Major	Ursae Majoris	UMa	Great Bear	1, 2, 5	6, 8, 90–92
Ursa Minor	Ursae Minoris	UMi	Little Bear	1, 2	8, 105–106
Vela	Velorum	Vel	Sails	9	22, 49
Virgo	Virginis	Vir	Virgin	6	12, 95–96
Volans	Volantis	Vol	Flying (Fish)	9	166
Vulpecula	Vulpeculae	Vul	Little Fox	7, 8	14, 134–135, 166

*indicates a proper name from classical mythology. For such constellations the "meaning" given in column 4 is the character of the constellation as envisioned by the ancient Greeks and Romans.

The
Bright Star Atlas 2000.0

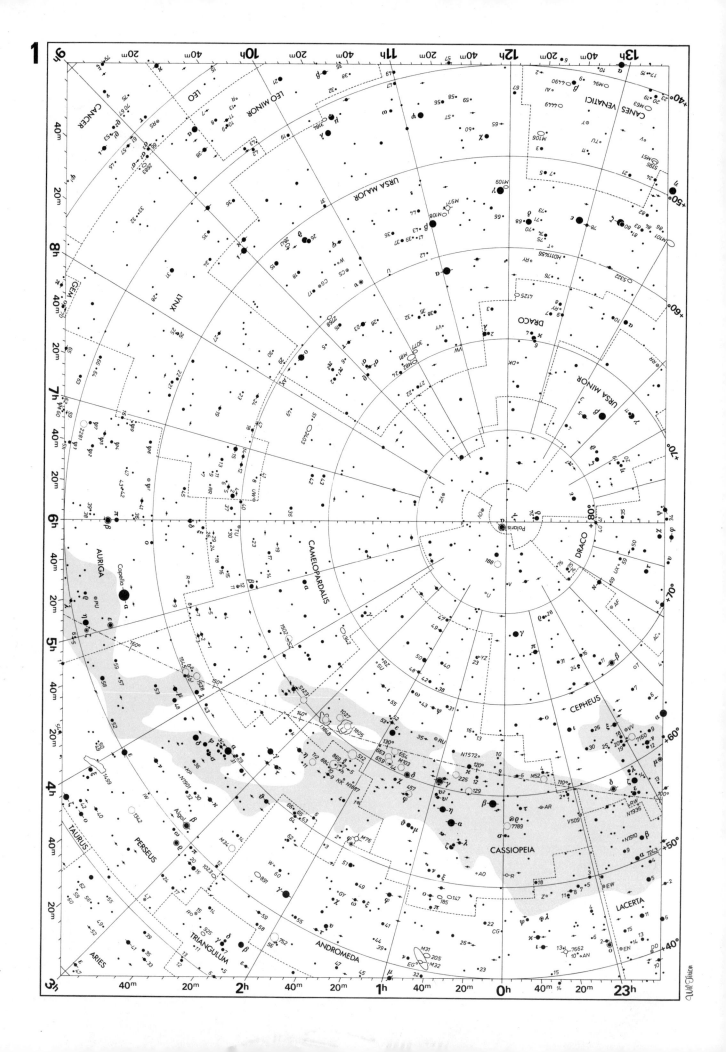

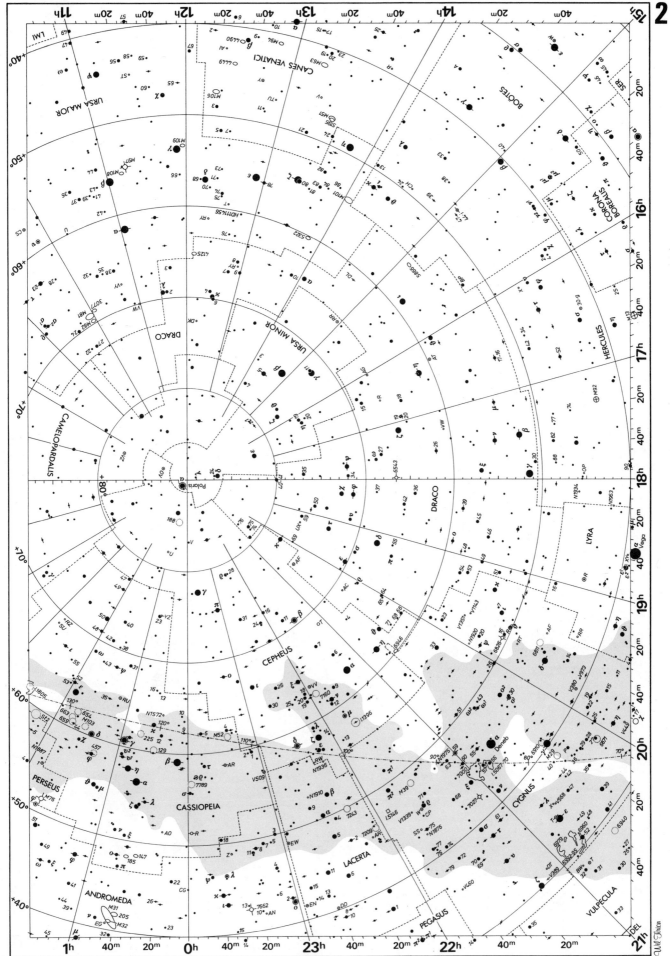

3

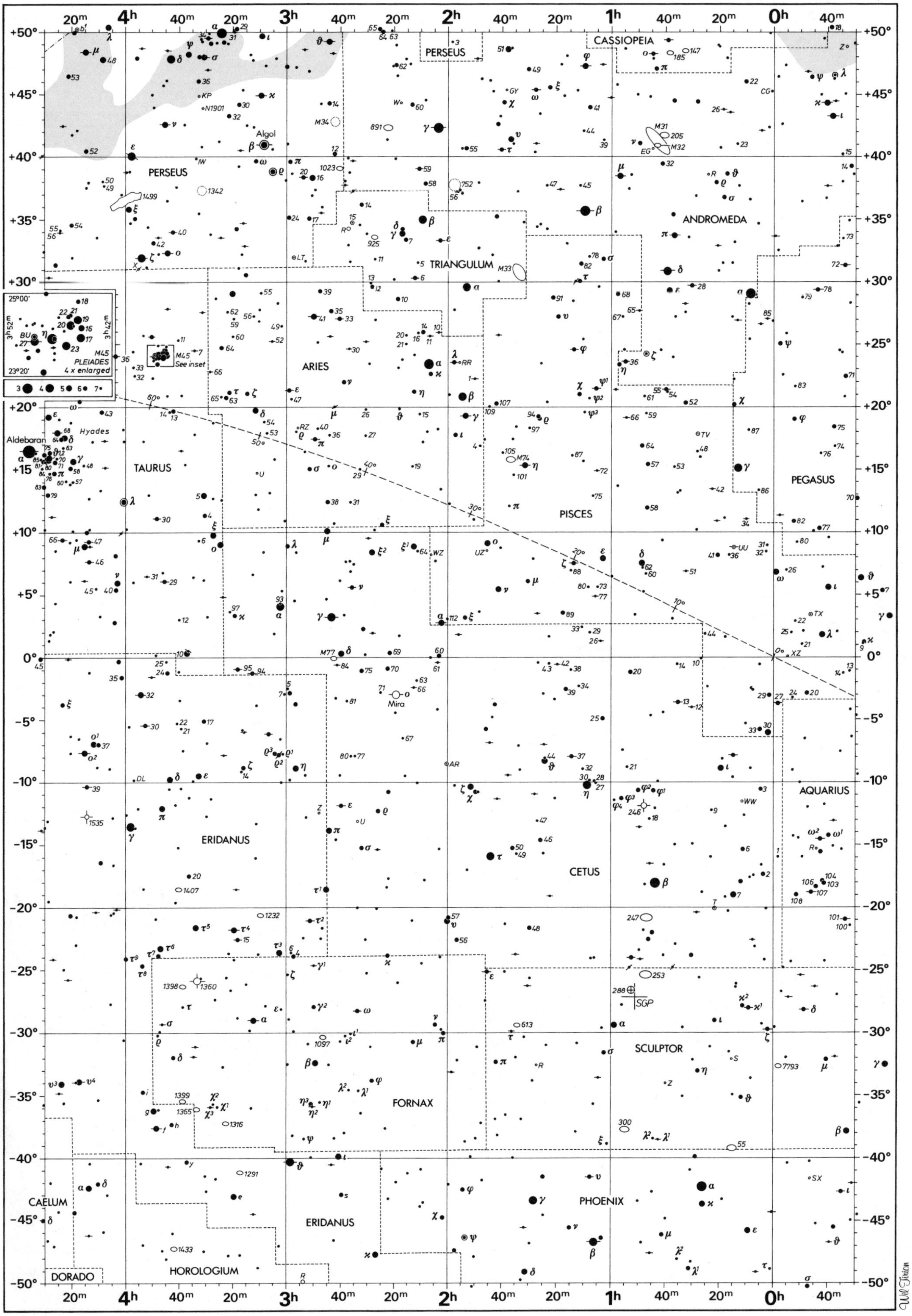

+50° +45° +40° +35° +30° +25° +20° +15° +10° +5° 0° −5° −10° −15° −20° −25° −30° −35° −40° −45° −50°

CASSIOPEIA

PERSEUS

Algol

ANDROMEDA

M31 M32 M205

M34

M33

TRIANGULUM

ARIES

PISCES

PEGASUS

Aldebaran Hyades

TAURUS

M45 PLEIADES 4 x enlarged

25°00' 3h52m 3h42m 23°20' BU η M45 PLEIADES 3 4 5 6 7

Mira

CETUS

ERIDANUS

AQUARIUS

SGP

SCULPTOR

FORNAX

CAELUM

ERIDANUS

HOROLOGIUM

DORADO

PHOENIX

Wil Tirion

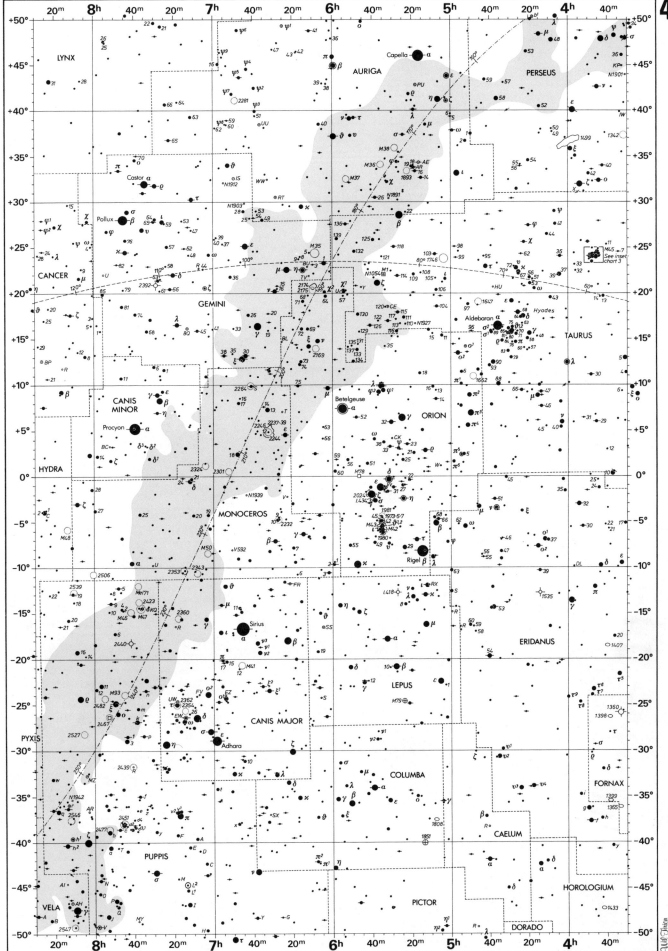

5

Top axis: 20m **12h** 40m 20m **11h** 40m 20m **10h** 40m 20m **9h** 40m 20m **8h** 40m

Left axis: +50° +45° +40° +35° +30° +25° +20° +15° +10° +5° 0° −5° −10° −15° −20° −25° −30° −35° −40° −45° −50°

Right axis: +50° +45° +40° +35° +30° +25° +20° +15° +10° +5° 0° −5° −10° −15° −20° −25° −30° −35° −40° −45° −50°

Bottom axis: 20m **12h** 40m 20m **11h** 40m 20m **10h** 40m 20m **9h** 40m 20m **8h** 40m

Constellation names: URSA MAJOR, LYNX, AUR, LEO MINOR, CANES VENATICI, GEMINI, CANCER, COMA BERENICES, LEO, CANIS MINOR, VIRGO, SEXTANS, HYDRA, MONOCEROS, CORVUS, CRATER, PUPPIS, PYXIS, HYDRA, ANTLIA, CENTAURUS, VELA

Selected star/object labels: M106, M85, M100, M98, M99, M87, M86, M84, M49, M61, M48, M67, M44, M47, M45, M93, Castor α, Pollux β, Regulus, Procyon α, Mel 71

Credit: Wil Tirion

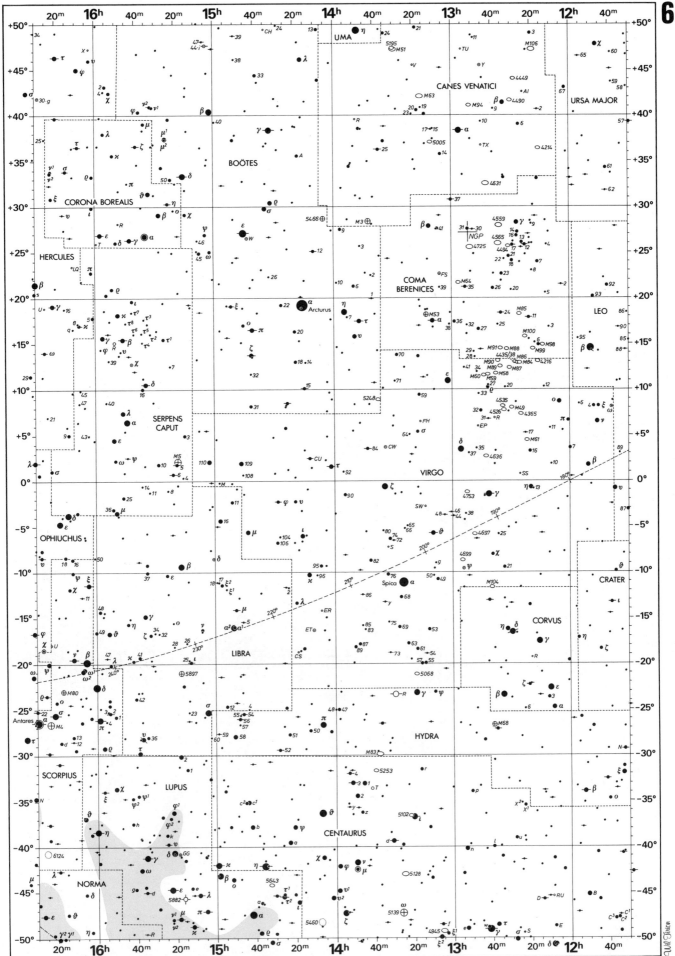

7

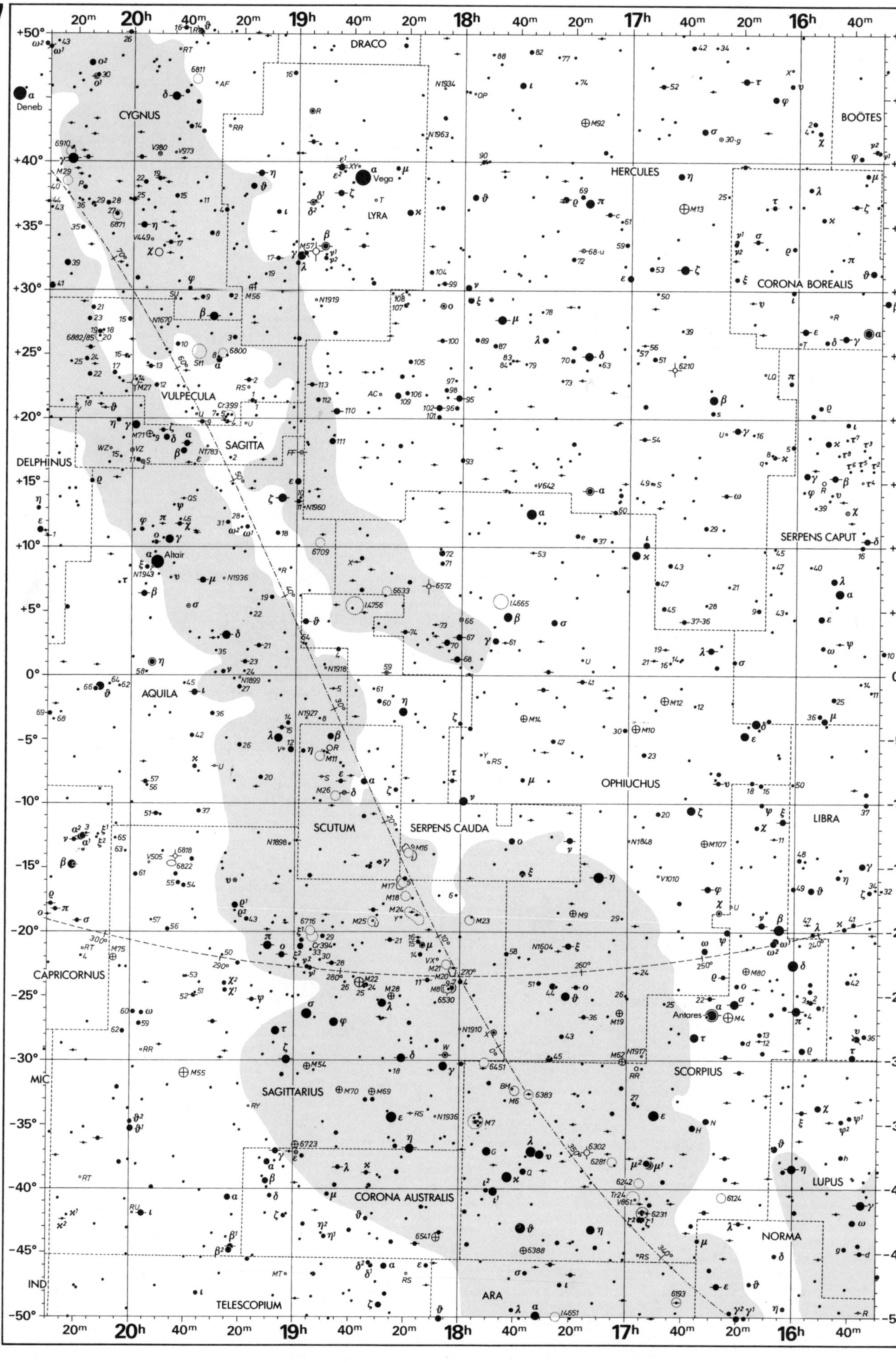

20h
19h
18h
17h
16h
+50°
+45°
+40°
+35°
+30°
+25°
+20°
+15°
+10°
+5°
0°
-5°
-10°
-15°
-20°
-25°
-30°
-35°
-40°
-45°
-50°
DRACO
CYGNUS
Deneb
BOÖTES
HERCULES
LYRA
Vega
CORONA BOREALIS
VULPECULA
SAGITTA
DELPHINUS
SERPENS CAPUT
Altair
AQUILA
OPHIUCHUS
SCUTUM
SERPENS CAUDA
LIBRA
CAPRICORNUS
SAGITTARIUS
SCORPIUS
Antares
MIC
CORONA AUSTRALIS
LUPUS
NORMA
IND
TELESCOPIUM
ARA
M92
M13
M57
M56
M71
M27
M11
M26
M16
M17
M18
M24
M25
M23
M21
M20
M8
M22
M28
M54
M70
M69
M55
M7
M6
M9
M10
M12
M14
M107
M80
M4
M19
M62
M75

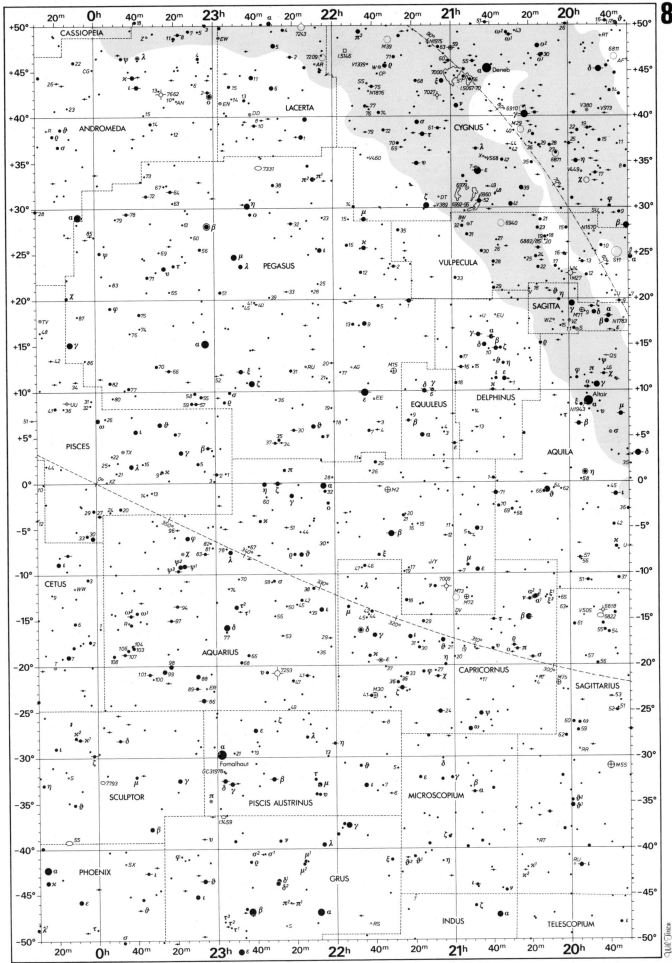

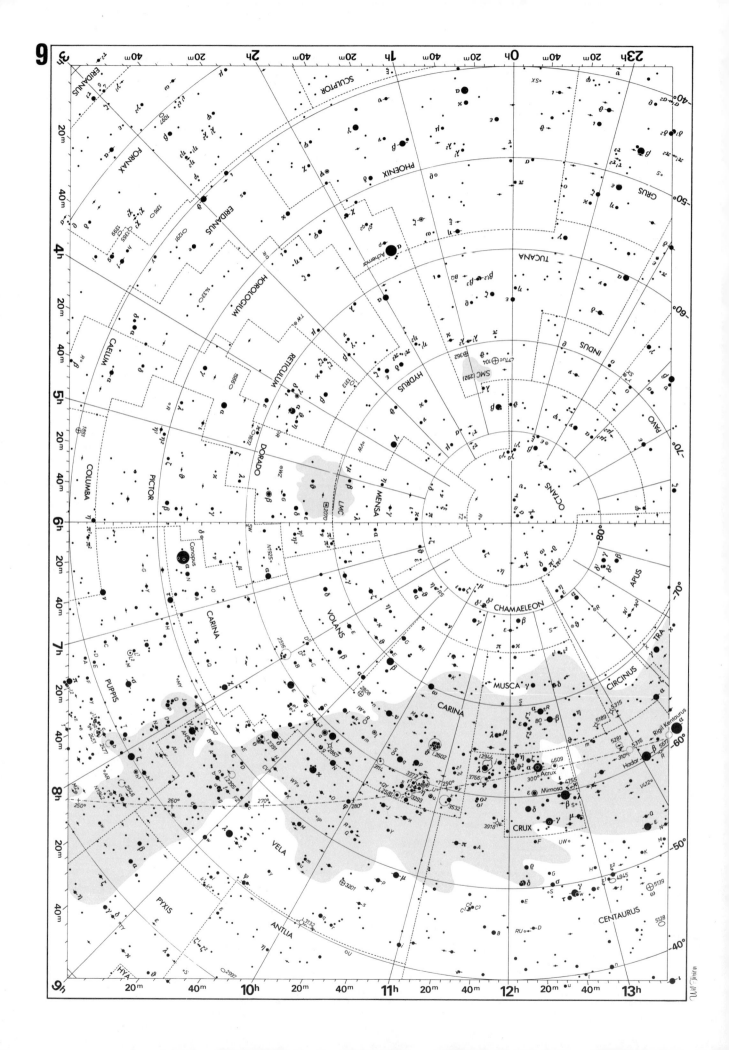

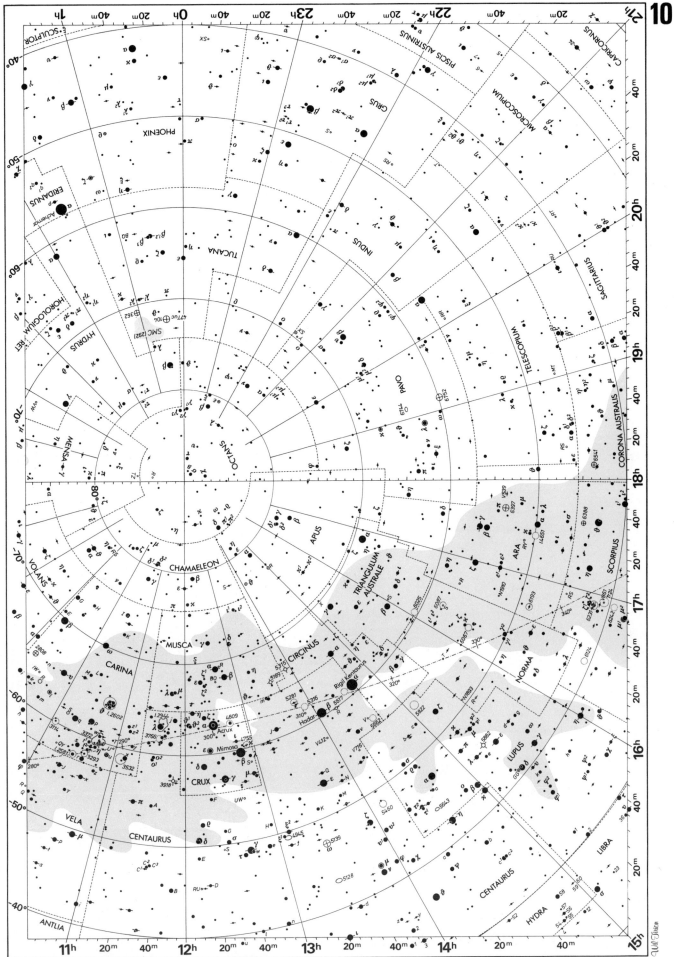